CONCISE COLLEGE TEXTS

TORT

AUSTRALIA
The Law Book Company Ltd.
Sydney : Melbourne : Brisbane

CANADA AND U.S.A.
The Carswell Company Ltd.
Agincourt, Ontario

INDIA
N. M. Tripathi Private Ltd.
Bombay
and
Eastern Law House Private Ltd.
Calcutta
M.P.P. House
Bangalore

ISRAEL
Steimatzky's Agency Ltd.
Jerusalem : Tel Aviv : Haifa

MALAYSIA : SINGAPORE : BRUNEI
Malayan Law Journal (Pte.) Ltd.
Singapore

NEW ZEALAND
Sweet and Maxwell (N.Z.) Ltd.
Auckland

PAKISTAN
Pakistan Law House
Karachi

CONCISE COLLEGE TEXTS

TORT

By

C. D. BAKER, B.C.L., M.A.
of the Inner Temple, Barrister,
Practitioner of the Supreme Court of South Australia;
Senior Lecturer in Law, University of Adelaide

THIRD EDITION

LONDON
SWEET & MAXWELL
1981

First Edition 1972
Second Edition 1976
Second Impression 1978
Third Impression 1979
Third Edition 1981
Second Impression 1983

Published by
Sweet & Maxwell Limited of
11 New Fetter Lane, London
and printed in Scotland

British Library Cataloguing in Publication Data

Baker, C.D.
　　Tort. — 3rd ed. — (Concise college texts)
　　1. Torts — England
　　I. Title
　　344.2063　　KD1949

ISBN 0-421-27030-6
ISBN 0-421-27040-3 Pbk.

PREFACE

The previous edition of this book was compiled while lawyers awaited the report of the Pearson Commission on compensation for personal injury. Some expected the Commission to recommend the complete replacement of the law of tort, so far as it concerned personal injury, by some type of compensation scheme not requiring proof of fault; most expected that some fundamental changes would be proposed. In fact, the Commission, which reported in 1978, recommended that the substance of the law should remain largely as it was before. The need to provide financially for those persons who received their injury in circumstances where no tort had been committed, or where no tort could be proved, should be met, at least in part, by an extension of the present social security system, leaving those who could establish a cause of action in tort free to pursue that remedy. It was possible, therefore, to prepare this edition in the confidence that a system was being described which would last for some, and probably a long, time.

The Pearson Commission did make a number of detailed proposals for reform of the present law, all of which await implementation by Parliament. These proposals are considered throughout this edition. A number of important Acts have been passed since the last edition, in particular, the Congenital Disabilities (Civil Liability) Act 1976, the Torts (Interference with Goods) Act 1977, the Unfair Contract Terms Act 1977, the Civil Liability (Contribution) Act 1978 and the Employment Act 1980. Of judicial decisions, *Anns* v. *London Borough of Merton* is of outstanding importance. It seeks to lay down the conditions under which public authorities may be held liable in tort for the improper discharge of their functions. Also significant are *Leakey* v. *National Trust, Pickett* v. *British Rail Engineering, Dodd Properties* v. *Canterbury City Council* and *McLoughlin* v. *O'Brien*. There have been a number of decisions exploring the ambit of the *Hedley Byrne* case. In view of the amount of judicial activity in the area of duty of care, I have rewritten and considerably extended that chapter. I also rewrote the chapter on causation and remoteness of damage, feeling that the existing account could be shortened and, it is hoped, simplified. Although the book has received no marked increase in size, a considerable amount of rewriting of passages has been

v

undertaken in a further attempt at clarification. The law has
been stated in accordance with materials available to me at the
middle of January 1981.

I would like to thank Simon Palk and Leni Green for helping
me at the proof-reading stage and eradicating a number of faults.
I would also wish to thank the publishers for preparing the
Tables and Index and for maintaining prompt and efficient communication with me out here.

C. D. Baker

Adelaide
February 1981

CONTENTS

TABLE OF CASES

TABLE OF STATUTES

1. INTRODUCTION

MEANING OF "TORT"; PURPOSE OF THE LAW OF TORT

The difficulty of defining the word "tort" is well recognised. In the words of an American authority (*Prosser on Torts*, 4th ed.), p. 1, "the numerous attempts which have been made to define the term [*i.e.* tort] have succeeded only in achieving language so broad that it includes other matters than torts, or else so narrow that it leaves out some torts themselves." The main reason for this difficulty is the extreme variety of behaviour which may constitute a tort. Intentionally or negligently to cause physical injury to another, to interfere with his enjoyment of his land, to defame him, or to conspire with another to cause him financial loss are examples of such behaviour. Such cases appear to have three elements. The first is human behaviour which the law categorises as wrongful. The second is that such behaviour infringes an interest of another person which is considered worthy of protection by the law. The third is that the person suffering the wrong is allowed to seek redress for it in the civil courts—it is a civil wrong. The law of tort may therefore be stated to be concerned with the protection of certain interests against certain types of wrongful conduct. Two points may be made in further elaboration of this. In the first place, in order that a tort be committed, it is essential that the relevant interest be protected against the particular type of wrongful conduct. Certain interests, for example the interests in personal security and property, are protected against both intentional and negligent conduct on the part of another, and in some cases against conduct which is free from fault. Other interests, such as the interest in economic security, are less well protected, being protected, generally speaking, only against their deliberate infringement by another. The second point is that, apart from the wrongfulness of the conduct involved in the tort, the type of person responsible for the conduct, and in some cases the relationship between the tortfeasor and his victim, may also be relevant. So, for example, to commit the tort known as *Rylands* v. *Fletcher* (*infra*, p. 194), it is necessary to be an occupier of land, and one who allows a dangerous thing to escape from land he does not occupy does not commit that tort. An example of relationship affecting the "wrongfulness" of conduct is the liability of an occupier of premises towards a visitor on those premises. Liability for negligent acts in relation to those premises under the Occupiers' Liability Act 1957 exists only when the relationship of occupier and lawful visitor is established between defendant and plaintiff.

It is recognised that the above in no sense provides a definition of tort. It fails to distinguish tort from other civil wrongs such as breach of contract, quasi-contract, and breach of trust. Each of these is definable in a broad sense by reference to some basic underlying principle (that underlying breach of contract and trust is obvious; in the case of quasi-contract the principle is that of unjustified enrichment). Tort, however, has no basic identifying principle and can therefore only be defined so as to include within itself the other categories of civil wrong. So, for example, the same act may be both a tort and a breach of contract. If a taxi-driver drives negligently and causes injury to his passenger, this is both the tort of negligence and a breach of the contractual duty to drive carefully. The same overlapping may occur with quasi-contract and with breach of trust.

It is especially difficult to distinguish tort from breach of contract. In both the right to claim unliquidated damages exists (*i.e.* damages measured only by the plaintiff's loss and not a predetermined amount of money). Such damages are not recoverable in actions for quasi-contract or breach of trust. A number of typical differences between tort and breach of contract exist but these are not conclusive. For example, tortious duties are said to be imposed by law, contractual by the contract. The obligation to perform the contract, however, is imposed by law. So also the law may impose contractual duties on contracting parties which cannot be excluded by the contract (as in the case of the duty under section 14 (2) of the Sale of Goods Act 1893 that goods sold should be of merchantable quality). Tortious duties are said to be owed to persons generally, contractual towards specific persons defined by contract. How insubstantial this distinction may be is shown by the case of the employer who owes the same duty of care to his employees for their physical safety while at work both under an implied term of the contract of service, and because of the operation of the tort of negligence. Again, tortious rights are said to be available against the world (often expressed as *iura in rem*), contractual against particular persons (*iura in personam*). Here again, there is no essential difference. The invitee on premises may look only to the occupier for protection under the law of tort against defects in the premises caused by negligent maintenance - his position is no superior to that of the visitor who has a contract with the occupier, and is owed the same duty. The law of tort typically compensates the plaintiff for loss of what he already had, the law of contract for what he expected to have. But there are numerous examples of contract protecting the former type of interest, and the tort of interference with contract is a clear example of a tort protecting the latter.

The *reductio ad absurdum* of the argument that no conclusive means exists for distinguishing breach of contract from tort is that every breach of contract is a tort. No court or legal writer has gone so far as to suggest this. There is no doubt, however, that overlapping between tort and contract may exist in a number of cases, particularly since the decision in *Donoghue* v. *Stevenson* (1932) which held that a contracting party might owe a duty of care in the performance of that contract which did not derive from the contract itself but from the law of tort. Important legal consequences may follow from the fact that an action in tort is available as an alternative to one in contract (for example, measure of damages, limitation periods may be different). Perhaps because of this, courts have tended to hold that the claim is one of contract alone without much beyond dogma or history in support (for example, liability of dentist (*Fish* v. *Kapur* (1948); of solicitors (*Clark* v. *Kirby-Smith* (1964); of architect (*Bagot* v. *Stevens, Scanlan & Sons* (1966)). The illogicality of this approach has been pointed out in *Midland Bank Trust Co.* v. *Hett, Stubbs & Kemp* (1978) which allowed a claim in tort to succeed against a solicitor who had negligently performed his contract with his client.

Where no contract exists, but a civil remedy lies the nature of which is in doubt, it is important to know whether unliquidated damages may be awarded for it since this will establish it as a tort. The elasticity of tort means that it acts as a residual category for civil wrongs which cannot be fitted in elsewhere. Doubtful torts of this kind are discussed in Chapter 27.

Between the law of tort and the criminal law, the difference is essentially one of purpose. The law of tort exists in order to give private redress to wrongs suffered by individuals. Criminal law exists for the public interest in the suppression of certain behaviour. There is, however, considerable overlapping between tortious and criminal behaviour. Most crimes are also torts. One tort, breach of statutory duty, requires proof of behaviour by the defendant which will normally be criminal. Even negligence, not normally a ground of criminal liability has its counterpart in crimes such as dangerous and careless driving of a motor vehicle and breaches of factory legislation.

CLASSIFICATION OF TORTS

Something must be said about classification in order to explain the order of treatment in this book. The emphasis of the courts has tended to be placed on the interest that is infringed, and on whether this was worthy of being protected against the defendant's conduct. This book has therefore adopted a classification of torts based upon the interest protected, beginning with the tortious infringement of the most important interests, those in personal security and property, and continuing with the protection of interests in reputation, in economic security, in domestic relationships and in various miscellaneous matters such as the right to vote. In view of the central importance at the present day of the tort of negligence, a classification based upon the mental element involved in the defendant's conduct into torts of intention, negligence and strict liability might seem logical. But negligence is preeminently of importance in protecting interests in person and property. It will therefore be treated as a whole in the part of the book dealing with torts to person or property, though this leads to a discussion of the negligent infringement of economic interests before such interests are dealt with as a whole. Otherwise, however, the classification of torts by reference to the interest protected is maintained. The difficulty with proceeding on the basis of a classification of torts by reference to the mental element required by the tort is that this fails to reflect the way in which the law developed and leads to completely disparate material being treated together. For example, the rules relating to the intentional invasion of economic interests are very different from those relating to the intentional invasion of bodily security.

NO UNITARY PRINCIPLE OF LIABILITY

It has been stated above that tortious liability is referable to no single principle. Mention must be made, however, of two attempts in which an attempt has been made to establish a principle which would constitute a sufficient though not a necessary condition for the existence of tortious liability. In *Allen* v. *Flood* (1898) it was argued that the malicious threat by the defendant trade unionists, lawfully to terminate their contracts unless the plaintiff was dismissed from his employment was not actionable in tort by the plaintiff who was dismissed by his employer. The presence of malice did not therefore make tortious what was otherwise a lawful act.

In the light of this case it would be surprising if any other general principle of liability could be established. In *Donoghue* v. *Stevenson* (1932) (for the ratio of this case, see *infra*,

p. 67) the judgements of the majority in the House of Lords, in particular that of Lord Atkin, were susceptible of the interpretation that the negligent infliction of damage or loss upon another person was invariably actionable by that person. Despite the extent of the tort of negligence, however, there are still exceptions to this rule (*infra*, p. 72), and it is therefore impossible to regard negligence as a universal ground of liability in tort.

REASONS FOR FAILURE OF TORTIOUS ACTION

An action in tort may fail for substantive or procedural reasons. The action will fail for substantive reasons where the facts relied on by the plaintiff do not in law amount to a tort. Generally speaking, this will mean the failure of the plaintiff's action, although there is the unlikely possibility of the court being willing to recognise a new tort. The most recent examples of such recognition appear to be of the tort of deceit, in 1789, of a general right to sue for inducing a breach of contract in 1853, and of the tort known as the rule in *Rylands* v. *Fletcher* in 1868.

The second substantive reason for failure of the action is that the defendant has a defence. Since the essence of a defence is that the defendant is alleging facts which make conduct of his lawful which would otherwise be tortious, the burden of proving the defence lies on the defendant.

An example of the failure of an action in tort for procedural reasons is failure in the plaintiff's evidence. Such evidence may fail to prove facts on which the plaintiff relies, or those facts which the plaintiff proves do not justify the court in reaching a certain conclusion, for example, that the defendant was negligent or malicious. In the case of those torts in which damage has to be proved as part of the cause of action the plaintiff's action may fail through his inability to show that he has suffered damage. Thus a passenger in a car which has been involved in a collision through its drivers's negligence does not establish a cause of action by proof of this. He must show also that he suffered damage in the form of personal injury or damage to his property. In the case of torts actionable *per se* (*i.e.* without proof of damage) the plaintiff succeeds upon proof of the commission of the tort by the defendant.

One procedural reason for failure that no longer exists is incorrect choice of the form of action. The forms of action were abolished in 1852, and under the Judicature Act of 1875, the plaintiff need only state the facts on which he relies without specifying any particular tort or torts. He will succeed if these facts are proved by him and show the commission of a tort by the defendant.

The failure of the plaintiff's action because of the expiry of a limitation period upon the action seems clearly procedural rather than substantive. This matter must be raised by the defendant as a defence; the court will not of its own motion take account of such expiry.

JURY TRIAL IN TORTIOUS ACTIONS

Jury trials are now rare in actions in tort. They can be demanded by either party in actions for libel, slander, malicious prosecution, or false imprisonment, and by the defendant when the action against him contains an allegation of fraud. In all these cases the court may refuse jury trial if it considers that the trial will involve a prolonged examination of documents or accounts or a scientific or local investigation. In all other cases the court has a discretion to order trial by jury but this discretion is exercised sparingly especially in actions for personal injury. In the case of these the Court of Appeal in *Ward* v. *James* (1966) laid down that there must be special circumstances before the court may order jury trial. The reason for this was the fear of excessive awards of damages against defendants on the ground that they were insured. *Ward* v. *James* also laid down as a general rule that the discretion to order jury trial is not a completely unfettered discretion but is one that must be exercised judicially. As a result of this case, jury trial in actions of tort, already uncommon, will come increasingly so.

FAULT AND COMPENSATION

In the majority of cases under English law, the plaintiff must show fault on the part of the defendant or someone for whose acts the defendant is in law responsible. Despite the advent of the age of machinery, and such inherently dangerous objects as industrial plant and high-speed locomotives, the courts have not adopted the view that those who carry on enterprises or activities in which such machinery plays a part should be liable without fault for the damage they cause. "Our law," said Scott L.J. in *Read* v. *Lyons* (1945, in the Court of Appeal), "is concerned not with [the defendant's] activities but with [his] acts." This rejection of enterprise or activity liability seems doubly unfortunate. First, it discards the justice of holding liable those who, though no fault can be proved against them in the individual case, have increased the risk of injuries by carrying on a certain activity. Secondly, the enterprise is normally in a better position than the victim to absorb the loss suffered by having to pay damages, either by passing it on to the public in the form of prices it charges for its product or by insuring against it. *Read* v. *Lyons* is significant in this respect. In it, the House of Lords rejected an attempt to argue a principle of strict liability for the carrying on of hazardous activities postulated on the basis of the rule in *Rylands* v. *Fletcher* (1868) which established that under certain conditions strict liability existed for the escape of dangerous things from the defendant's land. From the time of this decision, therefore, strict liability in the English law of tort could only exist in the logically unsatisfactory form of the rule in *Rylands* v. *Fletcher* itself, and in a few other unconnected instances (*infra*, p. 173).

Another problem which the law of tort has to face is that though liability in tort may be established, the means of the defendant may be insufficient to satisfy the judgement. Although no general rule of English law exists to avert this possibility, two important provisions ensure that in the large majority of tortious claims, the judgement will be satisfied. Under the provisions of various Road Traffic Acts the owner of a motor vehicle is compelled to insure against tortious liability to third parties. The master of a servant is at common law liable for torts committed by that servant in the course of his employment. These rules have the desirable effect of ensuring that in road and industrial accident cases, numerically the most important area of tort, the tortfeasor's liability will normally be met by a solvent person. These provisions do not cover the whole of tortious liability; and they are only applicable when tortious liability can be established. In cases of personal injury, it is generally speaking, only possible to establish liability by showing that the defendant was at fault.

The Royal Commission on Civil Liability and Compensation for Personal Injury was appointed in 1973 under the chairmanship of Lord Pearson. It published its report in 1978. Its terms of reference were: to consider to what extent, in what circumstances and by what means compensation should be payable in respect of death or personal injury (including antenatal injury) suffered by any person:

    (a)   in the course of employment;
    (b)   through the use of a motor vehicle or other means of transport;
    (c)   through the manufacture, supply or use of goods or services;
    (d)   on premises belonging to or occupied by another;
    (e)   otherwise through the act or omission of another where compensation is recoverable only on proof of fault or under the rules of strict liability, all this having regard to the cost and other implications of the arrangements for the recovery of compensation,

whether by way of compulsory insurance or otherwise.

The Commission was appointed in the wake of the disaster caused by the drug thalidomide, but its function was clearly to review the whole of the present system of compensation in tort for personal injury. The tort system has been criticised on the ground that it is expensive to operate, that it compensates only a small proportion of accident victims, and that the difficulty of proving fault makes it an arbitrary process (see, for example, Atiyah, "Accidents, Compensation and the Law"; Elliott and Street, "Road Accidents"). To abolish the action in tort would have the effect of freeing financial resources which could be used for the compensation of all accident victims. The figures quoted in the Pearson Commission Report tend to confirm these criticisms. They show that the cost of obtaining tort compensation is considerably greater than that of administering the social security system; that only a very small proportion of persons injured in accidents recover tort compensation; that over 90 per cent of tort payments are for less than £2,000 which presumably means that most tort actions are brought for pain and suffering over a fairly limited period, there being little in the way of residual disability affecting future earning power. The Commission however found itself unable to recommend abolition of the action in tort altogether. Instead they favoured a system of social security payments for the two main classes of accident victims under which the present scheme of compensation for industrial injuries would be improved and extended to the victims of road accidents. The Commission recommended a limited increase in the amount of strict liability in tort, by the introduction of strict liability for the manufacture of products, for medical experiments on volunteers producing severe injury, for vaccine damage caused by authorised vaccinations, and for certain "extra-hazardous" activities. Despite their recommendation that the action in tort should be retained, the Commission made two proposals which would markedly reduce its scope as a means of compensating minor injuries. The first is that damages for pain and suffering in the first three months after the injury should be abolished. The second is that there should be a total offset of social security benefits to the victim against damages in tort. The effect of the various recommendations of the Commission is considered at the relevant parts of this edition. For the moment it may be concluded that even if all the recommendations were implemented by legislation, the broad outlines of tort would remain unchanged.

2. INTENTIONAL INTERFERENCE WITH THE PERSON

In this chapter the law concerning intentional interferences by the defendant with the plaintiff's person will be considered. The law on this subject is still to some extent bound up with the former distinction between the action of trespass and that of case. It is therefore necessary as a preliminary matter to consider the distinction between the two.

TRESPASS AND CASE

The action of trespass had a requirement that the interference complained of by the plaintiff must be the direct or immediate result of the defendant's act. Case lay, on the other hand, where the interference was only a consequential result of the defendant's act. For example, if the defendant threw a log into the highway, striking the plaintiff, trespass was the appropriate action; if the log lay in the highway and the plaintiff rode his horse into it, the proper action was case. The distinction between the two actions, though clear-cut in many cases, might have give rise to argument. In the well-known case of *Scott* v. *Shepherd* (1773) the defendant threw a lighted squib into a crowded market-place. The squib was thrown on by two persons acting in self-preservation and for the protection of property. The second time it was thrown it hit the plaintiff in the face and exploded causing him to lose an eye. The majority of the court held the defendant liable in trespass, but Blackstone J. dissented on the ground that the action should properly have been one of case. This uncertainty was made more serious by the fact that an incorrect choice penalised the plaintiff by the failure of his action.

The distinction between trespass and case was not of purely procedural significance. Trespass was actionable *per se*, that is, without proof of damage; case needed such proof. There was however no association of any particular mental state with either form of action. Trespass may have involved strict liability, in other words, have been actionable without proof that the defendant either intended or should have foreseen the interference with the plaintiff's interest, but the matter is controverted. In any case it lay where the defendant had acted either intentionally or negligently. Case tended to be more closely connected with negligence, because the types of harm for which it lay were more likely to be committed negligently rather than intentionally, for example, actions for nuisance and for damage by fire. But it would lie for intentional injury; thus the modern tort of deceit evolved from the action on the case.

TRESPASS AND NEGLIGENCE

After the nineteenth-century legislation which abolished the forms of action and allowed a plaintiff merely to recite the facts of his case in his statement of claim provided these facts disclosed a cause of action, the plaintiff could no longer lose by making an incorrect choice of the form of action. From then on the term "trespass" came to be used in a substantive rather than a procedural sense; to describe a tort, rather than the form of action for enforcing the tort. There have been two important developments in the tort of trespass since that time. The first is that a number of cases have decided that trespass with the possible exception of trespass to land is no longer, if it ever was, a tort of strict liability (decided for trespass to the person by *Stanley* v. *Powell* (1891); for trespass to chattels by *National Coal Board* v. *Evans* (1951). Furthermore, it has been decided that the onus of proof is upon the plaintiff to show that the defendant either intended the trespass or was negligent in committing it, rather than upon the defendant to show that he acted without fault. In *Fowler* v. *Lanning* (1959) the plaintiff in his statement of claim alleged that "the defendant shot the plaintiff." It was held that the facts stated did not disclose a cause of action. The plaintiff also needed to allege (and therefore to prove) that the defendant shot him either intentionally or negligently.

The second development concerns the relationship between trespass and negligence. The frequency of actions in which negligence is the gist of the action, due to the increased mechanisation and industrialisation of society and the consequent multiplication of cases of personal injury caused by negligence, has led to the idea of negligence as a tort in itself, and not simply as a means of committing trespass or case. The tort of negligence has thus taken over much of the former area of trespass, namely, where it lay for personal injuries caused negligently though directly. Although trespass has been recognised as theoretically still available in such cases as the causing of personal injuries through the negligent driving of a motor vehicle, in practice such actions have usually been described as actions of negligence. Furthermore, the phrase "trespass to the person" has been more commonly applied to intentional invasions of the interest in bodily security such as assault, battery, and false imprisonment. In *Letang* v. *Cooper* (1965) this distinction appears to have gained Court of Appeal approval: the plaintiff was sunbathing in the car-park of a hotel. The defendant drove his car over her legs injuring her. Over three years later the plaintiff sued the defendant in negligence and trespass. There was no doubt that the claim in negligence was barred by the lapse of over three years after the accident under section 2 (1) of the Law Reform (Limitation of Actions etc.) Act 1954, which set up a three-year limitation period on actions for negligence, nuisance, or breach of duty, when the plaintiff has suffered personal injuries. The question in the action was whether the plaintiff's action in trespass was also barred under this subsection. The Court of Appeal held that it was, on the ground that it was an action for breach of duty within the meaning of the subsection.

The Court of Appeal also thought that the plaintiff's action could be dismissed on the ground that it was an action for negligence within the meaning of the subsection, since negligence was the basis of the plaintiff's allegation against the defendant. They made, during their judgements, observations about the relationship between trespass and negligence. Lord Denning M.R. thought that the old distinction between trespass and case had been replaced by a distinction between trespass, which lay only for intentional and direct invasions of the plaintiff's interest and was actionable *per se*, and negligence which lay only for negligent invasions and was actionable only upon proof of damage by the plaintiff. Diplock L.J. thought that it was still possible to call an action trespass where it was based on negligence. But no advantage could be gained by so doing. Where negligence was the gist of the cause of action, a plaintiff suing in trespass would still have to satisfy the requirements of the tort of negligence, for example, that the defendant owed him a duty of care or that he had suffered actual damage. Moreover, such an action was an action for negligence within the meaning of section 2 (1) of the Law Reform (Limitation of Actions) Act 1954, since the law looked to the substance rather than the form.

These opinions were wider than was necessary for the decision but they point the way to the law in the future. If followed, they would finally remove possible anomalies arising from the fact that a plaintiff injured by negligence might gain an advantage by framing his action in trespass. Although it is too early to conclude that trespass in all its forms can only be committed intentionally, it is suggested in this book that this should be the law.

BATTERY AND ASSAULT

In the remainder of this chapter, various forms of intentional interference with the person will be considered. Of these, battery, assault, and false imprisonment are forms of trespass.

Liability under the *Wilkinson* v. *Downton* (1897) principle (*infra*, p. 20) is on the other hand derived from the action on the case.

Assault and battery are both crimes as well as torts. It does not appear that the criminal law as to what constitutes an assault or a battery differs from the civil, with the exception that it is certain that neither crime can be committed negligently. Consequently many of the relevant precedents in civil actions of assault or battery are decisions in criminal cases.

Battery

Where the defendant, intending this result, does an act which directly and physically affects the person of the plaintiff, he commits battery.

It will be noticed that battery is here defined as an intentional tort. This reflects the views of the Court of Appeal expressed in *Letang* v. *Cooper* (1965). The effect is that where the defendant negligently though directly injures the plaintiff, by driving his motor-car against him, the plaintiff's action is not battery but negligence.

The battery need not be forcible but must be direct

Battery can be committed without the use of force. For instance it would be battery to move a sleeping man. But the requirement of directness excludes from the category of battery many intentional inflictions of physical harm upon another person. Thus it is not battery to poison another's drink, or to dig a hole intending another to fall into it, even though in each case the intended harm occurs. These cases are, however, clearly remediable by action based on the principle of *Wilkinson* v. *Downton* (1897) (*infra*, p. 20).

Consent

Many events of everyday occurrence such as a haircut, a surgical operation, and a passionate embrace would be batteries but for the fact that consent operates as a defence to an action of battery. But in order that consent should operate as a defence, it must be given to the act complained of by the plaintiff. A case illustrating this principle is *Nash* v. *Sheen* (1953): the plaintiff went to the defendant, a ladies' hairdresser for a permanent wave. The defendant applied a tone-rinse to the plaintiff's hair, which not only changed its colour but caused a rash all over the plaintiff's body. The plaintiff recovered damages for battery, since her consent did not extend to the application of the tone-rinse.

Implied consent appears to be the reason why a person who receives numerous physical contacts with his person of a trivial nature while standing in a large crowd, for example, at a football match, cannot sue those who touch him in battery.

It is assumed that consent in battery as in the case of other torts operates as a defence, the burden of establishing it therefore resting on the defendant. Certain nineteenth-century authority (*Christopherson* v. *Bare* (1848); *Latter* v. *Braddell* (1881) appears to suggest, however, that the plaintiff must establish his own want of consent. The matter awaits an authoritative decision.

Method of commission on battery

The battery need not be committed with the person of the defendant; it is battery to strike the plaintiff by throwing a stone at him. Equally provided the force used has its effect against the person of the plaintiff, it is not necessary that it should be aimed against his person, though to satisfy the definition of battery given above, the effect on the plaintiff's person must be intended by the defendant. For instance, it would be battery to throw over the chair in which the plaintiff is sitting. Equally it is probably sufficiently direct to constitute battery to remove the chair on which the plaintiff is about to sit, or to cut the rope up which he is climbing. It is more difficult when the defendant's act is committed against something in close proximity to the plaintiff, but has no effect upon his person, for example, to remove his hat or to throw water upon his clothes. In *Pursell* v. *Horn* (1838) it was held that the defendant's throwing of boiling water over the plaintiff's clothes, which he was wearing was not a battery, but the judgement gives little indication of the principles upon which it was decided. In any case such acts are actionable as trespass to chattels.

A positive act by the defendant is needed for the commission of a battery. Trespass could not be committed by an omission to act. In *Fagan* v. *Metropolitan Police Commissioner* (1969) the defendant accidentally drove his car on to the foot of a police constable. He then delayed in reversing the car in order to allow the constable to escape, knowing that his foot was trapped. The majority of the court held the accused liable for criminal assault, but one judge dissented on the ground that at the time the accused did the act complained of, he had no *mens rea*, and after he had formed the *mens rea*, he did not act. The decision seems justifiable, however, on the ground that at the time the accused formed a wrongful intention, the effects of his act in the form of a physical contact with the constable's person still persisted.

One situation that may cause difficulty arises where A intends to commit battery against B, but instead and by mistake strikes C. In criminal law, it appears that a battery is committed (in *R*. v. *Latimer* (1886) it was held that in similar

circumstances the crime of malicious wounding was committed by the accused). In America such conduct is regarded as
tortious on the ground that A's wrongful intent towards B is
transferred to C. But it is doubtful whether English courts
should adopt this doctrine. In every case, it appears, A's
conduct will be negligent towards C. The doctrine of tran-
ferred intent, though necessary in criminal law because of the
absence of a general principle of criminal liability for negligence, is unnecessary in tort.

Assault

A person commits assault if he intentionally and directly
causes the plaintiff to apprehend that he is going to commit a
battery against the plaintiff.

Although this tort, like the other variants of trespass, has
the requirements of directness, in practice it seems that difficulties about directness are unlikely to arise. As in the case of
battery, it is suggested that after *Letang* v. *Cooper* (1965)
assault can only be committed intentionally. The interest
protected by assault, that is, freedom from apprehension of a
battery, is unusual. The reason for the existence of a tort of
assault separate from battery is that, where two persons have
fought, the law can regard the aggressor as a tortfeasor and
the other as acting in self-defence, even though the aggressor
does not succeed in landing the first blow.

Can assault be committed verbally?

In *Mead's Case* (1823) which was a criminal prosecution
for murder, it was said, "no words or singing are equivalent
to an assault." It seems unsatisfactory to exclude the mere
threat as a means of committing assault, on the basis of this
flimsy *obiter dictum*, although if assault by threat is held
actionable it would be a question of fact in each case whether
the defendant intends to implement the threat. In *Read* v.
Coker (1753) the defendant, who had paid rent on behalf of
the plaintiff, visited the plaintiff with some of his workmen,
and threatened the plaintiff with physical violence in order to
make him leave the premises. The workmen clustered round
the plaintiff and committed such threatening actions as
tucking up their sleeves and aprons. This was held to be an
assault, but in the judgement of Jervis C.J. there is no indication that the threat by itself was not enough. He said, "There
was a threat of violence, exhibiting an intention to assault,
and a present ability to carry the threat into execution."

Words may qualify or explain an otherwise threatening
action, so as to render it no assault. In *Tuberville* v. *Savage*
(1669), the defendant did not commit assault by placing his
hand on his sword in the plaintiff's presence, because he said

the words, "If it were not assizetime, I would not take such language from you." Where, on the other hand, the words take the form of a conditional threat ("Your money or your life"), this seemingly constitutes assault, at least where it appears there is a present ability to carry the threat into execution.

Must the defendant intend to commit battery?

The old view of assault was that it was an incomplete battery. The question arose, if the defendant did not intend to commit battery, but nevertheless induced a reasonable belief in the plaintiff's mind that he was about to do so, would this amount to assault? The usual example is that of the defendant who points an unloaded gun at the plaintiff. This behaviour complies with the definition of assault given above, and in principle it seems that it ought to amount to assault. It is therefore to be hoped that a criminal case, *R* v. *St. George* (1840) which holds it to be assault, should be preferred to a civil case, *Blake* v. *Barnard* (1840) which holds it not to be. The analogy between assault and battery can, it seems, be overstated. Battery, for instance, can take place without prior apprehension of harm by the plaintiff, as, for example, where he is struck from behind. If battery is not necessarily a completed assault, there is no reason why assault should necessarily be an inchoate battery.

Must the plaintiff's apprehension be reasonable?

Suppose the plaintiff to be an unusually timorous person in whom the defendant's act has induced a fear of an imminent battery, though a reasonable man would not have feared in such circumstances. Does the defendant commit assault? The answer involves an examination of the mental element required of the defendant in assault. One answer is to say that the defendant is liable because he has intentionally done an act which has directly brought about apprehension of a battery in the plaintiff, whether or not the defendant knew or should have known that this would be the result. Another possible answer is to say that the defendant is liable only if he has intended to arouse such apprehension in the plaintiff, and, if he has so intended, he is liable whether or not he knew of the plaintiff's timorousness. An intermediate approach is to say that the defendant is liable only if he has intentionally acted in such a way as to cause apprehension in a reasonable person, an approach which would excuse the defendant in the case posed. The problem with the third approach is that liability in assault is made to depend upon ngeligence. Whether the first or second answer is correct seems to depend upon how specific the intention in trespass must be. In other forms of trespass (for example, trespass to land), an intention to do the act constituting the tort rather than an intention to commit the tort is sufficient.

Damages in assault and battery

Both torts, being forms of trespass are actionable *per se*. Where the defendant's act has caused no damage to the plaintiff, the plaintiff may in fact get only nominal damages. But it is quite possible for the court to give high damages in such a case because of the way in which the defendant acted. For instance, in *Loudon* v. *Ryder* (*No.* 2) (1953) the defendant entered the plaintiff's flat by climbing a ladder and entering through a window. He beat the plaintiff on her shoulders and head and dragged her downstairs. The plaintiff was not seriously injured. The following damages were awarded: £1,500 for the trespass, £1,000 for the assault and battery an £3,000 exemplary damages.

The exemplary damages could not now be awarded, but the other awards, consisting of aggravated damages for the manner in which the trespass and assault were committed, could still be made.

FALSE IMPRISONMENT

This tort is committed by one who intentionally and directly places a total restraint upon the liberty of the plaintiff. It is a form of trespass to the person, and is actionable *per se*.

Intention and directness

The tort is defined to exclude negligent imprisonment of another person. This is a reflection of the views of the Court of Appeal in *Letang* v. *Cooper* (1965) (*supra*, p. 10). There is also a requirement that the tort should be committed directly. This is of course a requirement of trespass to the person. Where for either reason the plaintiff cannot establish false imprisonment, an action in negligence may still be available. Thus in *Sayers* v. *Harlow U.D.C.* (1958) the plaintiff became imprisoned inside the defendants' toilet because of the negligent maintenance of the door lock by the defendants' servants. In trying to climb out of the lavatory, she fell and was injured. She recovered damages from the defendants because it was a reasonable act on her part to attempt to escape from the situation in which the defendants by their negligence had placed her. An action for false imprisonment would not have been available because there was not a sufficiently direct act of imprisonment.

Where the plaintiff has been imprisoned by the negligence of the defendant, but has suffered no damage, it seems that

he had no remedy if we define false imprisonment to exclude
negligence since negligence is actionable only upon proof of
damage. This may cause hardship to a person who has suffered
a fairly lengthy period of imprisonment. Even if such a person
has suffered financial loss, for example, in the form of loss of
wages, it seems that he could not recover these in an action
of negligence since negligence will not lie for purely pecuniary
loss. The solution may be to regard the period of imprisonment
itself, if it is not of merely trivial duration as damage, loss of
wages being then recoverable as consequential loss. Some
support for this exists in the case of *De Freville* v. *Dill* (1927).
The defendant, a doctor, negligently certified the plaintiff to
be insane, as a result of which she was detained in a lunatic
asylum for two days. Although false imprisonment was
probably not committed, because the defendant had not
directly imprisoned the plaintiff, she recovered £50 damages
from him. Since no damage other than the actual detention
was suffered, the court seems to have regarded this as sufficient
damage to support the action. In the tort of malicious prosecution, imprisonment counts as special damage.

The act of imprisonment

There must be a total restraint placed upon the plaintiff's
freedom of action. In *Bird* v. *Jones* (1845) the defendant
closed off the public footpath over one side of Hammersmith
Bridge. The plaintiff, wishing to use the footpath, was prevented by the defendant. In the plaintiff's action one of the
questions it was necessary to decide was whether the defendant's act amounted to a false imprisonment. The court held
that it did not (if the plaintiff could have proved special
damage arising from the defendant's act he could have sued
successfully on the case).

Provided the area of restraint is total, it does not seem to
matter that it is very large. False imprisonment on a large
estate or in a town seems possible. But there must be limits
to this. A wrongful deportation order which has the effect of
excluding the deportee from a particular country could hardly
be regarded as false imprisonment in the rest of the world.

Reasonable escape

There is no false imprisonment if a reasonable escape route
is available to the plaintiff. In *Wright* v. *Wilson* (1699) false
imprisonment was not committed where the plaintiff could
escape by trespassing on the land of a third party.

What is a reasonable escape route depends upon the circumstances of the case. The mere fact that the plaintiff is *able* to
take advantage of an escape route does not mean that he
must do so. An expert swimmer might be justified in not

taking advantage of an escape route offered by swimming if he thought that release by other means would soon become available.

Although an escape route which involves a risk of injury to the plaintiff may be regarded as unreasonable for the purpose of establishing the tort of false imprisonment it appears that an imprisoned person may not have acted unreasonably in taking that means of escape and suffering injury as a result. Thus in *Sayers* v. *Harlow U.D.C.* (1958) (*supra*) though it was regarded as reasonable, and therefore not a *novus actus* (*infra*, p. 115), for the plaintiff to attempt to escape from a lavatory in which she was locked by climbing over the wall, it seems likely that such an escape route would not have been held a reasonable one for the purpose of preventing her detention from amounting to false imprisonment. A person locked by the defendant in a room from which the only possibility of escape is a hazardous climb down a drain-pipe, is falsely imprisoned, and yet if he risks the climb and suffers injury, it seems that he might be held to have acted reasonably and therefore recover damages from the defendant. But whether he has acted reasonably depends upon a number of factors, in particular the possible duration of his detention and the degree of risk involved in trying to escape.

Despite the fact that false imprisonment is a form of trespass to the person, it does not require a physical act aimed against the person of the plaintiff. Imprisonment by show of authority is sufficient, for example, arrest by a constable, or restraint by persuasion used by a Commissioner of Lunacy to prevent the plaintiff, whom he believed to be insane, from leaving the room as in *Harnett* v. *Bond* (1925).

False imprisonment by omission to act

In *Herd* v. *Weardale Steel, Coal and Coke Co.* (1915) the plaintiff miners refused to complete their shift because they considered the work to be dangerous. The defendants' manager refused for some time to allow the lift to be used to take the men up the lift-shaft. The defendants were not in breach of contract because there was no obligation to remove men from the shaft except at certain times.

The House of Lords held that this did not amount to false imprisonment. The ratio appears to be that the defendants had committed no positive act of detention upon the plaintiffs and the plaintiffs were in breach of contract in asking for their liberty before the end of the shift. But the original imprisonment had been committed by an act of the defendants, to which admittedly the plaintiffs had given their consent. It would clearly have been false imprisonment to have refused to take up the miners *at the end of their shift*. This being so, it is not clear why the fact that the miners were in breach of contract should have made a difference, since the fact that a workman is in breach of contract in leaving his work early is no justification for imprisoning him. The case is probably wrongly decided.

What interest does this tort protect?

Although the obvious answer to this question appears to be, the interest in freedom, there is some force in the idea that it is the plaintiff's belief in his freedom that is protected. If the defendant informs the plaintiff that he is to be confined to his house, and that armed guards are placed outside the house with instructions to shoot the plaintiff if he attempts to leave, this appears to be false imprisonment even if no armed guards are present. In the same way, a police officer who induces in another person a belief that he is arresting him imprisons him even if he had no intention of preventing the departure of that person.

More difficult is the case where the plaintiff does not know that he is imprisoned. In *Meering* v. *Graham-White Aviation Co.* (1919) the plaintiff was being questioned at the defendants' factory in connection with certain thefts from the defendant company. He did not know of the presence outside the room in which he was being questioned of two works police who would have prevented his leaving if necessary. He succeeded in an action of false imprisonment against the defendants. It appears that the case can be supported on the ground that such imprisonment may conceivably affect the plaintiff's reputation. There seems little doubt that damages may be awarded in false imprisonment for loss of reputation caused by the imprisonment. This is a reasonable deduction from *Childs* v. *Lewis* (1924) in which it was held that damages might be awarded for the fact that the plaintiff, a director, had been compelled to resign by his co-directors, because of his wrongful detention in custody by the defendant.

Justification of imprisonment

It is clear that it is not in every case in which one person detains or imprisons another that such detention is wrongful. The detention may be justified because of a lawful arrest, or because there may have been a consent to the detention by the person detained.

There is, however, no power to arrest for a purely civil offence, for example the non-payment of a debt (*Sunbolf* v. *Alford* (1838)—defendant landlord committed false imprisonment by detaining guest for non-payment of his bill). The case of *Robinson* v. *Balmain New Ferry Co.* (1910) does not conflict with this principle—the defendant's forcible refusal to allow the plaintiff through the turnstile on his wharf unless he paid a penny was not false imprisonment since the plaintiff was attempting to leave the wharf by the exit on the side he had entered and in the words of the Privy Council "there is no law requiring the defendants to make the exit from their premises gratuitous to people who come upon a definite contract which involves their leaving by another way." The case is thus merely an illustration of the principle stated earlier that the restraint must be total (for criticism of the *Herd* and *Robinson* decisions, see G. Williams, *Justice, Equity and the Law*, Essays in tribute to G.W. Keeton), p. 47.

INTENTIONALLY CAUSING PHYSICAL HARM

In *Bird* v. *Holbrook* (1828) a trespasser succeeded in an action on the case against an occupier of land who had set a spring-gun on his land and thus caused injury to the trespasser. The principle underlying the case must have been liability for intentionally causing injury—there could have been no question of liability for mere negligence towards a trespasser.

A similar principle was applied in *Wilkinson* v. *Downton* (1897). The defendant, as a joke, told the plaintiff falsely that her husband had been seriously injured in an accident and that she was to take a cab with two pillows to fetch him home. The plaintiff suffered severe nervous shock as a result. The defendant was held liable under a principle which Wright J. expressed as follows: "where the defendant has wilfully done an act or made a statement calculated to cause physical harm to the plaintiff, and in fact causes physical harm, the plaintiff had a good cause of action."

The principle on which the case was decided gives rise to difficulty. The main trouble is with the words "calculated to cause." If these words mean no more than that harm was foreseeably likely as a result of the act or statement, there is great difficult in distinguishing the *Wilkinson* v. *Downton* (1897) principle from negligence. If the words mean more than foreseeable, such as certain or substantially certain, there is difficulty with the case itself since nervous shock, as distinct from mental distress, though a foreseeable result of the news imparted to the plaintiff, was hardly a certain or a substantially certain result. Only if the case is interpreted in this way, however, does it seem that the principle can have a separate existence independent of the tort of negligence.

It is clear that the law must impose liability for the intentional, non-trespassory infliction of personal injury, *i.e.* the *Bird* v. *Holbrook* situation. It is doubtful, however, whether the law needs a rule of liability so wide as that stated by

Wright J. in *Wilkinson* v. *Downton*, which, according to the likeliest interpretation of his judgement, has a considerable overlap with the tort of negligence. On the other hand, the liability imposed by the actual decision in *Wilkinson* v. *Downton* is defensible, because it is doubtful whether a duty of care exists in relation to the publication of words causing shock, and an action in negligence may, therefore, not be available (*infra*, p. 89). In America, a further use has been found for the *Wilkinson* v. *Downton* principle by extending it to cases of the intentional infliction of emotional distress, as opposed to nervous shock, by insulting behaviour or language. A like development in this country at the moment seems improbable.

3. INTENTIONAL INTERFERENCE WITH CHATTELS

The term "chattel" is generally taken to mean all forms of tangible property not regarded as realty, including goods, money, cheques, and other negotiable instruments.

The law relating to interference with chattels is full of difficulties, many of them arising from its evolution from three different forms of action, trespass, detinue, and conversion. Although each of these actions had a different function, there was a great deal of overlapping between them, and particularly in the case of detinue and conversion it was often a moot point whether the rules of one tort or the other should be applied. Some of this uncertainty has been removed by the Torts (Interference with Goods) Act 1977. Section 2 (1) abolishes the tort of detinue. Section 2 (2) preserves the liability it embodied as conversion. Section 1 of the Act defines the torts of conversion, trespass to chattels, negligence or any other tort that results in damage to chattels or to an interest in them as wrongful interference. Wrongful interference is regulated by the rest of the Act. It seems an unfortunate omission that the common law remedy of the bailor against the bailee does not seem to fall within Section 1 and is therefore not regulated by the Act. The effect of the Act will be considered in the course of this chapter. It should be mentioned that although the Act refers to "goods," the more precise term "chattel" will be used in this book except when dealing with the Act's provisions.

There is no doubt that the person principally protected by these tortious remedies is the owner of the chattel. He will normally be the person with a right to the immediate possession of the chattel as is required in conversion. He will also normally, though less often, be the person in actual possession of it as required in trespass. But the emphasis of the law on possession rather than title means that many others besides the owner of the chattel can sue in tort for interference with the chattel. These may include the wrongful possessor, even the thief. The extent to which the law has gone in protecting actual possession may be derived from the fact that such possession is a means of establishing a right to the chattel's possession, so that the person deprived of it may bring conversion or detinue. This fact has also meant a certain amount of overlapping between the latter two remedies and trespass.

TRESPASS TO CHATTELS

The tort may be defined as an intentional and direct act of interference by the defendant with a chattel of which the plaintiff was in possession at the time of the interference.

Plaintiff's interest; possession

The defendant's act must disturb the plaintiff in his possession of the chattel. Therefore it will be necessary for the plaintiff to prove his possession in order to succeed in trespass. Generally in order to prove possession of a chattel, it is necessary to prove that it is within one's control, either because it is in one's physical grasp or by other means. Thus a person continues to possess the goods that he has left in his house or car despite the fact that he himself is not in the house or car. It is also possible for possession to exist through another person; thus a master is in possession of goods held on his behalf by his servant.

It appears to be the law that there is no requirement in trespass that the possession should be lawful. Thus a thief may sue in trespass. But there must be some limits to this. The owner, or one with some genuine proprietary right over the chattel, cannot be successfully sued in trespass by a thief. This does not mean that an owner can never commit trespass to his own chattel. In *Rose* v. *Matt* (1951) the purchaser of some goods pledged his clock with the seller of the goods as security for a loan of the purchase price. Later he returned and took the clock away secretly. The owner of the clock was convicted of larceny. Since larceny (now called theft) was an offence which involved a trespassory taking, there is no doubt that the owner of the clock could have been sued in trespass by the pledgee.

Exceptions to the rule that the plaintiff must have possession

(i) *Bailment* is a transaction by which A, the bailor, transfers possession of a chattel to B, the bailee, both intending that at some future date, it should be transferred back to A. If no term is fixed for the bailment, it is said to be at will, and the bailor can demand possession from the bailee at any time. If a term is fixed, the bailor cannot demand possession from the bailee until the term has expired (or the bailment has otherwise been determined).

The bailor-at-will is allowed to sue for trespasses to his bailee's possession (*Lotan* v. *Cross* (1810); *Johnson* v. *Diprose* (1893)). The justification of this is normally expressed to be that the bailor here has a right to the immediate possession of the chattel, and in consequence may be regarded as being in actual possession through his bailee. The bailor for a term, who has no right to immediate possession of the chattel, cannot sue in trespass (*Gordon* v. *Harper* (1796)). It seems contrary to principle that the bailor can ever sue his bailee in trespass for doing an act contrary to the terms of the bailment, since there can be no question of the bailee infringing his own possession. There is support for this view in the Australian case of *Penfold's Wines Pty.* v. *Elliott* (1946), but in the English case of *Burnard* v. *Haggis* (1863) the court held that an act of the bailee which was not merely a wrongful perform-ance of the bailment but went completely outside its terms was trespassory at the suit of the bailor. The case seems difficult to support.

(ii)   The title of *executors and administrators of estates* relates back to the death of the deceased. This is the case with possession of chattels forming part of the estate. They are thus enabled to sue for trespass to such chattels committed before they actually take possession of the estate.

(iii)   The *owner of a franchise* in wrecks has been allowed to sue in trespass one who seized a cask of whisky from the wreck (*Dunwich Corporation* v. *Sterry* (1831)).

(iv)   A *trustee* may sue for trespass to chattels in the posses-sion of a beneficiary.

Jus tertii

Jus tertii may now be a defence to trespass to chattels under section 8 of the Torts (Interference with Goods) Act 1977. Its effect is considered on p. 31.

Acts constituting trespass

The defendant's act need not dispossess the plaintiff. A mere moving of the chattel, called an asportation, is sufficient.

In *Kirk* v. *Gregory* (1876) the defendant, the sister-in-law of a person recently deceased, removed his jewellery from the room where he lay dead to another room in the house, in order to safe-guard it. The jewellery was stolen by some unknown person. She was sued successfully in trespass by the executor of the estate, although the damages awarded against her were nominal.

Clearly a dispossession will amount to a trespass. Indeed it is the usual ground of complaint for which trespass is brought. It is uncertain whether a mere touching of the chattel, not amounting to an asportation or a dispossession is a trespass. If it causes damage it is clearly actionable as trespass, as for example where poison is adminstered directly to another's dog. Where no damage is caused, it is a little difficult to imagine circumstances in which the action of trespass would serve a purpose. It has been suggested that it might be useful for the purpose of preventing the handling of museum exhibits, but the action of trespass seems a somewhat heavy-handed way of dealing with this. Nevertheless the theoretical possibility of an action of trespass for mere touching probably should be preserved.

The defendant's act must directly cause the trespass

If the defendant has put poison down for the plaintiff's dog which the dog consumes, or placed a barrier across the highway into which the plaintiff drives his car, damaging the car, these acts will not amount to trespass because they are insufficiently direct. The courts have not yet decided whether, under an analogous principle to that on which *Wilkinson* v. *Downton* (1897) (*supra*) was based, a person can be sued for causing intentional, non-trespassory, damage to a chattel. There is probably liability here (*cf. infra*, p. 43).

As in battery, there is no need for the defendant himself to come into physical contact with the chattel. To throw a stone at a window and break it is therefore a trespass.

State of mind of defendant

It is suggested that after *Letang* v. *Cooper* (*supra*, p. 10) this form of trespass requires an intentional act on the defendant's part. It is true that *Letang* v. *Cooper* (1965) concerned trespass to the person, but there seems no reason why this should be treated differently from trespass to chattels.

National Coal Board v. *Evans* (1951) is authority for the proposition that in the absence of intention or negligence on the defendant's part, trespass to chattels will not lie. In that case the defendant's servant in the course of excavating the foundations of a building damaged the plaintiff's cable which was situated beneath the land surface. Because the presence of the cable could not have been foreseen by the defendant's servant, the defendant was held not liable in trespass.

It is assumed that after *Fowler* v. *Lanning* (*supra*, p. 10) the burden of proving fault in this form of trespass rests on the plaintiff.

Damages in trespass to chattels

The successful plaintiff who has actually been permanently deprived of the chattel by the defendant is entitled to its full value (even where as in *Wilson* v. *Lombank* (1963) the plaintiff has no title to the chattel, and the defendant's trespass involves restoring the chattel to its true owner). It may be assumed that consequential damages due to the plaintiff's being deprived of the chattel will also be awarded in trespass.

Where the defendant has not deprived the plaintiff of the chattel, but has damaged it, the damages awarded will be measured by the extent of the damage.

CONVERSION

This tort requires an intentional dealing with a chattel by the defendant which constitutes a sufficiently serious infringement of the plaintiff's right to possess that chattel as to amount to a denial of it.

Conversion is both more various in its method of commission than trespass, and more exacting in its requirement that the defendant's act must amount to a denial of the plaintiff's right to possess the chattel. Thus an infringement of actual possession is always trespass, but whether it is conversion depends upon the seriousness of the infringement (see the case on asportation, *supra*, p. 24). Conversion may take many forms other than an infringement of actual possession.

Conversion is the primary remedy by which proprietary interests in chattels are protected. Its reputation for difficulty owes something to this, since many disputes over title to chattels involve difficult questions of commercial law. Although it is largely an accident of history that proprietary claims to chattels are protected by actions in tort, the tortious aspect of conversion causes it to have characteristics which a purely proprietary action would not possess. Thus the judgment in conversion is for the value of the chattel, rather than for the return of the chattel itself. Where the plaintiff is the owner of the chattel, his title in the chattel passes to the defendant when the latter has satisfied a judgment obtained against him in conversion; for this reason conversion operates like a compulsory sale of the chattel to the defendant. A further distinctive feature of conversion is that it lies against anyone who has had dealings with the chattel provided they are sufficiently serious to amount to conversion; a purely proprietary action would lie only against the actual possessor of the chattel.

It must also not be overlooked that because the interest protected in conversion is the plaintiff's right to possess the chattel rather than his title to it, and because such right to possess may be established in other ways than by showing title to the chattel (*infra*, p. 27), the interest protected is more extensive than a merely proprietary one.

The distinction between right to possession and title can be observed in those cases where the owner has no right to possess his own chattel. On the facts of *Rose* v. *Matt* (1951) (*supra*, p. 23) for instance, the pledgee could certainly have sued the owner of the clock in conversion. This is because the pledgor, as a bailor for a term, had lost the right to possess the clock for the period of the pledge.

Plaintiff's interest; concept of right to possession

The plaintiff in conversion must have a right to the chattel's immediate possession. The force of the word "immediate" is that it serves to exclude cases where the plaintiff has some right over the chattel which will entitle the plaintiff to its possession at some future date. For example, the bailor for a term of a chattel will eventually become entitled to its possession. Since, however, his right is to eventual rather than immediate possession, he cannot sue in conversion.

The plaintiff may prove his right to immediate possession of the chattel in one of two ways:

1. He may show that he was in actual possession of the chattel at the time of the defendant's act. The mere fact of possession peacefully held is usually enough to confer a right to possession as against one who disturbs it. But this will not be the case where the person interfering with possession is the true owner or some other person with a title to the chattel which entitles him to its immediate possession. In some cases, however, even the owner can commit conversion against one in actual possession (the facts of *Rose* v. *Matt* (*supra*, p. 23) again present an example).

2. Where the plaintiff was not in possession at the time of the defendant's act, he must show that he has some right in relation to the chattel, entitling him to its immediate possession. Again ownership is the best example, with the proviso that as already explained, the owner does not always have the right to immediate possession of his chattel. It is difficult to state with certainty what, apart from ownership, confers the right to immediate possession of a chattel. Certain cases are clear. The bailee for a term of a chattel has such a right. The pledgee also has the right to immediate possession of the pledge; indeed pledge is a special type of bailment for a term. The holder of a lien also has the right to immediate possession of the subject-matter of the lien. For example, the seller of a chattel has a lien over it until the buyer has either paid or tendered the purchase price. Until that time, the buyer, though he normally acquires ownership of the chattel (section 18 of the Sale of Goods Act 1893) does not have the right to its immediate possession.

The following examples show the working of the law-

1. A bails a chattel for a term to B. It is stolen by C who sells it to D.

Under the principles laid down above, A has no action in conversion against anyone. B can sue either C or D in conversion (the receipt by D under a sale amounts to conversion).

2. A buys a chattel from B. It is stolen from B by C. The buyer of a chattel normally acquires ownership once the contract of sale has been concluded (Sale of Goods Act 1893, section 18) and therefore has the right to possession of the chattel. But he only has this right if he has paid or tendered the purchase-price to the seller; until that time the seller has a lien over the chattel. In the above example B could sue C in conversion, since C has infringed his actual possession. A could sue C in conversion if he had paid or tendered the purchase price to B, since only then does B's lien over the chattel terminate, (*cf. Lord* v. *Price* (1874) where the facts were similar to this example.)

Although the bailor for a term of a chattel has no right to its immediate possession during the term, at the end of the term or at the termination of the bailment, for example, where the bailee has committed an act repugnant to the bailment, the bailor acquires the right to the immediate possession of the chattel and can sue in conversion. If, for example, the bailee sells the chattel, the bailor may sue the bailee or the buyer in conversion. Complicated problems arise in the case of hire-purchase contracts in determining whether the hirer's disposal of the goods has the effect of determining the contract of hire-purchase, so allowing the hire-purchase company to sue in conversion (this normally depends upon the court's interpretation of the hire-purchase agreement—see *North General Wagon and Finance Co.* v. *Graham* (1950)).

Apart from these specific cases, there appears to be a general rule that possession of a chattel confers a right to possession of that chattel as against a later possessor. The clearest example of such so-called possessory title is that of the finder, but the doctrine does not appear to be limited to this case. So if A is in possession of a chattel, he has a right to its possession, not only as against B who steals it from him but as against C who buys it from B.

Right to possession of a wrongdoer

There appears to be no English authority upon whether a thief and other wrongful possessors can sue in conversion, but academic opinion leans in favour of their being able to do so where the thief is suing for an infringement of his actual possession, but less so where they are suing on the basis of a possessory title. In the Canadian case of *Bird* v. *Fort Frances* (1949) the plaintiff who had found money on land while trespassing on that land, was allowed to recover it from the police in an action of conversion. The court thought that whether or not he committed larceny as a finder was immaterial, since a thief could sue in conversion.

Finder
The finder is a somewhat special case. In those cases in which he gets possession, he can sue in conversion for an infringement of his actual possession, or on the basis of his possessory title.

In *Armory* v. *Delamirie* (1721) a chimney-sweep's boy found a jewel and handed it to the apprentice of a goldsmith for valuation. The latter extracted the jewel from its setting, and handing back the setting to the boy, offered him 1½d. for the jewel. This offer the boy refused and later sued the goldsmith in conversion. This action was successful, the court ruling that "the finder has such a property as will enable him to keep it against all but the rightful owner."

This went further than was necessary for the decision. In the first place, by property the courts clearly meant possession. In *Armory* v. *Delamirie* (1972), for example, there was an infringement of an existing possession, which the plaintiff had not surrendered by handing over the jewel for valuation. Secondly, the finder's possession will not always avail against all but the owner; for example, a previous lawful possessor from whom the goods had been stolen previous to the find would have a title superior to the finder's. Finally the courts have limited the possession of finders to cases where the finding is on the surface of land. Thus in *Bridges* v. *Hawkesworth* (1851) the plaintiff, a customer in the defendant's shop, found some banknotes on the floor of the shop. He then handed them to the defendant for the purpose of trying to discover the owner, but the notes were never claimed. The plaintiff successfully sued in conversion for the notes. The facts clearly illustrate the underlying principles. The plaintiff had obtained possession of the notes by finding, and although he surrendered them under a bailment to the defendant for the purpose of discovering the owner, the bailment became determinable on demand by the bailor when it was clear that the owner would make no claim. The defendant, therefore, committed conversion by refusing the plaintiff's demand for the banknotes. To the same effect is *Hannah* v. *Peel* (1945) (finder, a soldier, entitled to possession of brooch he found in house which had been requisitioned by the military authorities as against the defendant who was the owner of the house, and to whom the brooch had been handed by the police).

against the defendant who was the owner of the house, and to whom the brooch had been handed by the police).

On the other hand, where the chattel is attached to or lying beneath the surface of land, the possessor of land has possession of it. On this ground the possessor of land has been held entitled as against the finder to a pre-historic boat buried beneath the land surface (*Elwes* v. *Brigg Gas Co.* (1886), two rings lying on the mud at the bottom of a pool (*South Staffs. Water Co.* v. *Sharman* (1896) and bank-notes found by workmen in the wall safe of demolition premises (*City of London Corporation* v. *Appleyard* (1963)). It should be emphasised that possession of the land *at the time of the finding* is not necessary. Thus in *Elwes* v. *Brigg Gas Co.* (1886) the boat was found by the actual possessor of the land who had possession under the lease from the plaintiff. As it was clear, however, that the boat had been under the land at the beginning of the lease, the plaintiff was entitled to it.

The law on this matter is not particularly logical. The distinction between finding something on the surface of land, and finding something attached to it makes quite trivial matters important. If the chattel is lost on a dry patch of land the finder gets possession; if dropped into mud, the possessor of land. To allow the finder possession will encourage the finder to be honest and report his find, since otherwise he has no incentive for so doing. (He may have a further incentive since a finder in certain circumstances commits theft if he decides to keep the thing for himself—sections 3 (1) and 2 (1) (c) of the Theft Act 1968.) It is particularly necessary to provide this incentive in the case of finding on land to which the public has access, and for this reason the explanation of *Bridges* v. *Hawkesworth* (1851), in *South Staffs. Water Co.* v. *Sharman* by Lord Russell of Killowen, that the notes were found in the public part of the shop, though not justified by the judgment in the case. seems the most rational explanation of it. The policy argument in favour of allowing a finder possession of something found on the surface of private land seems weaker. Here it seems that the possessor of land should possess the chattel—*Hannah* v. *Peel* (1945) can be distinguished on the ground that the owner of the house had never been in possession of it prior to its requisition. (The Law Reform Committee has given its support to the view that in the case of a finding on land of a public character, the finder should acquire possession—Eighteenth Report of the Law Reform Committee, Cmnd. 4774 (1971)).

Treasure trove

The crown has a prerogative right to any gold or silver in coin, plate or bullion found in such circumstances that the owner is unknown (*cf. Att.-Gen. of the Duchy of Lancaster* v. *G.E. Overton Farms* (1980)).

Right of a proprietary nature

Whether the plaintiff's right to immediate possession of the chattel is based upon a right of property in it, or a right deriving from previous possession of it, it seems clear that a right of a proprietary nature is necessary—a mere contractual right to obtain immediate possession is not sufficient (see *International Factors Ltd.* v. *Rodriguez* (1979)).

Jus tertii (right of a third party)

In certain circumstances the defendant could rely as a defence on the fact that a third party had a better title to the chattel than the plaintiff. In such circumstances the defence was successful even though the plaintiff had a better title than the defendant. At common law the defence was only clearly available in two limited situations: (1) where the defendant defended the action under the authority and on behalf of the third party; (2) where the defendant had been evicted by the third party by title paramount (*i.e.* superior to that of the plaintiff). *Jus tertii* was certainly not available as a defence to conversion (or trespass) where the defendant had infringed the plaintiff's actual possession; it is a matter of academic dispute whether it was available where the plaintiff was relying on a right to immediate possession at the time of the defendant's act. The absence of the defence meant that the defendant might be subject to a double liability if he were sued first by one with a possessory title and later by the true owner. To allow the defence against one with only a possessory title would, however, be unfair if the true owner never made a claim for his chattel, since this would mean that the defendant succeeded against one with a better right to possession than himself. Section 8 of the Torts (Interference with Goods) Act 1977 attempts to resolve the problem. Section 8 (1) allows the defendant to plead the defence that a third party has a better title than the plaintiff in all actions for wrongful interference. Section 8 (2) provides for the making of Rules of Court to apply in proceedings for wrongful interference, requiring the plaintiff to give particulars of his title, and to identify any person who has or claims any interest in the chattel, and authorising the defendant to have the third party joined as a party to the action, and the court to deprive the third party of his right of action against the defendant if he fails to appear in the action. This has now been done (S.I. 1978, No. 579).

The effect of section 8 on double liability must be considered in connection with section 7. This regulates the case where two or more persons have interests in a chattel, but the court would be entitled to award the full value of the chattel to either party as damages for conversion. The example may be taken of the finder (who has a possessory title) and the true owner. The finder could undoubtedly recover the full value of the chattel in conversion or trespass from a third party on the basis of his possessory title. The position now is that the defendant is entitled under section 8 to have the true owner joined as a party. If the defendant complies with the requirements of section 8 and the true owner fails to appear, the court may deprive him of any further right of action against the defendant. Double liability is thus avoided. If the true owner appears as a party, section 7 (2) provides that the relief shall be such as to avoid double liability of the wrongdoer as between those claimants. The effect of this would be that the defendant would have to pay damages to the true owner alone, since a person with a possessory title could not succeed in conversion once the defendant has satisfied the true owner. Section 8 and section 7 (2) depend upon the true owner being identifiable. Where this is not the case, double liability would still be possible since the defendant might be held liable in successive actions by the finder and the true owner. To avoid this, section 7 (3) provides, in effect, that the finder has an obligation to account for what he has recovered in damages to the true owner, and section 7 (4) that the true owner, if at that time he also has recovered damages from the defendant must account to the defendant to the extent of the amount by which he is unjustly enriched. It should be noted that bailment does not present this problem of double liability, since satisfaction made to the bailee bars the bailor's action. The bailee has, however, a common law duty to account to the bailor.

The continued existence of the action of the bailment outside the bailment may cause a problem. The defence machinery of section 8 is not available in such an action. Nor does section 7 (2) apply since that is limited to actions for wrongful interference. Where the bailor and a third party made conflicting claims for the chattel against the bailee, the bailee ran the risk of converting it by delivering it to whichever had not got the superior title. His solution was to institute interpleader proceedings, the effect of which was that title to the chattel was determined by the court, and the bailee was protected from an action in conversion by handing over the chattel in accordance with the court's order. Interpleader proceedings are only available where the third party makes a claim. The absence of the machinery in sections 7 and 8 may therefore penalise the bailee where he is being sued on the bailment by the bailor, and a third party, whom he suspects to be owner, makes no claim.

Mental state of defendant in conversion

The defendant must intend to do the act which is relied on by the plaintiff as a conversion. This is quite different from intending to commit conversion. Where A does an act amounting to a conversion of B's chattel, in the mistaken belief that it belongs to him, he commits conversion. For this reason, conversion often operates like a tort of strict liability, in the sense that the defendant may be altogether free from fault.

Acts amounting to conversion

In order to constitute a conversion, the defendant's act must deny the plaintiff's right to possess the chattel. Around this somewhat vague requirement have centred most of the difficulties of conversion. Althought there will be no argument about most of the forms that conversion may take, there will always be a peripheral category of acts about which doubt must be felt. The following is a classification of the chief ways in which conversion can be committed. It is recognised that conversion may take other forms not here described.

Dispossession

Dispossession of another person is normally both a trespass and a conversion, since an infringement of another person's possession is usually sufficient to amount to a denial of that person's right to possess the chattel. Thus a thief commits both torts. Asportation, though invariably a trespass is not necessarily a conversion.

Thus in *Fouldes* v. *Willoughby* (1841) the defendant, in order to induce the plaintiff to leave the defendant's ferry-boat, removed the plaintiff's horses from the boat to the shore. The plaintiff remained in the boat and was transported across the river. This did not amount to a conversion; the defendant had done nothing inconsistent with the plaintiff's right to possess the horses. Where loss of the chattel is foreseeably likely as a result of the asportation, however, the defendent will be liable in conversion if such loss occurs. Thus, in *Forsdick* v. *Collins* (1816) the defendant took possession of land on which was lying a block of Portland stone belonging to the plaintiff. He removed the stone off the land to another place, and subsequently the stone was lost; the defendant was held liable in conversion to the plaintiff.

Destruction

Intentional and total destruction of another's chattel is a

conversion. Partial or negligent destruction will normally be actionable either in trespass or in negligence, but not conversion.

Dealing

1.   *After obtaining possession.* The first problem arises where the defendant has obtained possession of the plaintiff's chattel, knowing of the plaintiff's right, and then dealt with it, for example, by selling it to or pledging it with a third party. This is an obvious example of conversion. The law goes further by making the defendant liable in conversion, even where he is in ignorance of the plaintiff's right. Thus in *Hollins* v. *Fowler* (1875) the defendant, a cotton broker, sold and delivered some cotton belonging to the plaintiff, acting on behalf of a rogue who had obtained possession of the cotton fraudulently from the plaintiff. He was held liable for converting the cotton, despite the fact that he acted in the bona fide belief that he was acting on behalf of the owner.

The rigour of this principle is to some extent mitigated by the fact that it appears that the defendant is only liable if he himself has negotiated the transaction under which the goods are disposed of to a third party. Where he has only acted to facilitate another's transaction he is not liable in conversion, despite the fact that he knows the transaction affects the title of the goods. In *National Mercantile Bank* v. *Rymill* (1881) goods were given to the defendant, an auctioneer, for sale at his auction. The goods were sold privately by the seller himself, and the defendant handed them over to the buyer on the seller's instructions, knowing they had been sold. He was held not liable in conversion to the true owner of the goods. This case has been criticised by Lord Denning, M.R. and Roskill, L.J. speaking obiter in *R.H. Willis & Son* v. *British Car Auctions Ltd.* (1978) as being inconsistent with the principles laid down in *Hollins* v. *Fowler*. It seems correct that where the defendant delivers the chattel to a third party under a transaction which he knows is intended to transfer title to it, it should make no difference that he did not negotiate that transaction.

Similarly a carrier of goods does not convert them, even where the carrier knows that his act is a delivery of the goods under a sale or other transaction which affects the title to them (*Sheridan* v. *New Quay Co.* (1858)).

Whether a defendant who has himself negotiated the transaction under which possession of the goods passes to a third party is liable in conversion depends upon whether the transaction purports to create rights over the goods inconsistent with those of the plaintiff. Sale, pledge, and hire-purchase are obvious examples. A bailment-at-will by way of loan or deposit would not be. But if the bailment is for repair of the goods, the fact that the repairer has a lien over the goods for the amount of the repairs would probably make the act of bailment a conversion.

2. *Disposition without physical dealing.* A mere sale of another person's chattel without a physical dealing with it is not normally a conversion, though it may amount to slander of title to goods (*Lancashire Waggon Co.* v. *Fitzhugh* (1861)). Where, however, the sale has caused the plaintiff to be deprived of a possession he enjoyed or was entitled to, this is a conversion. *Van Oppen* v. *Tredegars Ltd.* (1921) illustrates the point. In the case the plaintiff delivered goods by mistake to a firm. The defendants' managing director purported to sell the goods to the firm, claiming to act on behalf of the defendants. The firm used and disposed of the goods in the course of their business. The defendants were held vicariously liable for their servant's conversion of the goods. In this case, although the managing director did not physically deal with the goods, he clearly caused their ultimate loss, since he induced a belief in the firm that it could deal with the goods as its own.

Receipt

To receive another's chattel under a sale amounts to a conversion of it, even though the recipient is ignorant of the other's right. This rule clearly reflects the view on which the tort of conversion is based, that ownership, even of chattels, should be inviolable. In a predominantly commercial society, however, a greater need is felt to uphold transactions, to protect the person who for value and in good faith has acquired the chattel. Thus numerous exceptions to the principle that receipt is a conversion have been established, principally by statute. For example, section 25 (1) of the Sale of Goods Act 1893 allows a seller of goods who has remained in possession of them to transfer a title to the goods under a disposition to one who takes them in good faith with the result that such a person is protected against an action of conversion by the buyer.

Receipt under a transaction which does not involve the assertion of any proprietary right over the chattel is not a conversion. For example, a carrier or warehouseman does not convert the chattel he receives. The doubt that existed whether receipt by a pledgee was conversion has now been stilled by section 11 (2) of the Torts (Interference with Goods) Act 1977, which makes it conversion if the pledgor himself committed conversion by making the pledge. An unauthorised pledge of another's chattel clearly constitutes conversion.

The doubt about receipt by the pledgee arose because although the pledgee does not assert a title to the chattel at the
moment of receipt, he asserts a future right to sell the chattel
should the pledge not be redeemed. This is, arguably, a sufficiently serious denial of the plaintiffs title to constitute
conversion, and explains the enactment of section 11 (2).

Involuntary receipt
Where the defendant has taken receipt of a chattel invol-
untarily (for example, unwanted goods sent through the post),
he is called an involuntary bailee of it. The term must be
limited to cases where, although the recipient does not want
the chattel, he may be taken to have consented to its being in
his possession (as when it is delivered through the post). If
there is no question of consent to the acquisition of possession,
for example, if the chattel is placed in a person's pocket
without his knowledge, or thrown on to his land, different
considerations arise (*cf. British Economical Lamp* case, *infra*,
p. 37).

The legal position of the involuntary bailee is a question of
some importance in view of the increasing use by high-pressure
salesmanship of the practice of sending unwanted goods
through the post and then claiming their price if they are not
returned. The involuntary bailee does not commit conversion
by his receipt of the goods. He is not bound to take steps to
return the goods, nor by failing to return the goods does he become bound to pay for them. He is probably not liable for negligence in their safekeeping. He would no doubt convert if he
unreasonably refused to return the goods to the sender on
request by the latter. He formerly had no right to use or dispose of the goods, but now under section 1 of the Unsolicited
Goods and Services Act 1971, he has a right, after six months
from receipt, or 30 days after giving notice to the sender, to
use, deal with or dispose of the goods as if they are an uncon-
ditional gift to him.

An involuntary bailee who takes reasonable steps to return
the goods to the sender is protected if they are lost. In *Elvin
and Powell Ltd.* v. *Plummer Roddis Ltd.* (1933) the delivery
by the bailee to a rogue who posed as the plaintiff's agent for
collection of the goods was held not to be conversion since
the bailee had acted reasonably and without negligence. But
in *Hiort* v. *Bott* (1874) where goods had been sent to a railway station, and were deliverable to the order either of the
plaintiff or defendant, the defendant committed conversion
by indorsing the delivery order to the rogue who posed as the
plaintiff's agent. The defendant was here not in the position
of an involuntary bailee, and his intermeddling had caused

the plaintiff to lose the goods. It was irrelevant that his action may have been reasonable.

Interference with the exercise of the plaintiff's rights

It is clear that the defendant's act may be a conversion even though the defendant has not physically dealt with the plaintiff's chattel (see *Van Oppen & Co. Ltd* v. *Tredegars Ltd* (1921) (*supra*)). But in such a case it must be quite clear that the defendant's act constitutes a repudiation of the plaintiff's right to possess the chattel. In *British Economical Lamp Co.* v. *Mile End Theatre* (1913) the defendants' refusal to allow the plaintiff to enter their premises and remove some lamps belonging to the plaintiff which their tenant had left behind at the termination of the lease, was held to be neither conversion nor detinue. The lamps were not present by the defendants' act nor was the mere refusal to allow the plaintiffs to enter their land a sufficient interference with the plaintiffs' right to possess the lamps (see *infra*, p. 64, for the right of recaption of chattels). *Oakley* v. *Lyster* (1931) shows that a refusal to allow the plaintiff to exercise his rights over the chattel coupled with other acts of the defendant may be actionable. The plaintiff had leased some land for the purpose of depositing on it a quantity of material which he owned. The defendant acquired the freehold, and subsequently wrote to the plaintiff, informing him that he would not be allowed to remove the material, claiming that it belonged to the defendant; he also used part of the material. The Court of Appeal held that he had converted all the material. He clearly converted the material he had used, but the judgments in the case do not make clear on what basis he converted the rest of the hard core. The defendant's actions went beyond that of the defendant in the *British Economical Lamp* case, because his letter amounted to an interference with the plaintiff's possession. But *England* v. *Cowley* (1875) shows that an interference with possession is not necessarily a conversion (defendant landlord wrongfully prevented the plaintiff from removing furniture belonging to her tenant and of which the plaintiff was in lawful possession under a Bill of Sale, from the premises. This was held to be no conversion). The defendant in *Oakley* v. *Lyster* had also denied the plaintiff's title to the material, but at common law it was not conversion merely to deny the plaintiff's title, even by asserting one's own inconsistent title, and this receives confirmation in section 11 (3) of the Torts (Interference with Goods) Act 1977. The case may therefore be authority only for what it actually decided-that to prevent the plaintiff from exercising an existing posssession of his material, at the same time denying his title to it by asserting one's own inconsistent title to the material and backing this up by using part of the material is conversion.

Demand and refusal

An action of conversion can be based on a demand for the return of the chattel, and a refusal to surrender it by the defendant. The action of detinue was the more typical remedy in this situation, and it was only by treating the defendant's refusal as evidence of a conversion by him that the availability of conversion could be justified by the courts.

Two conditions are necessary for the defendant's refusal to operate as a conversion:

1. The defendant must be in possession of the chattel. Where the defendant has lost possession, this may be because of his prior act of conversion. In such a case, the conversion dated for the purpose of the limitation period on the action from the act of conversion, detinue only from the demand and refusal (but see Limitation Act 1939, *infra*, p. 328). Where the defendant has lost possession in circumstances not amounting to a conversion by him the plaintiff's only possibility is detinue, since merely losing possession, even if negligently, is not conversion.

2. The defendant's refusal to surrender the chattel to the plaintiff must be unreasonable. In *Clayton* v. *Le Roy* (1911) where the defendant refused to return the plaintiff's watch on demand to the managing clerk of the plaintiff's solicitors, it was held that the refusal was not unreasonable because the clerk had shown no evidence of authority from the plaintiff to make the demand.

Conversion and detinue

Detinue was available in cases of wrongful detention of chattels. It applied in two cases. Where the defendant was in possession of the plaintiff's chattel and wrongfully refused to restore it to him this was detinue. It was also available against a bailee who was unable through his wrongful act of losing, disposing or destroying the chattel to restore it on demand to the bailor. The former case of detinue was identical with the liability in conversion just considered. The latter case was wider, since it applied where the bailee had merely been negligent in the safe-keeping of the chattel whereas conversion requires an intentional act. This case of detinue now becomes conversion under section 2 (2) of the Torts (Interference with Goods) Act 1977. In detinue the bailee had the burden of showing that he took proper care, and no doubt this will apply in conversion as well. Detinue had a further advantage over conversion in that in some cases the court would order specific restitution of the chattel to the plaintiff whereas damages were the only remedy for a conversion. The power to order specific restitution survives despite the abolition of detinue (*infra*, p. 41).

User

There is a certain amount of ancient authority (for example, *Petre* v. *Heneage* (1701)) to the effect that to use another's chattel without destroying or consuming it is conversion, and Australian case provides support, (*Penfold's Wines Pty. Ltd.* v. *Eliott* (1946)). The desirability of following these cases seems doubtful. If the defendant has caused damage to the chattel by using it, this would seem to be actionable under the residual principle mentioned below at page 43. Where the defendant has used the chattel without making any assertion of title to it (for example, where one person takes another's horse, rides it, and redelivers it to its owner), his act does not appear to be inconsistent with the owner's right to its possession, and should not expose him to an action for the chattel's value. The problem of use is more difficult in the case of bailment because of the introduction by the courts of the nebulous concept of an act repugnant to the bailment. If such an action of user is committed by the bailee, this terminates the bailment and the bailee can be sued in conversion. If the bailee's user is not repugnant to the bailment but is contrary to its terms, it is actionable on the case under the residual principle provided it causes damage (*Donald* v. *Suchling* (1866)).

Conversion and negligence

Although there is normally a great difference between the torts of conversion and negligence, it appears that negligence may have the effect of turning an otherwise innocent act into a conversion. One example of this is *Forsdick* v. *Collins* (1916) (*supra*) where the purely trespassory act of asportation was made into a conversion by the likelihood of loss of the chattel which it caused. Another example is *Moorgate Mercantile Co.* v. *Finch & Read* (1962). The defendant borrowed a car from a hirer at a time when the plaintiff hire-purchase company had the right to immediate possession of the vehicle because of the hirer's default in payment of instalments. The defendant used the car for the purpose of carrying smuggled watches, and when he was caught and convicted, the car was confiscated (permanently) by the customs under statutory powers.

The defendant was liable for conversion because he had intentionally done an act which was foreseeably likely to lead to the car's loss. The similarity of the ground on which this case was decided to the principle established in *Wilkinson* v. *Downton* (1897) may be noticed. It may give rise to difficulties in separating conversion from negligence.

Effect of judgment in cases of wrongful interference

Section 5 (1) of the Torts (Interference with Goods) Act 1977 provides that where damages for wrongful interference are being assessed on the footing that the claimant is being compensated for the whole of his interest in the chattel (or for the whole subject to a reduction for his contributory negligence), payment of the damages, or the settlement of a claim for damages, extinguishes the claimant's title to that interest. This section reproduces, with slight extensions, the common law rule concerning the effect of satisfaction of a judgment in conversion. Under section 5 (4) the same effect is produced as regards a third party's interest in a chattel where a claimant has accounted to him under section 7 (3) of the Act.

REMEDIES FOR WRONGFUL INTERFERENCE

The primary remedy in those torts representing the present wrongful interferences is the action for damages. Where the tort has caused the loss of the chattel to the plaintiff, damages are based on the value of the chattel together with any consequential loss suffered by the plaintiff. In conversion and trespass, the measure of damages was based on the value of the chattel at the date of the wrong. Since the wrong was complete at that time and the plaintiff in neither action could get his chattel back, the plaintiff would be expected to mitigate his loss by purchasing a replacement. In detinue, on the other hand, which was based on a continuing wrongful detention of the chattel until the date of judgment (which might take the form of an order for specific restitution of the chattel), the chattel was valued at the date of judgment. These differences were less absolute than theory might suggest. For example, it would not be reasonable to expect a plaintiff to mitigate his loss if he did not know his chattel had been converted. In such circumstances in *Sachs* v. *Miklos* (1948) the plaintiff was allowed as damages for conversion the higher value of the chattel at the date of judgment. In detinue also the notion of a continuing wrongful detention of the chattel until the date of judgment was a fiction in cases where the defendant had lost the chattel or negligently allowed it to be destroyed. The two supposed rules were probably no more than pointers to the court, the true rule being that the chattel was valued at the time most appropriate to compensate the plaintiff for his loss. This was the view of the Law Reform

Committee on whose report the 1977 Act was based (Eighteenth Report, para. 88). The silence of the act on this point seems also confirmation, since if it were assimilating two torts (*i.e.* conversion and detinue) with different rules as to their measure of damages, it would surely have stated which was to apply.

Section 3 of the Torts (Interference with Goods) Act 1977 deals expressly with the remedies available where the defendant is still in possession or control of the goods. The plaintiff may here be entitled to one of three remedies: (a) an order for delivery of the goods, and for payment of any consequential damages; or (b) an order for delivery of the goods, but giving the defendant the alternative of paying damages by reference to the value of the goods, together in either alternative with payment of any consequential damages; or (c) damages. Specific restitution under (a) thus survives as a remedy despite the abolition of detinue. Whether to grant it lies within the discretion of the court (see the judgment of Diplock, L.J. in *General and Finance Facilities* v. *Cooks Cars (Romford)* (1963) for the principles governing the exercise of the discretion). The plaintiff may, however, choose either (b) or (c) as a matter of right. It is submitted that the value of the goods in (b) must mean at the date of the judgment. If the date of the wrong were taken the defendant would always choose to hand back a chattel which had lost value since then and to retain one which had appreciated, so that the section would operate only to the benefit of the defendant. The overall effect appears to be that where the defendant is still in possession of the chattel, the plaintiff may get the benefit of an appreciation in the chattel's value at the date of judgment; where the chattel has lost value he will be entitled to the value at the date of the wrong under (c).

Munro v. *Willmott* (1948) was authority to the effect that where the defendant had in good faith improved the chattel, the expense of this was deductible from damages in conversion. Section 6 of the 1977 Act provides that in proceedings for wrongful interference against the improver, if the improver acted in the honest but mistaken belief that he had a good title to the chattel, an allowance must be made in assessing damages to the extent of the increase in value attributable to the improvement. Section 6 (2) extends this protection to bona fide purchasers from the improver. Section 6 narrows the protection available to the improver at common law, since the defendant in *Munro* v. *Willmott* had no honest belief that he owned the car though his actions were reasonable. The allowance is available only to a person who is a defendant in proceedings for wrongful interference (though the improver may establish a quasi-contractual claim against the owner in other cases-*Greenwood* v. *Bennett* (1973)). It is not discretionary, and is available for the whole value of the improvement even though this exceeds expenditure.

Damages could be awarded in conversion, detinue or trespass for consequential loss, and this continues to be the law. In *Bodley* v. *Reynolds* (1846), a carpenter was awarded damages for loss of earnings caused by the conversion of his tools of trade. Normally, however, the plaintiff will be required to mitigate such consequential loss by purchasing a replacement chattel. It may sometimes be excluded also on the ground that it was unforeseeable by the defendant and too remote (for example, loss of profit on a lucrative sale of the chattel by the plaintiff-*The Arpad* (1934)). In *Strand Electric* v. *Brisford* (1952), the defendants, who were in possession of the plaintiff's electrical equipment, wrongly refused to deliver it to the plaintiff on his demand. They were held liable to pay a reasonable hiring charge for all the equipment even though it was unlikely the plaintiff could have hired it all to customers. The profit-earning potential of the equipment was here obvious, and the plaintiff could not be expected to mitigate his loss by purchasing a replacement when the defendant was actually in possession of the equipment and refusing to give it back.

Plaintiff with possessory title

It is established law that the bailee, who is suing in conversion either on the basis of an infringment of his possession, or on the basis of his possessory title, may recover the whole value of the chattel despite the fact that his interest in the chattel is limited to the value of his services in relation to it (*cf. The Winkfield* (1902)). The same rule no doubt applies to persons in a comparable position, for example, carriers or pledgees. It is both just and convenient to allow the bailee, despite his limited interest, to recover the full value of the chattel, both because of his possible liability to account for its loss to the bailor under the contract of bailment and because of the desirability of finally disposing of the defendant's liability in one action. It is also clear that the holder of possession, or of a possessory title, which is not limited by any contract with a third party, is *a fortiori* entitled to recover the full value of the chattel in conversion. There is, however, a difference in the rule about satisfaction made by the defendant to the plaintiff. If the defendant makes satisfaction to the bailee by paying him the value of the chattel, this bars an action by the bailor against the defendant (no doubt because of the bailee's liability to account to the bailor for value of the chattel less the amount of his interest in it). In the case of a mere possessor, or holder

of a possessory title, satisfaction made to him by the
defendant does not bar action by the owner of the chattel
(*Attenborough* v. *London & St. Katharine Docks* (1878)—
this is the common law rule; whether it will change in the
light of section 7 (3) of the 1977 Act which requires the
holder of a possessory title to account to the owner for
damages recovered is a matter of conjecture).

RESIDUAL FORMS OF TORTIOUS INTERFERENCE WITH CHATTELS

Trespass, conversion, and detinue do not exhaust the forms
which a tortious interference with chattels may take. In these
torts the plaintiff must prove either an infringement of his
possession or a denial of his right to possession by the defendant. Where the plaintiff cannot fulfil these requirements, he
may still be able to sue. Thus, if the defendant has damaged
or destroyed the chattel, the owner may sue for the damage
to his reversionary interest in the chattel. This rule may be of
benefit to the bailor for a term (*cf. Mears* v. *L. & S.W. Ry.*
(1862)), the purchaser of a chattel where the seller has a lien
over it for its price, and other holders of reversionary interests
in chattels. Under a similar principle, the bailee who has
deviated from the terms of the bailment and thereby caused
damage to the chattel can be sued by the bailor by what was
formerly action on the case (*supra*, p. 39). Case was also available where the defendant's act did not constitute conversion
but had nevertheless caused damage, for example by interfering with the owner's freedom of using the chattel (*cf.
England* v. *Cowley*, *supra*). It is suggested that liability under
this principle extends to the causing of damage to the chattel
by wrongful user (*cf. supra*, p. 39).

Where the owner has no reversionary interest in the chattel
(*i.e.* is not entitled in future to its possession), he may be able
to rely on negligence. *Lee Cooper* v. *Jeakins* is an example of
this. The plaintiffs, who had sold goods to a firm in Eire,
arranged with X, another firm, for the reshipment and delivery
of the goods, on arrival in port in England, to Eire. The defendants, who were road-haulage contractors, agreed with X
to carry the goods from the English port of arrival to X's
warehouse. The defendant lost the goods through their negligence. It was held that this negligence was actionable by the
plaintiffs. Detinue was not available because the plaintiffs
had lost the right to immediate possession of the goods.

Replevin : distress

The existence of these should be noted. Distress refers to
any right which the law confers to seize and detain another's

chattel as a means of enforcing a debt. Where the plaintiff complains of a wrongful distress, he may apply to the registrar of the county court who will restore possession of the chattel to him on his giving security to bring proceedings in replevin. Replevin is thus a means of contesting the legal validity of a distress, and this is now its only function although originally it was wider. There is now a general power under section 4 of the Torts (Interference with Goods) Act 1977 for a county court or the High Court to restore possession of a chattel to a claimant pending the bringing of proceedings for wrongful interference relating to the chattel. Wrongful interference with a lawful distress is actionable as rescous or pound breach.

4. TRESPASS TO LAND

This tort, which is also called trespass *quare clausum fregit*, is committed by one who intentionally makes entry on the land of a person in possession of that land. It is also committed by one who enters in circumstances not amounting to a trespass, but who commits an act of trespass while on the land, for example, by refusing to leave when required to by the occupier.

Plaintiff's interest: actual possession of the land

The plaintiff must show that he was in actual possession of the land at the time of the defendant's act. It is clear, therefore, that the remedy of an owner of land out of possession of it against one who has entered it cannot be trespass. In this situation the owner must sue the intruder with the action of ejectment (*infra*, p. 50). The requirement of possession of the land in the plaintiff means also that trespass is available to persons other than the owner of the land. For example, a lessee who under the lease has possession of the demised premises may sue for trespass to them. So also may a mortgagee in possession of mortgaged land.

The law does not insist upon any legally recognised interest in the land entitling the plaintiff to possession of the land. To put the plaintiff to proof of his title to the land would penalise many persons whose peaceable and long-enjoyed occupation of land has been disturbed by a third party. But the wrongful possessor gets the benefit of the same rule, even seemingly the person who gained possession by his ejection of another person. Thus in *Graham* v. *Peat* (1861) the plaintiff who was in possession of land under a lease which was wholly void by statute was allowed to sue in trespass. But there are limitations to this doctrine. An unlawful possession, though sufficient against a third party, is not so against the true owner of the land. In *Delaney* v. *T.P. Smith & Co.* (1946) the plaintiff and defendant had orally agreed that the plaintiff was to acquire the tenancy of the defendant's premises. The plaintiff entered the premises secretly before a tenancy agreement had been executed, and was ejected forcibly by the defendant a week later. The plaintiff's action against the defendant in trespass failed. The oral agreement could not be relied on by the plaintiff as giving him the right to the possession of the premises since it was not evidenced by writing as required by section 40 of the Law Property Act 1925. Furthermore, the plaintiff's actual possession of the premises did not justify him in bringing an action of trespass against the owner of the premises.

Title to the land, though not conferring a right to bring trespass, is therefore nevertheless relevant in providing the holder of such title with a defence to an action of trespass. This does not mean that an owner of land cannot commit trespass thereto, *e.g.* a lessor can trespass against his lessee. Another limitation upon the rule that possession of the land confers title to bring trespass is that actual possession gained as a result of ejecting another is not sufficient to allow the possessor to treat a later entry of that other as trespass. The law allows the ejected person a reasonable time to reinstate himself in possession. If he succeeds in this, he does not commit trespass.

Title to the land also appears to be relevant where the exclusiveness of the plaintiff's possession is disputed by the defendant; if the plaintiff has title it will be more readily assumed in his favour that his actions in relation to the land show him to be in possession of it. Thus in *Fowley Marine (Emsworth) Ltd.* v. *Gafford* (1968) the plaintiffs were seeking an injunction against the defendant's trespassing on their tidal creek. Having found first of all that the plaintiffs could not establish a "paper title" to the creek, the court then ruled that the plaintiffs' actions in relation to the creek did not establish them to be in exclusive possession so that their action of trespass failed.

A licensee of land does not have possession of it, and his licence is revocable by the licensor at any time. Accordingly he is unable to sue in trespass. On the other hand the licence may be irrevocable by the licensor on the ground of estoppel, acquiescence, the fact that a proprietary interest is conferred or that the licence is contractual. It does not necessarily follow that in these cases the licensee can bring trespass against third parties, although *Mason* v. *Clarke* (1955) allowed such an action where the licensee had a proprietary interest in the land. Provided, however, that licensees of this sort have a sufficiently exclusive occupation of the land, they can probably bring trespass.

The act of trespass

The defendant by his act must cause a direct invasion of the plaintiff's land. Where the invasion is indirect, trespass will not lie, although nuisance or negligence may be available. In *Lemmon* v. *Webb* (1894) roots and branches of the defendant's trees projected from the defendant's land on to the plaintiff's. This was held to be nuisance and not trespass. In *Esso Petroleum Co.* v. *Southport Corporation* (1956) oil discharged from the defendants' ship was carried by the tide on the plaintiffs' foreshore. It was held that this was not trespass.

The entry on the land need not be that of the defendant. If he has thrown a stone on the land this is a trespass. But there must be some entry. In *Perera* v. *Vandiyar* (1953) the defendant turned off the plaintiff's gas and electricity from the meter in the defendant's cellar. This was not trespass because the defendant had caused no entry of anything into the plaintiff's premises although the effects of what he did were experienced there.

Trespass to the highway

The highway is in legal analysis a public right of way over land which remains in the ownership and possession of the adjoining landowners (although by statute ownership and possession of the surface and so much of the land above and below the surface as is necessary for the effective maintenance of the highway is often vested in a highway authority).

The public right over the highway is one of passage merely. One who uses the highway for a purpose other than that of passage may thereby commit a trespass against the adjoining landowners. Thus in *Harrison* v. *Duke of Rutland* (1893) the defendant who had scared off grouse as they were approaching a shooting-party on the Duke's land was successfully sued in trespass by the Duke. In *Randall* v. *Tarrant* (1955) the parking of a car on the highway was held not to be a trespass to the highway despite the fact that the occupants of the car after parking it committed trespasses on the plaintiff's adjoining land. The test appears to be whether the act committed on the highway can in itself be fairly objected to by the adjoining landowner.

State of mind of the defendant

The entry by the defendant on to the plaintiff's land will normally be intentional. This will be a trespass even if the defendant is under a reasonable though mistaken belief that he is entitled to enter (for example, because he thinks the land belongs to himself).

Trespass to land is not available where the defendant has acted neither intentionally nor negligently in entering the land. Support for this is provided by the ancient case of *Smith* v. *Stone* (1647) in which it was held that one thrown by another on to the plaintiff's land did not commit trespass, although he who threw did. It is also likely that after *Letang* v. *Cooper*, trespass to land cannot be committed negligently.

Subject-matter of trespass

The subject-matter of this form of trespass is land. This is wide enough to cover buildings, rooms in buildings, plants, and vegetables; indeed, anything attached to the land and capable of being separately possessed.

Possession of land was once thought to be *usque ad coelum*, *usque ad inferos*, *i.e.* extending to the air-space above the land as well as to the land beneath the surface. The latter proposition remains true but *Bernstein* v. *Skyviews Ltd.* (1977) has caused a modification of the *usque ad coelum* principle. That case held that the landowner's rights in the air-space above his land extend only to such height as is necessary for the use and enjoyment of the land. So the defendant's flight by aeroplane over the plaintiff's land for the purpose of photographing it was not trespass. The defendant also had a defence under section 40 of the Civil Aviation Act 1949, which provides that no action shall lie in respect of trespass by reason only of the flight of an aircraft over any property which, having regard to wind, weather and all the circumstances of the case, is reasonable. The same section provides that the owner of an aircraft if liable for all material loss or damage caused by it, or by a person in it, or by an article or person falling from it, while in flight, taking off or landing, whether the damage is to person or property and without proof of negligence, or intention or other cause of action. The Act applies to aircraft belonging to the Crown, except for military aircraft.

Trespass ab initio

Under the common law doctrine of trespass *ab initio*, one who has entered land under authority of law is liable as a trespasser in respect of his original entry if he commits some act on the land not justified by the authority under which he entered.

There is no doubt that the doctrine at its genesis was intended as a means of restraining abuse of power by officials who had a legal right to enter premises, and in particular sheriffs and bailiffs appointed to levy a distress on property within the premises. The fact that they could be treated as trespassers from the time of entry justified the award of greater damages. The same purpose can in many cases be achieved by the award of exemplary damages (*infra*, p. 312). The only importance of the doctrine apart from this is to make trespassory what is not in itself trespassory. So in *Oxley* v. *Watts* (1785) the defendant had worked a horse which he had taken as a lawful distress. It was held that this made him a trespasser *ab initio*, although the working of the horse was not trespass to chattels. But where the wrongful conduct is an omission, trespass *ab initio* cannot apply. It is also ruled out where a ground justifying entry remains, despite the misfeasance (*Elias* v. *Pasmore* (1934)—police lawfully entered premises to arrest plaintiff, and while there took documents some of which they were not entitled to take, but were not trespassers *ab initio* because of the arrest of the plaintiff). In *Chic Fashions Ltd.* v. *Jones* (1968) it was held that seizure by police lawfully on premises of goods on the premises reasonably believed by them to have been stolen was not trespass to chattels and the police were therefore not trespassers *ab initio*. The Court of Appeal appeared to doubt whether the doctrine of trespass *ab initio* had any continuing existence.

Defences

It is a defence that the defendant was on the land by permission or licence of the occupier. Such licence may be revoked by the occupier, and the entrant, having been given reasonable time to remove himself, ejected as a trespasser (the problems arising from revocation of contractual licences are not considered in this book).

The entrant also may have a legal right to enter, apart from the occupier's permission. This may be conferred by statute (for example, the powers given to officials of Gas and Electricity Boards), or may exist at common law (for example, public and private rights of way, and the right of recaption of chattels).

Remedies

The action of trespass to land, like that of conversion, is not a means of recovering the plaintiff's property. The remedies available to the plaintiff for trespass, damages, or an injunction, will not suffice to restore possession of the land to the plaintiff if at the time of the action the defendant rather than the plaintiff has possession. Furthermore, the measure of damages in trespass to land assumes the plaintiff either to have or to be able to recover possession of the land, since the plaintiff gets not the value of land but the diminution in value as the result of the trespass. The difference between conversion, on the one hand, where the plaintiff recovers the whole value of his chattel, and trespass, where he recovers only the reduction in value of his land, derives from the diffrence between chattels and land. Land is always identifiable—the plaintiff out of possession cannot therefore get the value of the land from the defendant but must bring action for the recovery of the land itself. All this points to the existence of another remedy if the plaintiff wishes to recover possession of the land rather than damages for an infringement of possession. This is the action of ejectment. It may be combined with an action for damages, called an action for mesne profits, which is merely another form of trespass *quare clausum fregit*. Where, therefore, the plaintiff is out of possession at the time of the action, even where he has been dispossessed by the defendant's act of trespass, he will sue in ejectment for recovery of the land and claim damages in the action of mesne profits. Where, on the other hand, he has possession at the time of the action, he will sue in trespass, claiming either damages from the defendant, or an injunction against further disturbance of his possession.

Measure of damages in trespass

The rule is that the plaintiff recovers from the defendant the loss he has suffered as a result of the trespass. Thus he will get the depreciation in the market value of the land (though not the cost of restoring it to its original condition). The plaintiff is further entitled to a reasonable rental for the land where the defendant has been in occupation of the land and has made use of it (*Whitwham* v. *Westminster Brymbo Coal and Coke Co*. (1896)—the two claims are cumulative— thus in the case itself the defendant had tipped refuse on part of the plaintiff's land. It was held that he must pay damages for the depreciation in the value of the land plus a reasonable amount of rental for that part of the land which the defendant had made use of for tipping).

Ejectment and the action for mesne profits

In all cases in which the plaintiff wishes to recover possession of his land from the defendant, he must use the action of ejectment. The action is wider in scope than trespass since it lies against a defendant who has come into possession of the plaintiff's land by other means than by committing trespass.

The action for mesne profits, as already pointed out, is merely a form of trespass *quare clausum fregit*. It is a claim in respect of damage of a trespassory nature done to the land by the defendant, together with a claim for profits taken from the land by the defendant during his occupancy, but unlike trespass is available where the plaintiff had a right to possession rather than possession at the time of the defendant's act. Since it is available in similar circumstances to the action of ejectment, it is normally combined with that action. The theoretical justification for allowing the plaintiff to sue in the action of mesne profits, which is a form of trespass, for acts of the defendant committed when the plaintiff had not possession of the land, is the doctrine of trespass by relation. Under this doctrine, the possession of one with a right to possession of land, who has recovered possession of it, is deemed to extend back to the date when the right to possession came into existence with the result that such a person can sue for trespass committed during the interim period. The theoretical objection against combining the action of mesne profits with the action of ejectment, *viz.* that possession of the land is not recovered until *after* the action of ejectment, with the result that the doctrine of trespass by relation cannot then operate, is now overlooked by the courts.

It may be helpful to set out the possibilities of action available to a person whose possession of land has been disturbed (it is assumed that he also has title to the land):

1. Trespass *quare clausum fregit* lies against the person who has actually infringed the plaintiff's possession, whether his act has dispossessed the plaintiff or not, and if he has dispossessed the plaintiff whether or not he is now in possession.

2. Where the plaintiff has been dispossessed of his land, it will be more normal to sue the person now in possession with the action of ejectment for recovery of the land, combining this with an action for mesne profits which lies against the present possessor whether or not he is the person who dispossessed the plaintiff.

3. Where the plaintiff has recovered possession of his land without suing in ejectment, or where he did not claim damages in the action of ejectment, it seems that he can now proceed in a claim for damages, either, in the case of the dispossessor, by an action of trespass, or against subsequent possessors, by the action for mesne profits.

4. Finally, there is a summary procedure for the recovery of land laid down by R.S.C. Ord. 113 (see also C.C.R. Ord. 26) and appropriate for the recovery of land from squatters. Where a person or persons have entered into or remained on land of which they are in *sole* occupation, a person claiming possession of such land may do so by means of an originating summons supported by an affidavit. This procedure is not only much quicker than the more traditional methods outlined above, but it has the advantage of being available against unidentifiable defendants (one of the features of the "squatters" cases being that the defendants refused to identify themselves thus making it impossible or at least very difficult for proceedings to be commenced against them). However, when recovery of land is sought by this method, no other claim, *e.g.* for mesne profits or damages, can be joined with the originating summons, and the procedure is in any case not available against a tenant holding over after the expiration of the tenancy.

Actions by those without possession or a right to immediate possession of the land

The typical case is that of the reversioner, for example the landlord or the person with an interest in remainder in land. The landlord has contractual protection against the tenant under the lease for damages to the premises. The remainder-man is protected against damage done by the tenant for life under the rules of waste. Reversioners also have an action against third parties who have damaged the land in such permanent fashion that the reversioner's interest is prejudiced.

Declaratory judgment

If for any reason it is impossible to prove the requirements of the tort of trespass, it may still be possible for a plaintiff to obtain a declaration of his rights in a declaratory action. A declaratory judgment, though not enforceable by the plaintiff, is of use in cases where the parties are in genuine doubt about their rights and wish the courts to remove this doubt. It therefore seems likely to be of use in disputes over title to land. In *Acton Bor. Council* v. *Morris* (1953) the defendant locked the door of his house thereby depriving the plaintiffs of access to their flat on the upper storey of the house. The defendant's act was not trespass, but the plaintiffs obtained a declaration from the court of their right of access to the flat.

5. DEFENCES TO THE INTENTIONAL TORTS TO PERSON AND PROPERTY

The defences that will be discussed in this chapter are those available where the defendant has committed an intentional invasion of the plaintiff's interest. Although some of these defences (for example, consent, contributory negligence) are equally applicable in the case of negligence and other non-intentional torts, most of the defences discussed here assume an intentional act by the defendant. The effect of the defence is that the defendant while admitting the commission of what would be a tort now seeks to adduce in evidence additional facts which will excuse what he has done. For this reason the burden of proving the facts that will establish the defence rests on the defendant.

CONSENT

The term consent is used to describe the defence available when the plaintiff has agreed to the commission of an intentional tort against himself. *Volenti non fit injuria* or voluntary assumption of risk is the defence available when the plaintiff has agreed to run the risk of being injured by the defendant's negligence. Consent may be express or implied. Whether it is implied will often be a difficult question of fact. The plaintiff in *Wilkinson* v. *Downton* (*supra*, p. 20) would no doubt have impliedly consented to being told the news about her husband had it been true. Consent must be given to the act complained of (for an example where consent was not a defence for this reason, see *Nash* v. *Sheen* (*supra*, p. 12)). Consent is invalid if it is obtained by fraud, duress or improper show of authority. In *Hegarty* v. *Shine* (1878) it was held that the consent of the plaintiff to having intercourse with the defendant, who did not reveal he was suffering from syphilis, was not obtained by fraud. The defendant had made no representation about his condition, and the plaintiff could therefore not establish that the terms of her consent excluded intercourse with syphilitic males.

In *Buckpitt* v. *Oates* (1968) it was held perhaps surprisingly that an infant of seventeen, though incapable of giving a contractual consent, could give a consent to another's negligence for the purpose of establishing the defence of *volenti non fit injuria*.

MISTAKE

Mistake appears to be no defence to the commission of an intentional tort against the plaintiff. The constable who mistakenly arrests the wrong man, however reasonable his mistake, has no defence to an action of false imprisonment. The rule is well settled but there is no doubt that it can cause hardship. Several examples of this have already been noted in the case of conversion, where it is clearly no defence that the defendant thinks that he has a right to do the act constituting the conversion.

Another case where hardship may be caused is where the defendant commits a battery through a reasonable though mistaken belief that he was acting in self-defence or to eject a trespasser—such belief is no defence.

INEVITABLE ACCIDENT

In an action of trespass, it appeared to be the law that the burden of proving that he acted neither intentionally nor negligently rested on the defendant—he had to prove inevitable accident. After *Fowler* v. *Lanning* (1959) (*supra,* p. 10) this defence is no longer necessary in an action of trespass.

DEFENCE OF PERSON

The fact that the defendant was acting in the defence of his person may be a valid defence to an action of battery brought by the plaintiff. The defence is made out if the defendant shows that he used no more than reasonable force in the protection of his person. Force may be unreasonable either because it is more than necessary to repel the plaintiff's attack, or because though necessary it is disproportionate to the harm the plaintiff threatened to inflict on the defendant.

Thus, suppose that the plaintiff repeatedly ruffles the hair of the defendant, a much smaller man, against his will, and the defendant eventually stabs the plaintiff. Although there is no authority on the use of disproportionate force, it seems doubtful whether the defendant could here rely on defence.

A case for self-defence must exist; a reasonable though mistaken belief by the defendant in his right to act in defence is not enough. But it may in this connection be pointed out that one who intentionally induces in another a belief that he is about to use force against him, even if he does not intend to use that force, probably commits assault. In such a case there is no doubt that a right of self-defence exists, as when the plaintiff has pointed an unloaded gun at the defendant, and the defendant has then used force against the plaintiff.

The courts have also recognised that a person may be justified in acting in the defence of his wife, his family, and his servants. Whether this would be extended to other persons is doubtful. The rule is probably that provided the defendant has acted reasonably in defending another person, he can use this is as a defence.

DEFENCE OF PROPERTY

It is well established that reasonable force may be used by one in possession of land to eject a trespasser from that land. A reasonable though mistaken belief that the person ejected is a trespasser is not sufficient. This may give rise to hardship, because there is often difficulty in drawing a line between the trespasser and the entrant under an implied licence. The occupier who ejects such a licensee thinking he is a trespasser, may it seems be acting perfectly reasonably, and yet be liable in tort.

Defence of property generally

As a matter of principle, it seems right that force might legitimately be used in the defence of one's own property in other cases than the ejection of a trespasser; for example against one who threatens a trespass, or where an owner of property not in possession of it uses force in its defence. The only decisions appear to be on the defence of property against the attacks of animals.

Thus in *Cresswell* v. *Sirl* (1948) the defendant, acting under the authority of the owner of livestock, shot the plaintiff's dog, which he believed to be about to renew an attack on the livestock. The court held that if the defendant's belief was reasonable, and if he acted reasonably in regarding the shooting as necessary to protect the livestock, he had a good defence. Under section 9 (3) (*b*) of the Animals Act 1971, the defendant is also provided with a defence if he has killed or injured a dog when it "has been worrying livestock, has not left the vicinity and is not under the control of any person and there are no practicable means of ascertaining to whom it belongs". *Cresswell* v. *Sirl* remains authority for a common law defence of defence of property.

The force used must be reasonable

As a general proposition it seems true that reasonable force in the defence of property means something less than reasonable force in the defence of person, but there is very little authority on how much force may be justifiable. In *Collins* v.

Renison (1754) in which the defendant pulled away a ladder on which the plaintiff a trespasser was standing this was held to be an unreasonable use of force. In *Bird* v. *Holbrook* (*supra*, p. 20) in which the defendant set a spring gun on his land which went off and injured the plaintiff, a trespasser, the force clearly was not used for the purpose of ejection, and was therefore unreasonable. The defendant was therefore held liable. On the other hand, in *Ilott* v. *Wilkes* (1820) where the plaintiff, a trespasser, knew of the presence of spring guns on the land, recovery against the defendant was not allowed. In so far as this case suggests that any amount of force is reasonable provided the occupier gives prior warning of it or the trespasser has notice that it may be used, it seems to go too far. The use of a spiked wall or one with broken glass seems, however, clearly justifiable. The purpose is deterrent not retributory and the trespasser has only himself to blame if he takes the risk (as to keeping a savage dog, see, *infra*, p. 209).

Distress damage feasant

This may be regarded as part of the protection which the law gives to an owner of property acting in its defence. If the plaintiff's chattel is unlawfully on the defendant's land, and has caused or is causing damage there, the defendant may seize the chattel and retain it until the plaintiff compensates him for the damage. This form of distress operates therefore as a defence to the plaintiff's action of conversion or detinue, which would otherwise be available if the defendant refused to return the chattel. The defence now applies only to the seizure of inanimate objects. In *Ambergate Ry. Co.* v. *Midland Ry. Co.* (1853) the plaintiff's railway engine which was encumbering the lines of the defendants' railway was distrained damage feasant by the defendants. The common law right of distress damage feasant in respect of trespassing animals has been abolished by section 7 of the Animal Act 1971, which provides, however, a new statutory defence based on similar principles except that the detainer of the animal is also given a right to sell it and to retain out of the proceeds his costs and the amount of any claim for damages he may have arising from the trespass.

Under the common law right, the chattel must have come on the land in circumstances amounting to a trespass or other tort. It must not be in use at the time of seizure, and the right to seize is only available as long as the chattel remains on the land.

NECESSITY

This defence differs from defence of person and property in that it purports to justify the infliction of harm on a person who is not himself threatening the person or property of the defendant.

The limits of this defence are ill-defined. The necessity of saving life was recognised as a defence in *Leigh* v. *Gladstone* (1909) in which it was held that prison warders, who forcibly fed the plaintiff, a suffragette, who was fasting in prison, were not liable in battery. Necessity would no doubt also be a defence for the surgeon who performs a necessary operation without consent (*cf. Beatty* v. *Illingworth* (1896) in which the defendant surgeon removed both the plaintiff's diseased ovaries though she had given consent to the removal of only one; the plaintiff was held to have impliedly consented to the removal. But necessity here appears a better ground for the decision). Where the defendant has acted in self-preservation, there is no authority on the availability of the defence. The two who threw on the squib in *Scott* v. *Shepherd* (*supra*, p. 9) could presumably have pleaded necessity, although the fact that they acted in the agony of the moment seems additionally important. What of cannibalism, where this is the only means of supporting life (*cf. R.* v. *Dudley and Stevens* (1884)). Certainly, homelessness does not give rise to a sufficient necessity to provide a defence to an action of trespass to land (*Southwark London Borough* v. *Williams* (1971)). The Court of Appeal in that case thought that the defence must be confined to an "urgent situation of extreme peril".

Where the defendant has acted to save property, necessity may be a defence. In *Cope* v. *Sharpe* (No. 2) (1912) the Court of Appeal excused for this reason the action of a gamekeeper who set fire to heather on the plaintiff's land in order to prevent a fire on that land from spreading to land over which has master had shooting rights. The case is unsatisfactory since the question of the liability of the plaintiff for the fire on his land is not considered so that defence of property cannot be ruled out. As a decision on necessity the case appears to be authority for two principles. The first is that the court will make a value-judgment as to which property deserved protection– the shooting-rights were valuable, the heather far less so. Secondly, it was important that the defendant was not a mere volunteer, being treated as having the same right to act as his master. It is uncertain whether a mere volunteer could ever rely on necessity as a defence in these circumstances.

Many cases which are sometimes explained as turning on this defence are better regarded as cases in which the defendant has committed no tort. Thus the defendant who erects barricades in order to keep flood-water out of his land, where the inevitable result of this is that the plaintiff's land is flooded (as in *Nield* v. *L. & N.W.Ry.* (1874)) is not liable to the plaintiff not because of the necessity of his action but because he has not committed any tort recognised by our law.

In order to establish this defence the defendant must have acted reasonably, firstly in deciding that his intervention was necessary, secondly in the steps he took to deal with the danger. *Cope* v. *Sharpe* shows that the necessity must be judged at the time of the defendant's action. In that case, the fire died out before reaching the land over which the sporting rights existed.

DISCIPLINE

It is recognised that parents and schoolteachers have a common law power, for the purposes of discipline, to inflict corporal punishment on children within their care. In all cases the force used must be for the purposes of discipline and correction and must be reasonable.

LAWFUL ARREST

The fact that the defendant is arresting the plaintiff for the commission of an offence is a defence to the plaintiff's action of battery or false imprisonment, provided the arrest is lawful. The powers of arrest of private citizens and police officers are now almost entirely statutory. The Criminal Law Act of 1967 has codified and to some extent extended the powers of arrest that existed at common law. The Act allows arrest only where the offence is "arrestable." This means an offence for which the punishment is fixed by law, or one for which under statute a sentence of five years' imprisonment may be imposed, or an attempt to commit such offences. When an offence is non-arrestable, arrest for such an offence is only possible if a power to arrest for that offence has been created by statute. There is now a common law power of arrest only in the case of one crime, breach of the peace.

Arrest under warrant

A policeman who arrests under a warrant issued by a magistrate is not liable for the arrest even if the magistrate had no jurisdiction to issue the warrant, or if it was defective in form. The policeman must however act within the terms of the warrant; he is not protected if, for example, he arrests the wrong person.

Arrest by policeman without warrant

The effect of section 2, subsections (2), (4), and (5) of the Act is to empower a policeman to arrest without a warrant in three cases:

(1) where he has reasonable cause to suspect that an arrestable offence has been committed and that the person he arrests is guilty of that offence (section 2 (4));

(2) where he has reasonable cause to suspect that the person he arrests is about to commit an arrestable offence (section 2 (5));

(3) where he has reasonable cause to suspect that the person he arrests is in the course of committing an arrestable offence (section 2 (2)).

It may be noted that in none of these subsections is it necessary for the policeman to show that his suspicion was correct, only that it was reasonable.

Section 2 (6) gives a policeman a power of entering and searching any place for the purpose of exercising these powers of arrest.

Powers of arrest of the private person

The private person has the same power as the policeman to arrest one whom he has reasonable cause to suspect to be guilty of an arrestable offence, but he has this power only if the offence has actually been committed (section 2 (3)). The common law rule in *Walters* v. *W.H. Smith* (1914) is therefore preserved. The private person has the same power as the constable under section 2 (2) to arrest one in the course of commission of an arrestable offence, but the power of arrest under section 2 (5) can only be exercised by a constable.

Reasonable cause

Where the power to arrest is dependent upon the person making the arrest having reasonable cause to suspect certain facts, it appears that he has the burden of proving reasonable cause in any action against him by the person whom he arrested.

Reasonable force

The Act of 1967 enacts the common law rule that reasonable force may be used in "effecting or assisting in the lawful arrest of offenders or suspected offenders" (section 3). It seems that a number of obvious factors are relevant to the degree of force that may be used, the seriousness of the offence, the likelihood of its repetition if the offender is allowed to escape, the seriousness of the harm the arrest inflicts upon the offender, the availability of other means of arrest. It appears that the burden of proving that the force used was reasonable rests upon the person making the arrest.

Manner of arrest

The arrest may be tortious, not because it is unjustified according to the principles discussed previously, but because it is conducted in an improper manner. *Christie* v. *Leachinsky* (1947) established that the person arrested is entitled to be informed of the offence for which he is arrested, unless this is in the circumstances obvious. Where the person making the arrest does not comply with this rule, he commits false imprisonment even if the arrest was justifiable for other reasons. In *Christie* v. *Leachinsky* itself the defendant policeman purported to arrest the plaintiff under a local Act. There were no grounds for making the arrest under this Act, but grounds did exist for arresting the plaintiff on reasonable suspicion of his commission of a crime. The defendant was held liable in false imprisonment. In *R.* v. *Kulynycz* (1970) the Court of Appeal held that though an arrest was unlawful because of a contravention of *Christie* v. *Leachinsky*, a lawful arrest could subsequently be made by informing the arrested person of the reason for which he was being held. *R.* v. *Inwood* (1973) shows that in order to effect a lawful arrest the fact of arrest must be made clear to the arrested person. If this is not done, any detention is unlawful and a false imprisonment. On the other hand, when arresting a deaf person who cannot lip-read, the arrester need do only what is reasonable in the circumstances to convey the fact of arrest and the reason for it to the person being arrested (*Wheatley* v. *Lodge* (1971)).

Another factor which can make an otherwise lawful arrest improper is the time taken before charging the plaintiff, or in the case of a private person, before bringing the plaintiff before a constable or magistrate.

In *Lewis & Co.* v. *Tims* (1952) it was held that a wait of between twenty minutes and an hour by the defendants before deciding to call the police in to charge the plaintiff who had been detained by the defendants on suspicion of shoplifting at their store, was reasonable. The police may go further than a private person and conduct inquiries and collect evidence before charging one whom they have arrested. So in *Dallison* v. *Caffery* (1965) the action of the defendant policeman in taking the plaintiff after arresting him to the plaintiff's house to see if any stolen property was there was held justifiable. But both these cases presuppose the lawfulness of the original arrest. Where, for example, the police have insufficient evidence to arrest upon reasonable suspicion in the first place, they cannot justify the arrest by the fact that it has allowed the collection of further evidence which would have made their suspicion reasonable.

POLICE POWERS OTHER THAN ARREST

The police possess a number of powers, in addition to their power of arrest, which may provide them with a defence to an action in tort. For example, they may lawfully enter premises in order to carry out an arrest which they are empowered to make under the Criminal Law Act 1967; or they may lawfully enter premises under the authority of a search warrant issued by a judge or magistrate. There is no general power to search persons without arresting them, although particular statutes such as the Metropolitan Police Act 1839 (stolen goods), and the Misuse of Drugs Act 1971, have conferred such powers on the police. There is some difficulty in deciding what the police are entitled to seize on premises which they have lawfully entered. Where they have entered under warrant to search for stolen goods, section 26 (3) empowers the seizure of any goods believed to have been stolen (whether or not the belief is reasonable, and whether or not the occupier appears to be the thief or handler of such goods, so extending the common law power of seizure conferred by *Chic Fashions (West Wales)* v. *Jones* (1968)). Furthermore as the result of a number of cases applying dicta of Lord Denning, M.R. in *Ghani* v. *Jones* (1969). it appears that where police are lawfully on premises there is a general common law power to seize articles if they are reasonably believed to be the fruits of a crime, or the instrument by which a crime was committed or material evidence of the commission of a crime. There is no necessity that the occupier himself should be suspected of involvement (*Frank Truman Export* v. *Metropolitan Police Commissioners* (1977)—documents, in the possession of a solicitor and subject to legal professional privilege, having come to light in the course of a lawful and reasonably conducted search of the premises by the police, were held to be lawfully seized by the police as being material evidence of the commission of a crime by a third party). Where the occupier himself is not suspected of involvement and refuses his consent to the seizure, the seizure will be a trespass unless the refusal is "quite unreasonable" (*cf. Wershof* v. *Commissioner of Police* (1978). These powers are not available if the entry on the premises is trespassory (*Jeffrey* v. *Black* (1978)).

ACTS DONE UNDER AUTHORITY OF LAW

The immunity of officials and other participants in the judicial process is considered below at page 332. Statutory authority may be a defence to an action in tort under the following circumstances: (1) the statute must confer either a duty or a power on the defendant to commit the act complained of; (2) the commission of the tort must be the inevitable result of acting under the duty of power. Statutory authority is thus no defence where the authorised act is committed negligently, unless the statute clearly excludes liability for negligence. Statutory authority is of chief importance in relation to the torts of nuisance and *Rylands* v. *Fletcher*, and receives separate consideration in the chapters dealing with those torts.

CONTRIBUTORY NEGLIGENCE

The chief scope of this defence will be where the tort complained of is one of negligence (*infra*, p. 123). It will rarely, for obvious reasons, be available where the defendant has acted intentionally, and no English case has yet applied it in such a situation. In *Lane* v. *Holloway* (1968), the Court of Appeal refused to make any deduction for contributory negligence where the plaintiff, a man of 64, had insulted and made a feeble attempt to strike the defendant in answer to which the defendant, aged 24, struck the plaintiff a very severe blow thus injuring him. The defendant acted disproportionately to the provocation received. In the case of a lesser blow the requisite causal connection between the provocation and the blow might have been established. On the other hand, the Court of Appeal thought it possible that a reduction for contributory negligence might be made in an action by the estate of a deceased person who had formed a plot with others to beat up the defendant and as a result the deceased met his death at the hands of the defendant (*Murphy* v. *Culhane* (1977)).

Section 11 (1) of the Torts (Interference with Goods) Act 1977 provides that contributory negligence is no defence in proceedings founded on conversion or intentional trespass to goods.

TORTS WHICH ARE ALSO CRIMES

It is now not a defence that criminal proceedings are yet to be instituted for the crime (the common law rule which made this a defence where the crime was a felony has disappeared with the abolition of felonies under the Criminal Law Act 1967).

In certain circumstances it is a defence to a civil claim for assault or battery that criminal proceedings in relation to the assault have been taken against the defendant. The circumstances are:

1. The criminal proceedings must have been summary.
2. The justices must either convict the defendant, and he must either have served a term of imprisonment or have paid a fine, or they must dismiss the complaint against him on the merits of the case. Such certificate of dismissal may be granted because the assault was not proved, or was justified or was too trivial to merit punishment (Offences against the Person Act 1861, s. 45).

ILLEGALITY

The principle of this defence is that no one can establish a right if it is necessary for him to rely on his own illegal act or one contrary to the public policy. The authorities on this seemingly simple matter are bewildering and the treatment of it here can only be brief. The first problem arises where an illegal contract exists. Such contract is unenforceable, but it is settled that where a cause of action in tort can be established without reliance on the contract, or the plaintiff's illegal conduct, illegality is no defence. Thus in *Bowmakers* v. *Barnet Instruments* (1944) the plaintiff company had let machine tools to the defendants under hire-purchase agreements which were illegal because they infringed a statutory order. The defendants sold all the machines except one, which they refused to return to the plaintiffs. They were held liable for the conversion of all the machines because the plaintiffs' cause of action in tort could be established without reliance on the illegal contracts. In the case of those machines which were sold, the decision is explicable on the ground that the court treated the sale as determining the bailment without reference to the terms of the agreement and the right to immediate possession of the machines therefore revested in the plaintiffs. In the case of the machine which was not sold, the mere refusal to return it would not seem *ipso facto* to determine the bailment, and the decision can therefore only be justified on the ground that a term in the contract caused it to have this effect. If this is so, it seems that, while reliance on the illegal contract may not be made by the plaintiff, he can at least refer to its terms in order to establish his cause of action. If the plaintiff cannot establish a cause of action in tort without disclosing his own illegal or immoral conduct, no action will lie. So in *Siveyer* v. *Allison* (1935) the plaintiff could not succeed in an action of deceit against the defendant, a married man who had promised to marry her (an illegal contract), because in establishing her cause of action she had to disclose her immoral association with the defendant.

Where no contract is involved, illegality may still be a defence. Much depends upon whether the illegality is a casual or incidental part of the main cause of action, or whether it is an integral part. So a person driving an unlicensed car could clearly sue another driver for his negligence in causing a collision. Also if one burglar picks another's pocket while proceeding to the premises they intend to burgle, that other may sue. If, however, they have agreed to open a safe by means of explosives, and one negligently handles the explosive charge so injuring the other, no action will lie (the latter examples are taken from *obiter dicta* of Lord Asquith L.J. in *National Coal Board* v. *England* (1954)).

So far the courts have made little attempt to distinguish the effects of different types of illegality. But such distinction is conveivably important. Would the decision in the *Bowmaker* case have been the same had the illegality been more than a breach of a fairly trivial statutory rule? In one case at least, the type of illegality is important. Where an employee who has aided and abetted his employer's breach of statutory duty is suing his employer for personal injury caused by that breach, illegality is no defence (*National Coal Board* v. *England* (1954)).

ENTRY ON LAND

In certain circumstances there is a right to enter another's land with a consequent defence to any action arising out of that entry. Three cases may be considered in all three of which the element of self-help as a *remedy* for tort is present, although the defence may be available where no tort has been committed by the occupier of the land which the defendant enters.

1. Recaption of chattels

An owner of a chattel may sometimes enter another's land in order to recapt it. The so-called right of recaption here operates as a defence to the owner of the land's action of trespass. This right of entry, however, appears to be limited to three situations:

(*a*) Where the chattel comes on the land by the act of the occupier.

(*b*) Where it comes on the land by the felonious act of a third party. How this will be interpreted with the abolition of the distinction between felonies and misdemeanours is uncertain.

(c) Where it comes on the land accidentally. In the case of *Thorns* (1466) thorns fell from a tree growing in a hedge on to another's land, and it was held that as they came there accidentally, they could be recapted. But there is room for doubt as to the meaning of "accidentally." Would it cover the situation where the chattel came on the land by the negligence of its owner or a third party? Can an owner ever recapt it when it is his act that has caused the entry of the chattel, whether negligent or not?

Recaption of the chattel may be a defence to an action of battery as well as trespass to land, since reasonable force may be used to effect recaption.

Where the right of recaption does not exist, the owner of the chattel may be without remedy, since the mere refusal by the occupier either to surrender the chattel, or to allow the owner to retake it does not appear to be conversion (*supra*, p. 37).

2. Re-entry on land

At common law a person entitled to the immediate possession of land could enter it and eject, using only reasonable force, the person in possession. This right operated as a defence to an action for trespass to land. Section 6 of the Criminal Law Act 1977 makes it an offence for anyone other than a "displaced residential occupier" to use or threaten violence for the purpose of securing entry into the premises, provided there is someone on the premises opposed to the entry. It seems likely that this section, like the Forcible Entry Act 1381 which it replaced, will not be interpreted as taking away the entrant's defence to an action of trespass by the occupier (*Hemmings* v. *Stoke Poges Golf Club* (1920)). Under section 3 of the Protection from Eviction Act 1977 it is unlawful for an owner of premises, which have been let under a tenancy which is not a statutorily protected tenancy, to enforce against the occupier of the premises upon the termination of the tenancy his right to recover possession of them except by court proceedings. This section appears to take away the owner's defence to an action of trespass by the occupier (*obiter dicta* of Ormrod, L.J. in *McCall* v. *Abelesz* (1976)).

3. Abatement of nuisance

The right of abatement of a nuisance enables one affected by the nuisance to take steps of his own in order to remove the nuisance. Where the abatement is effected by an entry on the land on which the nuisance exists, it affords a defence to the owner's action of trespass.

Abatement is not always advisable. The abater must be careful not to do any unnecessary damage, and where there is more than one method of abatement, he must choose the least mischievous. Furthermore, where he has exercised his right to abate, he cannot then sue for damages.

Notice of the abatement need not be given where there is no entry on the land on which the nuisance exists. Thus in *Lemmon* v. *Webb supra*, p. 46), abatement could be performed without notice because it simply required lopping off the offending branches. Notice is also not required in cases of emergency. Notice appears to be required in other cases.

So far it does not seem to have been stated by the courts that the abatement must be reasonable; that the harm inflicted by abatement must not be disproportionate to the harm caused by the nuisance. But such a requirement seems likely. Thus in *Perry* v. *Fitzhowe* (1846) the defendant purported to justify the pulling down of the plaintiff's house on the ground that the house interfered with the defendant's easement of pasture over the plaintiff's land and was therefore a nuisance. But the court held that abatement was not justified in these circumstances since it might lead to a breach of the peace.

It has been said that abatement is a remedy which the law does not favour (in *Lagan Navigation Co*. v. *Lambeg Bleaching Co*. (1927)). This appears to go too far. There may, however, be a tendency by the courts to decide matters of uncertainty (for example, as to the necessity of notice, reasonableness of the abatement) against the abater.

6. NEGLIGENCE

Negligence is a universal concept in legal systems. But as a ground of liability in itself for causing damage it is not so common. The evolution of negligence as a tort separate from trespass has already been considered (pp. 10-11, *supra*). It is now time to look at the tort of negligence itself.

At one time, although there were numerous instances of liability in negligence, there was no connecting principle formulated which could be regarded as the basis of all of them. In 1932, the House of Lords in *Donoghue* v. *Stevenson*, had to decide whether a cause of action in tort existed where the plaintiff alleged that, owing to the negligence of the defendant, a manufacturer of soft drinks, a bottle of ginger beer manufactured by the defendant and purchased for the plaintiff by a friend, contained a snail, which appeared in decomposed form when the plaintiff poured the contents of the bottle into a glass from which she was drinking, and as a result of which the plaintiff suffered personal injury in the form of gastro-enteritis and nervous shock. While the manufacturer was in contractual relationship with retailers of his products, he had no contract with the plaintiff and it had been supposed till then that a person in a contractual relationship with another person could owe no duty of care in the performance of that contract to persons not parties to the contract. This the majority in the House of Lords held to be not the law. They laid down the important rule that a manufacturer of products owes a duty of care in their manufacture to all persons who are foreseeably likely to be affected by those products. The "privity of contract" objection was therefore disposed of, and the so-called narrow rule in *Donoghue* v. *Stevenson* was established (for the effect of this rule *infra*, p. 163).

The case owes its chief importance, however, to the fact that it contains an attempt by the chief appellate court to provide a general formulation of liability in negligence. Lord Atkin's judgment is most important in this respect. He said that negligence depends upon proof that one person has committed a breach of duty of care binding upon himself and owed to another and has thereby caused injury to that other. Whether a duty of care is owed to another depends upon whether that other is in law a neighbour and Lord Atkin described a neighbour as a person "so closely and directly affected by [my] act that I ought reasonably to have [him] in contemplation as being so affected when I am directing my mind to the acts or omissions which are called in questions." This statement is often described, for convenience's sake, as "the neighbour principle." It is clear that Lord Atkin considered that a person was under a duty of care in respect of his actions or omissions whenever it could be foreseen that as a result of those actions or omissions another might be injured.

The existence of a separate tort of negligence was thus conclusively established. In the years since 1932, the tort has developed to such an extent that it is clearly now the most important tort. Quantitatively, actions in negligence far exceed those brought for any other tort. Besides this, negligence is in the process of absorbing other areas of tortious liability. Thus liability for defective premises and chattels is now governed almost exclusively by negligence. Negligence has taken over much of the area of liability formerly occupied by trespass, and appears at the moment to be in the process of doing the same thing to nuisance. On the other hand, the breadth of Lord Atkin's statement in *Donoghue* v. *Stevenson* has not received acceptance. It is not universally true that whenever there is foreseeability of harm the defendant is under a duty to so regulate his conduct that such harm is not produced. A number of so-called exceptions to the neighbour principle, the extent of which will be discussed in this chapter, have been established by the courts. In *Home Office* v. *Dorset Yacht Co.* (1970), the House of Lords gave its consideration to the question of the basis upon which such exceptions rest. In that case it was held by a majority of four to one that the Home Office owed a duty of care to the plaintiffs in respect of the detention of certain borstal trainees who had escaped from a borstal institution and had caused damage to the plaintiffs' yacht. Of those in the majority, Lords Reid, Morris and Pearson clearly thought that the neighbour principle of Lord Atkin had the status of a rule of law, subject only to exceptions based upon a "justification or valid explanation," or upon matters of policy. Lord Diplock thought, however, that foreseeability was only one element in determining the existence of a duty of care. In deciding whether to recognise a new duty, the court must also look at previous decisions by way of analogy and at the policy aspects of the case. Applying this to the facts of the case before him, Lord Diplock was prepared to extend the duty that already existed in respect of actions of prisoners committed inside the prison (*Ellis* v. *Home Office* (1953) to actions committed by the prisoner on escape in the vicinity of the prison. To the other judges in the majority, therefore, foreseeability as a determinant of duty has the force of a rule of law subject to exceptions, whereas Lord Diplock sees it as only an element in establishing such a rule. It is doubtful, however, whether there is much practical difference between Lord Diplock and the rest of the judges in the majority in the House of Lords. The broad basis upon which the latter rest the recognition of exceptions to the neighbour principle makes it clear that new duties will not be lightly imposed.

It is clear, therefore, that in deciding whether a duty of care exists, the court must decide two questions. First, whether there is a sufficient relationship of proximity or neighbour-hood between defendant and plaintiff so that the former reasonably contemplates that carelessness on his part may damage the latter, and secondly, granted that such proximity exists, whether there are any grounds why, despite that, the law should not impose a duty (see the judgment of Lord Wilberforce in *Anns* v. *London Borough of Merton* (1977)). The word "proximity" is coming to replace "foreseeability of harm" in the formulation of the first requirement. It emphasises that Lord Atkin thought that the duty of care only existed when the plaintiff was "so closely and directly affected" by the defendant's act that the defendant should reasonably have him in contemplation. The foresight required is that of a reasonable man who is not expected to foresee fantastic possibilities. Proximity is also a more plastic concept than foreseeability. It enables a court to lay down a more stringent test than foreseeability where the circumstances of the case require it. Thus in *Ross* v. *Caunters* (1980) (*infra*, p. 78), liability was imposed for a negligent statement causing the plaintiff financial loss only because the defendant actually had the plaintiff in mind when making the statement and the relationship between them was therefore sufficiently proximate.

CONSTITUENT REQUIREMENTS OF NEGLIGENCE

The tort of negligence is not merely carelessness. There must be a duty of care recognised by law in the situation in which the defendant finds himself. There must be a breach of that duty. There must be damage resulting from that breach. The damage that results must not be too remote a consequence of the breach. These constituent requirements of the tort will be examined in this and the succeeding chapters beginning with the examination of the requirement of duty of care.

DUTY OF CARE

Duty of care

We saw earlier that the questions of whether a duty of care exists depends upon whether there is sufficient proximity between the defendant and the plaintiff, and, if so, whether as a matter of law a duty should be recognised. It is customary and convenient to distinguish two aspects of the duty of care. The first is the existence of the duty of care as a matter of law. The second is the existence of a duty of care on the facts of a particular case. The first aspect may be referred to as duty of care in law; the second as duty in fact.

Duty of care in law

Whether a duty of care in law exists appears to be a mixed question of law and fact. Foreseeability of harm determines part of the answer and foreseeability is essentially a factual notion. The type of foreseeability involved here, however, is somewhat different from that involved in deciding the existence of a duty in fact. Here the question is whether the nature of the relationship between the defendant and plaintiff is such that it is foreseeable that lack of care on the defendant's part will lead to injury or damage to the plaintiff. The answers to such a question may be expressed in generalised terms rather than in relation to any particular individual. Thus a motorist owes a duty of care to persons on or in the vicinity of the road in relation to his driving. A manufacturer owes a duty of care to consumers of his chattels in relation to their manufacture. The law of negligence can conveniently be expressed in terms of a series of "duty-situations."

Objection was at one time made to this aspect of the duty of care on the ground that it was unnecessary. In other torts liability was not based on the breach of a duty not to commit the behaviour constituting the tort. Why was it necessary in negligence? (Buckland, (1935) 51 L.Q.R. 637). The answer to this criticism is that it ignores the fact that foreseeability is not the sole determinant of liability in negligence. In most cases where there is foreseeability of harm, liability will exist, but in some considerations of policy and justice will lead to a conclusion that A is not liable. The law rationalises this position by saying that in situations where liability exists A is under a duty of care in relation to his conduct; where it does not exist, he is under no duty of care. Thus duty of care may be regarded as convenient judicial shorthand for indicating those situations in which liability in negligence may exist and those in which it may not. The convenience of stating the law of negligence in terms of "duty-situations" must not be taken to mean that the whole of negligence can be classified in this way. Many factual situations have not yet been considered by courts for determination of the question whether a duty of care exists. When a novel situation is presented for the decision of a court, there is no way of telling in advance with certainty whether or not the court will recognise a duty of care-the court's decision on the point is in effect retrospective. It will, however, be expressed in terms that the defendant was, or was not, under a duty of care, a way of stating the result that fosters the impression that the law is more certain than it is. It may be that this is the reason for the judicial choice of the duty of care as their way of expressing the decision as to whether negligent acts should be legally actionable, in preference to the use of other legal concepts which could achieve the same purpose. Whatever the truth of this, the use of the duty of care has now been sufficiently sanctioned by the practice of all the courts that further analysis of it is unnecessary.

Duty in fact

The statement that a motorist owes a duty of care to another road-user is in effect a method of stating that, as a matter of law, if a motorist drives carelessly and foreseeably injures another road-user he will be liable to him in negligence. It does not say anything about the duty owed by a *particular* motorist towards a *particular* road-user. A motorist does not owe a duty of care to all road-users but only those who are within the foreseeable range of being affected of his careless driving. The decision whether a particular person was foreseeably likely to be affected by the careless driving of a particular motorist can only be determined retrospectively by a court. A decision by a court that the defendant owed the plaintiff no duty of care because he could not have foreseen harm to him clearly reflects a different aspect of the duty of care than that considered above. Clearly, as a matter of law, a duty of care was capable of arising. On the facts as found by the court, however, it did not exist. The second meaning of duty of care is conveniently referred to as the duty in fact.

The decision in *Bourhill* v. *Young* is an example of a court deciding a question whether a duty of care in fact existed. The defendant in that case was a motor-cyclist who was by his careless driving involved in an accident with another vehicle in which he himself was killed. The plaintiff, a pregnant housewife, was on the other side of a tram-car at the time of the accident, and was thus shielded from the effects of the defendant's negligence and the sight of the accident. Nevertheless she heard a loud noise, and on going to investigate she saw the plaintiff's blood on the road. She suffered nervous shock in consequence which caused her to miscarry. The House of Lords held that her action against the defendant's

estate failed. The defendant could not have foreseen any
injury whether physical or in the form of nervous shock to
her in the position she was. Therefore he owed her no duty
of care. The fact that he owed duties of care to numerous
other people in the vicinty and was in breach of those duties
did not assist the plaintiff.

SITUATIONS WHERE COURTS RELUCTANT TO IMPOSE A DUTY OF CARE

In the remainder of this chapter will be considered a number
of well-known cases where for policy reasons of one sort or
another, courts have been reluctant to recognise a duty of
care. In some cases the policy is expressed by an outright
refusal to impose a duty; in others, by the recognition of a
duty less extensive than that applying under the ordinary
principles of negligence.

1. Negligent statements

The courts have been reluctant to establish a rule that a
defendant who negligently makes a false statement is always
liable if the plaintiff foreseeably suffers loss as the result of
the statement. This has been because it was thought that to
some extent different considerations applied to words than
to acts. The statement may be made without any intention
that it should be acted on; the loss might be considered more
remote in that it usually arises from the plaintiff's acting in
reliance on the statement, rather than from the statement itself; finally "words travel faster than deeds"—to make the
defendant liable for all the foreseeable loss arising from the
statement might involve him in excessive liability. Thus until
recently the courts had refused to award damages for negligent statements causing financial loss to the plaintiff unless
the false statement constituted a breach of a contract made
between plaintiff and defendant, or unless the defendant was
in a fiduciary relationship towards the plaintiff. Where the
defendant's statement did not amount to a breach of contract
but had inducted the plaintiff to contract with the defendant
(called a misrepresentation) the plaintiff could not recover
damages from the defendant but was allowed the equitable
remedy of rescission of the contract. The position differed if
the false statement was made fraudulently by the defendant.
Then the plaintiff could get damages for the amount of his
loss in the tortious action of deceit.

The position thus summarised has been altered by two
important changes in the law, by means of which it is now
possible for the courts to make an award of damages for a
negligent statement. The first change was brought about by

the decision of the House of Lords in *Hedley Byrne & Co. Ltd.* v. *Heller and Partners Ltd.* (1964). The second change was the enactment of the Misrepresentation Act 1967.

The Hedley Byrne case
The facts of the case were:

The plaintiffs, *Hedley Byrne & Co.* who were advertising agents, asked their bank to inquire into the financial position of one of their clients, a company on behalf of which they wished to undertake certain advertising orders. The bank made inquiries on the defendants, the company's bank, which gave favourable references about the company, stating that these were made "without responsibility." As a result of relying on this advice, the plaintiffs lost money when the company went into liquidation. The plaintiffs' action in negligence against the defendants failed because of the defendants express disclaimer of responsibility for their reference.

The importance of the decision lies in the fact that all the members of the House of Lords thought that in appropriate circumstances an action for a negligent statement would lie, thus disagreeing with the contrary decision of the Court of Appeal in *Candler* v. *Crane, Christmas & Co.* (1951). The principle that negligent statements may be actionable in tort may be taken to be established, since the *Hedley Byrne* rules have been applied on a number of occasions both here and in Commonwealth jurisdictions.

It is a more difficult matter to deduce from the speeches of the House of Lords what circumstances are necessary in order to make the statement actionable. All the members of the House were agreed that mere foreseeability of harm by the maker of the statement was not enough; that a special relationship between plaintiff and defendant was necessary. There were differences in the explanations of what gives rise to this relationship. Lord Reid thought it arose where the "party seeking the information or advice was trusting the other to exercise such a degree of care as the circumstances required, where it was reasonable for him to do that, and where the other gave the information or advice when he knew or ought to have known that the inquirer was relying on him." Lords Morris and Hodson, more broadly, both based the existence of the special relationship on the basis of a voluntary undertaking by the defendant to exercise skill or use his knowledge, and a reliance on that by the plaintiff. Lord Devlin went no further than to say that a relationship "equivalent to contract" must exist between plaintiff and defendant. It is also possible to read into parts of the speeches in the House of Lords a further possible *ratio decidendi*, that the court was abolishing the rule that an action in negligence did not lie for purely pecuniary loss.

The last possibility has been rejected by the Court of Appeal (*infra*, p. 88) but it is now clear that the decision has been more wide-reaching than the narrow ratio of Lord Reid. Before examining the case law, it should be mentioned that a possible limitation on *Hedley Byrne* introduced by the Privy Council decision in *Mutual Life and Citizens Assurance* v. *Evatt* (1971) appears now to have been rejected by the English courts. In that case that Privy Council suggested a limitation upon *Hedley Byrne* to the effect that it only applied to advice given in the ordinary course of the business or profession of the adviser, unless there was an express undertaking by the adviser to exercise business or professional skill, or possibly that the adviser had a financial interest in the advice being taken. The Privy Council therefore held by a majority that a pleading which alleged that an insurance company had negligently misrepresented to the plaintiff the financial condition of one of its subsidiaries in which as a result the plaintiff invested his money and lost it disclosed no cause of action, since the case fell outside the three categories.

The *Mutual Citizen's* limitation appears inconsistent with the second *ratio decidendi* at the Court of Appeal in *Esso Petroleum Co.* v. *Mardon* (1976) although only one member of the Court of Appeal, Ormrod, L.J., expressly recognised the inconsistency. It was also expressly rejected as part of his ratio decidendi in *Howard Marine Dredging Co.* v. *Ogden* by Shaw, L.J., and disapproved obiter by Lord Denning, M.R. The likelihood is therefore that it does not represent English law. This is a good result since liability under *Hedley Byrne* is already subject to numerous restrictions. The case might have killed it off altogether.

Effect of the Hedley Byrne decision

The effect of the *Hedley Byrne* decision will now be considered in the light of the case law that has arisen in the years after it was decided.

(a) *Hedley Byrne and contract.* There is a clear possibility of overlap between liability for negligent mistatement and liability in contract. If the basis of the *Hedley Byrne* case is the plaintiff's reliance on the defendant's voluntary undertaking to use skill or knowledge, this could apply to many situations where there is an actual contract (a *fortiori* if a relationship "equivalent to contract" is required). The speeches of Lords Morris and Hodson in the *Hedley Byrne* case clearly envisage that there may be liability for negligence in the performance of a voluntary undertaking even if the negligence takes the form of action rather than words: furthermore that provided there is the necessary "reliance" the plaintiff need not act on the statement to his loss - it is enough for example if the defendant by negligence fails to improve the plaintiff's position. If this is so the line between tort and negligent breach of contract has become almost impossible to draw (*cf. Weir* (1963) C.L.J. 216). In *Midland Bank Trust* v. *Hett, Stubbs and Kemp* (1978), Oliver, J., after an exhaustive review of the authorities, held that a solicitor could be sued in tort for his negligence as well as in contract by his client (refusing to follow *Clark* v. *Kirby-Smith* (1964) which held that such liability lay in contract alone). The solicitor's negligence consisted in failing to register the plaintiff's estate contract, with the result that it did not bind a later purchaser of the land.

As regards negligent statements which induce the making of a contract the Court of Appeal decided in *Esso Petroleum Co.* v. *Mardon* that *Hedley Byrne* liability might exist in relation to such statements. There is here the possibility of overlap with the remedy under section 2 (1) of the Misrepresentation Act 1967, and with liability for breach of collateral warranty. The remedy under the Misrepresentation Act is in some respects more advantageous to the plaintiff than the action under *Hedley Byrne* (*infra*, p. 181).

(b) *Legal Advisers.* The *Midland Bank Trust* case held that the solicitor may be liable for his professional negligence in tort as well as contract. The barrister who is not in contractual relation with his clients, can only be sued in tort. The courts have accepted in principle that barristers may be sued in negligence as a result of the *Hedley Byrne* decision (thus tending to confirm the "reliance" ratio of Lords Morris and Hodson). However, a major exemption from liability exists, applying to both barristers and solicitors but peculiarly available to barristers. This is that an immunity from liability in negligence exists in relation to the conduct of litigation; this immunity extends to some pre-trial work (*Rondel* v. *Worsley* (1967); *Saif Ali* v. *Sydney Mitchell & Co.* (1977)). On the other hand, in relation to non-litigious work such as the drafting of wills and settlements and the giving of opinions, barristers, as well as solicitors, may be liable for negligence.

There are two questions arising concerning the immunity. First, why should it exist at all? Secondly, what is its extent? Among the reasons given by the courts in the *Rondel* and *Saif Ali* cases are the advocate's public duty to the court as well as to his client, the necessity to protect him while carrying out his task from the anxiety of a threatened law-suit, the public interest in there being finality to litigation, the exist-

ence of the system of appeals, and the immunity from suit
extended to other participants in the judicial process. Some
of these reasons are more convincing than others and none is
perhaps entirely convincing. In view of the considerable
extension of duties of care affecting professional classes and
public bodies, there may be considerable pressure on the
courts to remove the advocates immunity. Even if this is
done, there are likely to be few successful actions. As regards
the extent of the immunity, the test laid down in the New
Zealand case of *Rees* v. *Sinclair* (1974) was approved by the
majority of the House of Lords in the *Saif Ali* case:

> "Each piece of pre-trial work should be tested against
> the one rule - that the protection exists only where the
> particular work is so intimately connected with the con-
> duct of the case in court that it can fairly be said to be a
> preliminary decision affecting the way that the cause is
> conducted when it comes to a hearing."

The members of the majority were of the opinion that the
negligence alleged against the barrister in the *Saif Ali* case
itself - failure to advise institution of proceedings against a
person before the expiration of the limitation period against
that person - was well outside the scope of the immunity. On
the other hand the decision in *Rees* v. *Sinclair* that the
defendant's refusal to put forward his client's allegations of
misconduct by his wife before the court, on the ground that
he thought there was no evidence to support them, was within
the immunity, was approved by the House of Lords.

   (c) *Judges, arbitrators etc.* A judge is not liable for negligence in the performance of his duties, part of the general
judicial immunity from suit. It would, in any case, clearly be
difficult to find a special relation between a judge and the
parties to an action (*cf. Sirros* v. *Moore* (1975)). Arbitrators,
also, are not liable in negligence to the parties to the arbitration (an appeal may lie to the courts on fact or law from the
arbitrator's decision - Arbitration Act 1979). The mere fact,
however, that a person is to decide a question, rather than
resolve a dispute, as between two parties does not give him
the status of an arbitrator (*Arenson* v. *Casson, Beckman
Rutley* (1975)). Thus a person who agrees to value shares
owes a duty of care in respect of the valuation to both seller
and prospective buyer (*Arenson* case). So also the House of
Lords held in *Sutcliffe* v. *Thackrah* (1974) that an architect,
employed to certify to his client that building work undertaken for his client by a building contractor had been properly

completed, owed a duty of care to the client in respect of the certification.

(d) *Nature of statement.* The rules of equity placed a limit upon the motion of a misrepresentation. It had to be one of fact, not of law. It did not extend to a misrepresentation of opinion or of intention, unless at the time it was made the representor did not have that opinion or intention. There is some doubt whether these limitations affect liability under *Hedley Byrne.* It seems an inescapable deduction from the *Midland Bank Trust* case that negligent misrepresentation of law are actionable. There is, however, an analogous rule to the rule about misrepresentation of opinion in the case of *Hedley Byrne* liability. If the statement is made in circumstances in which it should be apparent to the plaintiff that care has not been taken by the defendant, the defendant is not liable for the statement. It may be made obviously off-the-cuff, for example, at a social occasion. But difficulties may arise in determining this question. In *Howard Marine Dredging Co.* v. *Ogden* (1978) members of the Court of Appeal differed about whether statements made during pre-contractual negotiations concerning the hire of two barges about the deadweight capacity of each barge were made in circumstances requiring care by their maker. Lord Denning, M.R., with whom Bridge, L.J. appeared to agree, thought the off-the-cuff-the circumstances in which the statements were made did not emphasise the "gravity of the enquiry" nor ought the plaintiff to have concluded this was considered advice. Shaw, L.J., more persuasively, thought that since the statements concerned matters vital to the plaintiffs decision whether or not to hire the barges, they could reasonably assume they had been made with due care. The defendant must of course give an honest answer and it has been suggested that honesty here requires more of the defendant than that he should abstain from telling lies, and that he has a duty to warn the plaintiff that care has not been taken (Honoré, (1965) 8 J.S.P.T.L. (N.S.) 284). The difficulty with this suggestion is that the defendant may quite reasonably take the view that the plaintiff could not possibly have expected a careful answer. The *Howard Marine* case shows that opinions may differ on this question. Perhaps the most that can be said is that if the defendant is aware of the plaintiff's reliance on a careful reply, he is under a duty to give a warning.

Argy Trading Development Co. v. *Lapid Development Co.* (1977) throws some light on the question whether statements of intention are actionable under *Hedley Byrne.* The defendant landlords had informed the plaintiff tenants that the demised premises were insured against fire with the result that the plaintiff's took out no insurance of their own on the premises. This statement was true. The policy was renewed once by the landlords, but was then allowed to expire with the result that when fire destroyed the premises they were uninsured. The defendant's were held not liable in negligence to the plaintiff's because the statement about insurance was true when it was made. In so far as the statement was one of intention, the case seems to exclude liability for such statement under *Hedley Byrne*, an unfortunate limitation on that principle. However, the statement was also one of existing fact and there is authority that when such a statement is known by the defendant to be continuing to influence the plaintiff, and the defendant discovers facts which make it untrue, he has a duty to communicate those facts to the plaintiff (*cf. Cherry* v. *Allied Insurance Brokers* (1978)).

(e) *Statements to third parties who act to them to the plaintiff's loss.* If A makes a negligent misstatement to B who acts on it to C's loss, can C successfully sue A? Clearly there is no reliance by C on A—equally there is no relationship equivalent to contract. In certain cases, however, it seems that C will succeed. In *Ministry of Housing* v. *Sharp* (1970) a local authority was held liable for the negligence of its clerk who issued a "clear" certificate to an intending purchaser of land, the result of which was that the purchaser bought the land, and the Ministry's development charge over the land was destroyed. Lord Denning, M.R. expressly based his judgment on *Hedley Byrne*; Salmond, L.J. expressly thought it did not fall within the principle; Cross, L.J. thought it unnecessary to decide the matter. The case is now, perhaps, better explained as one of negligence in the exercise of a statutory duty to which special considerations apply (*infra*, p. 84). However, the question fell for resolution before *Megarry*, V.C. in *Ross* v. *Caunters* (1980). He had to decide whether a solicitor, who had negligently advised a testator in the drawing up of his will with the result that a gift to the testator's intended beneficiary failed, was liable in negligence to that beneficiary. Holding the defendant liable, he did so on the basis that this was not *Hedley Byrne* liability but liability under general principles of negligence; that liability existed only if there was a sufficient degree of proximity between plaintiff and defendant, that this was present in the instant case because the defendant actually had the plaintiff in mind when advising the testator. Where no such proximity is present, the plaintiff must show that the defendant committed an intentional falsehood under the tort of injurious falsehood (*infra*, p. 285).

Extent of the Hedley Byrne special relationship

Granted that the problematical case just considered is not an example of *Hedley Byrne* liability, it is still a difficult question to determine whether a special relationship exists. The initial reluctance to impose liability for negligent statements arose partially from the potentially enormous range of such statements-"words travel faster than deeds." Under *Hedley Byrne*, for example, are newspaper proprietors to be held liable for the publication of negligent statements in their papers in circumstances in which it is foreseeable that members of the public will act on them to their loss? The answer appears to be probably not, although no English case has had to decide the point. Two New Zealand decisions give guidance on the matter. In *Scott Group* v. *McFarlane* (1975) accountants who had negligently audited the accounts of a public company were held not liable to the plaintiff who had lost money which he had invested in the company's shares on the strength of the accounts, even though the accounts were public documents. On the other hand, in *Dimond Manufacturing Co* v. *Hamilton* (1969) accountants were held liable for similar negligence, the difference being that one of the firm had actually shown the accounts to the plaintiff as the result of which he launched a take-over bid for the company. The principle these cases appear to establish is that the defendant must intend reliance on his knowledge or skill by the plaintiff-mere foreseeability of such reliance is not enough.

Exclusion of liability

The *Hedley Byrne* case itself decided that the defendant could exclude his liability to the plaintiff by a suitable term, a so-called "without responsibility" clause. A question now arises whether it is still possible to do this under the provisions of the Unfair Contract Terms Act, 1977. *Hedley Byrne* liability arises for breach of a common law duty to take reasonable care or exercise reasonable skill and is therefore within section 1 (1) (*b*) of the Act. Section 2 (2) requires a contract term or notice excluding or restricting liability in negligence for loss or damage other than death or personal injury to be reasonable. Section 2 (2) is extended by section 13 to terms or notices which exclude or restrict the duty to act carefully, rather than the liability which arises for breach of that duty. This is precisely what the "without responsibility" clause appears to do and unless the Act is given a strained interpretation it seems that such clauses are no longer effective. The validity of warnings that care has not been taken by the defendant in the making of the statement seems, however, clearly unaffected by the Act since here the defendant is not inviting reliance on his care by the plaintiff and is in fact performing his duty. The act also seems to leave available the exclusion of liability (or the duty itself) by reference to a term in a non-contractual agreement (*infra*, p. 133). Whether an exclusionary provision is reasonable will no doubt take into account the fact that the defendant may have acted gratuitously. In order to be effective, the defendant must take reasonable steps to communicate it to the plaintiff, though it seems that this can be done at any time before he acts upon the statement.

Liability for misstatement causing physical injury

Although no case seems directly to confirm this point, it seems clear that there may be liability in negligence when the statement causes personal injury or damage to property. A case such as *Clay* v. *A.J. Crump* (1964) comes close to confirming such liability. The defendant architect was held liable for leaving a wall on a demolition site standing without making a proper inspection of it, and thereby causing injury to the plaintiff, a workman on the site, when the wall fell. The defendant's conduct is clearly interpretable as a statement that the wall was safe. And the conduct of the defendant in *Sharp* v. *Avery* (*infra*, p. 84) can be regarded as a misdirection. The *Hedley Byrne* judgments were considered in *Clay's* case but the special requirements of liability under *Hedley Byrne* were not applied. It may, however, be unsafe to regard liability for negligent statements causing physical injury as turning entirely upon questions of foreseeability. Similar problems of limiting the extent of liability will occur as in the case of the negligent statement causing pecuniary loss. The problem is illustrated by the well known hypothetical case considered by Lord Denning in *Candler* v. *Crane, Christmas & Co.* (1951) of the marine cartographer whose negligently-drawn map having been relied on by mariners causes widespread injury and damage to persons at sea. Presumably liability would exist only if a special relationship could be proved on lines already suggested. Indeed, it may well be that the requirement of special relationship in cases of personal injury or damage to property applies in exactly the same way as it does in cases of financial loss. Certainly a special relationship wold have been discoverable readily enough on the facts of *Clay* v. *Crump* and *Sharp* v. *Avery*. There is, however, a difference as regards exclusion of the duty of care. Section 2 (1) of the Unfair Contract Terms Act, as extended by section 13, renders void exclusions of liability for negligence causing death or personal injury.

Misrepresentation Act 1967

The common law did not allow an action for damages for an innocent misrepresentation, even where it was made negligently. Any contract entered into by the representee with the representor as a result of the misrepresentation could be rescinded in equity, subject to the various limitations upon that right. But rescission remained the only remedy until the *Hedley Byrne* decision allowed an action for damages where the misrepresentation was negligent. Further changes have been made by the Misrepresentation Act 1967. Section 2 (1) of the Act provides as follows:

Where a person has entered into a contract after a misrepresentation has been made to him by another party thereto, and as a result thereof he has suffered loss, then if the person making the misrepresentation would be liable to damages in respect thereof had the misrepresentation been made fradulently, that person shall be so liable not withstanding that the misrepresentation was not made fraudulently, unless he proves that he had reasonable ground to believe and did believe up to the time that the contract was made that the facts represented were true.

The effect of this section is to prove an additional remedy by way of an action for damages where the misrepresentation is negligent. The following points may be noted about it:

(*a*) The subsection only applies where the defendant has made a misrepresentation. As has already been mentioned the term "misrepresentation" has acquired limitations under equitable principles. Representations of law, of opinion and of intention are excluded, at least where they are not made fraudulently. It has been pointed out also that *Hedley Byrne* liability probably extends to representation of law, but seems to have similar limitations to the second and third categories. However, under section 2 (1), the plaintiff is merely required to enter into a contract after a misrepresentation made to him and provided that the defendant would have been liable had the misrepresentation been made fraudulently. It may be, therefore, that the equitable limitations on the notion of the misrepresentation do not apply in the case of liability under section 2 (1). In *Howard Marine* v. *Ogden* (1978) Lord Denning thought that a misrepresentation made "off-the-cuff" could give rise to liability under the Act though not under *Hedley Byrne*. Equally there is no requirement of a special relationship under section 2 (1).

(*b*) The subsection only applies where the misrepresentation has induced the making of a contract between representor and representee. Where this is not the case, a person who suffers damage by acting on the misrepresentation must continue to rely on the *Hedley Byrne* case.

(*c*) The plaintiff suing on the basis of section 2 (1) has the advantage that he does not need to prove that the defendant was negligent, since the burden of proving lack of negligence is put upon the defendant.

(*d*) The fact that the defendant is to be liable as if the misrepresentation had been made fraudulently means that the other conditions of the tort of deceit must be satisfied. This means, *e.g.* that the sub-section imports the deceit rules as to damages into the cause of action.

It has now been held (*Esso Petroleum* v. *Mardon* (1975)) that where a negligent misrepresentation induces the making of a contract between defendant and plaintiff, the plaintiff can base his action upon *Hedley Byrne*, so that in this situation he has the alternative of suing in tort or basing his action on section 2 (1) of the Misrepresentation Act.

The 1967 Act made a further change in that section 2 (2) allows the court in its discretion, having regard to the nature of the misrepresentation and the loss that would be caused by it if the contract were upheld, as well as to the loss that rescission would cause the other party, to declare the contract subsisting and award damages in lieu of rescission. In particular, this allows the court to award damages for a non-negligent misrepresentation. There is as yet uncertainty about the measure of damages to be applied under this subsection; the Act does not make it clear whether it is to be the tortious or the contractual measure.

2. Omissions and undertakings

The problem of liability for an omission to act is not necessarily connected with the tort of negligence. The conduct of the person who, seeing a drowning man and being capable of saving him, makes no effort to do so, is deliberate rather than negligent. But since most of the problems concerning omission arise in connection with negligence, the topic will be treated here. The rule of English law is that pure omissions to act are not actionable in tort. The reason for this reluctance to impose liability for omissions (shared by other legal systems) is that legal obligations to take affirmative action ought not to be imposed upon people without their consent.

It must be emphasised that the omission must be a pure omission. When a person by some positive action has incurred a duty of care towards other persons, he may be liable for omissions in the performance of that duty. Thus a motorist by the act of driving incurs a duty of care towards other road-users and the fact that his negligence consists in an omission to give a signal will not prevent his being liable. Similarly the act of employing other persons puts the employer under a duty of care towards those persons; his obligation to provide proper machinery is not discharged by the provision of initially proper machinery which becomes defective through his failure to have it serviced. A further example is *Mercer* v. *S.E. Ry.* (1922) in which the defendant railway company had made a practice of locking the gates of a level crossing upon the approach of trains and, when the plaintiff was injured by a train while using the crossing with the gates open, it was held that the company was liable for its failure to lock the gates because of its previous positive practice of doing so on which the plaintiff relied.

Similarly, a person who acquires the ownership of land may be liable for a negligent failure to remedy a state of affairs on that land, although he did not create the state of affairs. Thus, in *Goldman* v. *Hargrave* (1967), the defendant was held liable for failing to prevent the spread of fire from his own land to that of the plaintiff, the fire having begun because of the ignition by lightning of a tree on the defendant's land, (*infra*, p. 183) (see under Nuisance).

Where a person who is under no duty to act in fact does so, the law takes the view that his only obligation is not to make matters worse by acting—he does not need to bring about an improvement. In *East Suffolk Rivers Catchment Board* v. *Kent* (1941) the defendants were emplowered by statute but had no duty to repair a sea wall. They exercised their power in such a way that the plaintiff suffered flooding of his land for five months, whereas had proper skill been shown the flooding would have been limited to fourteen days. The plaintiff's action failed because the defendants had merely failed to improve matters rather than made them worse; the plaintiff had suffered no damage.

This case, in so far as it concerned the negligent exercise of a statutory power is now of very dubious authority and has been more or less "explained away" by the House of Lords decision in *Anns* v. *London Borough of Merton* (*infra*, p. 84). Where a person is not exercising a statutory power, however, it still appears to be the law that where no duty to act exists, the only duty where action is taken is to take care not to make matters worse. A rescuer, for example, is not bound to exercise care so as to effect a rescue-he is required only not to aggravate the situation. However, there are two qualifications to this. Where a special relationship exists between plaintiff and defendant, the defendant is required to take care to improve matters. So in the *Hedley Byrne* case Lords Morris and Hodson thought that where a doctor gratuitously undertakes to treat an accident victim knowing that his professional skill is being relied on (which might even be the case where the victim was unconscious), he is liable for failure to take reasonable care, even though the victim's condition is no worse as a result. These dicta are open to the objection that they tend to discourage "good Samaritan" acts by professional persons. The other qualification is that where an antecedent duty of care exists, on principles explained above, the defendant is liable if his lack of care fails to improve matters. So in the Canadian case of *The Ogopogo* (1971) it was held that an occupier of a boat owed a duty to his invitee on that boat to attempt to rescue him when he fell overboard; that care must be taken in order to achieve the rescue; but that the standard of care required must take into account the emergency situation, and that in the circumstances the defendant's failure to achieve the rescue was not negligent.

Sharp v. *Avery* (1938) is an example of a case in which the negligent performance of a gratuitous undertaking actually caused damage. The defendant undertook to guide the plaintiff from London to Southend by road at night, each travelling on a different motor-cycle and the defendant travelling eight yards ahead of the plaintiff. The defendant negligently turned off the road at some stage; the plaintiff followed him and suffered injuries for which the defendant was held liable.

3. Negligence in the exercise of statutory powers and duties

The law on this topic was until recently impossible to state with any confidence. There was a well-known statement of Lord Blackburn in *Geddis* v. *Proprietors of Bann Reservoirs* (1878) to the effect that the person exercising a statutory power must not do so negligently so as to inflict damage. This was qualified by the House of Lords decision in *East Suffolk Rivers Catchment Board* v. *Kent* which appeared to hold that negligence in the exercise of a statutory power was only actionable where it caused damage and not where it failed to rectify damage which had already occurred. Then there was the virtually irreconcilable decision in *Dutton* v. *Bognor Regis U.D.C.* (1972) in which the Court of Appeal held a local authority liable for the negligence of its building inspector in failing to exercise with due care a statutory power of inspection of the foundations of a certain house, with the result that the house, which was eventually bought by the plaintiff, was allowed to be built and subsequently showed signs of damage. The distinction between this and the East Suffolk seemed to rest upon the thin line to be drawn between a failure to avert damage and a failure to arrest damage some of which had already occured. After the decision in *Anns* v. *London Borough of Merton* (1977) the law has been clarified and rationalised, although there remain some obscure areas. Again this case concerned negligence in the exercise of statutory powers of inspection of building foundations by a local authority, although here the allegation was both of a failure to inspect at all, and in the alternative of a failure to inspect properly. The question of law whether the local authority was under a duty of care to the plaintiffs, who had allegedly bought defective houses as a result was referred to the House of Lords for a preliminary opinion. The House of Lords held unanimously that a local authority owed a duty of care in the exercise of its powers of inspection of building foundations at least to the extent of ensuring that the foundations complied with byelaws regulating those foundations. The duty was owed to the class of future owners or occupiers of the premises whose safety or health was likely to be affected by defects in the building. The judgment of Lord Wilberforce which was concurred in by three members of the House of Lords must be taken to establish the relevant principles. On the question whether negligence in the exercise of a power which merely has the effect of failing to avert, or to improve, damage was actionable, the decision in Dutton was approved. The narrow distinction based on causation between it and the East Suffolk was not approved, and the latter case was explained either on the ground that there was there no negligence at all, or that the relevance of the principles of *Donoghue* v. *Stevenson* to the exercise of statutory powers was not sufficiently appreciated. On the question of what constituted negligence in the exercise of a power, the width of some of the statements in Dutton was disapproved on the ground that they took insufficient account of the discretionary nature of such powers and their public purpose. Councils could quite properly "fail" to exercise the power to inspect because they had taken a bona fide decision that to appoint a sufficient number of inspectors to inspect all sites was beyond their purse. The dictum of Du Parcq that public authorities have to strike a balance between the claims of efficiency and thrift (in the Court of Appeal decision in the *East Suffolk* case) was quoted with approval. Where this discretionary element entered into the decision, it therefore had to be shown that the decision was altogether outside the power, either because it exceeded its literal terms or because it was not a bona fide exercise of it. Where however the authority had exercised its discretion and reached its decision, and the negligence lay in the implementation of it, there was no reason to excuse the authority for this negligence. Thus there is liability where an inspector has actually inspected and failed to inspect properly. This "operational" negligence was present on the facts in Dutton so that the actual result of the case was right.

The *Anns* case therefore lays down both the conditions under which public authorities may be held liable for misuse of their powers and in addition a partial immunity from ordinary liability in negligence. Both aspects deserve comment. It is implicit in Lord Wilberforce's judgment that an action in negligence lies where the authority has acted outside the power (*ultra vires*) and the conditions for an action in negligence are present. The judgment even goes as far as to state that an authority may be held liable for a non-exercise of its discretion by failure to give due consideration to the exercise of its powers. A tort of negligent maladministration may well, therefore, have been created, a significant step since previously a doubt had existed whether even fraudulent maladministration was tortious (see below). As regards the immunity, it can hardly have been intended that the principles laid down should extend to the duties of care which public authorities owe, for example as occupiers, employers or as car-owners, even though in the performance of those duties the authority may be exercising discretionary powers. The judgment is not a charter to local authorities to save its rate-payers money by, for example, sending onto the highway improperly serviced fleets of vehicles. Where to draw the line between discretionary powers that can properly be exercised in such a way that damage may be caused and those which may not will cause difficulties. It is clear, however, that drawing simple lines between misfeasance and non-feasance, or between the infliction of damage and the failure to prevent it will not solve the problem. Thus a person, acting under a statutory power, may quite properly decide to set up an open prison in a certain neighbourhood, even though this sensibly increases the risk of damage to persons in the vicinty. A Parole Board may legitimately decide to release a certain prisoner into the community, even though this may involve some risk.

Anns is also important on the question of the negligent performance of statutory duties. The statutory duty is different from the statutory power. There is no discretion whether to perform it and so no question of *ultra vires* can arise. An action in tort for breach of statutory duty may also exist. There is no reason, however, why an action for negligent performance of a statutory duty should not be allowed, particularly in circumstances where no action for breach of statutory duty is available. This possibility is expressly recognised by Lord Wilberforce.

4. Purely pecuniary loss
There is no liability in the tort of negligence where the plaintiff has suffered purely pecuniary loss. This may be defined as pecuniary loss which is not consequent upon any physical damage to the plaintiff's person or property. It is clear that the rule has survived the *Hedley Byrne* case, despite dicta in that case throwing doubt it. In *Spartan Steel Alloys* v. *Martin* (1972) the defendant's servants negligently damaged

an electricity cable belonging to the local electricity board, and had thereby cut off the supply of electricity to the plaintiffs' factory for several hours. As a result a "melt" in the plaintiffs' furnace was damaged and four other melts were incapable of being performed. The plaintiffs recovered damages for the physical damage to the existing melt and for the loss of profit on that melt. They were not allowed damages for loss of profit on the four other melts since this was purely pecuniary loss unaccompanied by damage to property.

The rule rests on two main reasons of policy. Courts have always valued the interests in person and property higher than mere economic interests. There is also the need to restrict the defendant's liability. If all the persons who received a foreseeable pecuniary loss as the result of negligence were allowed to recover damages, liability might be excessive. Nevertheless in the individual case the rule may cause hardship. In *Caltex Oil* v. *The Dredge* "Willemstadt," the High Court of Australia refused to apply the rule where the plaintiffs suffered pecuniary loss through damage done to an oil pipeline belonging to a third party by the negligent navigation of the dredger by its crew and the negligent production of a marine chart by the second defendants. Both defendants knew of the existence of the pipeline and the fact that it led from its owner's oil refinery to the plaintiffs' terminal. They therefore had the knowledge or means to obtain knowledge that to damage it was likely to cause pecuniary loss to a particular and identified person or persons, and were therefore held liable. Clearly the High Court was trying to lay down a more restrictive test of liability than reasonable foreseeability, but the test of means of knowledge seems both uncertain in its application and dubious in its value.

Sometimes the court decisions on the rule have presented it as a rule of remoteness of damage, but the prevailing tendency at the moment is to say that no duty exists in respect of such loss. Since the rule is essentially one of policy, its juristic formulation is not really important.

A number of exceptions to the rule exist. The *Hedley Byrne* case is a major exception. The justification for this exception is that liability under that case is very close to liability in contract, where there is no doubt about the recoverability of purely pecuniary loss. Where the plaintiff's chattels are being transported in a ship belonging to another person, and the defendant by negligence damages the ship but not the chattels, the plaintiff may recover any pecuniary loss he suffers (for example, the general average expenditure of cargo owners in *Morrison Steamship Co.* v. *Greystoke Castle* (1947)). The reason for this is said to be that the shipowner and the owners

of cargo are in a joint venture, but the extent of the notion
of joint venture is hard to define (*cf. Atiyah*, (1967) 83 L.Q.R.
248). Exceptions are recognised also in the right of action of
the dependants of a deceased person against a tortfeasor who
caused his death (*infra*, p. 303), and in the various claims that
can still be brought for the loss of services of a person injured
as the result of a tort.

In *Dutton* v. *Bognor Regis U.D.C.* the Court of Appeal
held that where a house had been built upon defective foundations, the plaintiff who bought the house before the defect
in the house had been discovered could sue in negligence on
that basis that she had suffered damage to property. Surely,
however, since the house was always defective, the only injury
here was financial, *i.e.* the excessive amount paid for the
house? Nevertheless the House of Lords in the *Anns* case confirmed the Court of Appeal's ruling on this point, adding
only the requirement that the present state of the house
should be a danger to the health or safety of its occupants.
Although seemingly illogical, the decisions in these cases may
be justified by the hardship of applying the normal rule—purchasers are unlikely to be insured against the presence of
defects in houses of this sort. However, the Court of Appeal
has now compounded the illogicality by holding that a purchaser of a defective chattel has no remedy against its negligent manufacturer for purely pecuniary loss it has caused
him (*Lambert* v. *Lewis* (1980)—retailer of the chattel could not
recover an indemnity from the manufacturer against damages
he had to pay to a third person to whom he had sold the
chattel).

5. Nervous shock

The reasons for the courts' restrictions upon the right to
recover damages for nervous shock are different from those
denying a claim for purely financial loss. For a long time the
courts doubted the genuineness of nervous shock as a head of
damages. When finally the force of medical opinion could
admit of no further doubt as to the genuineness of physical
symptoms produced by nervous shock, the courts' recognition
of this was still somewhat gradual with the result that incon-
sistencies still exist in the law. Even now, the courts refuse to
recognise extreme distress or grief as compensable damage.
The term "nervous shock" means actual illness, whether in
the form of physical symptoms produced by the shock, or
genuine psychiatric illness (as in *Hinz* v. *Berry* (1970)—morbid
depression produced by plaintiff witnessing death of her husband and simultaneous injury to her children).

Actions for nervous shock were first allowed:

1. When it accompanied actual physical injury, where the courts were less inclined to doubt the genuiness of the symptoms of shock.

2. Where the plaintiff was put in fear of physical injury through the defendant's negligence and suffered nervous shock though not physical injury as a result (*Dulieu* v. *White and Sons* (1901)).

3. Where the defendant had intentionally done an act calculated to cause nervous shock to the plaintiff (*Wilkinson* v. *Downton* (1897)).

Whether the law should go further than this and compensate victims of shock who have neither suffered injury nor been in fear of such injury has been disputed (for a medical opinion to the contrary, see Havard, 19 M.L.R. 478) but actions in negligence have succeeded on a number of occasions where the plaintiff witnessed an accident caused by the defendant's negligence and he and the victim were in a sufficiently close relationship. Thus close relatives of the victim have been allowed to recover damages (*Hambrook* v. *Stokes Bros.* (1925). *Boardman* v. *Sanderson* (1964)); a fellow employee (*Dooley* v. *Cammell, Laird Ltd.* (1951); and a rescuer (*Chadwick* v. *British Transport Commission* (1967)). *Hambrook* v. *Stokes* is difficult to reconcile with another Court of Appeal decision in *King* v. *Phillips* (1953). The ratio of neither case is easy to determine, but it is suggested that there is no real basis for distinguishing them in point of fact and that *Hambrook* v. *Stokes* allowing damages to the relative is the preferable decision. Difficulties experienced by the court in *King* v. *Phillips* in deciding whether the relative's presence near the victim was foreseeable should not really cause problems in view of the extensiveness of foresight expected of defendants today (*infra*, p. 109). Equally it seems absurd that the relative should be in a worse position than the employee or rescuer. The plaintiff does not have to see the victim being injured, provided such injury is reasonably apprehended (*Hambrook* v. *Stokes*); nor does any injury actually have to occur, again if it is reasonably apprehended (*Dooley* v. *Cammel, Laird*). It does not seem to matter that the plaintiff has a predisposition towards suffering nervous shock. Mrs. Hambrook was pregnant, suffered a miscarriage and died. Both Dooley and Chadwick had a history of neurosis.

More difficult is the case of the casual spectator of an accident. In *Bourhill* v. *Young* the House of Lords held that the plaintiff could not recover for her nervous shock, since shock was not foreseeable to her in her position having seen and heard what she had. The case leaves open the possibility that the casual spectator might succeed if some gruesome sight were actually witnessed. The limitation may exist, however, that, unlike the case of the person in close relationship to the victim, the test is whether what is seen would produce nervous shock in a person of "ordinary phlegm and fortitude" (see especially the judgment of Lord Wright in *Bourhill* v. *Young*).

Other cases

In *McLoughlin* v. *O'Brian* (1981) the Court of Appeal refused to allow any damages for nervous shock to the plaintiff whose husband and three children were injured in an accident caused by the defendant's negligence and as a result of which the youngest child died. The plaintiff was not present at the scene of the accident, but was informed about it and discovered the truth when she visited the hospital to which her relatives had been taken. The Court of Appeal did not deny that nervous shock to the plaintiff was foreseeable. They concluded, however, that as a matter of policy the action should not succeed. It was necessary to draw a line somewhere in nervous shock cases. It was also necessary to spare the victims of nervous shock the prospect of its being exacerbated by the anxieties of litigation. These reasons of policy do not seem compelling. Assuming the case to be rightly decided, however, it seems to have finally ruled out the possibility of nervous shock being recoverable in any situation except those considered in the previous section (for example, shock caused by a negligent accident report in a newspaper would not be recoverable—the Canadian decision in *Guay* v. *Sun Publishing Co.* (1952) would be followed).

6. Duty in relation to human conduct

It has been abundantly clear for some time that a duty may exist to anticipate and guard against the conduct of other human beings. For a time it was thought that this may be limited to cases where the human being was not fully responsible for his actions, for example, a child. In *Stansbie* v. *Troman* (1948), however, the defendant painter and decorator, who had been employed by the plaintiff to paint his house, was held liable to the plaintiff for his negligence in leaving the house unattended and the door unlocked for a period of time during which a thief entered and stole some jewellery. The thief's action should have been foreseen and prevented by the plaintiff. It is clear that when damage caused by a third party is the only foreseeable damage arising from the defendant's conduct, the essential question is whether the defendant was under a duty in relation to the third party's act. Although cases such as *Stansbie* v. *Troman* were once thought to raise problems over a causation the court could hardly hold that a duty to prevent the act existed, but that the defendant's act was not a cause of the plaintiff's damage (causal problems may arise, however, in relation to the acts of third parties-*infra*, p. 115). If the essential question is one of duty it will be answered according to the principles outlined at the beginning of this chapter. Thus mere foreseeability of the third party's act is not enough; the court must think it appropriate that a duty should exist to prevent it. Employers for examples have no duty of care to their employees to prevent theft of their property (*Deyong* v. *Sherburn* (1946); nor does an occupier owe a duty of care to his visitors to prevent thefts of their property on his premises (*Tinsley* v. *Dudley* (1951)-these two cases lay down general rules which could no doubt be displaced by special circumstances). The keepers of prisons may owe a duty of care in respect of the acts of prisoners committed inside the prison (*Ellis* v. *Home Office* (1953); or outside the prison (*Home Office* v. *Dorset Yacht Co.* (1970)-Lord Diplock limited the latter duty to acts committed within the vicinity of the prison.)

The same principles determine liability where damage is brought about by the deliberate act of the plaintiff, and where it is brought about by a non-deliberate act, whether of a third party or the plaintiff. These cases will be separately considered.

(1) Deliberate act of the plaintiff-the rescuer

The rescuer is the paradigm example of this category. The earlier cases in which liability to rescuers was established were regarded as turning on the fact that the defendant was in breach of a duty of care to the person he had endangered rather than to the rescuer. The rescuer could nevertheless succeed in negligence if his rescue was reasonable and did not break the chain of causation (*Haynes* v. *Harwood* (1935). This approach caused problems where the defendant owed no duty of care to the person being rescued (*Videan* v. *British Transport Commission* (1964)-person whose rescue was attempted was a trespasser); or where the plaintiff had created his own need for rescue. In *Videan* the Court of Appeal allowed recovery by the rescuer on the basis of an independant duty of care owed to the rescuer himself not to create a situation where rescue was necessary. This was also the view of the Canadian Supreme Court in *The Ogopogo* (*supra*, p. 84). In that case another guest had dived into the water thinking that the rescue attempt of the defendant would fail; he also was drowned. The court held that the defendant

owed him a duty not to so mismanage his rescue attempt so
as to invite another rescue, but that in the circumstances no
negligence had been proved. Finally in *Baker* v.
Hopkins
(1959) the judge at first instance held that a person who put
himself into a position requiring rescue was liable to the
rescuer for any injury suffered by him on the basis of the
breach of a duty of care owed to the rescuer (it was unnecessary to decide this point on appeal where a different view of
the facts was taken).

Whether there is liability where there was no reasonable
necessity for the plaintiff to act, or to act in the way he did,
may again be analysed in terms of duty and breach, although
the traditional approach of the courts is to ask whether the
plaintiff was a volunteer, or, which is the same thing, whether
his act amounted to a novus actus interveniens. In *Cutler* v.
United Dairies (1933) the plaintiff went to the assistance of
the defendant's servant in order to help him pacify an unruly
horse and was injured. His action failed because he was a volunteer, the situation not being one requiring a rescue. Similarly
in *Sylvester* v. *Chapman* (1935) the plaintiff attempted to extinguish a fire near a caged leopard belonging to the defendants by stamping on it and consequently was mauled by the
leopard. His action failed since the fire could easily have been
extinguished by the use of water. (Whether the alternative
solution of a reduction of damages for contributory negligence
is open to the court in cases of this sort is discussed at p. 129).

(2) Non-deliberate conduct

Clearly a duty may exist to gaurd against negligent conduct
of another person. In *Hale* v. *Hants. and Dorset Motor Services*
(1947) the defendants allowed branches of their trees to over-
hang the highway. The second defendants' servant negligently
drove their bus too near the side of the road and the plaintiff passenger received injury. Both defendants were held
liable in negligence. Where the negligence that should have
been anticipated is that of another tortfeasor, an apportionment of damages between tortfeasors is possible under the
provisions of the Civil Liability (Contribution) Act 1978.
Where it is that of the plaintiff, damages for his negligence
can be reduced under the Law Reform (Contributory Negligence) Act 1945. The actions of irresponsible persons such as
children are often required to be anticipated (*cf. Shiffman* v.
Order of St. John (1935)-defendants held liable to plaintiff
upon whom children had pulled down defendants' flagpole;
Carmarthenshire C.C. v. *Lewis* (1947)-defendants held liable
to plaintiff lorry-driver injured in accident caused by child
negligently allowed to escape from defendants' school.

Other exceptional cases

In other cases formerly recognised as clear exceptions to the neighbour principle, the exceptions have recently either been removed or have weakened in force. Thus, although an occupier still owes a trespasser on his land no duty of care, he now owes him a duty of humanity which is quite a stringent duty (*infra*, p. 155). Many of the exceptions relating to premises which existed at common law have been removed by the Defective Premises Act 1972 (*infra*, p. 158). There is now, under section 8 of the Animals Act 1971, a duty of care in relation to the straying of domestic animals on to the highway from private land (*infra*, p. 215). It seems likely though it has not yet been conclusively established, that there is a duty of care in relation to a chattel not dangerous in itself (*infra*, p. 163). Many anomalous gaps have thus been closed either completely or in part. It is still possible, however, for a court to refuse to find a duty where there is a clear foreseeability of harm, and no obvious reason of policy against imposing a duty. Thus in *Moorgate Mercantile Co.* v. *Twitchings* (1976) the House of Lords held that the plaintiff finance company, which was a member of an organisation which registered details of hire-purchase agreements and with which 98 per cent. of all hire-purchase agreements relating to cars were registered, owed no duty of care to another member of the organisation to ensure that details of its hire-purchase agreements were supplied to the organisations. It was therefore not estopped from asserting its title to a car which another member had bought, relying on a statement by the organisation that no hire-purchase agreement existed over it.

Introduction

In the case of some torts, of which battery may be given as an example, the definition of the tort allows us to form a clear mental picture of the defendant's conduct in committing it. Negligence is not like this. To say that a person has acted negligently tells us nothing about the type of conduct involved. It merely evaluates that conduct as against some ideal standard. The standard against which the defendant's actions are judged is that of *reasonableness*; to be more precise, the question is asked whether the defendant has acted as a reasonable man would have acted in the situation in which he found himself. If the defendant's conduct fails to pass this test, he is said to be in breach of his duty of care. The phrase, "standard of care," which is often used to indicate the standard of reasonable conduct by which the defendant's conduct is measured is misleading in that it suggests that a pre-existing standard is available to determine whether or not the defendant is negligent. In fact, the court always reaches its decision by an *ex post facto* adjudication that on the actual facts of the case the defendant acted reasonably or unreasonably. Previous decisions on similar facts, though they are evidence of what has in the past been regarded as reasonable or unreasonable conduct will not bind the court in its decision in the instant case.

How breach of duty is established

The vagueness of the rule that the judge has to apply in deciding whether a person was negligent and the lack of binding force in previous judicial determinations of the same question inevitably create a measure of judicial discretion and therefore of uncertainty in the law. Negligence is not alone in this respect. Unreasonableness (though not necessarily the unreasonableness of the defendant's conduct) is the central requirement of the tort of nuisance. Furthermore, the uncertainty is mitigated by the existence of certain guiding principles of law which control the exercise of the judicial discretion. Thus, in arriving at his decision, the judge must take into account:

1. The degree of risk to the plaintiff created by the defendant's conduct. In this matter, the question of the foreseeability

of the plaintiff's injury by the defendant is important.

2. The seriousness of the harm that the plaintiff may suffer.
3. The social utility of the defendant's action.
4. The expense and practicability of taking precautions against the risk.

These criteria for deciding the reasonableness of the defendant's conduct are interrelated, and cannot therefore be separately assessed. Thus, it is impossible to decide the question whether the degree of risk created by the defendant is sufficient to involve him in liability without also examining the seriousness of the harm that may result from the risk materialising. Equally the social importance of the defendant's conduct may justify the creation of a higher degree of risk than is normally permissible. Essentially the court's decision is an attempt to strike a balance between these various factors.

(1) *Degree of risk*
In order to decide whether the defendant has created a sufficient risk of the harm which the plaintiff suffers, it is not enough to ask whether this harm was a foreseeable result of the defendant's conduct. The harm must be *reasonably* foreseeable: it must therefore result from a risk which a reasonable man would regard as one against which precautions ought to be taken. Clearly the inquiry involved in deciding whether a certain danger was so sufficiently likely that the defendant ought to have taken care to prevent it happening is similar to the question of whether a "duty in fact" existed (*supra*, p. 71). It is not quite the same, however. Foreseeability is here not the sole determinant. The court must decide whether the degree of foreseeable risk of danger was sufficiently great that, bearing in mind factors 2, 3 and 4, the defendant acted unreasonably in failing to regulate his conduct to avert it.

For example, in *Bolton* v. *Stone* (1951), the defendants were occupiers of a cricket ground. The plaintiff who was standing on the highway outside the ground was struck by a cricket ball hit during the course of a match on the ground. The plaintiff's action of negligence against the defendants was unsuccessful.

The House of Lords took the view that in view of the distance from the wicket to the fence which marked the perimeter of the ground, the upward slope from the wicket to the fence, the infrequency with which balls had been hit into the road (estimated at six times in the previous thirty years), the plaintiff had not established that the defendant had created a sufficient risk of the injury she suffered happening. It may be noted that in this case the defendants took no precautions whatsoever to prevent balls being struck into the road. This shows again that the expression "standard of care" may be misleading since the defendant may have acted reasonably although he had taken no precautions whatsoever against the risk. If the risk is sufficiently slight he is justified in ignoring it altogether.

In recent cases the courts have taken a more stringent attitude where the defendant has created only a slight risk of harm.

In *The Wagon Mound* (No. 2) (1967) the defendants' servants carelessly allowed furnace oil to spill into Sydney harbour. The oil drifted towards a wharf (owned by the plaintiffs in *The Wagon Mound* (No. 1)) where oxyacetylene welding was being carried out by their servants, in the course of repairing a ship belonging to the present plaintiff. The oil was ignited by the fall of pieces of hot metal from the welding operations. The plaintiff's ship was damaged in the resulting fire. The defendants were held liable to the plaintiff for this damage in negligence. The finding of fact by the trial judge in Australia was that a reasonable man in the position of the defendants' servant would have regarded the ignition of furnace oil on water as a possibility but one which could become an actuality only in very exceptional circumstances. This did not excuse the defendants. In the words of Lord Reid, delivering the judgment of the Privy Council: "If a real risk is one which would occur to the mind of a reasonable man in the position of the defendants' servant, and which he would not brush aside as far-fetched, and if the criteria is to be what that reasonable man would have done in the circumstances, then surely he would not neglect such risk if action to eliminate it presented no difficulty, involved no disadvantage and required no expense."

This raises the problem of distinguishing this case from *Bolton* v. *Stone*. It seems impossible to separate the two cases on the question of the degree of likelihood of the harm occurring. Equally it seems wrong to regard the damage in *The Wagon Mound* (No. 2) as more serious than that in *Bolton* v. *Stone*—the cricket ball could have caused serious injury. The difference seems to be that in *Bolton* the defendants were carrying on a lawful activity, arguably of social benefit, and would have been put to expense in providing precautions against the risks of the activity. The discharging of oil by the servants of the *Wagon Mound* was on the other hand antisocial, unnecessary and unlawful (as a public nuisance). In the circumstances the defendants were not entitled to ignore any risk involved provided they should have foreseen it. This comparison shows how factors 3 and 4 (*supra*) can impinge on the question whether the degree of risk created by the defendant was sufficient.

Another case which shows that a court may be prepared to find negligence though the risk of injury is slight is *Haley* v. *London Electricty Board* (1965). In that case a blind person recovered damages in negligence from the defendants for personal injuries received through falling into an excavation made by the defendants' servants in the pavement. The House of Lords found that the defendants' duty of care was not discharged by safeguarding, as they had, normal persons from falling into the excavation; they must also take into account the use of the pavement by blind persons, for whom the excavation was not reasonably safe.

Foresight or hindsight? Some of the cases already dealt with in this book indicate that the reasonable man is expected to foresee some quite improbable events. The presence of a relative near an accident victim, the presence of a blind man near a hole in the ground, the action of a rescuer in throwing himself into the path of a runaway horse are all within the range of his foresight. The element of foresight is that which determines the necessity to use care on the part of the defendant. But it is not a simple notion to apply. Take the case of the car driver. The reasonable driver, if asked why he should drive with care, would reply that otherwise he might hit somebody or something on the road. To ask whether he should also take into account as a reason for driving carefully the possibility that he may cause nervous shock to the relative of a person he hits (or narrowly misses), or that his bad driving may cause a fire which burns down a shop three hundred yards from the scene of the accident, is to ask a meaningless question of him. Yet because of the rule of English law that duties of care cannot exist in the abstract but must be owed to the particular person who suffers harm, such questions will often need to be answered. The real test here seems to be not whether a reasonable driver would actually have borne the unlikely risk in mind, but whether, assuming the injury or damage that occurred were the only possible result of bad driving, the reasonable driver if asked at the time of his driving would have said that the existence of such a risk was sufficient to impose an obligation on his part to exercise care. A complicated question of this sort looks much more like a test of hindsight rather than foresight and this seems to be the truth of the matter in a number of cases. The advantage of this approach is that persons who by carelessness have created obvious risks should not escape on the ground that the result of their carelessness is unusual rather than obvious. In other cases the only risk created by the defendant is an unusual one, and in such cases it seems the defendant is only liable if a reasonable person in his position would actually have borne that risk in mind. *Haley* v. *London Electricty Board* is a good example of this.

(2) *The seriousness of the injury*

It is an obvious proposition that the defendant's obligations become greater with the greater seriousness of the injury his actions may threaten. The more serious the injury or damage, the less the defendant will be entitled to argue that the degree of risk involved in his actions was insufficiently large, or that he would have needed to incur considerable expense in order to avoid the risk.

In *Paris* v. *Stepney Borough Council* (1951) the House of Lords held that the defendants' omission to provide protective eye goggles for their servants while not negligent in the case of a two-eyed man was negligent in the case of the plaintiff who had only one eye. Such omission clearly did not increase the risk of injury to the plaintiff but only the risk that if he did suffer injury it would be more serious.

(3) *The social utility of the defendant's action*

It has become apparent in the present century that certain inventions, such as the train, the motor-car and various forms of industrial machinery, though by and large regarded as beneficial to humanity, inevitably by their operation involve danger to human life and limb. When the first cases of train and motor-car accidents came before the court, it would have been possible for them to have laid down a rule that the mere operation of the train or motor-car involved so great a risk of injury that it was in itself negligent. Instead the courts decided that there was no negligence provided the vehicle was operated with proper care. The courts reached this result by balancing the social utility of the inventions against the risk of injury where they were operated with due care. Cases in which the defendant is excused on the ground of the usefulness of the activity he is carrying on are therefore somewhat rare, because it will be unusual for such a consideration to excuse what would otherwise by negligence in the activity itself. The only English case in which a plea of utility has been unequivocally recognised is *Daborn* v. *Bath Tramways* (1946) (and even this is a decision on contributory negligence rather than negligence itself). In that case the driver of a left-hand drive ambulance in wartime was held not contributorily negligent in failing to signal a right turn prior to a collision with a bus driven by the defendants' servant, because the shortage of ambulances in wartime conditions justified the use of a vehicle in which it was impossible to give such a signal. In *Watt* v. *Hertfordshire Corporation* (1954) the plaintiff, a fireman, was injured when a heavy jack in a lorry belonging to his employers, the defendants, and in which he was travelling, moved on to him. Although the jack was insecurely tied on, the court held that there was no negligence because the jack was urgently needed in order to save a person trapped under a lorry, and the emergency justified the risk of travelling with the jack insecurely tied. The most acceptable explanation for the case appears to be that given in the judgment of Singleton, L.J. to the effect that firemen are deemed to accept the risks incidental to dealing with such an emergency as part of their employment. It seems doubtful whether the emergency would have justified the defendants' action had the jack injured a member of the public. In *Gaynor* v. *Allen* (1959) a police constable who knocked down a pedestrian while riding a motorbicycle in excess of the speed limit was held liable although he had been riding his motorbicycle in pursuance of his police duties.

(4) *The expense and practicability of taking precautions*

From the dearth of decisions where the relevance of the practicability and expense of taking precautions against the risk has been discussed, it appears that the courts do not look with favour upon an argument by the defendant along these lines. In *Latimer* v. *A.E.C.* (1952) it was argued on behalf of the plaintiff that the defendants should have shut down their factory, the floor of which had been flooded in a thunderstorm, rather than subject the night-shift workers, who included the plaintiff, to the risks caused by the resulting slipperiness of the floor, on which the plaintiff slipped and suffered injury. The House of Lords accepted this argument in principle, though finding that insufficient evidence had been presented by the plaintiff to show that such a step was necessary.

Where the defendant is being sued in negligence for failing to remedy the state of affairs on his land, where that state of affairs arose without his default, the expense of remedying the state of affairs is a relevant factor in deciding whether a defendant is negligent. Thus, in *Goldman* v. *Hargrave* (*supra*, p. 83) since the fire could have been extinguished at nominal expense, the defendant was held liable for its spreading from his land to that of the plaintiff. It seems reasonable to regard expense as a relevant factor where the defendant has done nothing to create the risk, but is liable merely because of his occupation of land upon which the risk spontaneously arises. It has also been held that expense is a relevant factor in deciding whether an occupier has committed a breach of his duty of humanity towards a trespasser on his land (*infra*, p. 156).

The objective standard; the reasonable man

In imposing a requirement on a defendant that he should have acted reasonably, the law is judging him by a standard external to himself. The standard by which the defendant's conduct is assessed is that of a reasonable man in the same situation as that in which the defendant finds himself. It is sometimes said that the standard is an objective rather than a subjective one; but the defendant could hardly be judged by his own standards—this would not be a standard at all. It is important to note that the standard by which the defendant is judged though objective is also hypothetical; the court must imagine what a non-existent reasonable person in the position of the defendant would have done. In effect the court must make up its own mind as to what is reasonable in the light of the evidence.

Difficulty arises where the defendant has some defect, whether physical or mental, which makes it impossible for him to show the same standard of care as a normal person. Are these defects engrafted upon the reasonable man, so that the question is what is it reasonable to expect of a person with those defects? On this matter it seems there are two competing viewpoints. The first is that, unless the defect is taken into account, the "fault" basis of negligence will be ignored, and it will operate as a tort of strict liability. Against this it is argued that unless the test is largely objective, liability in negligence will be hard to establish because all sorts of trifling defects might be put forward in excuse for what is in fact a careless act. To a great extent the problem may be solved by application of the principle that one who, with knowledge of his own defects put himself into a position where those defects made it impossible to display a proper standard of care, is negligent. So a car-driver with slow reactions cannot plead that in an accident caused by his slowness of reaction he was not negligent. On these matters there is a dearth of English authority, and a paucity of discussion of principle in those authorities that exist. The cases, such as they are, tend to support those who argue for a subjective interpretation of negligence. Many of the decisions are, however, on contributory negligence rather than negligence itself and it may be that different considerations apply (a court might excuse a child for failure to look after itself—but what of a failure to look after the safety of other people?). The following is a discussion of the more common factors which might defeat an allegation of negligence.

Defects caused by immaturity

Clearly very young children have a different standard of care from adults both in matters of negligence and of contributory negligence. But the courts have also applied a different standard of care, at least in contributory negligence cases, to older children. In *Gough* v. *Thorne* (1966) a thirteen-year-old child was held to be not contributorily negligent in crossing the road on a signal from a lorry driver without checking that the way was clear beyond the lorry. Where the child is nearing adulthood, however, the same leniency will not be shown him. In *Gorely* v. *Codd* (1967) the court held a boy of 16½ liable for his negligence in "larking about" with an air-rifle as a result of which he shot the plaintiff.

Defects caused by age

There is little authority about the effect of old age. Old people are not expected to show the same agility as the young (*Daly* v. *Liverpool Corporation* (1939) in which an old person who was struck by a bus while crossing a street was held to be not contributorily negligent where a younger person would have succeeded in crossing). Clearly, however, an old person must not put himself in a position which calls for the reactions or agility of a younger person; also he must make allowances for the slowing-up processes of age (for example, when driving a car).

Illness

In *Ryan* v. *Youngs* (1938) a driver who had a heart attack and lost consciousness at the wheel prior to an accident was held not negligent in causing the accident. Although it has been argued that even in such a case the defendant should bear the loss because he is insured against it, there does not seem any sense in which the defendant's conduct could be described as negligent. There is a difference, however, if the driver of the car retains consciousness. In *Roberts* v. *Ramsbottom* (1980), the defendant driver suffered a cerebral haemorrhage which caused a clouding of consciousness with the result that he was, through no fault of his own, unable to drive properly but also incapable of realising this. He was held liable in negligence for a collision with another car. The decision reflects a tendency to impose what is virtually strict liability on car drivers (*cf. Nettleship* v. *Weston*, below 103). There is of course no difficulty in imposing liability in negligence if the defendant knows of his illness or its likelihood in advance.

Intelligence and character

It seems certain, although there is no authority, that a defendant, is not excused by such defects as stupidity, absent-mindedness, accident-proneness, inability to learn from experience, and the like. This is not surprising because if these were regarded as excusing factors few actions in negligence would succeed.

Knowledge

Every adult is expected to possess a certain quantum of knowledge. That petrol is highly inflammable, that dynamite explodes, that acid burns, that toadstools are dangerous, are matters of common knowledge. Apart from this a person may be expected to acquire knowledge by observation from his surrounding circumstances. Expert knowledge is not required of a defendant unless he has acted on the footing that he is an expert. A landowner who has trees growing on his estate is not expected to possess scientific knowledge of diseases that may affect the trees—the knowledge required of him is "somewhere between that of an urban observer and a scientific arboriculturist" (*Caminer* v. *Northern and London Investment Trust* (1951)). But such a landowner also owes a duty to call in experts to inspect the trees from time to time to assess their safety, especially where, as in that case, one of the trees is an elm, which a reasonable landowner ought to know possesses special hazards and the elm in question overhangs or adjoins the public highway. Equally, although expert knowledge is not required of a ship's engineer, he is expected to know that furnace oil might in exceptional circumstances be ignited on water (*The Wagon Mound* No. 2) (1967), knowledge that clearly would not be expected of the average person.

Skill

Skill is very often interrelated with knowledge, although of course a skill may exist which does not require a body of knowledge. Sometimes the skill and knowledge of an expert is required of a person, for example, a surgeon in performing an operation. In other cases only ordinary skill or knowledge is required, for example, that required of a motorist in driving a car. In general it may be said that the person who holds himself out as possessing the skill and knowledge required for performing a certain task must show that skill and knowledge in the exercise of the task.

The courts have not been too ready to decide that a person must show more than ordinary skill. In *Philips* v. *Whiteley* (1938) it was held that a jeweller who pierced the plaintiff's ears at her request was not bound to show proper medical skill in performing the operation—he need only show the standard of care of a reasonably competent jeweller. In *Wells* v. *Cooper* (1958) the defendant was held not negligent in fitting a new door-handle, the plaintiff suffering injury because it came away when he pulled on it and he fell down some steps. The defendant had shown the standard of care of a reasonably competent amateur carpenter, and professional expertise was not required of him. Both cases seem open to the objection that they encourage the doing by amateurs of tasks which involve danger to others. In *Nettleship* v. *Weston* (1971), on the other hand, the Court of Appeal held that a learner-driver must show the standard of driving skill of a reasonably competent qualified driver and was therefore liable to a passenger for injuries the passenger received through his failure to do so. The case is a strong pointer towards "object-ifying" the fault element in negligence, although the fact that the defendant was insured against liability clearly influenced the decision (there can be no real objection towards this decision now that insurance against liability towards passengers is compulsory).

Superior qualities

There seems no English authority on the question whether the person of superior intelligence or skill is liable for failing to use those qualities in a situation where such person is not holding himself out as possessing these qualities. Is a racing driver liable for causing an accident in ordinary traffic in which he showed the skill of an ordinary motorist, but had he driven with the skill to be expected of a racing driver the accident would have been averted? The answer to this question depends upon a resolution of the uncertainty as to whether the fault element in negligence is assessed subjectively or objectively.

Sportsmen

There is authority that participants in a sport are not required to show the same standard of care as is normally required. In *Woolridge* v. *Sumner* (1963) Diplock L.J. said, "if the participant does so concentrate his attention and con-sequently does exercise his judgment and attempt to exert his skill in circumstances of this kind which are inherent in the game or competition in which he is taking part, the question whether any mistake he makes amounts to a breach of duty to take reasonable care must take account of these circum-stances." Thus in that case, the defendant who was riding a horse in a competition was held not liable to the plaintiff, a photographer, standing inside the competition area, who was injured when the horse took a wrong turn as the result of an error of judgement on the part of the rider. This decision, which appears to impose liability upon the sportsman only if he has acted in reckless disregard of the spectator's safety, has been criticised (by Goodhart (1962) 78 L.Q.R. 490), and in *Wilks* v. *Cheltenham Car Club* (1971), Edmund Davies, L.J.

speaking *obiter*, disapproved the rule laid down and said the proper test should be whether the spectator's injury was caused by an error of judgment that a reasonable competitor, being a reasonable man of the sporting world, would not have made." The criticism seems sound, particularly since the plaintiff will often have difficulty in establishing liability on the part of the organisers of the sporting event (*infra*, pp. 131-132).

General practice of those engaged in the activity

It is relevant evidence of the fact that the defendant acted reasonably to show that he acted in accordance with the general practice of those who carried on the same activity. For example, in order to decide whether he showed proper medical skill, it is relevant to show that the defendant acted in accordance with approved medical practice. But such evidence is not necessarily conclusive. It is not enough to act in accordance with general practice if it ought to be apparent to a reasonable man that it is a negligent practice. In *Cavanagh* v. *Ulster Weaving Co.* (1960) the plaintiffs employers were held to be negligent in providing him with an unsafe system of work despite the fact that the system was in accordance with accepted practice.

8. CAUSATION AND REMOTENESS OF DAMAGE IN NEGLIGENCE

The question of whether damage suffered by the plaintiff is too remote to be actionable arises, in the case of torts other than negligence, only when it has been established that the defendant has committed the tort. In negligence, however, the question arises as soon as it has been established that the defendant was in breach of his duty of care to the plaintiff. In order to show that the damage he suffered was not too remote, the plaintiff under the present law must prove both that the damage was caused by the defendant's breach of duty to him, and that this was foreseeable. The two issues of causation and foreseeability will be examined in this chapter. Remoteness of damage must be distinguished from measure of damages. The former concept is concerned with what damage suffered by the plaintiff the defendant must compensate the plaintiff for; the latter with the amount of money the defendant must pay in order to produce that compensation. Since negligence does not, generally speaking, lie for purely pecuniary loss, the question of remoteness of damage in negligence is normally concerned with for what physical consequences of the defendant's breach of duty the plaintiff can recover damages.

Legal cause-causation in fact and in law

(1) *Causation in fact*

The plaintiff must prove that the defendant caused the damage. He must first of all show that the defendant's conduct was a cause in fact of his damage. This he satisfies by showing that but for the defendant's negligence the damage would not have occurred. In *Barnett* v. *Chelsea Hospital Management Committee* (1969) the defendants' servant carelessly failed to examine the plaintiff who attended their hospital for treatment complaining of vomiting. The plaintiff was suffering from arsenical poisoning and later died. The action of his estate against the defendant failed because it could not establish that proper treatment would have diagnosed the plaintiff's condition in time to save him. In *McWilliams* v. *Arrol Ltd.* (1962) the plaintiff had been injured in an accident at work. The defendants, his employers, had in breach of their duty to him, failed to supply him with a safety-belt which would have prevented his injury. The plaintiff's action failed because he could not prove that on the balance of probabilities he would have worn the belt. Finally, in *Cutler* v. *Vauxhall Motors* (1971), the plaintiff, an employee of the defendant's, grazed his ankle in an accident at work for which the defendants were liable in negligence. The graze caused ulceration of the leg necessitating an immediate operation for the removal of varicose veins in it. The plaintiff could not recover damages in respect of this operation because the court found as a fact that he would in any case have needed the operation within five years.

The last case illustrates that the tortfeasor takes the benefit of his victim's condition. It is cheaper to injure a person who has a week to live than a healthy person. This caused a problem in *Baker* v. *Willoughby* (1970). The plaintiff had received an injury to his leg through the defendant's negligence, and the leg was partially disabled as a result. Later the plaintiff was shot in the leg by another person and the leg was in consequence amputated. The need for amputation did not arise because of the existing disability in the leg. Nevertheless the House of Lords held that the plaintiff should recover compensation from the defendant on the basis of a continuing disability in the leg arising from the earlier injury. Since it is difficult to see that any part of the disability the plaintiff suffered from at the time of the trial would not have arisen but for the defendant's negligence, the decision looks like one of policy rather than logic. The second tortfeasor would have had to pay compensation to the plaintiff for the loss of an already injured leg. If the first tortfeasor had had to pay for the disability he inflicted only until the plaintiff lost his leg, the plaintiff would have received less than the total value of his leg even though he hd received two tortious injuries to it. The first tortfeasor's liability is perhaps best explained on the basis that the measure of damages for the first injury takes into account the reduction in compensation that the plaintiff may obtain from a later tortfeasor. So explained the case is distinguishable from that in which the later cause of damage is a natural event. In *The Carslogie* (1952) the plaintiff's ship had been damaged in a collision with the defendant's ship that occurred through the negligence of the defendant. Beofre it was repaired it suffered further damage in a storm. Thirty days were necessary for the repair of the storm damage, but during this period the collision damage, which itself would have taken 10 days to repair, was also repaired. The House of Lords held that the plaintiff's loss of use of the ship was wholly attributable to the storm damage (for confirmation of the view stated in the text here, see the Court of Appeal decision in *Jobling* v. *Associated Dairies* (1980)).

A slightly different problem in relation to factual causation is that in which the evidence makes it impossible to say whether or not the defendant's act caused the plaintiff's damage. Normally this means that the action will fail. But in the Canadian decision of *Cook* v. *Lewis* (1952), the plaintiff was shot by one of two members of a hunting party both of whom had fired their rifles in the plaintiff's direction at the same time. The Canadian Supreme Court held that if it could be established that both persons were in breach of their duty of care to the plaintiff in firing their rifles, the plaintiff's action would succeed against both, even though the plaintiff could not establish which had hit him. The decision is supportable on the ground that where it is clear that the plaintiff has been injured as the result of a tort committed by someone, and all possible tortfeasors have been careless towards the plaintiff, and the result of that carelessness is to prevent the plaintiff proving which person committed the tort, the plaintiff should succeeed against all. In *McGhee* v. *National Coal Board* (1975), however, the House of Lords went a good deal further. The plaintiff had contracted dermatitis through working in some brick kilns belonging to the defendants. The defendants were found to have been careless in not installing showering facilities. The state of medical knowledge did not enable the court to decide whether the taking of showers would have prevented dermatitis. Nevertheless the defendants were held liable in negligence. The court refused to draw a distinction between materially increasing the risk of injury and materially contributing to injury. This distinction seems, however, to be fundamental, unless the law relating to proof of negligence has been rewritten to the extent that the plaintiff need only prove a breach of duty of care by the defendant. The decision is distinguishable from *Cook* v. *Lewis* on the ground that there was no certainty that the cause of the plaintiff's injury was a tort. The other possibility was that the plaintiff's injury was accidental—the defendant's negligence made it impossible to decide whether this was so.

(2) Causation in law

The "but for" test merely serves to eliminate certain factors as causes of the plaintiff's damage. It does not identify those causes in respect of which legal liability exists. A test for determining what causes in fact are also causes in law of the plaintiff's damage is therefore required. Under the decision of the Court of Appeal in *Re Polemis* (1921) the defendant was liable for damage which was the direct or immediate consequence of his negligence to the plaintiff. This test gave way in certain cases to allow the defendant to be held liable for indirect consequences provided they were foreseeable. The decision in *The Wagon Mound* (No. 1) (1961) replaced the *Polemis* rule with a rule that the defendant was liable only for the foreseeable consequences of his breach of duty to the plaintiff. The decision at the time it was made appeared to introduce a more restrictive test for remoteness of damage than *Re Polemis*. Whether it has done so is for consideration in this chapter. It may be pointed out here, however, that the *Wagon Mound* (No. 1) appears to allow the defendant to be held liable for all the foreseeable consequences, direct or indirect, to the plaintiff of which the defendant's breach of duty is a cause in fact whereas, generally speaking, under *Polemis* liability existed only for damage arising directly.

The present law and its evolution

The *Wagon Mound* (No. 1) was a decision of the Privy Council on appeal from the courts of New South Wales. Such a decision is not in theory binding on any English court, though it has undoubted persuasive force. Decisions of the Court of Appeal bind all English courts apart from the House of Lords, including the Court of Appeal itself. Despite this, and as support for those who argue that there are no binding rules of precedent in English law, the cases subsequent to the Privy Council decision have applied the rule for remoteness it laid down rather than the rule in *Re Polemis*. This has happened in a number of first instance decisions and at Court of Appeal level in *Doughty* v. *Turner Manufacturing Co.* (1964). The House of Lords has not yet had to consider the correctness of the decision in *The Wagon Mound* (No. 1) (*Hughes* v. *Lord Advocate* (*infra*, p. 111) was a decision on Scots law which never accepted *Re Polemis*). It is assumed that the decision in *The Wagon Mound* (No. 1) now represents English law.

A comparison between the two cases remains of interest. In *Re Polemis* the defendants were charterers of a ship belonging to the plaintiffs. The defendants' servants carelessly allowed a plank to fall into the hold of the ship. The hold contained petrol vapour which was present because of leakage of petrol from tins in the hold. The fall of the plank caused a spark which ignited the vapour, and in the ensuing conflagration the ship was totally destroyed. The defendants were admittedly responsible for the breach of duty of care by their servant since some damage to the ship was foreseeable. But the presence of the petrol vapour was found as a fact to be unforeseeable. Nevertheless the defendants were liable to the plaintiffs for the loss of the ship. The fire was the direct result of their breach of duty of care. Foreseeability was irrelevant once a breach of duty had been established.

It is significant that 40 years elapsed before a case came

before the courts in which the correctness of the decision in
Re Polemis had to be examined. The facts of *The Wagon
Mound* (No. 1) were similarly extraordinary. The defendants
were charterers of the ship "The Wagon Mound." By the carelessness of their servants, who were ship engineers, a spillage
of a quantity of furnace oil into Sydney harbour occurred.
The oil spread to a wharf owned by the plaintiffs and on
which the plaintiffs were carrying out welding operations.
After taking advice that the oil was not ignitable, the plaintiffs' servant continued to carry on these operations. The oil
was ignited by the fall of hot metal from the wharf, and extensive damage by fire occurred to the plaintiffs' wharf. The
trial judge found that the defendants were in breach of a
duty of care to the plaintiffs since damage to the wharf
through the fouling of its slipways by oil was foreseeable, and
had actually occurred. Damage by fire was, however, unforeseeable, because furnace oil has a high ignition point, and it
was unforeseeable that it would ignite on water. The presence
of the oil was nevertheless found to be a cause of the fire
damage. On these findings the Privy Council refused to apply
the *Polemis* rule and held the defendants not liable for the
damage by fire since this was not a foreseeable consequence
of their breach of duty to the plaintiffs.

The plaintiffs in *The Wagon Mound* (No. 1) were reluctant
to argue that the defendants should have foreseen the possi
bility of the oil being ignited, because if that had been found,
it would have been arguable that their own servant should
have foreseen this possibility, and that therefore the welding
operations should have been discontinued. The failure to do
so would therefore have operated as a cause, and possibly the
sole cause of the damage. No such problem confronted the
owners of the ship, the *Corrimal*, which was moored at the
plaintiffs wharf and which was extensively damaged in the
fire. In a later action (*The Wagon Mound* (No. 2) (*supra*,
p. 96), brought by the owners of that ship against the
defendants in the earlier case, the court made a different
finding as to foreseeability and the defendants were held liable.

The concept of foreseeability

Foreseeability is a more flexible notion than that of causation. It will be easier for the courts to take into account
matters of policy in their decisions than before, and on the
whole this seems desirable. But the flexibity of foreseeability
is both its strength and its weakness. The unpredictability of
foreseeability as a test of duty of care has been seen, in particular, in the nervous shock cases. With foreseeability now the
test both of breach of duty and of remoteness of damage

there is a real danger of uncertainty in the law producing lack of confidence in the courts' decisions.

It has also been suggested that, now that the test both of the defendant's breach of duty and of remoteness of damage is one of foreseeability, there is no longer any need to answer the two questions, "Should the defendant have foreseen any damage to the plaintiff?" to decide whether he was in breach of duty, and "Was the damage the plaintiff suffered a foreseeable consequence of that breach?" A single question such as "Was the plaintiff's damage a foreseeable consequence of the defendant's act?" should be sufficient. But in deciding whether there has been a breach, the court does not simply ask the question whether the defendant's conduct created a foreseeable risk to the plaintiff. The degree of risk to the plaintiff must be sufficiently great that the defendant should have taken steps to prevent its occurrence, bearing in mind also that the defendant's conduct may have social value, or that the elimination of the risk may present great difficulty. The balancing operation that courts perform in deciding whether there has been a breach can, it seems, be performed only once. Once the defendant's conduct has been adjudged negligent as against the plaintiff in respect of a certain risk, it is not possible to weigh its utility or the difficulty of its removal against the degree of likelihood of other risks occurring, even though those other risks are less likely. It may be therefore that in deciding what is foreseeable for the purposes of remoteness of damage factors that are relevant to the question of breach, such as degree of risk, the knowledge and circumstances of the defendant, the utility of his conduct and the difficulty and expense of averting the risk are irrelevant. The court must merely ask itself whether the damage was foreseeable within the confines of universal human knowledge. The courts have not yet had to consider this point, but at the moment there is nothing to indicate that different tests of foreseeability exist. A decision such as that in *Tremain* v. *Pike* (1969) seems directly contrary to such a view. In that case, in considering a question of remoteness of damage, the court had to consider the foreseeability of a disease called Weil's disease which is caught by contact with rat's urine. There was evidence that the disease was known to medical officers of health and public health inspectors, but that it was very rare and would not be known about by the ordinary, reasonable farmer. The defendant was a farmer. The court found that Weil's disease was unforeseeable.

It is relevant to remind the reader here that if two different tests of foreseeability are to be applied, one in deciding the issue of breach, and the other the issue of remoteness of damage, the plaintiff must, in order to raise the question of remoteness at all, establish a breach of duty of care to himself by the defendant. He cannot rely on any breach of a duty of care which the defendant may have committed towards other persons.

Foreseeability and risk

If the defendant is liable for the foreseeable consequences of his breach of duty, how precise does this foreseeability have to be? Clearly exact foreseeability is not required. In the words of Lord Denning, M.R. in *Steward* v. *West African Air Terminals* (1964):

> "It is not necessary that the precise concatenation of cir-
> cumstances should be envisaged. If the consequence was
> one within the general range which any reasonable person
> might foresee (and was not of an entirely different kind
> which no one would anticipate) then it is within the rule
> that a person who is guilty of negligence is liable for the
> consequences."

For a case in which the defendant did not even contest the foreseeability of the harm he had produced despite the bizarre sequence of events which led up to it, the case of *Salsbury* v. *Woodland* (1970) should be read. The so called "risk principle," which as far as English law is concerned is more an academic theory than something deriving from established authority, would take matters a little further. The theory would hold the defendant liable for any *type* of harm, which was a foreseeable result of his conduct, even though the *manner* in which the harm occurred was unforeseeable. Risks would, therefore, be classified broadly and in terms of their effects rather than their causes. Some risks lend themselves easily enough to differentiation in this way. The foreseeable risk of impact damage to property is distinguishable from the risk of fire (as in *Polemis*); the risk of oil fouling slipways from the risk of fire through its ignition on water (as in *The Wagon Mound* No. 1). But the cases of *Hughes* v. *Lord Advocate* and *Doughty* v. *Turner Manufacturing* show the difficulties the process involves. In the former case workmen employed by the defendant left a manhole shelter unattended during their tea-break. Four lighted paraffin lamps were placed at the corners of the shelter. The plaintiff, a boy aged eight, took one of the lamps into the shelter to explore the manhole. He tripped over the lamp which fell into the hole. An explosion occurred in which the plaintiff suffered severe burns. The trial judge held that though the workmen were negligent in leaving the shelter unattended, in that they had created a risk of the plaintiff being burned by the lamp, injury by explosion which occurred through vaporisation of the paraffin in the lamp and its subsequent ignition was not foreseeable. Nevertheless the House of Lords held the defendants liable in negligence. They had created a foreseeable risk of injury by burning, and this risk included burning by explosion, which though itself unforeseeable was sufficiently similar to the foreseeable risk created to count as part of it. In *Doughty's* case, the defendants kept on their premises a large bath containing sulphuric acid heated to a temperature of 800 degrees centigrade. The bath had a loose cover made of a compound of asbestos and cement. This cover was knocked into the bath by the plaintiff's fellow workman. A chemical reaction took place between the acid and the cover and an eruption of acid followed in which the plaintiff received burns. This was found to be unforeseeable. The Court of Appeal held the defendants not liable in negligence. Even if there had been a breach of duty when the cover was knocked into the acid because of the risk of splashing (which was not determined), it was unrealistic to regard the eruption which occurred as a mere variant of the perils of splashing. The court described the eruption in the words of Lord Reid in *Hughes* v. *Lord Advocate* as "the intrusion of a new and unexpected factor."

The latter case seems to deny any wholesale incorporation of the risk principle into English law. Whether it occurred by splashing or eruption the risk in terms of its effect on the plaintiff was the same. There has it seems, therefore, to be some measure of similarity between the manner of occurrence of the actual harm and the foreseeable manner of occurrence. If this is so, the difference between the two cases appears to be one of degree. Foreseeability, as suggested above, has introduced uncertainty into the law. This has received some confirmation by later decisions. In *Bradford* v. *Robinson Rentals* (1967) the plaintiff received frostbite as a result of being instructed by the defendants, his employers, to make a journey of 500 miles in a van without a heater during exceptionally severe winter weather. Frostbite itself was unforeseeable, but the plaintiff recovered damages in negligence because frostbite lay within the general class of risk arising from exposure to cold weather. In *Parsons* v. *Uttley, Ingham* (1978) (a contract case but one which could have been argued in tort to which similar principles would apply), the defendants supplied the plaintiff with a defective "hopper" which was to be used for the purpose of storing animal fodder. Some nuts stored in the hopper became mouldy and the plaintiff's pigs developed a rare disease called E-coli infection through eating them. Since some form of internal disorder in the pigs was clearly foreseeable, the unforeseeability of E-coli did not prevent the defendants being held liable. On the other hand, in *Tremain* v. *Pike* (1969) the court held that, had the defendant been negligent in keeping a rat-infected farm (which on the facts he was not), he would not have been liable to his employee who contracted Weil's disease from contact with rats' urine. The foreseeable dangers were disease from rat-bite or from eating contaminated food, and the catching of Weil's disease, which was unforeseeable, was not a mere variant of these. Under *Re Polemis*, all these cases would have admitted of a straightforward solution; it may be significant that in the two cases in which the defendant escaped liability, a breach of a duty of care was negatived in one (*Tremain*) and not established in the other (*Doughty*).

Cases where the damage is aggravated by physical peculiarities of the victim

While *Polemis* was law it was never doubted that the principle was that the tortfeasor took the victim as he found him, so that the greater amount of damage suffered by the haemophiliac or the man with an egg-shell skull was recoverable. After *The Wagon Mound*, it was arguable whether the peculiarities of the victim which were probably unforeseeable could be allowed to affect the extent of the defendant's liability. But the courts have made it clear that the rule remains unchanged.

In *Smith* v. *Leech, Brain & Co* (1962) the Court of Appeal allowed the deceased's estate to recover damages from the defendants for his death from cancer of the lip. The lip had been in a pre-malignant condition and cancer broke out when the deceased received a burn from molten metal owing to negligence by the defendants.

It is not necessary that the extra damage suffered by the plaintiff should arise through an aggravation of the first injury. It is enough if there is causal connection between the plaintiff's thin skull condition, and the effect of injury on it, and a later event inflicting another injury. In *Wieland* v. *Cyril Lord Carpets* (1969), the plaintiff received personal injuries in a car accident through the defendant's negligence. Because of the shakiness induced by the accident, she could not adjust to the wearing of bi-focal glasses and suffered further injury in a fall soon after the first injury. She recovered damages for the second injury as well. In *Robinson* v. *Post Office* (1974), the plaintiff suffered minor injuries to his leg through the defendant's negligence. He was given an anti-tetanus injection but suffered an unusual adverse reaction to it and was seriously affected. He recovered damages for the resulting condition from the defendant. (These cases should be contrasted with *McKew* v. *Hannen, Holland & Cubitts Ltd.* *infra*, p. 116).

The thin-skull rule probably has as its justification the analogous though distinct rule concerning measure of damages. In assessing measure of damages, the tortfeasor must take the victim as he finds him, paying, *ceteris paribus*, more to the millionaire than to the bank clerk. So also in evaluating the extent of the injury suffered by the plaintiff the courts do not make any reduction for the fact that the plaintiff's injury has been aggravated by his own condition. So explained it seems essential that the plaintiff should have suffered an injury for which the defendant is liable in negligence. It does not seem enough that the defendant has committed a breach of duty of care to the plaintiff, and the plaintiff's pre-existent condition has caused the injury to happen. But in *Tremain* v. *Pike*, the court thought that if the defendant had been guilty of keeping a rat-infested farm, and the plaintiff through his own abnormal susceptibility had caught Weil's disease, the rule would have been applied. There are dicta to this effect, also, in *Bradford* v. *Robinson Rentals*. If this is so, the basis of the rule is far less clear and it is more difficult to reconcile with the principles laid down in *The Wagon Mound* (No. 1).

Two further points about the rule may be made. The "condition" of the victim does not include his surrounding circumstances. Otherwise the decision in *Re Polemis* would be decided in the same way despite *The Wagon Mound* (No. 1). Where, on the other hand the damage that was foreseeable occurs in the manner that was foreseeable, an increase in the extent of that damage caused by the victim's surrounding circumstances is not too remote. The extent of foreseeable damage does not itself need to be foreseeable (*Vacwell Engineering Co.* v. *B.D.H. Chemicals* (1971)). So in *Great Lakes S.S.Co.* v. *Maple Leaf Milling Co. Ltd.* (1923) as a result of the defendants' negligent failure to lighter the plaintiffs' ship, the ship ran aground. The damage was increased by the fact that the ship came to rest on a submerged anchor, the presence of which was unforeseeable by the defendants. The plaintiffs recovered the full extent of their damage from the defendants. On the other hand, and perhaps illogically, though neurosis is a foreseeable result of an injury, the fact that it is perpetuated by the victim's family circumstances does not enable the victim to claim for the increased amount. (*McLaren* v. *Bradstreet* (1969)). The second point about the rule is that it is doubtful whether it extends to property damage. It is generally assumed that it does not, but there is no clear authority.

Liability for intervening causes

Cases where the only negligence alleged against the defendant is his failure to anticipate and prevent the act of another human being raise questions of duty rather than remoteness of damage, *Stansbie* v. *Troman* (*supra*, p. 90) is an example of this type of case. Where the breach of duty committed by the defendant is not of this nature, a question arises whether an intervening act of a human being excuses the defendant. This raises a true question of remoteness of damage and will be discussed in this chapter. Where the defendant is excused by the later human act, it is referred to as a *novus actus* (or *nova causa*) *interveniens*, and it is commonly said to "break the chain of causation" between the defendant's negligence and the plaintiff's damage.

The same principles now govern the question what is a *nova causa interveniens* as governs all other issues of remoteness of damage. The damage the plaintiff suffers must be both foreseeable and a consequence (*i.e.* caused in fact) by the defendant's breach of duty to him.

In the case of deliberate actions of a third party (or of the plaintiff himself), these are generally regarded as unforeseeable and as breaking the chain of causation. In *Philco Radio* v. *Spurling Ltd*. (1949) the defendants' servants had negligently delivered by mistake some packing-cases containing highly inflammable celluloid film scrap to the premises of the plaintiffs. The film had been set alight by a typist after one of the cases had been opened by the defendants' servants. The court found that the typist had acted negligently rather than deliberately and her act was therefore not a *nova causa interveniens*. Even a deliberate action may be held to be not a *nova causa* if it is not truly voluntary and is foreseeable. In *The Oropesa* (1943), the defendants' ship negligently collided with another ship, the *Manchester Regiment*. The captain of the *Manchester Regiment* decided to put to sea in a lifeboat along with others including the plaintiff in order to discuss the possibility of salving the *Manchester Regiment* with the defendants' crew. The lifeboat capsized in heavy seas and the plaintiff was drowned. His estate recovered damages for his death from the defendants. The captain's decision was a reasonable reaction to a situation of peril created by the defendants and could not be likened to the deliberate infliction of harm by a third party. In the case of later negligent conduct by a third party or the plaintiff, such conduct will seldom if ever be regarded as a *nova causa*. Negligence is always foreseeable. If the defendant by lack of care has put the plaintiff into a position of danger from which the exercise of due care on the part of a third party or himself could have saved him, there is little reason for completely excusing the defendant. This is particularly so under a system of law which permits apportionment of liability among tortfeasors (*infra,* pp. 118), and a reduction in the plaintiff's damages because of his contributory negligence.

Similar principles determine the defendant's liability where his negligence has actually inflicted damage on the plaintiff, and that damage has been increased in extent by later human conduct. *McKew* v. *Hannen, Holland & Cubitts* (1969) shows that deliberate actions will generally break the chain of causation. The plaintiff had received an injury to his leg for which the defendants were legally liable. He attempted to descend some steps, which had no handrail, without assistance which was at hand. The House of Lords refused to hold the defendant liable for his further injury, because the plaintiff's act was unreasonable and therefore a *nova causa interveniens.* It is suggested that unreasonable here meant deliberate, and that if the plaintiff had merely negligently failed to appreciate the disabling effect of his first injury, this would not have broken the chain of causation (though justifying some reduction of damages). Again, where the plaintiff's action, though deliberate, is not truly voluntary, and is foreseeable, it does not break the chain of causation. In *Pigney* v. *Pointer's Transport Services* (1957), the plaintiff committed suicide less than two years after receiving a head injury through the defendants' negligence. The suicide was found to be the result of an acute anxiety neurosis and depression produced by the head injury. The defendants were held liable to the plaintiff's estate for his death, which was a foreseeable result of the earlier injury. Unlike McKew, Pigney was not fully responsible for his later deliberate act.

In cases where the earlier injury is aggravated by later negligence, it might be thought that the defendant is liable for this since negligence is always foreseeable. It must be remembered, however, that the earlier injury must operate as a cause in fact of the later one. If, without the earlier injury, the later negligence would in any case have injured the plaintiff, the defendant is not liable for it. Two cases will illustrate the distinction. In *S.S. Singleton Abbey* v. *S.S. Paludina* (1927) the *Paludina* was in collision with the *Singleton Abbey* due to the negligent navigation of the *Paludina.* The *Singleton Abbey,* having been cast adrift, caused another collision in which another ship, the *Sara* was cast adrift. Later the *Sara* again collided with the *Singleton Abbey* and was sunk. The *Sara* was found to be negligent in respect of the last collision. The House of Lords held the owners of the *Paludina* not liable for the sinking of the *Sara.* There was no more reason for the last collision to have occurred than if the *Sara* had been on a normal voyage—the effects of the earlier negligence were spent.

In the *Calliope* (1970), on the other hand, a collision occurred between a ship called the *Calliope* and another called the *Carlsholm*, for which the negligence of the latter was 45 per cent to blame. The *Calliope* was grounded and suffered damage but was refloated. On the following day, while executing an "exceptionally difficult" turning manoeuvre in fog, which was necessary for it to resume the original voyage, it grounded twice and collided with its tug, thus suffering further damage. The *Calliope* was found to be negligent in the execution of this turn. Nevertheless the owners of the *Carlsholm* were held to be partially legally liable for the later damage. The *Calliope* had not acted unreasonably in attempting the manoeuvre despite its difficult nature. The defendants' earlier negligence was clearly still operative in producing the later damage, even though by proper skill the plaintiffs could have surmounted the difficulty presented them by the defendants. Similar principles to those applied in these cases will no doubt determine the thorny question of the defendant's liability for an injury that is aggravated by later medical negligence. No English case on tort exists, but in *Hogan* v. *Bentinck Collieries* (1949) (a decision on workmen's compensation), the House of Lords answered the causal point in the defendant's favour in a case where the plaintiff's injury presented no unusual problem to the surgeons.

The two rules of remoteness of damage compared

At the time of the decision in *The Wagon Mound* (No. 1), its correctness divided academic opinion, and it was the subject of a voluminous literature. Supporters of *Re Polemis* argued that where the question arose as between innocent plaintiff and negligent defendant who should bear the loss caused by that negligence, the defendant should be chosen. They were fortified in their stance by the consideration that defendants in tort suits generally had the means to satisfy liability; most plaintiffs were impecunious. Supporters of *The Wagon Mound* (No. 1) founded themselves on a moralistic argument that a defendant should not be held liable in negligence to an extent greater than the foreseeable amount of the damage. They also disliked the "mechanical" test of causation laid down by *Polemis*. Foreseeability was a more flexible notion in which the requirements of justice and policy could be taken into account. Some of the cases decided since *The Wagon Mound* (No. 1) have indicated that this flexibility is bought at a price, and that there is now more uncertainty in the law than formerly. The cases deriving from *Hughes* v. *Lord Advocate* are not easily reconcilable with each other. The extent of the thin skull rule and its harmonisation with principles of foreseeability remains doubtful. The overriding impression, however, is how little change has actually resulted from the Privy Council decision. The thin skull rule has survived it. *Hughes* v. *Lord Advocate* shows that not every aspect of the plaintiff's damage need to be foreseeable. No case decided since 1961, with the possible exception of *Doughty* v. *Turner Manufacturing Co.* would have produced a different result under *Polemis* principles. It is interesting to note that the finding on foreseeability which led to the decision in *The Wagon Mound* (No. 1) was reversed on the same facts (but as between different parties) in *The Wagon Mound* (No. 2).

MULTIPLE CAUSES AND THE APPORTIONMENT OF DAMAGE

The cases on liability for intervening causes show that the law recognises that an event may have more than one cause. Where two tortfeasors have combined to produce the same damage to the plaintiff, each is liable for the full amount. A further question then arises whether a tortfeasor held liable in full for that damage is entitled to recover a contribution from another tortfeasor also liable for the same damage. This question will be examined in this chapter. It is felt that to deal with the law's handling of multiple causation in tort in the chapter on causation in negligence, the tort which most commonly produces the problem, should be an aid to understanding. It must be remembered, however, that the principles governing this question are applicable to all torts, not just negligence. The present law is laid down in the Civil Liability (Contribtion) Act 1978, which replaces and extends the Law Reform (Married Women and Tortfeasors) Act 1935.

Although cases of multiple causation appear to demand a mechanism for apportioning responsibility among tortfeasors, the recognition of this has been slow to occur in England. There are two reasons for this. First, tortfeasors were thought to be immoral persons to whom the courts should not lend their aid in enforcing claims against each other. This reasoning has lost most of its validity with the expansion in the tort of negligence and the recognition of torts of strict liability. It is no doubt still true that a tortfeasor who was malicious or fraudulent would be unable to claim contribution from other tortfeasors because of the *ex turpi causa* rule. Secondly, the phenomenon of multiple causation is generally found in cases where the various parties have been negligent, and only in the present century has negligence become established as a tort.

Before discussing the introduction of the rule allowing apportionment of damage, it may be said that the problem only arises where two or more have tortiously contributed to the *same* damage, and it is impossible to allocate different parts of that damage to different persons. Where the plaintiff's damage can be separately allocated, there is no problem of apportionment. Thus if A and B simultaneously commit battery against C, it may be possible to show that A caused one injury and B another (but the harm will not be divisible if A and B have acted in the furtherance of a common design— see *infra*).

The damage may, however, not be readily divisible among the tortfeasors responsible. In a motor accident caused by the negligent driving of X and Y and in which Z, a pedestrian, suffers personal injuries, it would obviously be impossible to attribute any particular part of Z's injuries to X or Y. In such a situation X and Y are said to be separate concurrent tortfeasors (they will be referred to hereafter as concurrent tortfeasors). Each is liable for the whole of Z's injuries and Z may choose to sue either of them for his damage.

In English law a distinction is drawn between concurrent tortfeasors and joint tortfeasors. The distinction may be explained as follows. Concurrent tortfeasors are responsible for different torts producing the same damage, whereas joint tortfeasors in law commit the same tort. The most important examples of joint tortfeasors are:

(i) In cases of vicarious liability, the person vicariously liable is a joint tortfeasor with his servant, an employer with his independent contractor.

(ii) In cases where there has been concerted action in the furtherance of a common design, those participating are joint tortfeasors. Thus conspirators are joint tortfeasors. So are the author, publisher, and printer of a defamatory work. *Brooke* v. *Bool* (1928) furnishes another illustration: the defendant landlord invited his lodger to help him look for an escape of gas by striking a match in the vicinity of the escape. The landlord and the lodger were held to be joint tortfeasors in respect of the damage caused by the ensuing explosion.

(iii) Where one person has instigated or authorised another to commit a tort, the two are joint tortfeasors. Thus the landlord who authorities his tenant to commit a nuisance is a joint tortfeasor with the tenant.

(iv) The partners in a firm are jointly and severally liable for the torts of a partner acting in the ordinary course of business of the firm. The basis of this may be vicarious liability, or community of design among the members of the partnership.

The distinction between joint and concurrent tortfeasors must still be drawn, although it has lost much of its importance. The rule in *Brinsmead* v. *Harrison* (1872) that judgment obtained against one or more of several joint tortfeasors released all of them was abolished by the 1935 Act. Section 3 of the Civil Liability (Contribution) Act 1978 provides that judgment recovered against any person liable in respect of any debt or damage shall not be a bar to an action, or to the continuance of an action, against any other person who is (apart from any such bar) jointly liable with him in respect of the same debt or damage. The common law rule about the effect of judgment did not apply in the case of concurrent tortfeasors.

The common law rule that release of one joint tortfeasor released all the rest remains unchanged, so that it is still necessary to distinguish joint from concurrent tortfeasors. But the courts have lessened the effect of the rule by distinguishing a release from a covenant not to sue, the latter having no effect on the continuance of liability of other joint tortfeasors. The test for drawing the distinction is whether it can be inferred from the language used by the plaintiff that he intended to reserve his rights of action against other joint tortfeasors-if so, it will be construed as a covenant not to sue rather than a release.

Contribution

Section 1 (1) of the 1978 Act provides: subject to the following provisions of this section, any person liable in respect of any damage suffered by another person may recover contribution from any other person liable in respect of the same damage (whether jointly or otherwise).

Who may recover contribution?

Any "person liable" may recover contribution. In this context "liable" will normally mean held liable. But section 1 (2) says that this includes a person who has ceased to be liable, provided that he was so liable immediately before he made or was ordered or agreed to make the payment in respect of which contribution is sought. Section 1 (4) removes a problem that existed under the former law by providing that a person who makes a bona fide settlement or compromise of a claim against him in respect of any damage may recover contribution without the need for proving his own liability for that damage, provided that "he would have been liable assuming the factual basis of the claim against him could be established."

From whom may contribution be claimed?

The person from whom contribution may be claimed is defined by section 1 (2) of the Act to be any other person liable in respect of the same damage (whether jointly or otherwise). Section 6 (1) expands this by providing that the requirement of liability is satisfied whatever the legal basis of liability, whether tort, breach of contract, breach of trust or otherwise. The 1935 Act only allowed contribution between tortfeasors so that this is a considerable extension. A tortfeasor, for example, liable in respect of certain damage may now recover contribution from one liable in breach of contract for the same damage. A further extension is section 1 (3) which provides that contribution may be claimed from one who has ceased to be liable, unless this was through the expiry of a limitation period which extinguishes the right on which the plaintiff's claim is based. One example of that sort of limitation period is that applying to actions for conversion, but most limitation periods merely operate to make the plaintiff's right unenforceable rather than to extinguish it. Under the former law, where the tortfeasor had the defence of limitation he was immune to liability to make contribution, so here again the Act effects an important change. Contribution proceedings themselves must be brought within two years of the date on which the right to recover contribution accrues. Section 1 (3) also extends to allowing contribution to be claimed from one who has reached an out-of-court settlement with the plaintiff, or from one against whom the plaintiff's action has been dismissed for want of prosecution.

Amount of contribution

Section 2 (1) and (2) of the 1978 Act provide: subject to section 2 (3), in any proceedings for contribution under section 1, the amount of the contribution recoverable from any person shall be such as may be found just and equitable having regard to the extent of that person's responsibility for the damage in question: (2) subject to section 2 (3), the court shall have power in any such proceedings to exempt any person from liability to make contribution, or to direct that the contribution to be recovered shall amount to an absolute indemnity.

It is now established that in exercising its discretion under these subsections, the court must take into account both the causative potency of the defendant's act and its degree of blameworthiness. The test is the same as that established for assessing for the plaintiff's contributory negligence under the Law Reform (Contributory Negligence) Act 1945 (*infra*, p. 124).

Section 2 (3) provides for certain limitations upon the court's discretion under section 2 (1) and (2). Section 2 (3) (*a*) provides that where the liability of any person is "subject to any limit imposed by or under any enactment or by any agreement made before the damage occurred," the right to recover contribution is limited in the same way. It may be noted that, although the case may not be a suitable one for ordering an indemnity under section 2 (2), the provisions of a contract may produce this effect under section 2 (3) (*a*). (Thus in *Sims* v. *Foster, Wheeler* (1966), an employer and his sub-contractor were adjudged to be at fault to the extent of 25 per cent and 75 per cent respectively on the claim of the plaintiff employee. Nevertheless the employer obtained under the terms of his contract with the sub-contractor a complete indemnity.) Section 2 (3) (*b*) provides, in effect, that where the amount of damages recoverable from a tort-feasor is subject to a reduction for the plaintiff's contributory negligence, the amount recoverable in contribution proceedings from that tortfeasor shall not exceed the reduced amount. Normally all defendants will get the benefit of such a reduction, but it is still a disputed question whether a reduction for contributory negligence is possible where the plaintiff's claim is for breach of contract. If not, the following result would emerge from the Act's provisions. Suppose that D1, by his breach of contract, and D2 by his tort have caused the same damage, amounting to £1,000 to the plaintiff, and the plaintiff is 75 per cent contributorily negligent. Assume also that D1 and D2 are equally at fault. D1 must satisfy the plaintiff's claim in full, but can recover only £250 contribution from D2 (*i.e.* the full amount of his liability to the plaintiff, less a 75 per cent reduction).

Nature and machinery of contribution proceedings
The right to claim contribution is an independent, statutory right, having its own period of limitation. It is, however, uncommon for separate proceedings to be brought for enforcement of the right. Where the plaintiff has not joined all possible tortfeasors as defendants to his action, the defendant actually sued may issue a third-party notice against anyone from whom he is claiming relief whether by way of contribution or indemnity, under Order 16, Rule 1 of the Rules of the Supreme Court (a similar right exists in the county court). The effect of this is to make the third-party a defendant to the plaintiff's action, so that the court may apportion responsibility for the damage among him (if found liable) and all other defendants similarly liable. The plaintiff is provided with an incentive to join all possible tortfeasors as defendants to his action by section 4 of the 1978 Act which allows the court a discretion to deprive the plaintiff of the costs of any actions brought by him subsequent to the first.

9. DEFENCES TO NEGLIGENCE

DEFENCES TO NEGLIGENCE

The two defences to be dealt with in this chapter may operate as defences to negligence as such, as well as in situations where negligence is the gist of the action, such as employers' liability, occupiers' liability and liability for chattels. Their applicability to other torts is considered in the relevant sections of the book.

CONTRIBUTORY NEGLIGENCE

Introduction

The rules of contributory negligence deal with the situation where the plaintiff has suffered damage through the negligence of the defendant, but has also contributed to that damage through his own negligence. The law on this seemingly straightforward situation was formerly full of complications, but now, because of the courts' power to apportion responsibility for the damage as between the plaintiff and defendant, generally works satisfactorily.

Before the Law Reform (Contributory Negligence) Act 1945, where the defendant successfully established contributory negligence on the part of the plaintiff, this was a complete defence to the plaintiff's action. The basis of the defence appeared to be that the plaintiff's negligence destroyed the causal link between the defendant's negligence and the damage, rather than that, where both the parties had been negligent, in the absence of a power to apportion the damage, the loss should lie where it fell. Where the defendant's negligence post-dated that of the plaintiff it could be seen effectively as the cause of the damage; in the reverse situation the plaintiff was regarded as having caused his own downfall (*cf*, the old cases *Davies* v. *Mann* (1842) with *Butterfield's* v. *Forrester* (1809)).

The courts therefore applied, more or less mechanically, a rule of letting the loss fall on whichever of the plaintiff or defendant had the last opportunity of avoiding the accident.

The decisions on this so-called rule of last opportunity are no great credit to our jurisprudence. But the courts were faced with the difficulty that, in the absence of a power to apportion the damage, they were forced to take the negligence of one party as the only cause of the damage. Even so, there was no reason why the later negligence should always have been chosen. The problem was recognised in *Swadling* v. *Cooper* (1930) in which a trial judge's direction to a jury in a case involving a road accident that the question was, if both plaintiff and defendant were negligent whose negligence substantially caused the accident, was upheld by the House of Lords.

The Court of Admiralty, which had to deal with similar problems of dual responsibility in connection with collisions at sea, was not so hamstrung in its approach to the problem, because of its power to apportion damages under the Maritime Conventions Act 1911. In a famous judgment in *The Volute* (1922) Viscount Birkenhead made it clear that there was no rule of admiralty law corresponding to the rule of last opportunity. It was therefore to be expected that with the provision in 1945 of a general statutory power to apportion damages in all cases of contributory negligence, the last opportunity rule would disappear. Cases decided since then have borne out this expectation.

Law Reform (Contributory Negligence Act) 1945
Section 1 (1) provides as follows:

> "Where any person suffers damage as the result partly of his own fault and partly of the fault of any other person or persons, a claim in respect of that damage shall not be defeated by reason of the fault of the person suffering the damage, but the damages recoverable in respect thereof shall be reduced to such extent as the court thinks just and equitable having regard to the claimant's share in the responsibility for the damage."

Fault of the plaintiff
In order that the power of apportionment be exercised in his favour, the defendant must show both that the plaintiff was at fault and that this fault contributed to his damage. "Fault" is defined by section 4 of the Act to mean negligence, breach of statutory duty or other act or omission which gives rise to a liability in tort, or which would, apart from the Act, give rise to the defence of contributory negligence. Although, therefore, it is possible that the plaintiff's contributory negligence may consist in a tort or breach of a duty of care owed to someone else, it is celar that this is not necessary, and that it may consist simply in a failure to look after his own safety. For example, in *Davies* v. *Swan Motor Co. Ltd.* (1949) the plaintiff was held to be contributorily negligent in that he

rode on the back of a dust lorry contrary to his employer's instruction and thus unnecessarily exposing himself to danger.

The defendant must also show that the plaintiff's fault contributed to the damage he suffered. In the first place, *dicta* in *Jones* v. *Livox Quarries* (1952) show that the present rules of remoteness of damage in tort that the plaintiff's damage must be a foreseeable consequence of the defendant's negligence, applies also in determining whether the plaintiff's damage is contributed to by his own fault. For example, Singleton L.J. thought that there would be no reduction of damages where the plaintiff negligently sat on an unsafe wall, and the defendant negligently drove into the wall and injured the plaintiff. This view appears correct.

Apart from being within the risk of the plaintiff's negligence, the defendant must also show that the plaintiff's damage is *caused* by that negligence. With the court's power to apportion damages, there has been a great deal of simplification of the causal problems connected with contributory negligence. The courts are now able to recognise that an event may have more than one cause, and by their apportionment to reflect the comparative importance of each cause. Thus in *Davies* v. *Swan Motor Co.* (*supra*) the plaintiff was injured while riding on the back of a dust lorry in an accident caused by the combined negligence of the driver of the lorry and the driver of a bus. Liability was apportioned among the two defendants, the employers of the bus driver and the lorry driver (under section 6 (1) of the Law Reform (Married Women & Tortfeasors) Act 1935) and the plaintiff was found to be contributorily negligent to his own damage.

Several cases have made it plain that, because the negligence of either party occurred later than the other, this does not excuse the earlier negligent person. Thus, in one case, *Henley* v. *Cameron* (1949), the defendant left his car without lights on the highway at night. The plaintiff's husband, carelessly drove his motor-cycle into the car and was killed. The plaintiff recovered damages on behalf of his estate subject to a reduction for his contributory negligence. It is now clear, therefore, that there is no such thing as a rule of last opportunity. Of course it is still possible for a court to regard the negligence of one party as so pre-eminently the cause of the damage, that the other, despite being negligent, is totally excused. Furthermore, this situation seems most likely to arise where a clear margin of time exists between the two acts of negligence. But whether this is so depends upon the normal principles of causation and remoteness of damage, already outlined, not on a rule which always takes the last act of negligence as the sole cause.

Thus, in *Rushton* v. *Turner Bros. Asbestos Co.* (1960), the defendants, in breach of their statutory duty under section 14 (1) of the Factories Act 1937, failed to fence a dangerous part of their machinery. The plaintiff attempted to clean the machine while it was in motion by inserting his hand into it despite instructions by the defendants never to clean the machine while it was in motion. It was held that the plaintiff was solely responsible for his own injuries.

Fault of the defendant

Section 4 of the Act of 1945, in so far as it refers to the fault of the defendant, requires him to have committed negligence, breach of statutory duty, or other act or omission which gives rise to a liability in tort. The latter words clearly permit the power of apportionment in the case of all torts. So far, however, contributory negligence as a defence has had virtually no application outside negligence, the torts deriving from it, and breach of statutory duty.

It is not yet settled whether the statutory provisions allowing an apportionment of damage apply where the defendant has committed a breach of contract rather than a tort. Because of the use of the word "other" before "act or omission which gives rise to a liability in tort," the regrettable likelihood is that, even in the case of a negligent breach of contract causing damage, there is no power to apportion damage under the Act for the plaintiff's contributory negligence. The point has not yet arisen directly for decision (*cf*, however, *Quinn* v. *Burch Bros.* (1966); *Sole* v. *W.J. Hallt* (1973)). The gap is less serious in view of the fact that many negligent breaches of contract will also be actionable in tort (*Midland Bank Trust Co.* v. *Hett, Stubbs & Kemp.*

Basis of apportionment

The plaintiff's damages will be reduced "to such extent as the court thinks just and equitable, having regard to the plaintiff's share in the responsibility for the damage." It is now settled that the courts apply two tests in deciding the extent of the reduction of damages the plaintiff must suffer. They must assess (i) the causative potency of the acts of the plaintiff and defendant; (ii) the degree of blameworthiness to be attached to these acts (*per* Lord Reid in *Stapley* v. *Gypsum Mines* (1953)). Degree of blameworthiness appears to mean, at least as far as negligence is concerned, degree of departure from the requisite standard of care rather than degree of moral blameworthiness. Although the two tests have been criticised (the causative potency test was criticised by Glanville Williams (1954) 17 M.L.R. 66, at p. 69, on the ground that causation itself was difficult enough, and that degrees of causation would be a nightmare), they seem just-

ifiable on the ground that in some torts there is no element
of blameworthiness so that no other basis of assessment than
causative potency exists; also that it seems sensible to assess
the causative force of factors such as, for example, dangerous
machinery, independently of the degree of blameworthiness
in the operation of such machinery. But very few cases have
produced a conflict in the operation of the two tests.

One such case was *Cavanagh* v. *London Transport Executive*
(1956). The plaintiff was injured by a bus negligently driven
by the defendants' employee. The plaintiff was contributorily
negligent. Devlin J found that on the causative potency test
the plaintiff should recover half his damages, but found the
bus driver only 20 per cent blameworthy on the second test.
He therefore compromised by holding the defendants 33 and
one-third per cent responsible for the plaintiff's damages.

The mathematics of apportionment are by no means
difficult, typical reductions being one-fifth, one-third,
one-half and three-quarters. It is unusual for a court to find a
plaintiff less than 10 per cent responsible for his damage, nor
more than 90 per cent. But in *Laszczyk* v. *National Coal
Board* (1954) where the plaintiff's contributory negligence
consisted in a breach of statutory duty binding on himself
and committed under instructions from a superior, his
damages were reduced by 5 per cent.

Particular cases of contributory negligence

(1) *Workmen*
In *Staveley Iron and Chemical Co.* v. *Jones* (1965) it was
suggested by Lord Tucker that in cases of liability for breach
of statutory duty not every "risky act due to familiarity with
the work or some inattention due to noise or strain" amounted
to contributory negligence. The suggestion was concurred in
by Lord Reid. Lord Tucker thought that this applied even if
the particular risky act might involve the employer in liability
to third parties. It is difficult to say whether the same doctrine
applies in the case of actions for common negligence by the
workman. There appears no reason to differentiate such
actions and some of the statements in the *Staveley* case
appear to support the application of the doctrine.

(2) *Children*
It has already been pointed out (*supra*, p. 100) that a lower
standard of care is expected of children than adults and that
this applies to both negligence and contributory negligence.

(3) *Agony of the moment*
Where the plaintiff has been put into a position of peril by

the defendant's negligence, compelling him to choose one
of two or more risky alternatives, he is not guilty of contributory negligence if his choice turns out to be a mistaken one.

Thus, in *Jones* v. *Boyce* (1816), the plaintiff, a passenger
in a coach owned and driven by the defendant, reasonably
believed that the coach was about to overturn through the
defendant's negligent driving. The plaintiff jumped off the
coach, breaking his leg. The coach did not overturn, but the
plaintiff was found not to be contributorily negligent. The
requirement for the operation of this principle is often stated
to be that the plaintiff must have acted in the agony of the
moment. But it may be that the principle applies in all cases
where the defendant has by his negligence placed the plaintiff in a difficult dilemma, even where the plaintiff has time to
stop and think. On the other hand it is clear that the plaintiff
may be found negligent in the *operation* of a self-rescue.
Mrs. Sayers had her damages reduced by 25 per cent because
in descending from the top of the lavatory she placed her
foot on the toilet-roll and thus slipped to the floor (*Sayers* v.
Harlow U.D.C., *supra*, p. 16).

(4) *Contributory negligence by rescuer*

Sayers v. *Harlow U.D.C.* is clear authority that a deduction
for contributory negligence may be made where the rescuer
has injured himself through his negligent performance of the
rescue attempt. But the standard of care required of rescuers
must take account of the emergency in which they act. "It is
well established that the court, recognising the need to
encourage salvors, should take a lenient view where negligence
or lack of skill is alleged against salvors." (*per* Willmer, L.J. in
the *Tojo Maru* (1970); see also *The Ogopogo* (1971)). It is
also clear that the dilemma principle will apply to rescuers. If a
rescuer is presented with a choice between two or more risky
modes of rescue and makes what turns out to be a mistaken
decision, this will not be regarded as contributory negligence.
It is also clear that a rescuer who chooses to incur the virtual
certainty of injury will not have his damages reduced for con-
tirbutory negligence if he reasonably considered this to be
the only effective means of rescue (see, for example, *Haynes*
v. *Harwood* (1935) where the plaintiff who dived in front of
the defendant's runaway horses pulling a van was found not
to be contributorily negligent). Even where only damage to
property is foreseeable, the rescuer who chooses to incur a
considerable risk of injury may recover the whole of his loss
(see, for example, *Hyett* v. *G.W. Ry* (1948)). Where, however,
there was no reasonable necessity for the plaintiff to act, or
to act in the way he did, his action fails altogether (*Cutler* v.
United Dairies (1933); *Sylvester* v. *Chapman* (1935)). This is

variously explained on the basis that the plaintiff is a volunteer; that his action breaks the chain of causation; that his injury is self-inflicted. Both these cases were decided however before the power to apportion damages as between plaintiff and defendant became available to courts in cases of contributory negligence, and it may be that there would now be a different decision, particularly on facts such as those in *Cutler*. His action hardly looks like that of a true volunteer and it may be that where the defendant by his negligence has created a foreseeable likelihood of another person acting, even where viewed objectively there was no reasonable necessity for that action, the defendant should be regarded as having committed a breach of his duty of care to that person and the plaintiff's conduct should be regarded as contributory negligence rather than a *novus actus interveniens*.

(5) *Seat belts, crash helmets*
Where the negligence of the plaintiff had the effect merely of failing to mitigate damage, some of which would in any case have occurred to him, there is considerable doubt whether the defence of contributory negligence would have been available to the defendant at common law. Furthermore section 1 of the 1945 Act does not increase the range of contributory negligence beyond what would have been regarded as giving rise to the defence at common law. This difficulty has been ignored by the courts in deciding whether failure to wear a crash helmet or a seat belt justifies an apportionment of damage under the Act. *Froom* v. *Butcher* (1976) in holding that failure to wear a seat belt was contributory negligence under the Act, indicated that the appropriate deduction was 25 per cent if wearing the belt would have prevented the injury altogether, and 15 per cent if it would have reduced its extent. The defendant who has the burden on this issue, fails unless he shows that some injury would have been avoided by wearing the belt *Owens* v. *Brimnells* (1977)). It is assumed that the principles as to apportionment laid down in *Froom* v. *Butcher* apply also to failure to wear a crash helmet (held to be contributory negligence in *O'Connell* v. *Jackson* (1971)).

Imputed contributory negligence
Under a largely discredited common law doctrine, the contributory negligence of one person might be imputed to another so as to constitute contributory negligence on the part of that other. Several decisions have whittled away the doctrine, so that now the only important case of it is that the negligence of a servant acting in the course of his employment is imputed to his master. But the negligence of a carrier

is not imputed to his passenger, that of an adult is not imputed to a child of whom he is in charge, and that of an independant contractor is not imputed to his employer.

It is not easy to see why the rule should survive in the case of master and servant. It cannot be explained on the ground of the master's vicarious liability for the negligence of his servant committed in the course of his employment, since the basis of policy underlying the doctrine of vicarious liability is that the servant's liability is transferred to a financially solvent defendant, whereas imputed negligence affects the case where the employer is the injured party, and there is no reason of policy requiring financially solvent plaintiffs to meet part of their own loss out of their own pockets. By an unwarranted extension of the doctrine, it applies also in those cases where the owner of a car is vicariously liable for the negligence of the person driving the car (*infra*, p. 234). Thus, in *Lampert* v. *Eastern National Omnibus Co.* (1954), it was held that the plaintiff who had delegated the driving of a car which she owned to her husband was contributorily negligent as to the amount of his negligence in an accident caused also by the negligent driving of the defendant. This is less serious now that the liability of the person driving the car towards passengers is required to be covered by insurance under section 145 (3) (*a*) of the Road Traffic Act 1972.

VOLENTI NON FIT INJURIA

Introduction

The defence of *volenti non fit injuria* was of importance during the nineteenth century, when it was confined within less narrow limits than it is today. In particular it was used to defeat actions by workmen who had suffered injuries in the course of their employment as the result of their employer's negligence; it was enough to establish the defence that the workmen knew of the negligence and had remained in his employment. This doctrine was removed by *Smith* v. *Baker* (1891) which held that an employee who chose to stay in his job, knowing of a dangerous situation created by his employer's negligence was not volens to that negligence. The present century has seen a further narrowing down of the defence. Clearly behaviour which might give rise to the defence of volenti may also amount to contributory negligence, and it now seems correct to say that the courts look with disfavour on the former defence, preferring to apply the apportionment provisions of the 1945 Act. This tendency may receive a further impetus from the Unfair Contract Terms Act 1977, which considerably limits the right to contract out of liability for negligence.

Volenti applies to the unintentional torts

The basis of the defences of consent and of *volenti non fit injuria* is the same—the plaintiff has in effect consented to his own injury. But the defence is normally called consent where the plaintiff has consented to the commission of an actual tort against himself, for example, the licensing of a battery by one who agrees to have a haircut; the defence is called *volenti non fit injuria* where the plaintiff consents to tortious behaviour which may injure him in the future. This distinction means in effect that the defence of consent is confined to the intentional torts, since only in these torts can there be certainty that the tort will be committed. *Volenti* is confined to torts of negligence and strict liability, since in such cases an actual tort is a risk rather than a certainty. Both consent and *volenti non fit injuria* are, however, derived from the same general principle. The rules determining the effect of consent given by minors, and the effect of fraud and duress on consent, will therefore apply to *volenti*.

Extent of defence

Volenti may arise from an inference from the plaintiff's conduct, or because he has given his consent to an express exclusion of his duty by the defendant. The latter case is governed by the provisions of the Unfair Contract Terms Act 1977. The former is unaffected by the Act. It will be dealt with first.

(1) *Volenti based on inference from plaintiff's conduct*

Two decisions of the Court of Appeal indicate that the defence will very rarely be established when it is based on the plaintiff's conduct. In *Wooldridge* v. *Sumner* (1963) the plaintiff, a photographer, was standing at the edge of a show-jumping arena taking photographs. He was injured when a horse ridden by the defendant in a competition galloped off the course and crashed into him. The trial judge found that the defendant was doing his best to win but had committed an error of judgment. He held the defendant liable in negligence. The Court of Appeal reversed his decision. The standard of care owed by the sportsman to the spectator at a sporting event must take into account the risks incidental to the sport. Provided the sportsman was concentrating on the game and doing his best to win he was not liable for an error of judgment. This was not because of *volenti non fit injuria*, which requires an individual consent by the plaintiff, but because the law fixes the standard of care in the light of what the average spectator is entitled to expect. Thus the plaintiff's knowledge of the risk and his ability to give a binding consent to it are irrelevant (*cf, Murray* v. *Harringay Arena* (1951) in which a

six-year old boy, who had been injured while watching a
game of ice-hockey, was unable to succeed in negligence
against the occupiers of the stadium, because his injury had
occurred through a risk incidental to the playing of the game).
Diplock L.J. said in *Wooldridge* v. *Sumner*:

> " the maxim (*i.e. volenti non fit injuria*) has no applica-
> tion to negligence simpliciter where the duty of care is
> based solely on proximity or "neighbourship" in the
> Atkinian sense."

Where the alleged consent preceded the act of negligence, the
plaintiff could not have the necessary full knowledge of the
nature and extent of the risk he ran. When it came after, the
case was governed by ordinary principles of foreseeability and
causation. These remarks went further than was necessary for
the decision, but they found support in the second Court of
Appeal decision, *Nettleship* v. *Weston* (1971). The court
there decided that a learner-driver was liable in negligence to
his instructor for an injury caused by his failure to show the
skill of a reasonably competent driver. Before entering the
car, the instructor had asked whether the defendant had a
liability insurance policy, and was told he had. Lord Denning
M.R. thought that *volenti* could only be established as a
defence by express agreement between plaintiff and defendant.
Salmond L.J. thought that the plaintiff's consent by conduct
might be relevant to the production of a special relationship
under which a lesser standard of care was owed by the defendant to the plaintiff but not to establishing *volenti non fit
injuria* (the *Wooldridge* v. *Sumner* "doctrine"). In any case
the plaintiff's question about insurance ruled out such
consent on the facts before him. Megaw L.J. thought that in
a proper case the defence might still be established in the
absence of express agreement between plaintiff and defendant,
but the mere decision by the instructor to enter the car with
knowledge of the risk could not establish such a case.

These cases are some support for the view that the defence
of *volenti* does not exist at all apart from express agreement.
At the very least they show that mere knowledge of the
possibility of future negligence by the defendant, even where
such negligence is likely, does not establish the defence (for
further confirmation of this, *cf.* the failure of the defence in
Dann v. *Hamilton* (1939). The plaintiff passenger was injured
by the negligence of the driver of a car in which she was
travelling. He was known by the plaintiff to be drunk and to
be driving badly.) Nevertheless on the unusual facts of *I.C.I.* v.
Shatwell (1965) the defence succeeded. The plaintiff and his
brother agreed to disregard instructions of their employer
(and to commit a breach of a statutory obligation) by testing

some detonators without taking the necessary precautions. The plaintiff was injured in an ensuing explosion. He sued his employers on the ground that they were vicariously liable to him for his brother's negligence. The House of Lords dismissed his action on the ground that *volenti non fit injuria* applied. A stronger case for its application could hardly be imagined. The plaintiff not only willingly ran the risk of his brother's negligence at the very time it was happening but also part-icipated in it. Even so the case admits of an alterantive ratio—the actions of joint tortfeasors when participating in a common, unlawful design are legally indistinguishable. In effect the plaintiff blew himself up (see the judgment of Viscount Radcliffe).

Whatever the common law status of the defence, it has statutory survivals. Section 2 (5) of the Occupier's Liability Act provides the occupier with the defence that the visitor willingly accepted the risk; section 5 (2) of the Animals Act 1971 preserves the defence in the case of liability for animals under the Act.

(2) *Consent to express exclusions of liability*

Before considering the provisions of the Unfair Contract Terms Act 1977, the common law position must be set out. Subject to certain specific statutory exceptions (*infra*, p. 134), it has until now been possible to exclude liability in negligence by a provision in a contract or other agreement. In the case of contractual provision, this could become a term of the contract either because the plaintiff had expressly agreed to it, or because the defendant had taken reasonable steps to bring it to the plaintiff's attention as the basis on which he was con-tracting. Where the defendant was relying on a provision of a non-contractual agreement, the basis of his defence was *volenti non fit injuria*. This defence was therefore available to infant car drivers who displayed exclusionary notice in their cars which they took sufficient steps to bring to the plaintiff's attention (see *Buckpitt* v. *Oates* (1968); *Bennett* v. *Tugwell* (1971); *Birch* v. *Thomas* (1972)). The defendants, in those cases, could not form binding contracts; nevertheless the exclusionary notice bound the plaintiff because they had consented to them (for special difficulties concerning the basis on which occupiers of premises may exclude liability by displaying a notice, see *infra*, p. 151). The common law position now holds goods only to the extent that it has not been changed by the Unfair Contract Terms Act 1977.

Unfair Contract Terms Act 1977. Under this Act certain exclusions of liability in negligence are either rendered wholly inoperative or subjected to a test of reasonableness.

Negligence is defined by section 1 (1) as the breach: (a) of any obligation arising from the express or implied terms of a contract to take reasonable care or exercise reasonable skill in the performance of a contract; or (b) of any common law duty to take reasonable care or exercise reasonable skill, or (c) of the common duty of care imposed by the Occupier's Liability Act 1957. The ambit of the Act's provisions is restricted to "business liability" which is defined by section 1 (3) as liability for breach of obligations or duties arising from things done or to be done by a person in the course of his own business or another's; or from the occupation of premises used for business purposes of the occupier. Section 2 (1) prevents a person excluding, by reference to any contract term or to a notice given to persons generally or to particular persons, liability in negligence causing death or personal injury. In the case of negligence causing other loss or damage, section 2 (2) requires that the contract term or notice must satisfy the requirement of reasonableness. Section 2 (3) abolishes the defence of *volenti non fit injuria* in cases covered by section 2 (1) and (2). A person's agreement to or awareness of the contract term or notice does not give rise to that defence. Section 13 extends the notion of excluding or restricting liability contained in section 2. In particular exclusion or restriction of liability extends to terms or notices making the liability or its enforcement subject to restrictive conditions, excluding the remedy for enforcement of the liability, or excluding or restricting the duty breach of which gives rise to the liability. It seems a curious loophole in the Act that it does not cover terms in an agreement not having contractual force, for example, agreements with infants and agreements binding in honour only. Unless such terms may be regarded as "notices," which seems unlikely, they will continue to give rise to the defence of *volenti non fit injuria*.

Other statutory restrictions upon the power to exclude. A number of specific restrictions upon the power to exclude liability in tort continue to exist outside the 1977 Act. Two examples may be given. Section 1 (3) of the Law Reform (Personal Injuries) Act 1948 prevents an employer from contracing out of his vicarious liability for the torts of employees committed in the course of their employment against their fellow employees. Under section 148 (3) of the Road Traffic Act 1972, a car driver cannot by any agreement exclude or restrict his liability towards his passengers. Furthermore the fact that the passenger has "willingly accepted as his the risk of negligence on the part of the driver" is not to be treated as negativing the driver's liability. The defence of *volenti non fit injuria*, whether based on agreement or on the conduct of the passenger is therefore excluded altogether.

10. PROOF OF NEGLIGENCE

Judge and jury

It was at one time important to differentiate between the functions of judge and jury in the trials of civil actions for negligence. Appellate courts, while willing to overrule the judges' decisions on points of law would seldom disturb the findings of the jury unless they were completely unreasonable having regard to the evidence in the case. This was a quite serious limitation upon the function of the appellate court, since juries were not confined to determining the actual facts of the case, but also had to perform the evaluation of the defendant's conduct (in the light of the judge's direction to them about what standard was demanded of the defendant) required in order to decide whether he was negligent. But with the virtual disappearance of the jury in actions of negligence, it is no longer of much importance to attempt to distinguish "jury questions" from those which the judge has to decide. The judge sitting alone will decide all the issues in the case, the actual facts, the inferences to be drawn from those facts, and matters of law, such as the existence of a duty of care, the standard of care required by the defendant in discharging that duty, and questions of remoteness of damage. Furthermore, the appellate court will not regard itself as precluded from reviewing decisions of the trial judge on matters which were formerly left exclusively to the jury, for example, the decision whether the defendant has acted reasonably, and the award of damages in the action, though the appellate court will invariably accept the judge's finding on the actual facts of the case rather than inferences to be drawn from those facts. The differentiation in function between judge and jury remains in those cases where the action is heard before a jury, and is also relevant in the case of appeals from the County Court to the Court of Appeal which lie on points of law if the action is for £200 or more. In both these cases the appellate court will accept the jury's findings both of fact and of the inferences to be drawn from them unless satisfied that the latter are wholly unreasonable. It should be pointed out finally, that despite the virtual disappearance of juries in tort actions, it is still normal to refer to the fact-finding process at the trial as a "jury question" and to define a prima

facie case of negligence as one where there is sufficient
evidence of negligence to be left to a jury.

No evidence of negligence

It is a matter of law whether there is sufficient evidence of
negligence on which a judge might decide that the defendant
was negligent. Accordingly an appellate court may reverse a
judge's decision that there was, or was not, sufficient evidence
of negligence to be left to the jury. The decision that there is
no evidence of negligence may be reached either because the
facts proved by the plaintiff do not tend to support his
allegation of negligence against the defendant, or because he
has given insufficient evidence to be left to a jury of facts
whcih if proved would clearly establish negligence on the
defendant's part. An example of the former situation is the
case where the facts proved by the plaintiff are equally consistent with negligence or no negligence by the defendant.
Thus, in *Hammack* v. *White* (1862), the defendant was riding
a horse he had purchased the previous day in a busy street.
The horse for no apparent reason became restive, and, despite
the defendant's efforts to control it, ran upon the pavement
and killed the plaintiff's husband. There was held to be no
evidence of negligence, since the facts proved might have
pointed to a negligent failure to control the horse by the
defendant, but were equally consistent with no negligence at
all by him.

A different situation exists where the plaintiff has given
sufficient evidence to be left to a jury of facts which if
proved would establish negligence by the defendant. Here the
trial court's decision as to whether the plaintiff's evidence is
sufficient proof of these facts is not a matter of law and its
verdict will not be disturbed by an appellate court unless it is
clearly unreasonable. Equally conflicts of evidence as to such
facts must be resolved by the trial court.

Burden of proof

The legal burden of proving negligence rests upon the plaintiff. He must show, in accordance with the general rule for
civil trials, that on the balance of probabilities the defendant
was negligent and that this negligence caused the plaintiff
injury. The burden of proving the facts establishing both
breach of duty and causation thus rests on the plaintiff.

It used to be thought that the plaintiff who had established
a prima facie case of negligence might still fail, even if the
defendant provided no explanation. In *Henderson* v.
H.E. Jenkins & Sons (1970), however, Lord Pearson said in
the House of Lords,

"But if in the course of the trial, there is proved a set of
facts which raises a prima facie inference that the
accident was caused by negligence on the part of the
defendants, the issue will be decided in the plaintiff's
favour, unless the defendants by their evidence provide
some answer which is adequate to displace the prima
facie inference."

The defendant achieves this by satisfying the so-called
evidential burden of proof. He must show that the accident
was at least as likely as not to have occurred not through his
negligence. This is enough for him to succeed since the legal
burden of proving that on the balance of probabilities the
defendant was negligent rests on the plaintiff.

Res ipsa loquitur

The effect of this rule of evidence is to allow the plaintiff
to treat the actual facts of the case as evidence of the defendant's negligence—the facts speak for themselves. The rule is
an important concession to plaintiffs since it recognises the
difficulty that exists in the case of many accidents of furnishing
direct evidence that they were the result of negligence. In
order that the rule should operate three conditions are
necessary: (1) the plaintiff's injury must be such as does not
in the ordinary course of things happen in the absence of
negligence; (2) the facts proved must point to negligence by
the defendant; (3) the court must not have facts before it
which enable it to make up its mind on the issue of negligence
independently of *res ipsa loquitur*. Whether the rule applies
to the case before it is a question of law for the judge to
decide.

(1)   *The plaintiff's injury is one that would not in the ordinary
course of things have happened without negligence*

The rule has been applied to the case of objects falling
from upper storeys of buildings on to the highway below (for
example, in *Byrne* v. *Boadle* (1863), flour bags falling from
the upper window of the defendant's building). Numerous
cases have established the applicability of the rule to motor
vehicles going out of control (for example, *Laurie* v. *Raglan
Building Co. Ltd.* (1942)—a lorry driven at 10 m.p.h. skidded
and mounted the pavement, killing the plaintiff's husband)
and it has been applied to stones found in buns (*Chaproniere*
v. *Mason* (1905), to sulphites found in underpants (*Grant* v.
Australian Knitting Mills Ltd. (1933) and to the effects of a
surgical operation upon the plaintiff (*Cassidy* v. *Minster of
Health* (1951), disposing of doubts whether *res ipsa loquitur*
applied in medical cases.

(2) *Facts proved must point to negligence by the defendant*
If facts proved merely point to negligence by one of a
number of persons of whom the defendant is one, this is
insufficient (for qualifications upon this when negligence is
proved to be committed by one of the defendant's servants
or independent contractors, see *infra*, p. 226). The second
requirement is sometimes stated to be that the *"res"* must be
under the defendant's control. So in *Easson* v. *L. & N.E. Ry
Co.* (1944) the fact that a door of the defendants' train fell
open when the train, an express, was in between stations, did
not raise a presumption that the defendants' servants had
failed to close it on leaving its last stop. But in *Gee* v. *Metropolitan Ry. Co.* (1873) when the train door fell open shortly
after the train had left a station, it was held that *res ipsa
loquitur* applied. In *Lloyde* v. *West Midlands Gas Board*
(1971) the members of the Court of Appeal appeared to
agree that exclusive control by the defendant is not necessary
to establish *res ipsa loquitur*. The plaintiff would, however,
have to establish the improbability of outside interference in
order that the doctrine should apply.
   The rule is qualified to some extent in the case of collisions
between motor vehicles. Where a collision occurs between
two such vehicles and there is nothing in the evidence on
which the court can make up its mind as to which driver was
to blame, or as to the proportions in which each driver was to
blame, then the court will hold each driver equally responsible.
This result was arrived at in *Bray* v. *Palmer* (1953) (head-on
collision near centre of road) and *France* v. *Parkinson* (1954)
(collision on cross-roads of equal status). This is in fact a case
of *res ipsa loquitur* where the fact establish a balance of probability of two people sharing equally in the responsibility for
the damage.

(3) *Facts must not be present before the court which enable
it to make up its mind on the issue of negligence independently
of res ipsa loquitur*
   Barkway v. *South Wales Transport* (1950) established
that where actual evidence is given of the defendant's negligence, *res ipsa loquitur* can no longer apply (evidence of negligent system of tyre inspection excluded *res ipsa loquitur* in
case where type of defendant's bus had burst causing the bus
to go out of control).

Effect of res ipsa loquitur
   What is the effect of *res ipsa loquitur* being held to
apply? In the first place it seems likely that once that
happens, as with direct evidence of negligence, the defendant
will fail unless he furnishes evidence to show that his negli-

gence did not cause the plaintiff's damage. He can do this in one or both of two ways. He can show that he took reasonable care so that the court may infer that the damage to the plaintiff had some other cause; or he may actually prove that the damage had some other cause. What is the nature of the burden of proof? In principle, it seems that, as with direct evidence of negligence, it should be an evidential burden only he succeeds if he leaves, at the end of evidence, the balance of probabilities equal as between negligent conduct on his part or some other cause being responsible for the damage to the plaintiff. If he had the legal burden of satisfying the court on the balance of probabilities that his negligence did not damage the plaintiff, this would produce the anomaly that the burden of proof had shifted during the course of the trial, and *res ipsa loquitur* would acquire the force of a rule of law rather than one of evidence. It would also be most unsatisfactory to distinguish *res ipsa loquitur* from direct evidence of negligence which clearly does not effect a transference of the burden of proof. Surprisingly, however, court formulations of the rule appear to support the anomaly (see, for example, the remarks of Asquith L.J. in Barkway's case, and of Sir Raymond Evershed M.R. in *Moore* v. *Fox & Sons* (1956). In neither decision, however, was the question directly in point. Furthermore, in *Ward* v. *Tesco Stores* (1976), Megaw L.J. took the view that a defendant who wished to satisfy the court that he took reasonable care must do so on the balance of probabilities, though Lawton L.J. did not appear to put the defendant's obligation as high as this.

Where the defendant is relying on evidence to show that he operated a careful system among the persons under his employment, it is not enough for him to convince the court that personally he was not at fault, if the likelihood is that there was fault by someone in his employment. Thus in *Grant* v. *Australian Knitting Mills* (1936) the plaintiff contracted dermatitis because of the presence in his underwear manufactured by the defendant's excess sulphites. The defendant's evidence proved that he had manufactured 4,737,600 pairs of underpants previously without complaint. Nevertheless, he was held liable because the likelihood was of lack of care by someone in his employment for whose acts he was legally liable. Furthermore, the plaintiff does not have to identify the actual person at fault, if he can show the likelihood that it was the defendant's servant. Few manufacturers of defective chattels will therefore escape liability for the damage they cause. *Daniels* v. *R. White* (1938) was an unsatisfactory decision which appeared to run contrary to these principles. It held that when the defendant chose to show that he had taken reasonable care to establish a safe system

of manufacture, if he succeeded in showing this, the plaintiff
failed even though the likelihood was of negligence in the
operation of that system by someone employed by the
defendant. The case was expressly not followed by another
court at first instance in *Hill* v. *James Crowe (Cases) Ltd.*
(1978). Where the defendant is relying on evidence of the
operation of a careful system, he may have to give evidence
of his knowledge or means of knowledge of a certain fact,
since this may affect his standard of care. in *Henderson* v.
Jenkins (1970) the defendant's lorry had gone out of control
and injured the plaintiff because of brake failure. The cause
of the failure was a corroded brake pipe underneath the lorry.
The defendants gave evidence of a system of visual inspection
of the pipe which would have shown adequate care provided
the lorry had not been subjected to any unusual risks of
corrosion such as contact with acid or sea-water. Since,
however, they chose to call no evidence to show whether
they knew or had the means of knowing whether the unusual
risk had occurred, the plaintiff succeeded.

Res ipsa loquitur and causation

The plaintiff in an action of negligence must prove not
only that the defendant was negligent but also the existence
of a causal connection between that negligence and the
damage he suffered. Thus, in *Wakelin* v. *L. & S.W. Ry. Co.*
(1886), the plaintiff's husband was killed by the defendants'
train which was negligent in failing to whistle. But as no
evidence was given of the way in which the accident occurred,
no causal connection could be established between the negligence and the death and the action failed. As it appears that
the factual inference allowed by *res ipsa loquitur* is only as to
the defendant's negligence and not as to causal connection
between the negligence and the plaintiff's damage, it cannot
be used to prove such causal connection. But in certain cases
where causal connection is very likely the plaintiff is allowed
to succeed even though he cannot prove the exact way in
which his accident occurred (see, for example, *Thurogood* v.
Van den Burghs and Jurgens Ltd. (1951), and *Allen* v. *Aeroplane and Motor Aluminium Castings* (1965)—do not these
decisions ignore possible contributory negligence by the plaintiff?—The discussion in an earlier chapter of *Cook* v. *Lewis* and
McGhee v. *National Coal Board* (p. 107) is also relevant
to the question of proof of causation).

Section 11 of the Civil Evidence Act 1968

The Civil Evidence Act 1968 removed the rule of the
common law that a conviction could not be used as evidence
in civil proceedings. Section 11 allows the conviction to be

used as evidence of the facts which constituted the offence, although allowing the defendant to controvert such evidence by evidence of his own (*cf. Stupple* v. *Royal Insurance Co.* (1971) for the nature of the evidential burden which this casts on the defendant). A conviction for careless or dangerous driving may now, therefore, be used as evidence of negligence in a civil court. The effect of the section is to place the legal burden of proof on the defendant (*Stupple* v. *Royal Insurance Co.* (1971)).

11. LIABILITY FOR PREMISES

Liability for defective premises (the term includes land itself) is in the process of being assimilated to liability in negligence. But it justifies separate treatment because to some extent special rules still apply to it. In particular the common law distinguished the liability of the occupier towards those injured when on his premises from those who were injured when outside the premises. The latter could if they could prove injury from a dangerous condition in the premises, sue in nuisance or negligence. The former made use of the special rules of occupiers' liability. Whatever the logic of the distinction, it has been preserved because the Occupiers' Liability Act of 1957 has rendered the obligations of the occupier towards his visitors statutory while leaving untouched his obligations to those outside his premises. But as the Act has gone a long way towards making the liability of the occupier turn entirely on his negligence the divergence is now no longer very marked.

In this chapter there will be considered the rules concerning the liability of occupiers and other persons towards those who suffer personal injury or damage to property while they or their property are on premises.

OCCUPIER'S LIABILITY

PRE-1957 LAW

The old law recognised five different classes of entrant: (1) the invitee; (2) the licensee; (3) the person entering under a contract with the occupier; (4) the person entering as of right; (5) trespassers and others.

The invitee was a person who was both permitted to enter and whose entry was in the interests of the occupier, for example, a customer entering a shop. The licensee was one merely permitted to be on the land, for example, a person permitted to take a short-cut over the occupier's land. The importance of the distinction was that more onerous obligations were owed to the invitee than to the licensee, to whom the occupier's only obligation was to warn of concealed dangers of which the occupier was aware. Criticism of the distinction between invitee and licensee, and of the injustices it led to, in particular by the Law Reform Committee in 1954, was the chief reason for the passing of the Occupiers' Liability Act in 1957.

The person entering under contract with the occupier might himself be in contractual relationship with the occupier, or might be permitted to enter under the terms of the occupier's contract with another. In the former case the occupier's duties depended on the terms of the contract, and in the absence of an express term, the courts would imply a term that the premises were to be reasonably safe for the purposes for which entry was made. The latter type of entrant was treated as a licensee of the occupier.

Various persons have a right to enter premises, without obtaining the permission of the occupier. For example, factory inspectors, Gas and Electricity Board officials, and policemen acting under a search warrant or in the course of effecting an arrest have such a right, whether under statute or at common law. Private individuals may also in some situations enter land without committing trespass, for example, in order to recapt a chattel on that land, or to abate a nuisance. A private individual may also enter land in the exercise of a public or private right of way. The duty owed to the person entering as of right was probably the same as that owed to the invitee, although in the case of an entrant under a public or private right of way, the only duty appeared to be not to commit acts of misfeasance rendering the right of way dangerous.

The fifth type of entrant is the person who enters without permission of the occupier and not in exercise of a right conferred by law. The trespasser is by far the most important case, but there are others. For example, a person thrown on to the land by another person is not a trespasser but comes within this category. Also section 1 (4) of the Occupiers' Liability Act 1957 has added the case of the person who enters under an access agreement or order under the National Parks and Access to the Countryside Act 1949. The Act of 1957 has not affected the occupier's duty to trespassers and other entrants of this type. Their rights will be considered later in this chapter.

OCCUPIERS' LIABILITY ACT 1957; THE COMMON DUTY OF CARE

The distinction between invitees and licensees has now been abolished by the Occupiers' Liability Act 1957. The occupier now owes the same duty, the "common duty of care," to all his lawful visitors, defined by the Act as comprising those persons who would at common law be treated as his licensees or invitees (this result is achieved by sections 1 (1), 1 (2) and 2 (1) in combination). The common duty of care is defined by section 2 (2) as a duty to take such care as in all the circumstances of the case is reasonable to see that the visitor will be reasonably safe in using the premises for the purposes for which he is invited or permitted by the occupier to be there. The Act has therefore created a tort of statutory negligence to replace the special rules which an occupier owed to his invitees and licensees at common law. It seems to be the effect of section 2 (6) of the Act that all persons entering as of right are to be treated as if they are licensees and are therefore owed the common duty of care. *Greenhalgh* v. *British Railways Board* (1969), however, shows this view to be fallacious. Section 2 (6), treats the entrant as of right as a licensee only "for the purposes of this section," and section 2 is concerned with the definition of the content of the common duty of care, rather than the persons to whom it is owed. It does not therefore extend the class of entrants as of right who are to be treated as licensees to those entrants who would not be treated as licensees at common law. In the case of the entrant under a public right of way, for example, the occupier merely had a duty not to commit acts of misfeasance rendering the right of way dangerous (a less onerous duty than that owed to licensees), and it was held in *Greenhalgh* that this rule had survived the Act. The same reasoning would apply in the case of an entrant under a private right of way. On the other hand, a railway corporation over whose lines a public right of way exists, has a duty to keep its stiles in good repair so as to keep out young children-*Thomas* v. *British Railways Board* (1976).

Section 1 (3) (*b*) appears to be intended to preserve the common law position relating to liability for damage to property. In so far as such damage could be claimed at common law, it is now possible to claim it in an action for breach of the common duty of care. The Act expressly envisages that the property damaged need not be that of a visitor. No doubt such property must lawfully be on the premises. The common law rule whereby the occupier was not liable for loss of property, for example by theft, on the premises, remains unaffected by the Act (*Tinsley* v.*Dudley* (1951) *cf.* the comparable rule in the case of the employer in *Deyong* v. *Sherburn* (1946)). There may be liability where the property is bailed to the occupier or the occupier is an innkeeper. The basis of the rule in *Tinsley* v. *Dudley* is not clear. It may be that the occupier is never liable for loss of property or it may be that, although there is generally no duty to safeguard property on the premises, special circumstances may place the occupier under such a duty (for example, frequent thefts on the premises or a structural defect in the premises likely to cause loss of property).

Activity duty

The pre-1957 law distinguished between the occupier's duty in respect of the static condition of his premises (occupancy duty) and his duty in respect of his activities carried out on those premises (activity duty). In particular, the distinction between invitee and licensee was not relevant in the case of the latter, the occupier's liability being governed by principles of ordinary negligence (*Slater* v. *Clay, Cross & Co.* (1956)). With the removal of the distinction between invitees and licensees by the Act of 1957, it is now hardly necessary to distinguish the two duties. The Act, however, unfortunately fails to make the fate of the activity duty clear. It may continue to exist at common law, unaffected by the Act's provisions; or it may have become statutory. The answer depends upon the interpretation given to section 1 (1) and 1 (2) of the Act. Subsection (1) states that the rules made by the two following subsections shall have effect in place of the common law duties of the occupier regarding the state of his premises *or things done or omitted to be done on them*, but section 1 (2) states that the rules so enacted shall regulate the nature of the duty imposed by law in consequence of a person's occupation or control of premises. Since the activity duty is hardly imposed in consequence of a person's occupation or control of premises, the bizarre result of the Act might be that it has abolished the activity duty without replacing it. For this reason, it seems better to confine the ambit of section 1 (1) to "things done" on the premises which affect their static condition, thus allowing the activity duty to survive outside the Act.

Conditions for the application of the Act: "occupier"; "premises"

The defendant must under section 1 (2) be in occupation or control of the premises in order that the statutory obligation be demanded of him. As it is clear that no legal or equitable interest in the premises is necessary to satisfy the requirements of the statute, the circumstances of each case will have to be considered to decide whether such occupation or control exists.

In *Wheat* v. *Lacon & Co*, (1966) the plaintiff, a guest staying in a public house owned by the defendants, was killed in a fall from a defective staircase, the staircase being in the part of the public house which was occupied as his private living-quarters by the defendants' manager. The court decided that the brewery retained sufficient control over the premises to be in occupation within the meaning of section 1 (2), although it was held that the manager, also a defendant, was also an occupier.

The case makes it clear, therefore, that exclusive occupation of the premises, such as is necessary to maintain an action of trespass, is not required. Equally there can be more than one "occupier" of the premises at a given time. It has also been decided that a person does not necessarily lose occupation or control by having an independent contractor do work on the premises. But it may be that the contractor is also an occupier. Thus, in *Hartwell* v. *Grayson Docks Ltd.* (1947), it was held that a contractor converting a ship into a troopship in dry dock was an occupier of the ship. This is clearly not inconsistent with occupation by the shipowner.

"Premises" included at common law not only land and buildings on the land, but also other erections and structures on the land, such as electricity pylons, diving-boards and grandstands. Movables such as ladders, ships and aeroplanes were also included provided they were occupied by the defendant, and provided the plaintiff's injury resulted from some structural defect in them. If, for example, a ladder is lent by A to A, and B suffers injury because of a defect in the ladder, A's liability is governed by the principles of liability for chattels, since he no longer occupies the ladder. And negligent operation of any locomotive was governed by ordinary negligence, not occupier's liability. These rules are preserved by section 1 (3) (*a*) of the Act—the rules of the Act regulate the obligations of a person occupying or having control of any "fixed or movable structure, including any vessel, vehicle or aircraft," "in like manner and to the like extent" as the common law rules of occupiers' liability regulated the liability of persons occupying such structures.

SPECIAL PROVISIONS ABOUT THE COMMON DUTY OF CARE

It is clear that most cases on occupiers' liability will turn on questions of negligence indistinguishable from negligence at common law. There are, however, certain provisions in the Occupiers' Liability Act about the nature of the common duty of care, its discharge, and the defences available to an action for breach of it, which need to be specially considered. Section 2 (3) provides that the circumstances relevant for the purpose of deciding whether the occupier has committed a breach of his duty of care, include the degree of care, and of want of care, which would ordinarily be looked for in a visitor, so that in proper cases (a) an occupier must be prepared for children to be less careful than adults; and (b) an occupier may expect that a person, in the exercise of his calling, will appreciate and guard against any special risks ordinarily incidental to it, so far as the occupier leaves him free to do so.

Duty towards children

The first problem concerns the occupier's liability towards children who are lawfully present on his land. He must not have on his land objects that are dangerous but are also an allurement or invitiation to them. Thus, in *Glasgow Corporation* v. *Taylor* (1922), the plaintiff, a child aged seven, died through eating some poisonous berries which he picked from a tree in the defendants' public gardens. The defendants were held liable despite the commission by the plaintiff of an otherwise trespassory act in picking the berries. The allurement therefore appears both to have nullified the trespass and established liability on the defendant's part. The concept of an allurement involves the idea of "concealment and surprise, of an appearance of safety under circumstances cloaking a reality of damage" (*per* Hamilton L.J. in *Latham* v. *Johnson and Nephew Ltd.* (1913)). Thus in that case a child who was injured while playing with a heap of stones on the defendants' land was held to have no remedy against the defendants. Equally, in *Perry* v. *Wrigley Ltd.* (1955), a hole in the ground into which a child fell was held to be no allurement to a child who was injured by falling into the hole. It is perhaps questionable whether this emphasis on the concealment of the danger is desirable. The obviousness of the danger may increase its attractions to a child. This seems to be recognised by *Gough* v. *National Coal Board* in which slow-moving railway trucks were held to be an allurement and also in *Holdman* v. *Hamlyn* (1943) in which the same was held on a threshing machine.

The question whether there is an allurement on the land is also relevant to the question whether the child is a trespasser or licensee on the land. This is discussed below at page 154.

Very young children

To the very young child, almost anything can be dangerous. Furthermore, the obviousness of the danger will not prevent the child from encountering it. It might be expected therefore that the law would differentiate between the occupier's duty to the young and to the very young child. This was confirmed in *Phipps* v. *Rochester Corpn.* (1955)—

The plaintiff, agred five, and his sister, aged seven, were licensees on the defendants' land. There was a trench on the land, nine feet deep by two-and-a-half feet wide. The plaintiff fell into this and broke his leg. The defendants were held not liable because they could not anticipate that a child of this age would not be accompanied by a responsible person and so had not broken their duty of care.

There is a lack of precision about the nature of the occupier's duty towards very young children. In particular these questions may be asked:

(1) At what age does the very young child become a young child?

(2) Is the age of the child alone relevant in determining whether the occupier can expect him to be accompanied by a responsible person? The answer seems to be probably not, since the judgment of Devlin J. in the above case takes into account the fact that the land in question was not a playground in a slum area, where the presence of unaccompanied very young children could be foreseen.

(3) In what circumstances does an occupier break his duty to very young children? The rule in *Phipps* appears to relate only to dangers which arise because of the extreme youth of the child visitor. Where the occupier by his negligence has allowed a dangerous situation to arise and that situation would have endangered adults as well as children, the occupier should not be able to rely on the rule in Phipps even where by proper care the accompanying adult would have averted the danger. Where the danger is one which proper care on the part of an accompanying adult would not have averted, the occupier alone is liable. Where proper care on the part of an accompanying adult would have averted the danger, his absence should be regarded as negligence contributing to the child's injury to the same extent as he would have been adjudged contributorily negligent if he himself had been injured. The proper solution is therefore an apportionment of damages as between the occupier and the person who should have been in charge of the child.

(4) Who is a responsible person for the purposes of the rule? *Coates* v. *Rawtenstall B.C.*(1937) regarded a child of fourteen as sufficiently responsible, and this seems reasonable.

Risks incidental to calling

Section 2 (3) (*b*) was judicially considered in *Roles* v. *Nathan* (1963)—

The plaintiffs, two chimney-sweeps, were employed by the defendants to block up holes in the flues of a heating-system which employed coke. They attempted to block up one of the holes while the coke-fire was lit, despite a warning against this by their employer's agent. Both were killed by the escape of carbon monoxide gas. One of the grounds for the Court of Appeal's decision in favour of the defendants was that this was a risk incidental to their calling which they appreciated and should have guarded against.

Volenti non fit injuria; contributory negligence; warning

The defence of *volenti non fit injuria* is expressly provided for by section 2 (5) of the Act. Where the visitor has entered the premises with knowledge of the danger it seems clear that this in itself does not make him *volens* in respect of it. But in such a case the occupier may rely on a special defence provided by section 2 (4) of the Act. Under this section, a warning of the danger given by the occupier to the visitor, although not automatically absolving the occupier for liability, has this effect if in all the circumstances it is enough to enable the visitor to be reasonable safe. The subsection appears to have reversed the common law rule in *London Graving Dock* v. *Horton* (1951) in which it was held that the occupier was not in breach of duty towards an invitee who knew of the danger, even though such knowledge was not enough to make him reasonably safe. The subsection was applied in *Roles* v. *Nathan* (*supra*, p. 149) in which an additional ground for the decision was that the warning given to the plaintiffs by the occupiers' agent was enough to have enabled them to have been safe.

It seems that the effect of knowledge of the danger by the visitor can have one of three effects:

1. It may give rise to the defence of *volenti non fit injuria*, if the court finds a willingness by the visitor to run the risk of the occupier's negligence.

2. Where the knowledge is the result of the occupier's warning, section 2 (4) contemplates that this in itself may be a sufficient discharge of the occupier's duty of care.

3. The Act leaves open the question what is the position when the visitor has knowledge of the danger gained otherwise than through the warning of the occupier. If such knowledge is enough to make the visitor reasonably safe, he should, it seems, be treated no more favourably than one who is in a similar position as the result of the occupier's warning and should therefore recover no damages from the occupier if he receives injury. (This reasoning receives support from O'Connor J. speaking *obiter* in *Bunker* v. *Charles Brand* (1969)). The legal formulation of this result will, however, differ. There is no doubt that the occupier, unless he is relying on the visitor's knowledge of the danger, is in breach of his duty of care to him. The visitor's knowledge of the danger may therefore go to establish either that he willingly accepted the risk so that a defence arises under section 2 (5) of the Act, or that he was contributorily negligent thus justifying a reduction of damages (*cf.* section 2 (3) 0f the Act). In order to achieve the result mentioned above the contributory negligence should be assessed at 100 per cent. If the visitor's knowledge is not sufficient to make him reasonably safe, it may

still go towards establishing that he willingly ran the risk, or that he was contributorily negligent (though here the occupier's breach would also be causative and the result would be an apportionment of damage under the 1945 Act—this was the actual decision in *Bunker* v. *Charles Brand*).

Exclusion of liability by the occupier

Section 2 (1) of the Occupiers' Liability Act provides that the occupier owes the common duty of care to all his visitors, "except in so far as he is free to and does extend, restrict, modify or exclude his duty . . . by agreement or otherwise."

The power to exclude liability is thus made subject to any legislative or judicial restrictions that may be imposed on it. A major restriction has now been imposed by the provisions of the Unfair Contract Terms Act 1977 which expressly regulate exclusion of the common duty of care. The Act is limited to "business liability" which in the case of occupiers means liability arising from the occupation of premises used for business purposes of the occupier. Liability to trespassers is also outside the Act since it is not based on common law negligence or breach of the common duty of care.

It is clear that at common law the occupier could exclude his liability for breach of both occupancy and activity duties, and as regards both licensees and invitees (see *Ashdown* v. *Samuel Williams* (1957); *White* v. *Blackmore* (1973)). Exclusion could be based on express agreement between occupier and entrant, but it could also be achieved by the display of a suitably prominent notice at the entry to the premises. The words "by agreement or otherwise" in section 2 (1) of the Occupiers' Liability Act preserve the common law position. This common law power to exclude liability continues to exist except where "business liability" of the occupier applies. The juridical basis of the power of exclusion by notice causes some problems. Courts have generally regarded the exclusion clause as a term of the licence under which the visitor enters. This causes difficulties with trespassers and entrants as of right who do not enter under licence. An alternative basis is that the defence of *volenti non fit injuria* is available to the occupier against one who enters with knowledge, or presumed knowledge of the notice. Again, the trespasser presents a problem since the method of his entry may make it impossible for him to have read the notice. But he can hardly be in a better position than the lawful entrant. If *volenti* is the basis, the consent must be a real one. A prisoner, for example, could hardly be held bound by an exclusionary notice displayed outside the prison. This is supported by *Burnett* v. *British Waterways Board* (1972).

The plaintiff was not bound by an exclusionary notice displayed outside the defendants' dock since he had an obligation under his contract of employment to enter the dock.

Liability for independent contractor

Section 2 (4) (b) has settled a question which caused uncertainty at common law, by allowing, subject to certain conditions, the occupier to discharge his duty of care by delegating its performance to an independent contractor. The section provides that the occupier is not to be treated without more as answerable for the danger if in all the circumstances he has acted reasonably in entrusting the work to an independent contractor and has taken such steps (if any) as he reasonably ought in order to satisfy himself that the contractor was competent and that the work had been properly done.

The subsection has confirmed the decision in *Haseldine* v. *Daw and Sons Ltd.* (1941) in which the defendant occupier was held not liable to the plaintiff, his licensee, who had been injured through the fall of a lift negligently repaired by a third party, the occupier's independent contractor. It appears not to have affected *Woodward* v. *Mayor of Hastings* (1945) which held that the clearing of snow from a school steps was not a task which involved technical knowledge and was therefore not reasonably delegated to an independent contractor.

Liability to contractual visitor

Section 5 (1) regulates the occupier's duty to one who enters under contract with him. Section 3 (1) regulates the liability of the occupier to those whom he is bound by contract to permit to enter, but who are not under contract with him.

Liability to contracting party

Clearly if there is an express term in the contract regulating the occupier's liability to the other party, this will be conclusive. In the absence of such a term, section 5 (1) implies a term that the occupier's duty is to be the common duty of care. Liability whether under an express or implied term is contractual rather than tortious, and can therefore be excluded only by subsequent variation of the contract with the agreement of the other contracting party—unilateral notice of exclusion of liability given by one contracting party to the other is not sufficient. *Sole* v. *W.J. Hallt* (1973) allows the contractual entrant the choice of proceeding for breach of contract or in tort for breach of the common duty of care (contractual entrants clearly qualify as visitors, whether as invitees or licensees). This seems important in the case of "business liability." The prohibition against exclusion of liability in section 2 of the Unfair Contract Terms Act 1977, only applies in the case of section 1 (1) (*a*) to obligations arising under the express or implied terms of the contract, and if the contract makes clear there is no such express or implied term, this does not infringe section 2 (even as extended by section 13 to terms which exclude the duty rather than liability for breach of it). The prohibitions under section 2 apply also, however, to terms excluding liability for breach of the common duty of care, so that the alternative basis of claim allowed by *Sole* v. *W.J. Hallt* may be necessary where the occupier's "business liability" is in question.

Liability to persons permitted to enter under contract with occupier

Since persons entering under the terms of a contract with the occupier formerly came within the class of licensees, they are now his visitors within the meaning of the Act of 1957, and are therefore owed the statutory common duty of care by the occupier. But section 3 (1) reinforces this by providing that the occupier cannot restrict the duty of care he owes to such visitors by a provision in the contract, and also that if in the contract he has undertaken obligations going beyond the common duty of care, the duty of care he owes to them "shall include the duty to perform his obligations under the contract." Section 3 (4) makes it clear that a lease is within the provisions of section 3 (1). This means that a landlord, who will normally retain occupation and control of common staircases, passage-ways and lifts in such demised premises as a block of flats, owes the visitor of his tenant the common duty of care and cannot contract out of this by provision in the lease. This is a twofold improvement on the former law, since the duty he formerly owed was that towards licensees, and he could expressly exclude this by provision in the lease.

A further question remains, whether the landlord can exclude his liability to persons entering the premises under contract by exhibiting a notice to this effect on the premises. Clearly the policy arguments which found the exclusion of the visitor's rights by provision in the contract undesirable, on the ground that the visitor would lose his rights without his knowledge, do not apply to an exclusionary notice. Further there seems no reason why the entrant under contract should be in a better position than other visitors. Both Street and Winfield, however, take the view that exclusion by notice is impossible (Street, p. 190; Winfield, p. 210). Street's arguments are: (1) The words "shall include" in section 3 (1) are mandatory, and cannot be evaded by the occupier by any means. But these words appear to make mandatory the inclusion of further contractual obligations going beyond the common duty of care. They do not appear to rule out exclusion of liability under the duty as eventually constituted. (2) A notice given subsequent to the execution of a contract is not sufficient to vary its terms. But this may be answered on the ground that the duty of care owed under section 3 (1) does not rest upon contract, although it may include contractual obligations, and may therefore be excluded by notice. On the whole it seems that the view of Payne (21 M.L.R. 369) that the occupier may by exhibiting a notice exclude the duty under section 3 (1) is probably correct. (Even so, in the case of "business liability," the common duty of care cannot be excluded by notice.)

OCCUPIER'S LIABILITY TOWARDS THE TRESPASSER

Liability towards the trespasser is still governed by the rules of common law unaffected by the Occupiers' Liability Act 1957. In the first place, it is necessary to consider what is meant by trespasser. It may be noted that one permitted to enter may exceed the terms of that permission by trespassing on another part of the premises (for example, *Lee* v. *Luper* (1936)—licensee in hotel trespassed by going through door marked "private"). It is vital to distinguish the trespasser from the implied licensee, since express permission of the occupier is not the only way to establish a licence to enter. Two cases on children illustrate the fine lines that are drawn in this area of the law.

In *Cooke* v. *M.G.W. Ry. of Ireland* (1909), the plaintiff was a child of four who was injured while playing with his companions on a turntable on the defendants' railway premises. The turntable was kept unlocked and was close to a public road. The defendants' servants knew that children were in the habit of entering the premises from the road for the purposes of playing on the turntable, but they took no precautions to exclude the children or lock the turntable. It was held that the plaintiff was a licensee, and that the defendants were liable for his injuries. The case may be compared with *Edwards* v. *Railway Executive* (1952). The plaintiff was a boy aged nine who made his way through a fence between the public recreation ground and a railway embankment to fetch a ball on the other side of the railway line. He was injured by a passing train. For several years children had broken through the fence and used the slope of the embankment for purposes of tobogganing. The defendants had always repaired the fence when as a result of the children's activity it was found to be in need of repair, and there was no evidence that it was in disrepair at the date of the accident. It was held that as the plaintiff was a trespasser the defendants owed him no duty of care.

The latter case can be distinguished from the former in two respects: (1) in *Edwards'* case, even if the allurement of the embankment had imported a licence to go on the embankment, it would not extend to crossing the railway line. In the *Cooke* case, the allurement actually caused the accident; (2) the defendants in the latter case had not passively acquiesced in the acts of trespass as had the defendants in the *Cooke* case. They had repaired the fence although it appeared to be inadequate to keep out children. These differences are clearly not very considerable. The occupier is under no obligation to make his land child-proof even when there is an intrinsically dangerous operation on the land such as the running of trains.

It seems likely that courts will be less willing to find that a person is an implied licensee in view of the decision in *Herrington* v. *British Railways Board* (1972) which considerably extended the occupier's duty towards trespassers.

Liability towards the trespasser

The law on this matter has recently undergone a transformation. Until 1972 the occupier was liable to the trespasser only for intentionally injuring him or for acting in reckless disregard of his presence on the land. This state of the law, imposed by the House of Lords in *Addie & Sons* v. *Dumbreck* (1929) was unchangeable by judicial decision until the House of Lords in 1966 announced its capacity to review its own decision. In *Herrington* v. *British Railways Board* (1972) the action was brought by a child trespasser who had been electrocuted and severely injured by a live rail on land occupied by the defendants. There was evidence that the fence guarding the line on the side from which the plaintiff had entered was in a state of disrepair and had been trampled down, and that a short cut led over the line to a park on the other side. The House of Lords, in affirming the decision of the Court of Appeal that the defendants were liable, did so on the ground that the rule that an occupier is liable to a trespasser only for intentionally or recklessly injuring him is an inadequate one in the light of present social conditions. As a substitute the House of Lords used a test of humanity. Had the defendants done all that a humane person would have done for the safety of the trespasser? In view of the high degree of danger, the likelihood of trespass and the ease with which, granted their financial resources, the defendants could have maintained the fence in repair, the defendants had not shown due humanity in this case. How does the duty of humanity differ from the duty of care? In the first place it will allow the courts to do that which Viscount Radcliffe said was impossible in *Commissioner for Railways* v. *Quinlan* (1964). He said that the law relating to liability to trespassers had to be a comprehensive formulation. Distinctions could not be drawn between different types of occupier and different types of trespasser. This "all or nothing" approach has now been abandoned by the House of Lords. For example, the financial resources of the occupier will be particularly relevant in deciding whether he has acted humanely, a fact which weighed against the defendants in the case itself. So also will the type of "fault" alleged to have been committed. In particular an occupier could hardly plead a lack of financial resources where he is alleged to have carried out carelessly activities on his land. His financial resources are, however, clearly relevant to the question what should be required of him in remedying a static condition of his premises. Distinctions will also be drawn according to the character of the entrant. More humanity must be accorded to the child trespasser, less, if any, towards the burglar. Finally the degree of likelihood of the trespasser's presence on the land appears not to be governed by ordinary principles of foreseeability. In *Herrington* tthe House of Lords spoke of substantial probability of the trespasser's presence as the requirement, but in *Southern Portland Cement* v. *Cooper* (1974) the Privy Council (applying law that was "substantially in line" with *Herrington*) found an occupier liable to a trespasser of whose presence on the land there was no substantial probability. Whether or not this is correct, it seems probable that something more than mere foreseeability of presence is required in the case of the trespasser.

The workings of the law laid down in *Herrington* can be seen in *Pannett* v. *P. McGuiness & Co.* (1972). Demolition contractors were occupiers of a site in a busy urban area where large numbers of children were to be expected. At the completion of demolition it became necessary to burn a quantity of rubbish on the site. The defendants realised that this activity would be an attraction to children and so employed three workmen to keep children away. The latter had chased children, including the plaintiff, a child of five, away on several occasions. One afternoon the three men absented themselves from the site at a time when a fire was burning and during this period the plaintiff entered the site and was burned. The Court of Appeal, in holding the defendants liable stressed the hazardous nature of the activity and its attraction to children together with the substantial likelihood of trespass. In these circumstances the occupier's duty went beyond merely chasing the children away and the defendants were therefore vicariously liable for the default of their men in absenting themselves from the site.

Pannett v. *P. Mcguiness & Co.* seems to have regarded the servant's liability towards the trespasser as turning upon the same test as that of the occupier, *viz.*, that of humanity. There seems no reason, however, why the servant should enjoy the same dispensation from the ordinary principles of negligence as does the occupier, and this was recognised in the later Court of Appeal decision in *Rose* v. *Plenty* (1976). If this is so, the occupier may be held vicariously liable for his servant's negligence towards a trespasser (though difficulties may arise about the course of employment, see Chap. 13).

The Pearson Commission proposed that occupiers should owe a duty of care to trespassers and other uninvited entrants. The duty would exist only in respect of dangers against which "in all the circumstances of the case, the occupier can reasonably be expected to offer him some protection" and would be a duty to take such care as is "reasonable in all the circumstances of the case." They also proposed that this duty should be extended to the entrant under a private, but not a public, right of way.

LIABILITY OF NON-OCCUPIER IN RESPECT OF PREMISES

The law on this topic has always been complex and to some extent remains so. The only way it can be understood is to set out the common law position first, dealing separately with three cases, the vendor, the lessor and the builder; then to examine the Defective Premises Act 1972.

Common law position

(1) *Vendor*

The vendor of premises had complete immunity from an action in tort for defects in the premises. He was not liable in tort for injuries to the buyer, other persons in the premises, or to persons injured outside the premises. He might incur liability to the buyer in contract for breach of an express or implied warranty that the house was fit for human habitation.

(2) *Lessor*

He had the same immunity as the vendor from actions in tort for injuries to his lessee or other persons injured inside the disused premises. He might be held liable in public nuisance or negligence to persons injured outside the premises by reason of their defective condition (*infra*, p. 159). He might incur contractual liability to the lessee in the case of furnished premises for breach of an implied warranty that the premises and furniture were fit for occupation at the commencement of the tenancy. Also, if he undertook the duty of repair, the lessee might sue him in contract for injuries suffered by reason of his failure to perform it. This, however, gave no remedy to any person other than the lessee (*Cavalier* v. *Pope* (1906). The lessor had an obligation in respect of the condition of his own premises to persons generally. Thus in *Cunard* v. *Antifyre* (1933) some defective roofing and guttering forming part of the premises retained by the defendant lessor fell on to premises let by him to the plaintiff's husband. The plaintiff suffered personal injuries and recovered damages in negligence from the defendant.

(3) Builder
The builder was liable in tort for his negligence in the building of premises on ordinary *Donoghue* v. *Stevenson* principles, and in the same way as other person who did work on premises (*Sharpe* v. *Sweeting* (1963); *Billings* v. *Riden* (1957)). However the vendor/builder had the same immunity from an action in tort as the vendor, and the lessor/builder as the lessor. In the case of a building contract, the builder could be liable in contract to the buyer on the basis of an implied warranty that (a) work would be done in a good and workmanlike manner; (b) good and proper materials would be used; (c) the completed house would be reasonably fit for human habitation. The common law position of vendor/ and lessor/builders has now been radically changed. In *Anns* v. *London Borough of Merton* (1977), Lord Wilberforce thought *obiter* that a lessor/builder should be liable for negligence in building. In *Batty* v. *Metropolitan Realisations Ltd.* (1978) the Court of Appeal held a vendor/builder liable in negligence to a subsequent purchaser of the house he built for choosing as a site for the house land which he should have known was liable to subsidence. The builder in this case had sold the building to a development company which had sold it to the plaintiff. The development company also was held liable to the plaintiff for similar negligence to that of the builder. Here again, the common law position appears to have changed-but— it is clear that the development company was not a mere vendor of the property but a joint venturer with the builder in the building enterprise.

Defective Premises Act 1972

(1) Vendor
It should be noted that the position of a vendor, who is not a builder, and who has done no work on or in relation to premises, is not touched by the statute.

(2) *Lessor*

In the case of the lessor of premises, the combined effect of section 4 (1), (2), and (4) of the Defective Premises Act is to make the lessor liable in respect of defects in the state of the premises to "persons who might reasonably be expected to be affected by" such defects, for personal injury or damage to their property, provided the lessor has an obligation under the tenancy agreement to keep the premises in repair, or has under the tenancy agreement an express or implied right to enter and do repairs, and provided the lessor knows or ought to know of the defect needing repair. Section 4 (1) of the Occupiers' Liability Act 1957, is expressly repealed. The new obligation goes further than section 4 (1) of the 1957 Act in that it may be owed to trespassers, it covers cases where a lessor has a mere right to enter and do repairs, and notice of the need for repair by the lessee to the lessor is unnecessary. Under section 4 (5) of the Defective Premises Act 1972, statutory obligations to repair premises imposed upon lessors (for example, that arising under section 32 of the Housing Act 1961) are to be treated as being imposed by the tenancy agreement. Where the lessor has a mere right to enter and do repairs, and the obligation to repair is imposed on the lessee by the tenancy agreement, the lessor will not be liable to the lessee if the latter is injured because of defects in the premises due to want of repair.

Certain gaps still remain. If the premises which have been let have fallen into a state of disrepair prior to the let, the lessor is not liable under the Act for damage caused by defects in the premises unless he has an obligation to repair under the tenancy agreement, or has a statutory obligation to repair, or has a right to enter and do repairs. A lessor who actually enters and does repairs after the commencement of the lease is liable for damage caused by defective repair. His liability is based on ordinary principles of negligence from which in this instance there is no reason to exempt him (*cf. A.C. Billings & Sons* v. *Riden* (1958) in which the House of Lords recognised that persons who do work on premises are liable for negligence to those foreseeably present on the premises). It is not yet clear whether the reasoning in *Billings* v. *Riden* extends to the negligent installation of a defective chattel not dangerous in itself, thus overruling the Court of Appeal decision in *Ball* v. *L.C.C.* (1949) which held that the lessor was liable only if he knew of the defect in the chattel.

(3) *Builders*

The Defective Premises Act 1972 was passed at a time when it was thought that vendor/ and lessor/builders were immune from liability in negligence at common law. Sections

1 and 3 of the Act attempt to repair the gap, but in view of the fact that a common law action has now become available, much of the legislative repair-work has become redundant.

Section 1 of the Act provides that persons who "take on work for or in connection with the provision of a dwelling" owe a duty to see that the work is done in a workmanlike, or as the case may be, professional manner, with proper materials, and so that as regards that work the dwelling will be fit for habitation when completed. The duty is owed to the person for whom the dwelling is provided and to persons who subsequently acquire an interest whether legal or equitable in the dwelling. The cause of action arises on the completion of the building. The nature of the duty under this section, and in particular whether it is one of care only (which it looks like), or a strict duty, await judicial interpretation. The section may be wider than the common law remedy in that it covers defects which render the dwelling unfit fot habitation, whereas the common law remedy requires that the house be a danger to person or property. The latter requirement seems, however, fairly easy to satisfy. In other respects, the common law remedy seems both wider and superior. It covers all buildings, not just dwellings. The limitation period on the common law claim is far more favourable (see below). Section 1 is excluded where the dwelling is protected by the National House Building Council Scheme, which covers most new houses. Section 1 extends, however, to conversions or enlargements of existing dwellings to which the Scheme would not apply.

Section 3 (1) of the Act was designed to remove the immunity which vendors and lessors of premises, which they had built or done work on prior to the sale or lease, enjoyed at common law. With the courts' own removal of that immunity, the subsection seems wholly redundant and does not require consideration.

Comment

The development of the law regarding the protection of the public against buying or being injured by defective houses has not been satisfactory. There are it is true, some difficult considerations of policy involved. Courts were, for example, anxious to protect private vendors of houses from having to undertake onerous inspections of their properties prior to sale, when the buyer might be in just as good a position to make such an inspection. The law is similarly reluctant to impose duties of care on private sellers of. chattels (see Chap. 12). There seems, however, no good reason why the principles of *Donoghue* v. *Stevenson* were not immediately applied to all builders of houses, yet this development took forty years, and in the event an unfortunate duplication of legislative and judicial effort has occurred. The courts have now so far overthrown the old principles that there is liability in negligence for building a defective house, even though the house has caused no damage to person or property, and even though in the case of the negligent manufacture of a chattel, the very case with which *Donoghue* v. *Stevenson* was concerned, there is no liability unless the chattel has caused damage.

Liability of the non-occupier towards the trespasser

The non-occupier did not enjoy the same immunity from liability in negligence towards the trespasser as did the occupier (*cf. Buckland* v. *Guildford Gas, Light & Coke Co.* (1949)). His liability continues to be governed by ordinary principles of negligence.

12. LIABILITY FOR CHATTELS

The whole subject of liability for chattels needs to be considered in the light of the judgments of the majority in *Donoghue* v. *Stevenson* (*supra*, p. 67). The narrow ratio of that case is concerned with the question of the liability of the manufacturer of the chattel. The wide ratio, applicable to persons other than the manufacturer, may be used in the case of anyone who has been negligent in connection with a chattel. But it is too early to state that the topic of liability for defective chattels, whether that of the manufacturer or of some other person, is simply an application of the general principles of negligence to a specific field. Some anomalous exceptions to these general principles may still exist.

LIABILITY OF PERSONS OTHER THAN THE MANUFACTURER

In considering liability for negligence in relation to chattels, it may be noted that this phrase may cover a number of factual situations. The negligence may be that of the person who has manufactured or produced the goods, or of one who for reward has done repair work on the goods, or of a person who has merely transmitted the chattel to another person, for example, the seller, bailor, donor or lender of the chattel. It seems that the standard of care to be expected of a defendant will vary according to what he has done in relation to the chattel. The manufacturer and the repairer are expected to ensure that the chattel when it leaves their possession is reasonably safe (they both are covered by the narrow rule in *Donoghue* v. *Stevenson*). The seller and other transmitters are subject to no such onerous duties. In general, they appear to have no duty to inspect the goods they are selling (although a dealer in second-hand cars is expected to inspect them to ensure their safety before sale—*Andrews* v. *Hopkinson* (1957)). Their liability would therefore appear to be limited to failure to notice patent defects in the chattel, and allowing a defect in the chattel to arise by negligently failing to look after it. In the case of the person who transfers a chattel to another purely for that other's benefit, for example, by way of gift or gratuitous loan, there is nineteenth-century authority (for instance, *Gautret* v. *Egerton* (1867) that the transferor was not liable for a defect in the chattel unless he actually knew of the defect and had failed to warn the transferee of it. But it seems doubtful whether the principle of this case has survived *Donoghue* v. *Stevenson*. It seems that the gratuitous transferor should be judged by the same standard as other transmitters of a chattel. He should therefore be liable if he has failed to notice obvious defects in the chattel, or where by neglect he has allowed the chattel to become defective.

DANGEROUS CHATTELS

The law in relation to liability for negligence in respect of chattels has been confused by the distinction drawn between the dangerous and the non-dangerous chattel. The distinction has received judicial criticism (for example, by Scrutton L.J. who did not "understand the difference between a thing dangerous in itself, as poison, and a thing not dangerous as a class, but by negligent construction dangerous as a particular thing. The latter if anything, seems the more dangerous of the two; it is a wolf in sheep's clothing rather than an obvious wolf" (*Hodge and Sons* v. *Anglo-American Oil Co.* (1922)).

The effect of the distinction in cases where it applies is that liability in the case of the dangerous chattel is based on ordinary negligence, whereas, in the case of the non-dangerous chattel, it is based upon knowledge by the defendant of a defect in the chattel. Although in several cases since *Donoghue* v. *Stevenson* (1932) the defendant has escaped liability on the ground that the chattel was non-dangerous and there was no question of the narrow rule in that case applying (for example, *Ball* v. *London County Council* (1949)—defendant landlords not liable for negligent installation of defective boiler which exploded and injured plaintiff on ground that boiler was not dangerous chattel and landlords did not know of defects in it), in others it has been ignored (for example, in the cases on liability of parents for son's use of a gun— *Donaldson* v. *McNiven* (1952); *Newton* v. *Edgerley* (1959)). The present-day position is therefore one of uncertainty whether the distinction survives, and if so in what cases it applies. In view of the arbitrary nature of the distinction and its unjust consequences, it seems time that the defendant's standard of care was assessed according to the capacity for doing harm of the particular chattel in the particular situaation, and not of the class of chattel in the abstract.

LIABILITY OF THE MANUFACTURER OF A CHATTEL

Lord Atkin expressed the narrow ratio of *Donoghue* v. *Stevenson* as follows:

"A manufacturer of products, which he sells in such a form that he intends them to reach the ultimate consumer in the form in which they left him with no reasonable possibility of intermediate examination and with the knowledge that the absence of reasonable care in the preparation or putting up of the products will result in injury to the consumer's life or property, owes a duty to the consumer to take that reasonable care."

The liability of the manufacturer is best treated by considering this formulation in sections.

"Manufacturer"

The rule has been extended to persons other than the manufacturer who do work on chattels, *e.g.* repairers (*Stennett* v. *Hancock* (1939)). It seems that it will not apply to the mere retailer of goods although an exception was recognised in the case of the dealer in second-hand cars who was held in *Andrews* v. *Hopkinson* (*supra*, p. 162) to have a duty to inspect such cars before selling them. This decision is justifiable both because of the public interest in keeping defective vehicles off the road, and because there will normally be no question of manufacturer's liability in relation to such vehicles. It has been suggested above that in general the retailer of goods is liable for defects which should be obvious to himself and for allowing the goods to become defective while in his care. It may be thought that the law should go further than this and make the retailer take some steps to ensure that the goods are safe, at least by buying them from what he considers to be a reputable source. Such a duty has been imposed on the distributor of goods. Thus, in *Watson* v. *Buckley, Osborn, Garret & Co.* (1940), the defendants supplied a hair dye which was used on the plaintiff's hair by a hairdresser. The dye contained excessive acid and the plaintiff caught dermatitis as a result. The defendants were held liable because though they had advertised the dye for its safety, they had bought from a manufacturer who was unknown to them, and had failed to carry out a simple test which would have ascertained the quantity of acid in the dye. The case probably turns on its own special facts, but it seems that a general duty on distributors to take reasonable steps to ensure the safety of the goods would be an acceptable extension of it.

"Products which he sells in such a form, etc."

The words "in such a form" do not mean that the goods must reach the consumer in the same container in which they left the manufacturer. They mean that the manufacturer contemplates nothing of substance being done to the goods after they leave him.

"Possibility of intermediate examination"

It is now clear that the mere possibility of intermediate examination of the goods after they have left the manufacturer is not enough; it must also be a reasonable expectation of the manufacturer. Thus, in *Grant* v. *Australian Knitting Mills Ltd.* (1936) (*supra*, p. 140) the defendants argued that the underpants should have been washed before use. Lord Wright dismissed this by saying: "It was not contemplated that they should first be washed." Where the manufacturer reasonably contemplates intermediate examination, it seems that he is totally absolved if such examination does not take place, even though through negligent manufacture of defect exists in the goods as in *Kubach* v. *Hollands* (1937) in which the defendants had been supplied with a mislabelled and, in the circumstances, highly dangerous chemical which had been accompanied by an invoice stating that the chemical must be tested before use (*quaere*, the effect of a negligent examination which fails to reveal the defect). In both cases it appears that in accordance with principles already discussed on page 118, there should be an apportionment here between the manufacturer and the person responsible for the later negligence.

A different problem arises where the examination has been successful in revealing the defect in the goods. Here it seems that, on causal principles, the manufacturer ought to be excused since to use the goods (or to pass them on) after discovering the defect seems a clear *novus actus*. So in *Taylor* v. *Rover Car Co.* (1966), where the plaintiff's foreman discovered a defect in a hammer manufactured by the defendants but continued to allow it to be used, the plaintiff's employers were liable to him but the defendants were not. (To similar effect is *Farr* v. *Butters Bros. & Co.* (1932) in which the plaintiff himself discovered defects in the parts of a crane manufactured by the defendants, but nevertheless attempted to assemble it and was killed as a result.) But knowledge of the defect by the plaintiff does not help the manufacturer where there is no safe way of dealing with the chattel, but it is necessary to do so (as in *Denny* v. *Supplies & Transport Co.* (1950)—plaintiff had to unload badly stowed timber as part of his employment. Although he realised the danger he recovered in full for the injuries he suffered from the defendants who had stowed the timber, because no safe way of unloading the timber existed).

"Ultimate consumer"

These words received an extremely liberal interpretation by the court in *Stennett* v. *Hancock and Peters* (1939) in which it was held that a pedestrian could recover damages from the defendants who were repairers of a lorry. Due to the defendants' negligence in the course of repair the flange of the lorry came apart from the lorry while it was being driven, and struck and injured the plaintiff. In view of this decision, it may be that anyone foreseeably injured because of the defect in the chattel is a consumer within the meaning of the rule.

Pearson Commission Report

The Pearson Commission made important recommendations concerning liability for chattels. They proposed that producers (*i.e* manufacturers) should be strictly liable in tort for death or personal injury caused by defective products. Producers of both the finished product and of components should be subject to strict liability, but not distributors. A distributor would have an obligation to reveal the name of the producer of the goods or the name of his own supplier, and failure to do so within a reasonable time should render him strictly liable in tort. Importers would be treated as producers for these purposes. The producer would be allowed the defence either that he did not put the product into circulation; or that the product was not defective when he did so; or that he did not put it into circulation in the course of a business. Contributory negligence of the plaintiff would also be a defence. The producer's strict liability in tort would terminate 10 years after the initial circulation of the product.

These proposals are largely in line with a draft EEC directive of 1976, and a treaty called the Strasbourg Convention of 1977. United States law also favours strict product liability. Arguments which also influenced the Pearson Commission in favour of strict liability were the fact that the seller of the product already is subject to strict liability in contract, that the producer aims his product at the consumer rather than merely foreseeing it might injure him, and the fact that the change would involve low costs, most of which would be borne by consumers as a whole. It may also be pointed out that because of the operation of the *res ipsa loquitur* principle, producers are subject to what is tantamount to strict liability already (see Chap. 10). Nevertheless, the recommendations concerning strict liability in this area of the law seem to symptomise the piecemeal approach of the Commission. If strict liability is thought to produce desirable results in one field, it is surprising that its claims were so readily dismissed in more significant areas of tort compensation such as road accidents and industrial injuries.

13 EMPLOYERS' LIABILITY

Introduction

It is now necessary to consider the duties which the employer owes at common law towards the persons he employs. The employer's common law duties are now considerably supplemented by the vast number of statutory duties which are imposed upon employers for the protection of workmen, particularly in the industrial field. A detailed account of these duties is beyond the scope of this book, and the general topic of breach of statutory duty is postponed to a later chapter.

The common law duties of the employer towards his workmen co-exist with the employer's vicarious liability for the torts of his workmen committed in the course of their employment against their fellow workmen so as normally to ensure the employer is liable where an employee has been injured through negligence at the place of work. At one time this was not so, because under the doctrine of common employment an employer was not vicariously liable for the negligence of one workman committed in the course of his employment and injuring his fellow. The rule of common employment was abolished in 1948, but it has left its traces in the law. Thus, it could be by-passed if the employer was shown to be in breach of a personal duty owed to the workman. So, a workman injured by the negligence of another workman could succeed against an employer for the latter's negligence in choosing that workman. The necessity of placing emphasis upon the employer's personal duties rather than on his vicarious liability no doubt explains the completeness of formulation of such duties and the tendency to regard them as a separate branch of negligence rather than as an example of a duty of care based upon Atkinian proximity. The absence of vicarious liaiblity no doubt also accounts for the personal duties of the employer being construed as non-delegable—they could not be performed through the medium of his servants or independent contractors, no matter how reasonable such delegation might be. The concept of non-delegability has survived the abolition of the doctrine of common employment.

As far as his personal duties are concerned, the employer's duty is only to take reasonable care for the safety of his workmen. There is no question of his being subject to strict liability at common law, although he may be subject to strict duties imposed by statute. Although the employer clearly has a general duty to take reasonable care for the safety of his workmen, it is customary both in decided cases and in works of reference to make a tripartite division of such duty. On the basis of this division the employer must provide (1) competent staff; (2) proper plant and premises; (3) a safe system of work. These individual duties must now be examined.

Competent staff

The importance of this duty has considerably lessened with the abolition of the doctrine of common employment, since it will normally be possible to rely on the vicarious rather than the personal liability of the employer where the plaintiff has been injured by the negligence of a fellow workman. The duty, however, came to the assistance of the plaintiff in *Hudson* v. *Ridge Manufacturing Co.* (1957). The plaintiff was injured in the course of horseplay committed against him by a fellow workman. The latter was known to be addicted to such behaviour and had several times been reprimanded for it. The employer was held to be in breach of his personal duty to the plaintiff to provide competent staff. It seems that in this case the employer would not have been held vicariously liable for the workman's negligence, which was not committed in the course of his employment.

Proper plant and premises

The employer's common law duty is to take reasonable care to provide proper tools, machinery, working places and premises generally, and to maintain them as such. The duty in respect of equipment has now been statutorily strengthened. *Davie* v. *New Merton Board Mills Ltd.* (1959) had held that the employer's duty to provide proper equipment is satisfied by the purchase of such equipment from a reputable source. So in that case where the plaintiff suffered injury through the use of a tool which had a defect in it because of the negligence of its manufacturer, it was held that the plaintiff's employer was not liable to him since he had purchased the tool from reputable suppliers who themselves had purchased from reputable manufacturers. The law as a consequence of this decision was hard for the workman who received injury in this way and was unable to discover the manufacturer's identity or found the manufacturer not worth suing. Accordingly the Employers' Liability (Defective Equipment) Act 1969 makes the employer liable to the workman where the latter has suffered personal injury in the course of his employment in consequence of a defect in equipment provided by the employer for the purposes of his business, provided that the fault is attributable wholly or partly to the fault of a third party whether the latter is identified or not. The Act thus imposes strict liability upon the employer but only if the workman can prove the defect was due to the fault of a third party. In view of the acceptance in principle of strict liability and the difficulty often involved in establishing fault, it is hard to see why the Act did not go further and make the employer liable for all defects in equipment which cause injury to his employers.

Safe system of work

The distinction between an unsafe system and dangers caused by "isolated and day-to-day acts of the servant of which the master is not presumed to be aware and which he cannot guard against" appears to be one of degree, and is today of vastly reduced importance now that the master is liable for casual acts of negligence committed by a servant against another servant in the course of operating an otherwise safe system of work. It is established that an unsafe system of work may exist in an operation which is to be performed once and for all and may never again arise. *General Cleaning Contractors* v. *Christmas* (1953) is an example of an employer's liability for an unsafe system of work. The defendants required their workmen who were window cleaners to work on a narrow sill twenty-seven feet above the ground without instructing them to keep one section of the window open or providing any appliance to enable this to be done. They were held liable to the plaintiff who fell and was injured when the sash of a window fell on his fingers compelling him to release his hold on the other sash.

Delegability of the duty

The personal nature of the employer's duties has led to some doubt whether, if ever, they can be delegated to a third party. It is clear that delegation of the employer's personal duties to his servant is not a discharge of these duties (*Wilsons and Clyde Co. Ltd.* v. *English* (1938)). Thus the employer's duty to prove a safe system of work cannot be delegated to a servant, however competent and however high his position, and the employer is liable even if the servant is not personally negligent in bringing about the unsafe system. (It must of course be shown that it would have been negligent of the employer himself to operate such a system.) It is clear therefore that the employer's duty, though expressed as only one to take reasonable care, may in certain cases involve him in liability when he is not personally at fault if he acted reasonably in delegating. This is *a fortiori* the case if delegation to an independent contractor is also not permissible since many of the duties of an employer are not only reasonably but also necessarily delegated to an outside agent. At one time it was thought that the employer was liable in every case for the fault of an independent contractor, but *Davie* v. *New Merton Board Mills Ltd.* (*supra*) shows this may not be the case. The reasons for the decision of the House of Lords in that case were two: (1) purchase of the tool from a third party was not delegation to an independent contractor; (2) the employer's duty was to provide, not to manufacture, proper equipment and this duty was satisfied by purchasing the equipment from a reputable source. The latter reason opens up the possibility of vicarious performance of certain of the employer's duties through a competent contractor being permissible but it is difficult to say whether this would extend from cases of purchase of equipment (now in any case covered by the 1969 Act) to other contracts (for example the building of factory premises on the employer's land. In *Sumner* v. *William Henderson & Sons* (1964) it was held that an employer was liable for the negligence of any of a number of independent contractors employed to instal an electric cable, purchased by the employer, in his factory, but not liable if the negligence was in the manufacture of the cable).

Duty one of reasonable care

It must always be remembered that the employer's duty in respect of his workmen's safety is not an absolute duty. It is discharged by the exercise of reasonable care on the employer's part, and the question whether he has committed a breach of duty is decided in exactly the same way as it is in actions of negligence generally.

Extent of employer's duties

Some of the employer's duties are self-limiting, for example, the duty to provide proper plant and premises and the duty to provide a safe system of work. But it may be doubted how far the duty to provide proper equipment extends. If the workman takes home a defective tool and is injured in using it, can he sue the employer? There may be a limitation that the plaintiff must be acting in the course of his employment, but this is not so in the analogous tort of breach of statutory duty (*infra*, p. 219). No doubt a line must be drawn which would probably rule out liability in the above example, but it seems difficult to formulate a test other than that the injury must have some reasonable connection with the performance of the plaintiff's duties.

Employees are not the only persons who may be present on the premises of an employer. There may, for example, be persons present employed by the employer's independent contractor or self-employed persons. The nature of the employer's duty to such persons is by no means clear. There is clearly no liability *qua* employer, but there may be liability *qua* occupier or under ordinary principles of negligence. What is not clear is to what extent the employer must take positive action to ensure the safety of such persons, as he must in the case of his own employees. In the analogous tort of breach of statutory duty, persons other than employees have generally been held to be unable to sue the employer for breach of factory safety legisation (see Chap. 19). The Health and Safety at Work Act 1974, has introduced a duty (section 3 (1) on the employer to take reasonable care for the health or safety of such persons, but civil liability for breach of this duty is expressly excluded.

Pearson Commission Report

The Commission recommended no change in the basis of employers' liability to employees. In particular they were against the introduction of strict liability because the present action for breach of statutory duty goes far enough in this direction. This is hard to follow. If strict liability is desirable, it is not sufficiently achieved by the action for breach of statutory duty, which is a hybrid, sometimes involving strict liability but more often operating as a form of statutory negligence. Very similar arguments as to the cost of introducing strict liability apply in the case of employers' liability as exist in the case of products liability. The employer is required under the present law (Employers' Liability (Compulsory Insurance) Act 1969) to be insured against liability to his employees; any increase in the cost of insurance brought about by introducing strict liability could no doubt be transferred to the consumer at a very low cost per head.

14. TORTS OF STRICT LIABILITY—INTRODUCTORY

Strict liability is liability which arises without fault—*i.e.* the defendant need have acted neither intentionally nor negligently. The instances of strict liability in the English law of tort are of a somewhat unconnected nature. Although it might be possible to deduce a principle of strict liability for carrying on an extra-hazardous activity under the rule in *Rylands* v. *Fletcher* (1868) and liability for animals, the courts have refused to recognise any such general principle (*cf. Read* v. *Lyons & Co., infra*, p. 195). The strict liability involved in breach of statutory duty depends upon interpretation of the relevant statute. Vicarious liability for the acts of servants is justified mainly by reason of the fact that the employer is a financially responsible person, whereas the servants who commit the torts while carrying on his business are generally speaking not worth suing. In nuisance and liability for fire there appear now to be only vestigial traces of original strict liability. It must be remembered that other torts, not regarded as torts of strict liability, may operate as such. Conversion and defamation are examples.

The Pearson Commission Report disappointingly makes little attempt to analyse the merits of introducing strict liability into areas of personal injury traditionally requiring proof of fault. The Commission rejected its introduction for road accidents, chiefly for the reason that strict liability together with the recommended no fault social security-type scheme would place an unfair burden of cost on the motorist. Surely, however, the two should have been considered as alternatives to each other? In the previous chapter of this book it was pointed out that the reason given by the Report for rejecting strict liability in the case of industrial accidents also seems unsatisfactory. Once these two areas of tort are excluded, there was clearly no scope for a general proposal concerning strict liability. The nearest the Report gets to making such a proposal is its recommendation concerning exceptional risks. The Report recommended that liability should be strict in respect of those things or operations which either, by reason of their unusually hazardous nature require close, careful and skilled supervision, the failure of which may cause death or personal injury; or, although normally by their nature perfectly safe, are likely if they do go wrong to cause serious and extensive casualties. In view of the considerable scope for argument about what falls into these categories, the Report wisely recommended a system of listing of dangerous things or activities falling within the two categories by means of statutory instruments under the authority of a parent statute. This form of liability would also co-exist with the existing cases where strict liability exists at common law. It seems safe to conclude that the law would not change greatly if this proposal were implemented. The Commission also favoured the introduction of strict liability into three additional areas; products liability; the liability of an authority to a volunteer for medical research of clinical trials who has suffered severe damage as a result; the liability of the Government or local authority concerned in relation to severe damage suffered by anyone as the result of vaccination which has been recommended in the interests of the community. It may be noted that statutory forms of strict liability in tort already exist. Section 40 of the Civil Aviation Act has already been mentioned (see above). Other examples, which have practical importance though details of them are beyond the scope of this book, are the Nuclear Installations Act 1965, the Merchant Shipping (Oil Pollution) Act 1971, and the Control of Pollution Act 1974.

15. NUISANCE

Much of the confusion that centres round the word "nuisance" in the law of tort is caused by the fact that the term covers two concepts, those of private and public nuisance, which, while not totally dissimilar, are not too closely related. In private nuisance the central idea is that of invasion of land: the defendant causes the entry into the plaintiff's land of such things as noise, smell, vibrations, water or chattels. However, in the *British Celanese* v. *A.H. Hunt,* a *withdrawal* of power from the plaintiffs' land causing physical damage to property there was found to be actionable as nuisance. In the words of Lord Macmillan in *Read* v. *Lyons & Co.* ((1947)—spoken of *Rylands* v. *Fletcher,* but true also of private nuisance), the tort "derives from a conception of mutual duties of adjoining or neighbouring landlowners," (this does not mean that the nuisance must always emanate from the defendant's land—it may emanate from land belonging to another, from the highway, or presumably, from the airspace above or adjoining the plaintiff's land—*cf. Lyons* v. *Wilkins* (1899)—watching and besetting the plaintiff's premises (presumably from the highway) in the course of picketing held to be a private nuisance; *cf.* also *Hubbard* v. *Pitt* (1975)). Public nuisance derives from the criminal law, its place in the law of tort depending upon the fact that a member of the public who can prove that he has suffered special damage from the defendant's commission of the common law crime of public nuisance may sue the defendant in tort. It does not require the invasion of private land, but the annoyance of the public by such acts as the obstruction of the highway, the pollution of the public water supply, and the keeping of a common gaming-house. The generic concept underlying both forms of nuisance, which may be expressed by saying that the defendant must have acted to the annoyance of another person or persons, is so broad as to be valueless.

The difference in origin of the two torts explains certain differences between them. For instance, the inability to sue in private nuisance for personal injury is explained because that tort protects exclusively the plaintiff's interest in his land; the same limitation does not exist in public nuisance. Generally speaking, however, the courts appear to assume that the two aspects of nuisance are governed by similar rules.

PRIVATE NUISANCE

One requirement of the tort of private nuisance, mentioned already, is that the defendant's act must interfere with the defendant's use and enjoyment of his land. This in itself is not enough to constitute private nuisance—the interference must also be unreasonable. What is an unreasonable interference is often a difficult question to decide, and one in which matters of law and fact are involved. Besides this, private nuisance, being derived from the action on the case, has the attribute that it lies only for an indirect interference.

The type of interference required by the tort of private nuisance may be either actual damage to the plaintiff's land or property thereon, or an interference with the enjoyment of such land not accompanied by any actual damage, or both.

The use interferred with by private nuisance may be the normal one of residing on the land and putting it to domestic use, but it is possible for other types of use to be protected, for example, agricultural, commercial or industrial use. The interference may be caused by a variety of different types of invasion: by vibrations, flooding, electricity, fire, smell, noise, dust, and sewage. Even an offensive sight has been held to be an actionable nuisance. Thus, in *Thompson-Schwab* v. *Costaki* (1956), the defendants were prostitutes who used premises adjoining the plaintiff's for the purposes of prostitution. The plaintiff sued them successfully in nuisance.

There is, however, no right to a particular view from one's house, provided that the defendant does not replace this with such an eye-sore that this is in itself a nuisance. Equally, nuisance does not protect a monopoly of view of what takes place within one's land. Thus, in *Victoria Park Racing Co.* v. *Taylor* (1937) (an Australian case which would probably be followed in this country), the defendant, by broadcasting commentaries of racing held on the plaintiff's premises, which he was able to view from an adjoining building, did not commit nuisance. Privacy may be protected by the tort of nuisance, but only where in infringing it the defendant has also substantially interfered with the plaintiff's enjoyment of his land.

Private nuisance and other torts

Nuisance has to be distinguished from other torts, with some of which it may overlap. The difference between nuisance and trespass to land is the difference between indirect and direct interference with the plaintiff's land: there is no possibility of an overlap between these two torts. On the other hand, nuisance and *Rylands* v. *Fletcher* (1968) are often available on the same set of facts. The differences between the two are dealt with in the chapter on *Rylands* v. *Fletcher*.

The greatest difficulty is experienced in distinguishing between the torts of nuisance and negligence. Clearly negligence is much wider than nuisance, in the sense that the interests which it protects are not limited to the use and enjoyment of land. Apart from this the following differences exist between the two torts:

(i) In negligence, the plaintiff must establish that the defendant was under a legal duty to take care. In nuisance, there is usually no difficulty in showing that the defendant had a duty not to interfere unreasonably with the plaintiff's enjoyment of his land. Where, however, the nuisance arises by omission to act, the plaintiff must normally show that the defendant was under a duty to act carefully (*infra*, p. 183).

(ii) Nuisance may be committed intentionally, or, perhaps, without negligence (see below). It is certain that in nuisance, negligence does not have to be *proved* by the plaintiff, though it may be relevant to show the unreasonableness of the interference.

(iii) It seems unlikely that mere interference with the enjoyment of land would be sufficient to constitute damage for the purpose of an action in negligence.

(iv) In nuisance, the question whether there has been an unreasonable intereference must be determined both in the light of the defendant's conduct and of the seriousness of the interference suffered by the plaintiff. In negligence, any damage, however small, is always sufficient to support the action, although the triviality of the anticipated damage may be a factor in the court's decision that the defendant did not need to take precautions against the risk of its occurence.

Unreasonableness

Interference with the enjoyment by the plaintiff of his land is not, as such, actionable. The plaintiff must show that such interference is unreasonable. The question of unreasonableness in nuisance is Janus-like: the court must consider *both* the conduct of the defendant in creating the interference *and* the effect that such interference has upon the victim, the plaintiff. These factors are not considered in isolation from each other. Thus the fact that the defendant has acted carelessly or maliciously may tip the scales in favour of showing an unreasonable interference. Equally, however carefully the defendant may have acted, if it is proved that the interference is sufficiently unreasonable, he will be liable in nuisance. Besides this, the court may take into account factors external to the parties, such as the locality in which the alleged nuisance takes place and the public interest in whether the defendant should be restrained from carrying out the activity. In the light of these factors, the court must then ask itself the question that is central in all nuisance actions, "Is it reasonable that the plaintiff should have to put up with this interference?"

Conduct of defendant

In some cases, the mental state of the defendant may make his conduct nuisance, although, had that mental state been different, nuisance would not have been committed. Where, for example, he is actuated by spite or malice toward the plaintiff, nuisance may be committed for that reason. Thus, in *Christie* v. *Davey* (1893), the plaintiff was a music teacher who held lessons in her house. The defendant, a neighbour, made a variety of noises during these lessons, solely, as the court found, for the purpose of annoying the plaintiff. The defendant was held liable in nuisance. In *Hollywood Silver Fox Farm Ltd.* v. *Emmett* (1936), the defendant caused his son to discharge guns on his land for the purpose of interfering with the breeding of the plaintiff's silver foxes. The defendant was held liable in nuisance.

It may be that the court would have found, in each case, that the interference was unreasonable also by reason of the annoyance to which it subjected the plaintiff. The nature of the defendant's conduct, however, made it possible to regard his action as unreasonable without reference to the degree to which it interfered with the plaintiff's enjoyment of his land. The two cases are not inconsistent with the earlier decision in *Bradford Corpn.* v. *Pickles* (1895). The right to appropriate water from an underground stream is not, like the right to make a noise on one's land, a right limited by the requirements of reasonableness. It is an absolute right, and the fact that it was exercised maliciously could not make it a nuisance.

Another factor which may go towards rendering the defendant's conduct unreasonable is that he has not taken reasonable care to prevent the interference of which the plaintiff complains. If a factory emits smell or noise which could be circumvented by some reasonable outlay or trifling precaution by the defendant, this might well determine the court's mind that the interference caused by the smell or noise is unreasonable. On the other hand, the fact that the defendant has taken all reasonable care to prevent the nuisance arising does not necessarily exclude liability. Whether this makes private nuisance a tort of strict liability is discussed below.

Where the defendant is carrying out an activity which has public utility and has taken all reasonable care to prevent a

nuisance arising, it is a moot point whether the utility of his
activity is relevant in deciding on his liability in nuisance. It
may be that in such a case, a greater degree of interference is
justifiable than where the defendant's activity has no utility.
The point awaits authoritative resolution (*cf. Munro* v.
Southern Dairies (1955); *Bellew* v. *Cement Co.* (1948)). It is
certain that where a sufficient degree of interference has been
reached, nuisance will be established whatever the utility of
the defendant's conduct. In *Miller* v. *Jackson* (1977) the
public interest in recreational facilities did not excuse a
nuisance created by the playing of cricket and the hitting of
balls into the plaintiff's garden. But it partially explained the
Court of Appeal's refusal to issue an injunction. On this point
a later Court of Appeal decision has refused to follow it
(*Kennaway* v. *Thompson* (1980)).

Another factor which may influence the court is the temporary nature of the disturbance. In the case, for example, of
demolition or construction work on buildings, what might
appear an intolerable interference with the plaintiff's enjoyment of his land if committed in perpetuity may be justifiable
on the ground that the plaintiff need only suffer it for a short
time. The defendant must not however abuse the position
and must take reasonable steps to safeguard the plaintiff
from unnecessary interference. Thus in *Andreae* v. *Selfridge
& Co. Ltd.* (1938), the plaintiff, a hotel owner, recovered
damages from the defendants who in the course of demolition
operations carried out by them had subjected the plaintiff's
premises to an unnecessary amount of noise and dust.

Seriousness of the interference

In *Walter* v. *Selfe* (1851) Knight Bruce V.C. stated the test
to be whether the interference was an "inconvenience
materially interfering with the ordinary comfort physically
of human existence, not merely according to elegant or
dainty modes and habits of living, but according to plain and
sober and simple notions among the English people." Thus
stated it is clear that questions of degree must be resolved in
order to decide whether the interference was sufficiently
serious. The reports are full of examples of courts' decisions
on the seriousness of the interference but as in each case the
question is one of degree, these cases will not be examined
here (a good example is *Halsey* v. *Esso Petroleum Co. Ltd.*
(1961), in which Veale J. found proved against the defendants private nuisances by noise, smell and invasion of acid
smuts).

An unresolved question is whether the degree of interference is taken into account where the plaintiff has suffered
damage to his property (*contra*, Clerk & Lindsell, para. 1394;

pro, Street, p. 230). Such slight authority as there is supports Street (in *Halsey's* case Veale J. appeared to assess degree in the case of the damage caused by acid smuts; and in the Scottish case of *Watt* v. *Jamieson* (1954) the court found an insufficient interference where the defender had, by discharging a considerable amount of water periodically from his house through a gable common to his property and to that of the pursuer caused damage to the walls of the pursuer's house). Against this the exclusion of locality as a factor where the interference consists in damage to property justifies the opinion that degree is far less important where actual damage occurs. The justification for its having to be assessed at all may be that in every case of nuisance interference with the *enjoyment* of land must be established. Trivial damage not sufficient to support an action in nuisance is no doubt recoverable in negligence, in which as we have seen the degree of damage is irrelevant.

Locality of nuisance

In *St. Helens Smelting Co.* v. *Tipping* (1865) the plaintiff complained of a nuisance by fumes from the defendants' factory which had caused damage to his shrubs. The defendants argued that, since the locality in question was an industrial one, the plaintiff must put up with the invasion of industrial fumes into his land. The court held, however, that though locality was an important consideration where the alleged nuisance took the form of interference with the occupier's comfort and enjoyment of his land, it was irrelevant where physical damage to proerty had been occasioned. In the case of this factor, therefore, the distinction between physical damage to property and mere interference with the enjoyment of property is vital. An example of locality influencing the decision that the defendant's act was a nuisance is *Sturges* v. *Bridgman* (1879). In this case the plaintiff was a physician whose use of his consulting room at the foot of his garden was interfered with by noise from the defendant's machinery which he used in his business of confectioner. The court found that the interference was unreasonable in view of the fact that the area was one in which numerous medical practitioners had their consulting rooms.

The distinction between physical damage to property and interference with enjoyment

As we saw above, where the plaintiff can establish actual damage to his land or other property, it may be that he is not required to do more in order to show a sufficient degree of interference for nuisance. It is certain, also, that the locality of the alleged nuisance is then irrelevant. It therefore becomes

important to distinguish between what is actual damage for
the purposes of the tort and what is a mere interference with
the enjoyment of land. This distinction, though easy to state
and to appreciate, is not without difficulty. In the first
place, the courts insist on visible change in the property and
require such change to be palpable to the ordinary observer.
Scientific evidence of the damage is therefore excluded, presumably on the ground that if the plaintiff's damage can only
be detected by scientists the damage is not sufficiently substantial. But may not such serious damage as the undermining
of the foundations of the plaintiff's house be only capable of
being established by scientific evidence?

Damage to property includes damage to the land itself, to
buildings on the land, to plants and shrubs and to chattels on
the land (*Halsey* v. *Esso Petroleum Co. Ltd.* (1961)). It
appears to exclude financial damage such as loss of the plaintiff's business profits, or depreciation in the value of his land.
In the case of the latter this is not surprising. If this were
allowed to rank as damage to property, for the purpose of
the rule, the distinction would lose most of its foundation,
since in few cases in which there is a substantial interference
with the comforts of the occupier will his property retain its
value.

In some cases it may be uncertain whether the nuisance is
of the "physical damage" or "interference with enjoyment"
type. Nuisance by dust, which is arguably within either
category, appears to be treated by the courts as a mere interference with enjoyment (in *Andreae* v. *Selfridge*, locality was
considered a relevant factor in such a nuisance, but this
would not have been so, had the court found damage to
property).

Unusually sensitive plaintiffs

Where the plaintiff has put his land to some special use,
nuisance will not lie for interference with such use, if it is
shown that the amount of protection required goes beyond
that required by persons generally. So, in *Robinson* v. *Kilvert*
(1889) it was held that nuisance was not available where heat
rising from the defendant's flat damaged brown paper manufactured by the plaintiff on his premises. There was no allegation that the heat was excessive, and the process of manufacture was exceptionally sensitive to heat (but n.b. that
locality might operate to make such use "normal" rather
than special). Opinions clearly may differ as to what is a
special use. In *Bridlington Relay Ltd.* v. *Yorkshire Electricity
Board* (1965) the court said *obiter* that the reception of television by the private householder was a special use of land. In
the same case it was doubted *obiter* whether nuisance would

ever lie for interference with a purely recreational use of land. Both opinions are clearly debatable.

Once nuisance has been established, the plaintiff can recover for interference with a special use, even where such use is not foreseeable (because the victim is taken as the defendant finds him—*cf. McKinnon Industries Ltd.* v. *Walker* (1951)-damage to hypersensitive orchids recoverable).

Damage

The generally-held view that nuisance is actionable only on proof of damage must be understood in the sense that the plaintiff does not have to show physical damage to his property to succeed-any substantial interference with his enjoyment of his land will suffice. Even where the requirement of damage is stated in this way, it is difficult to reconcile certain cases on projections with it. In *Fay* v. *Prentice* (1845) the court held that nuisance was established in relation to a cornice on the defendant's building which projected over the plaintiff's land. The plaintiff attempted to prove actual damage to his land through rain-water dripping from the cornice but failed to do so. Nevertheless the defendant was held liable since damage was to be presumed from the mere overhanging of the cornice. This looks very like saying that in cases of this sort nuisance is actionable *per se*.

The plaintiff in private nuisance does not appear to be able to recover for his personal injuries. The explanation generally given for this, that private nuisance protects only the plaintiff's interest in the enjoyment of his land, does not seem adequate in a case where there is an interference with enjoyment leading to personal injury (where, for example, fumes cause physical illness). Certainly damage to chattels is recoverable in private nuisance, not only where there is a sufficient degree of interference to constitute nuisance apart from the damage to chattels (*Halsey* v. *Esso Petroleum Co.* (1961)), but also where there is an isolated escape producing damage to chattels (*British Celanese* v. *A.H. Hunt* (1969)). If the analogy between personal injury and damage to chattels is correct, the latter case would suggest that personal injury, even where produced by an isolated escape which gives rise to no other interference is actionable in nuisance.

Strict liability in nuisance

Differences between the torts of nuisance and negligence have already been noted. In this section, the question will be examined when, if ever, private nuisance operates as a tort of strict liability. Nuisance differs from negligence in that most nuisances are of a continuing nature whereas the damage complained of in negligence generally occurs once and for all.

This fact means that in the majority of nuisance actions the defendant either knows of the nuisance (in which case he may be regarded as intending it) or should be aware of it (in which case he is negligent). There appears to be no authority to indicate whether the plaintiff may recover damages in respect of interference from a continuing nuisance for the period during which the defendant neither knew nor ought have known of the interference. In the case of the continuing nuisance created by the defendant, the possibility of strict liability seems in any case remote.

Two other situations may give rise to the possibility of strict liability. The first is the case of the non-continuing nuisance, or nuisance created by the isolated escape. It is settled that an action in nuisance will lie for such an escape provided the escape is the result of a state of affairs of some permanency on the defendant's land (for example, defective electric wiring causing an escape of fire (*Spicer* v. *Smee* (1946). In *Kiddle* v. *City Business Properties* (*infra*, p. 187), the court assumed that liability for such an escape was strict, though this was *obiter*, the action failing because of the plaintiff's consent. Despite this decision, in those cases in which liability has been imposed for an isolated escape, the defendant has been negligent (*Midwood* v. *Manchester Corporation* (1905); *Spicer* v. *Smee* (1946); *Castle* v. *St. Augustine's Links* (1939); *British Celanese* v. *A.H. Hunt* (1969)).

The second situation in which strict liability is possible is that in which the defendant is held liable for a nuisance created by another. No case, however, points unequivocally to strict liability for such nuisance and the effect of the House of Lords decision in *Sedleigh-Denfield* v. *O'Callaghan* (1940) appears to be that negligence on the defendant's part is necessary.

One clear instance of strict liability in nuisance is provided by the rule in *Wringe* v. *Cohen* (1940) discussed below, at page 191. It seems likely, however, that this form of liability is in public nuisance only, and is based on the necessity of protecting users of the highway from the dangers from unsafe constructions on the highway.

The authority mainly relied on for regarding nuisance as a tort of strict liability, *Rapier* v. *London Tramways Company* (1893), does not carry the point. In that case the plaintiff complained of a nuisance by smell caused by overcrowding of horses in the defendants' stables. The court rejected the defendants' plea that they took all possible precautions. "If they cannot have 200 horses together, even where they take proper precautions, without committing a nuisance, all I can say is, they cannot have so many horses together" (*per* Lindley C.J.). In other words, given the existence of a sufficiently serious interference by smell, it was beside the point that the defendants might have done everything possible to prevent it.

Failure to remedy a nuisance

The liability of the occupier on whose land a nuisance has arisen without any act on his part has caused problems. Does he have to take steps to remove the nuisance, and, if so, what is the extent of his obligation? Although once complicated, the law on this point seems now relatively easy to state as the result of three decision of the higher courts. In *Sedleigh-Denfield* v. *O'Callaghan* (1940) the House of Lords held that an occupier of land who had knowledge of a nuisance created there by a trespasser had a duty, in so far as he was able, to remove it. If he failed to do so, he was liable for "continuing" the nuisance. It should be noted that removal of the nuisance involved the simple task of placing a grid over a culvert-pipe to prevent the accumulation of refuse, and the judgments of the House do not explore the extent of the occupier's obligations. In *Goldman* v. *Hargrave* (1967) the defendant, a landowner in Western Australia, discovered that a redgum tree on his land had caught fire. He decided to fell the tree and let the fire burn itself out, but a sudden change of wind caused the fire to spread to the plaintiff's neighbouring land and cause damage there. The fire could have been extinguished at minimal expense to the defendant by the use of water. Holding the defendant liable in nuisance, the Privy Council did so on the basis that liability in nuisance was in this situation indistinguishable from liability in negligence. A duty to take careful action to remove the nuisance had to exist. There was no rule that such duty could not exist in the case of conditions arising naturally on land. But whether the duty existed and the extent of it should take into account the means and resources of the particular occupier on whose land the nuisance has arisen. If, for example, the only way of removing the nuisance was through expensive works, no duty might exist at all, except to invite the assistance of neighbours in dealing with the problem. *Goldman* v. *Hargrave* has been followed by the Court of Appeal in *Leakey* v. *National Trust* (1980). The defendants owned and occupied land on which existed a hill known as the Burrow Mump. Because of its soil basis, it was "peculiarly liable to cracking and slipping as a result of weather." The defendants knew of this but had refused to undertake repairs, with the result that the plaintiff's land suffered damage on a number of occasions. The defendants were held liable in nuisance, their means being more than sufficient to undertake the necessary protective work.

It may now be assumed that the same principles determine

liability whether the nuisance arises naturally or through the
act of a third party. All three cases have concerned occupiers
with actual knowledge of the nuisance, but dicta in the *Sedleigh-Denfield* case suggested that the occupier may be liable
if he ought to have known of the nuisance.

It should be mentioned here that the former doubt that
existed about whether there was any obligation to remedy
nuisances arising naturally did not affect structural premises.
The occupier of such premises has a duty of care to persons
outside the premises to keep them in good repair (see *Payne*
v. *Rogers* (1794); (*St. Anne's Well Brewery* v. *Roberts* (1929)
(1929)). His liability for failure to do so lies in nuisance or
negligence.

Who can sue in nuisance?

The plaintiff in nuisance must, with rare exceptions (see
Newcastle-under-Lyme Corporation v. *Wolstanton Ltd.*
(1947)), show that he was in occupation of land affected by
the nuisances under some legal or equitable title. So the tenant
of land may sue in nuisance, but his wife and children resident
with him are excluded. Similar considerations no doubt will
determine the ability of a licensee with exclusive occupation
to sue as were indicated in connection with trespass to land
(*supra*, p. 46). A reversioner may sue if he can show that his
interest in the land has been affected (where, for example,
the nuisance has caused permanent damage to the land).

Who can be sued in nuisance?

(1) *Creation; authorisation of nuisance*

The person who creates a nuisance on land is liable although
he may have given up occupation of the land, and cannot
enter it in order to remove the nuisance. It is, however, an
unsettled question whether the creator must have been in
occupation or control of the land at the time of the creation.
A dictum of Devlin J. in *Southport Corporation* v. *Esso
Petroleum Co. Ltd.* (1953) supports the view that a nuisance
can be created by a licensee or even a trespasser. In principle
this seems correct.

The person who authorises the commission of a nuisance
by another is also liable for creating that nuisance. Where a
landlord let a field, knowing it was to be used as a lime
quarry, he was held liable for authorising the nuisance created
by working the quarry, since it was clear that such working
would inevitably create a nuisance (*Harris* v. *James* (1876)).

The principle of this case has been extended to the situation
where it is foreseeable that acts of nuisance may be committed
by other persons on one's land. In *Att.-Gen* v. *Stone* (1895),

the landowner was held liable in nuisance where he had permitted gypsies to camp on his land, and create a nuisance
there. On the other hand, where a local authority let property
to a family which was known by the authority to be a
"problem" family, it was held that the authority was not
liable for nuisance in respect of physical damage and noise
committed by the family, since the tenancy agreement
expressly prohibited the commission of a nuisance by the
tenant, and the authority could therefore not be said to have
authorised the nuisance (*Smith* v. *Scott* (1972)).

(2) *Continuation, adoption of nuisance*
The cases considered under the heading, "failure to
remedy a nuisance," are examples of liability for continuing a
nuisance. There may also be liability for continuing a nuisance
created by a predecessor in title, for example a negligent
failure to repair a defect in premises created by that predecessor (*St. Anne's Well Brewery* v. *Roberts*). "Adopting" a
nuisance is stronger than continuing it. The person who makes
personal use of a nuisance created by another person, or of
one created by natural forces, is liable for adopting the
nuisance.

(3) *Vicarious liability*
The employer is liable for nuisances created by his servant
or independent contractor on principles discussed below
(Chapter 20).

(4) *Lessor and lessee*
Special rules govern the respective liabilities of the lessor
and lessee for nuisances created by the condition of the demised premises. The rules have become complex, largely
because liability may exist under three separate heads, for
failure to repair arising from negligence, under section 4 of the
Defective Premises Act 1972, and under the strict liability imposed by the case of *Wringe* v. *Cohen* (1940). The latter case
imposes strict liability in respect of defects arising through
want of repair in premises situated on the highway. Its substance will be considered under public nuisance of which it
appears to be an example, but something must be said about
it in this connection.
The lessee as occupier must take reasonable care to keep
the premises in good repair. He is liable to persons outside
the premises in negligence if they are injured through his
failure to maintain the premises in good repair, and in negligence or private nuisance if they receive damage to property
as a result of the failure. He is also strictly liable
for defects arising from want of repair under the rule in

Wringe v. *Cohen*. The fact that the lessor has covenanted to
repair does not relieve the lessee of liability to third parties
who are not bound by the contract. On the other hand, this
would be a good case for a full indemnity of the lessee by the
lessor.

There are clearly many reasons of policy and equity for
also holding lessors liable in respect of nuisances on the
premises even though they do not occupy them. The lessor is
liable in the following circumstances:

(i) He is liable in nuisance to a third party if he knew or
ought to have known of the nuisance at the commencement
of the lease (*Brew Brothers Ltd.* v. *Snax (Ross) Ltd.* (1970).
In such a case he is not excused where he has taken a repairing covenant from the lessee - otherwise he could defeat his
obligations by letting to a man of straw.

(ii) He has a duty of care of "all persons who might reasonably be expected to be affected by defects in the state of the
premises" (which, of course, includes persons outside the
premises) under section 4 of the Defective Premises Act,
provided two conditions are fulfilled. The defect must be one
of which he knows or ought to know. He must have an obligation under the lease to carry out repairs. This requirement
is satisfied by express or implied provision in the lease itself,
by obligations to repair arising under statute (for example,
section 32 of the Housing Act 1961), or even where the lease
gives the lessor an express or implied right to enter and do
repairs.

(iii) He is strictly liable in nuisance under the rule in
Wringe v. *Cohen* for defects arising from want of repair in
premises situated on the highway, if he has covenanted to
repair (*Wringe* v. *Cohen*), or if he has reserved, expressly
(*Wilchick* v. *Marks and Silverstone* (1943) or impliedly (*Mint*
v. *Good* (1951), the right to enter and do repairs. The rule in
Wringe v. *Cohen* probably extends, also, to breach of the
obligation to repair imposed by section 32 of the Housing
Act 1961.

Defences to private nuisance

Prescription
The right to commit a nuisance may be acquired by prescription, that is, by 20 years' exercise of the acts constituting
the nuisance, provided that this exercise is *nec vi, nec clam,
nec precario* the owner of the servient estate (neither done
violently, nor secretly, nor by his permission). The content of
the nuisance must be capable of existing as an easement.
Whether it is or not is a question that the law of real

property decides. It was stated *obiter* in *Sturges* v. *Bridgman* (1879) that the right to cause vibrations could be acquired by prescription, but this is open to doubt (and see Megarry and Wade, *Law of Real Property* 4th ed. p. 880 where the case is criticised).

Conduct of the plaintiff

It is no defence that the plaintiff acquired the land with knowledge of the nuisance existing there, *i.e.* that he "came to the nuisance." In *Miller* v. *Jackson*, however, part of the reason for refusing the plaintiff an injunction was that she had come to the nuisance, since she knew about the playing of cricket on the field adjacent to her property before she acquired it. But if coming to the nuisance is to have this effect, the properties of many persons who have not come to the nuisance will be rendered less marketable. The fact that they have a remedy at law does not appear a good answer to this. As *Sturges* v. *Bridgman* illustrates, the fact that the nuisance only arises because the plaintiff has put his land to some particular use is not a defence, provided that this is not a special use which nuisance would not protect. Once the nuisance has been established, the normal duty in tort to take reasonable steps to mitigate damage no doubt applies. Could this be used to inhibit a person from putting his land to an otherwise reasonable use? The question was put in argument by Jenkins L.J. in *Davey* v. *Harrow Corporation* (*infra*, p. 196) whether he who sees encroaching roots on his land can build a house and wait for it to fall. It seems likely that the duty to mitigate operates to prevent this use of the plaintiff's land.

Consent may be a defence to nuisance. In *Kiddle* v. *City Business Properties Ltd.* (1942) it was held that the tenant of part of premises consents to run the risk of nuisances due to the condition of the premises retained by the landlord provided there is no negligence on the part of the latter; so in that case the plaintiff tenant could not succeed in nuisance when the landlord's gutter became flooded and water poured into the plaintiff's premises, damaging his stock.

Contributory negligence on the part of the plaintiff is an unlikely factor in private nuisance where the wrong complained of is an interference by the defendant with the plaintiff's enjoyment of his land. It is not contributory negligence on the plaintiff's part to "come to the nuisance," nor to put his land to the use with which the nuisance interferes. Where the nuisance consists of an isolated escape, contributory negligence of the plaintiff may well be relevant, since liability here is essentially one for negligence.

Statutory authority

Statutory authority is a defence where the statute imposes an obligation upon the defendant to act, the inevitable result of such action being to create a nuisance (even though the statute expressly preserves liability in nuisance). Where, however, the nuisance is created by negligence on the defendant's part, statutory authority is no defence to an action of nuisance, and the defendant has the onus of showing that he took due care (*Manchester Corporation* v. *Farnworth* (1930)). Where the statute is merely permissive rather than mandatory, it again is the law that statutory authority is a defence if the creation of the nuisance is the inevitable result of carrying out, without negligence, the statutory permission. Where wide, rather than specific, powers are conferred, they will generally be construed to mean that they must not be exercised so as to create a nuisance. Thus in *Metropolitan Asylum District* v. *Hill* (1881), it was held that a general power to construct hospitals did not authorise the construction of a smallpox hospital where it would create a nuisance. This was so even where the discretion to build the hospital in the particular place had been exercised in good faith and without abuse, and even where it might be impracticable to build such a hospital without creating a nuisance. Where a specific power is conferred, the courts will lean against an interpretation that other powers must be implied, even though this may seem to be a natural interference. Thus in *Allen* v. *Gulf Oil Refining Co.* (1980), Gulf Oil had been empowered by statute to acquire certain land for the purpose of establishing an oil refinery. The Court of Appeal held that this did not empower them to *operate* the oil refinery on that land so as to create a nuisance there.

Fires Prevention (Metropolis) Act 1774

The effect of this statute upon actions in nuisance will be considered in a later chapter.

Remoteness of damage in nuisance

In *The Wagon Mound* (No. 2) (1966) (*supra*) the Privy Council held that, in order to establish public nuisance, the plaintiff must show that the infringement of which he complains is a foreseeable consequence of the defendant's act. There seems little reason to doubt that the foreseeability test for deciding questions of remoteness of damage will apply also in private nuisance.

Remedies

Damages

The plaintiff is entitled to compensation for the damage he has suffered as a result of the nuisance. Thus he may recover for physical damage to his property, for depreciation in the value of his property, and for business loss resulting from the nuisance. In the case of the latter, the plaintiff may not recover the whole amount of the loss if the court considers that some loss would have been suffered even though no actionable nuisance had been committed. Thus in *Andreae* v. *Selfridge & Co. Ltd.* (1938) (*supra*), the court quantified the loss of custom which might have been expected had the defendant's interference been reasonable, and this amount was deducted from the total damages. The reasoning of this case would also seem to apply to depreciation of the plaintiff's land.

Where the nuisance is a continuing one, the award of damages in an action for the nuisance does not bar subsequent actions, since a cause of action in respect of the nuisance arises from day to day so long as it persists. It is otherwise when the nuisance is complete; then all the damages the plaintiff claims must be obtained in one action.

Injunction

It is common for the plaintiff in nuisance to ask for an injunction against further continuance of the nuisance by the defendant. This may be combined with a claim for damages. The injunction is a discretionary remedy and in some cases of actionable nuisance may be refused by the court (see, for example, *Att-Gen.* v. *Sheffield Gas Consumers* (1853) where an injunction was refused on the ground that the nuisance would only be repeated at long intervals and would on the occasion of each repetition be of short duration). The court may grant a *quia timet* injunction in cases where no nuisance has actually been committed by the defendant, but the commission of one by him in the future is reasonably apprehended by the plaintiff. The court may grant damages in lieu of a *quia timet* injunction by virtue of their jurisdiction under Lord Cairns' Act 1858, though this leads to the startling result that one who has suffered no tort may recover damages (*Leeds Industrial Co-operative* v. *Slack* (1929)).

PUBLIC NUISANCE

A public nuisance is, in the words of Romer L.J. in *Att-Gen. v. P.Y.A. Quarries* (1957):

"any nuisance 'which materially affects the reasonable comfort and convenience of life of a class of Her Majesty's subjects.' The sphere of the nuisance may be described generally as the 'neighbourhood'; but the question whether the local community within that sphere comprises a sufficient number of persons to constitute a class of the public is a question of fact in each case."

This definition makes it clear that no absolute line can be drawn between public and private nuisance so that overlapping between the two may exist. So, in the above case, a nuisance by the quarrying operations of the defendants which caused vibrations and dust to affect houses in the vicinity was held to be a public nuisance; clearly on the facts the individual householders could have sued in private nuisance. In fact an action in public nuisance by a private individual may not have succeeded on these facts (the actual action was brought by the Attorney-General—see below), because of the rule that the plaintiff in public nuisance must show damage to himself greater than that suffered by the public generally. Public nuisance is a common law crime, and is also restrainable at the instance of the Attorney-General by a civil proceeding known as a relator action. Apart from this there is the rule that one who suffers special damage as the result of the nuisance may sue in tort.

Basis of liability

The basis of liability in tort for public nuisance remains in doubt. In *The Wagon Mound* (No. 2) (*supra*, p. 96), the Privy Council found that, although the charterers committed the crime of public nuisance by discharging the oil into the harbour, their liability in tort depended upon whether they should have foreseen the risk of fire. Further, although Lord Reid appeared to regard the question of liability as turning on whether the fire was a foreseeable consequence of the nuisance, in deciding this question he took into account all the factors relevant to deciding whether a person has committed a breach of duty of care (*supra*, pp. 94-95). On this approach, it seems that the "wrongfulness" of the conduct involved in committing a public nuisance is irrelevant to the question of liability in the tort, and that in order to succeed the plaintiff must prove that the requirements of the tort of negligence are fulfilled.

In *Dymond* v. *Pearce* (1972) the Court of Appeal considered the liability in public nuisance of the defendant who had parked his lorry for several hours on one side of a dual carriageway. The plaintiff, a passenger on a motorcycle, had been injured when the motorcycle was driven into the back of the lorry. The lorry had been properly lighted and the street lighting was excellent. The Court of Appeal concluded that, although the defendant had committed a public nuisance through obstructing the highway by parking his lorry on it, he was not liable in tort to the plaintiff since the accident which occurred was not a foreseeable result of the nuisance but was due entirely to the fault of the driver of the motorcycle. The issue was treated by the Court of Appeal as one of causation, a different approach from that of the Privy Council in *The Wagon Mound* (No. 2) in which liability in public nuisance seems to be treated as identical with negligence, so that breach of a duty of care must first be established. Since the issue of causation was regarded as turning on foreseeability of danger arising from the nuisance, the practical difference between these approaches may be minimal. Two members of the Court of Appeal, however, thought that cases might occur in which it was possible to establish causal connection between the nuisance and later damage even where such damage was not a foreseeable result of the nuisance, so that the theoretical possibility of public nuisance operating as a tort of strict liability remains (though the tentative examples given by Sachs L.J. of supervening fog and unexplained rear light failure appear to be cases where the risk though slight is foreseeable).

Special cases of public nuisance

(1) *Buildings and projections on or over the highway*

The classic type of public nuisance is interference with the public right of passage along the highway, for example, by obstructing it, or by rendering passage unsafe by erecting dangerous structures on or near the highway. In *Wringe* v. *Cohen* (1940) the Court of Appeal held that "if owing to want of repair, premises on a highway become dangerous and therefore a nuisance, and a passer-by suffers damage by their collapse, the occupier, or the owner if he has undertaken the duty of repair, is answerable whether he knew or ought to have known of the danger of not." The defendant landlord was therefore held liable for the collapse of the demised premises, which he had covenanted to repair, on to the plaintiff's premises. It seems fairly certain that the ratio is limited to public nuisance, and that where there is no element of danger to the highway the decision does not apply. The strict liability laid down by the case is of a somewhat special kind, since it only applies where the danger arises through want of repair, not through some secret, unobservable process of nature, nor through the act of a trespasser (*Cushing* v. *Walker & Son Ltd.* (1941)—enemy action caused tile to fall

from roof). Liability is strict, therefore, only where the need
for repair accrues faster than a reasonable man would appreciate. It would follow logically from *Wringe* v. *Cohen* that the
same liability should exist in respect of defects arising from
want of repair in artificial constructions projecting over the
highway, and *Tarry* v. *Ashton* (1876), although the ratio of
this case is disputed, appears to impose such liability on the
occupier of the house to which the construction is attached.
In the case of projecting trees, however, there is no liability
for the fall of the tree in the absence of negligence, whether
the trees are planted by the defendant, by a predecessor in
title, or are self-sown (see *Noble* v. *Harrison* (1926); *Caminer*
v. *Northern and London Investment Trust* (1951); *British
Road Services* v. *Slater* (1964)).

(2) *Failure to maintain highway by highway authority*
      Although section 44 of the Highways Act 1959, imposed
an absolute obligation on the authority to maintain its highways, no action lay for breach of this obligation. Section 1
(1) of the Highways Act 1961 removed the immunity of the
highway authority for nonfeasance in relation to highways
thus rendering the authority open to an action for breach of
the statutory duty in section 44. Section 1 (2) of the 1961
Act provides the authority with the defence to such an action
that it took reasonable care. (Five criteria are provided by
section 1 (3) for deciding whether such care has been shown).
The plaintiff must therefore show an injury to himself resulting from a condition of the highway which made it dangerous
to traffic (which includes pedestrian traffic), and that this
condition was the result of a failure to maintain the highway.
If he succeeds in doing this, the authority is only excused if it
shows that it took reasonable care. It is not enough for it to
show that even if it had taken reasonable care the plaintiff
would have received his injury (*Griffiths* v. *Liverpool Corporation* (1967)-Diplock L.J. speculated that the defence of
inevitable accident might still be available to the authority
here). In *Haydon* v. *Kent C.C.* (1978) a majority of the Court
of Appeal thought that the word "maintain" in section 44 of
the 1959 Act was wider than "repair" and could extend to
the clearance of ice and snow from the public highway. The
standard of care of the authority must, however, take into
account such factors as the time available to it, its means and
the amount of clearance work overall it had to do.

Special damage
The plaintiff must show special damage over and above
that which is suffered by the public as a result of the nuisance. This may take the form of personal injury, damage to

property, or loss of business profits. It seems that special damage includes inconvenience provided this is greater than is suffered generally. So the plaintiff may recover for being delayed at a level-crossing (*Boyd* v. *G.N. Ry. Co.* (1895)—an Irish case) or for loss of sleep caused by vehicular noise (*Halsey* v. *Esso Petroleum Co. Ltd.* (1961)). The overall limit on the recovery of damage is that it must be a foreseeable consequence of the nuisance (*The Wagon Mound* (No. 2)).

Where nuisance to the highway is complained of, the special damage complained of by the plaintiff does not have to be sustained in his capacity as user of the highway. If, for example, the nuisance consists of an obstruction of the highway, the plaintiff may recover loss of profits due to the interference with the access of the public to his shop (*Wilkes* v. *Hungerford Market Co.* (1835)).

But where the plaintiff suffers personal injury, he must show that he suffered it on the highway or in the course of a slight deviation from it (*Jacobs* v. *L.C.C.* (1950)—plaintiff injured by falling over projection on forecourt of shop not forming part of the public footpath had no action in nuisance).

Relationship with private nuisance

Differences between the two forms of nuisance do exist. Thus prescription is no defence to an action based on public nuisance. In public nuisance it is possible to claim for personal injury. But the rule applicable to the two torts are generally speaking treated by the courts as similar, if not identical. The rules concerning liability for the nuisance, for example, do not appear to discriminate between public and private nuisance.

Statutory nuisances

The above account does not exhaust the rights of the citizen to complain of a nuisance. Various nuisances have been created by statute under which the individual may bring a complaint, though this is not quite the same thing as bringing a civil action for damages . Statutes deserving particular mention are the Public Health Act 1936, Part 31 (*cf. Coventry City Council* v. *Cartwright* (1975); *Salford City Council* v. *McNally* (1975), the Clean Air Act 1956 and the Noise Abatement Act 1960).

16. THE RULE IN RYLANDS v. FLETCHER

The decision in Rylands v. Fletcher

The facts in *Rylands* v. *Fletcher* (1868) were as follows:
the defendant, a millowner, employed independent contractors to build a reservoir on his land for the purpose of
supplying water for his mill. In the course of making excava-
tions upon the defendant's land, the contractors came upon
some disused mine-shafts which, unknown to them, connected with mines underneath adjoining land. The plaintiff
had taken a lease of this land in order to work the mines. The
contractors negligently failed to seal up these shafts and
when the reservoir was filled with water, the mines were
flooded.

The case came upon appeal to the Court of Exchequer
Chamber, where the plaintiff succeeded, and this decision
was upheld by the House of Lords. The ground for the
Exchequer Chamber's decision is contained in this extract
from the judgment of the court, delivered by Blackburn J.:

> "We think that the true rule of law is, that the person
> who for his own purposes brings on his lands and collects
> and keeps there anything likely to do mischief if it
> escapes, must keep it in at his peril, and if he does not
> do so is prima facie answerable for all the damage which
> is the natural consequence of its escape."

This sentence makes it clear that the defendant's liability
was personal, not a mere vicarious liability for the negligence
of his independent contractor, and that such liability was
strict.

In the House of Lords, a qualification was put by Lord
Cairns upon this statement of the rule by Blackburn J. to the
effect that the defendant was only liable if he brought the
thing on his land in the course of non-natural use of the land.
This qualification has been accepted by later cases as an
essential part of the rule.

The importance of Rylands v. Fletcher

At the time of the decision *Rylands* v. *Fletcher* did not
appear to lay down new law. In the course of his judgment,
Blackburn J. drew analogies from recognised cases of cattle-
trespass and nuisance to justify his decision. Thus he compared the plaintiff's case to that of the person whose grass or

corn was eaten by escaping cattle of his neighbour, or whose land was invaded by smells from his neighbour's alkali works or filth from his privy. He stressed that the defendant was liable for the escape of the thing even in the absence of any personal fault on his part but there is nothing to suggest that he thought there was anything new about this; such strict liability existed also in the examples which he gave of cattle-trespass and nuisance. What was important at the time about the decision in *Rylands* v. *Fletcher* was that a comprehensive rule was laid down governing the incidence of strict liability in the case of the escape of dangerous things from a man's land. This rule was accepted by the courts and applied by them in numerous cases following *Rylands* v. *Fletcher*, but it still remained doubtful whether the rule was merely a special branch of the law of nuisance or whether it established a separate tort. Now that the courts are moving away from the conception of nuisance as a tort of strict liability, it seems that a real difference may exist between it and *Rylands* v. *Fletcher*. The difference may be summed up by saying, that whereas in nuisance the defendant is only liable if as the result of a state of things he has created on his land an escape of something on to the plaintiff's land is foreseeable, in *Rylands* v. *Fletcher*, the defendant is liable even if the escape of the thing which he has brought on his land is totally unforeseeable.

At one time it was thought that the decision in *Rylands* v. *Fletcher* might have introduced into English law a general principle of strict liability for the carrying on of dangerous activities. In *Read* v. *J. Lyons & Co.* it was necessary to examine the question whether such a principle had been established. The defendants operated a munitions factory as agents of the Ministry of Supply. The plaintiff was an inspector appointed by the Ministry. In the course of her duties she was in the shell-filling shop in the factory when an explosion occurred in the shop causing her serious injuries. She based her claim against the defendants on *Rylands* v. *Fletcher*, making no assertion that the defendants had been negligent. The House of Lords held that she could not succeed under *Rylands* v. *Fletcher* because her injuries had been suffered *on the premises of the defendants;* the explosives had not escaped within the meaning of the rule. The case is important because it shows that the courts treat the rule in *Rylands* v. *Fletcher* like a statute, and have applied to it the literal rather than the mischief rule of statutory interpretation.

Requirements of the rule in Rylands v. Fletcher
(1) *The defendant must bring the thing on his land; he must do this for his own purposes*

The first point to note is that the defendant need not own the land on to which he has brought the thing. A temporary occupier of land such as a lessee, or a person physically present on the land but not in legal occupation of it such as a licensee, is equally within the scope of the rule (*Rainham Chemical Works Ltd.* v. *Belvedere Fish Guano Co.* (1921). In *Charing Cross Electricity Supply Co.* v. *Hydraulic Power Co.* (1914) the rule was applied to one who had a statutory right to lay electric cables under the highway. It has been decided that where the thing is brought on to the land by a licensee, the licensor is also liable under *Rylands* v. *Fletcher* at least where it is brought there for his purposes (*Rainham case, supra*). Whether this would be extended to an owner of land out of occupation is uncertain.

The requirement that the things must be brought on the land for the purposes of the defendant does not mean that it must benefit the defendant, according to *Smeaton* v. *Ilford Corporation* (1954), where it was stated *obiter* that a local authority which was under a statutory duty to collect sewage, collected it for its own purposes within the rule in *Rylands* v. *Fletcher*. On the other hand in *Dunne* v. *North Western Gas Board* (1964) it was doubted *obiter* whether the defendant Board which was under a statutory duty to supply gas collected it for its own purposes within the meaning of the rule. Doubtless a gratuitous depositee of the thing would be within the rule.

Where the thing is naturally present on the land of the defendant, he cannot be liable for its escape under *Rylands* v. *Fletcher*. The escape of such things as weeds, vermin, rocks, and flood-water is thus normally outside the scope of the rule (*Giles* v. *Walker* (1890); *Stearn* v. *Prentice Brothers Ltd.* (1919); *Pontardawe Rural District Council* v. *Moore-Gwyn* (1929); *Whalley* v. *Lancashire and Yorkshire Ry. Co.* (1884). Recent decisions, however, have established the possibility of an action in nuisances in such circumstances (*Davey* v. *Harrow Corporation* (1958); *Goodman* v. *Hargrave* (1967); *Leakey* v. *National Trust* (1980)).

(2) *The thing must be likely to do mischief if it escapes*

The rule does not require that the thing should be both likely to escape, and likely to do mischief on escaping. If this were the rule there would be little difference between *Rylands* v. *Fletcher* and negligence. Furthermore, the *Rylands* v. *Fletcher* "thing" need not be a thing dangerous in itself. The most harmless object may cause damage on escape from a man's land. The rule has been applied to a large class of objects including gas, electricity, explosives, the poisonous leaves of a tree, a flag pole, a revolving chair at a fair ground, and acid smuts from a factory (*Batcheller* v. *Tunbridge Wells Gas Co.* (1901); *National Telephone Co.* v. *Baker* (1893); *Rainham Chemical Works Ltd.* v. *Belevedere Fish Guano Co. Ltd.* (1921); *Crowhurst* v. *Amersham Burial Board* (1878); *Shiffman* v. *Order of St. John* (1936); *Hale* v. *Jennings Bros.* (1938); *Halsey* v. *Esso Petroleum Co. Ltd.* (1961)). The courts have established the sensible rule that the thing brought on the land need not be the thing which escapes. Thus a defendant who kept a motor-car in his garage with petrol in the tank was held liable for a fire which spread from the tank (*Musgrove* v. *Pandelis* (1919)). The rule has even been applied to human beings. In *Att-Gen.* v. *Corke* (1933) a land-owner who permitted caravan dwellers to camp on his land was held liable when they committed insanitary acts on neigh-bouring property. But this case would make the keepers of a prison strictly liable for the acts of escaping prisoners, a view that seems difficult to reconcile with the tenor of the speeches in *Home Office Co.* v. *Dorset Yacht Co.* (1970). In principle it seems that liability should exist only if the escape itself is foreseeable, and should, therefore, lie only in negli-gence or nuisance.

(3) *The defendant's use of the land must be non-natural*
Non-natural use of land was explained by the Privy Council in *Rickards* v. *Lothian* (1913) as follows:

> "it must be some special use bringing with it increased danger to others, and must not merely be the ordinary use of the land or such a use as is proper for the general benefit of the community."

Ordinary use cannot simply be equated with domestic or agricultural use; the working of mines is a natural use of land (*Rouse* v. *Gravelworks Ltd.* (1940)). Most domestic and agricultural uses of land are in fact outside the rule, for instance, the planting of trees (*Noble* v. *Harrison* (1926); but the planting of a poisonous tree is a non-natural use; *Crow-hurst* v. *Amersham Burial Board* (1878)). The lighting of a household fire (*Sochaki* v. *Sas* (1947)), the installation of water pipes for a water closet (*Rickards* v. *Lothian (supra)*), the wiring of a building for the supply of electric light (*Collingwood* v. *Home and Colonial Stores Ltd.* (1936)) are examples of natural use.
Non-natural use of land is constituted by such activites as the storage on the land in bulk of water, gas or electricity and the collection of sewage by a local authority (*Smeaton* v. *Ilford Corporation* (1954)). It is arguable that all the above examples should be saved by the second party of the Privy Council's definition as being for the general benefit of the

community. The opinion of certain members of the House of Lords (*e.g.* Viscount Simon in *Read* v. *Lyons* (1947)) that running a munitions factory in wartime was a natural use of land may be supported on this ground although this was not the reason advanced in the judgments. This is supported by the judgment of Lawton J. in *British Celanese* v. *A.H. Hunt* (1969) in which he held that the benefit derived by the community from the defendant's business of manfacturing electrical components made the use of land for this purpose and the storing of strips of metal foil thereon a natural use of the land. If this case is followed it seems to mean that the rule in *Rylands* v. *Fletcher* can only be applied in exceptional circumstances.

(4) *The thing must escape*
This requirement has already been illustrated by *Read* v. *Lyons.*

Status of the plaintiff: type of damage recoverable
In the judgment of Blackburn J. in *Rylands* v. *Fletcher*, there was no requirement that the thing should escape on to land in which the plaintiff had an interest. However, in *Read* v. *Lyons* (1947) the opinion was expressed by Lord MacMillan that the doctrine of *Rylands* v. *Fletcher* "derives from a conception of mutual duties of adjoining or neighbouring landowners." In *British Celanese* v. *A.H. Hunt*, however, Lawton J. refused to limit the rule in this way, holding that there is liability provided there is an escape from a place over which the defendant has occupation or control to a place which is outside his occupation or control. So, in that case, liability would have existed for the escape of strips of metal foil from the defendants' land which caused a power failure and consequent damage to machinery in the plaintiff's factory by being blown on to a power station owned and operated by a third party (but for the fact that there was natural use).

This divergence of opinion also affects the question of what damage is recoverable. If Lord Macmillan's view is correct, only damage to land occupied by the plaintiff and his chattels on that land is recoverable, by analogy with nuisance, *supra*, p. 181). On the view that the plaintiff need not be an adjoining landowner, it appears that every type of damage is recoverable provided it is not too remote. There is a certain amount of authority suggesting that the latter view is correct. Thus successful actions have been brought under *Rylands* v. *Fletcher* for personal injuries, both where the plaintiff had an interest in the land on to which there was an escape (*Hale* v. *Jennings Brothers* (1938)) and where he had no such interest (*Shiffman* v. *Order of St. John* (1936)). It is suggested that the basis of the cause of action under *Rylands* v. *Fletcher* is not the defendant's interference with the plaintiff's enjoyment of his land, but the fact that the plaintiff has suffered damage as the result of an escape of a noxious thing from the defendant's land.

It seems probable that the damage recoverable under the rule is limited to damage to person or property (*Cattle* v. *Stockton Waterworks Co.* (1875) in which it was held that purely pecuniary loss was not recoverable).

There must be proof of actual damage. This appears to mean actual physical damage to property (or possibly person), and to exclude a mere interference with the plaintiff's enjoyment of his land, such as would ground an action in nuisance. However in *Eastern & S.A. Telegraph Co.* v. *Cape Town Tramways Co.* (1902) such an interference was thought to be actionable in *Rylands* v. *Fletcher*, although the plaintiff's action failed because his use of the land was abnormal (*i.e.* receipt through a submarine cable of telegraphic messages, with which electricity from the defendants interfered). Where physical damage to the plaintiff's property is sustained only because of its weak condition, this appears to be recoverable (held *obiter* in *Hoare* v. *McAlpine* (1923)—no defence that damage to plaintiff's hotel through vibrations occurred because of its allegedly unstable condition).

Defences to Rylands v. Fletcher

(1) *Act of God*
The basis of this defence, and of act of a stranger, is that the defendant ought not to be held responsible for an escape which is caused by something beyond his control. They show that the obligation of the occupier is not an absolute one. Act of God has been defined as an operation of nature "which no human foresight can provide against, and of which human prudence is not bound to recognise the possibility." (*Tennent* v. *Earl of Glasgow* (1864)). The definition of act of God in terms of human foresight tends to assimilate *Rylands* v. *Fletcher* with negligence and this has been criticised (Goodhart, *Current Legal Problems* (1951) 177). However, not every event which is not reasonably foreseeable may constitute an act of God since the requirement is that the event be one against which no human foresight can provide. The defence was successful in *Nichols* v. *Marsland* (1876) where an extraordinary rainfall caused flooding from some artifical lakes on the defendant's land. It was rejected in very similar circumstances by the House of Lords in a Scottish case, *Greenock Corporation* v. *Caledonian Ry. Co.* (1917), on the

ground that rainfall, however heavy, is not sufficiently unprec-
edented to be an act of God.

(2) *Act of a stranger*

If the escape is caused by the unforeseeable act of a
stranger, and not by such persons as the occupier's servants,
independent contractors, members of his family and possibly
guests, this is a defence to *Rylands* v. *Fletcher*. Thus, where
the plaintiff's premises were flooded because an unidentified
person had turned on a water tap in the defendant's premises
there was no liability under the rule (*Rickards* v. *Lothian*
(1913)). Where the act of the stranger, whether it is deliberate or negligent, is foreseeable, there is liability under
Rylands v. *Fletcher*, although here it will normally co-exist
with negligence (*Perry* v. *Kendricks Transport Ltd.* (1956);
Hale v. *Jennings Brothers* (1938)). In relation to the defence
of act of a stranger, there seems greater force in Goodhart's
criticism that its effect is to assimilate *Rylands* v. *Fletcher*
with negligence. Even so, there may be a difference since it
may be that the burden of establishing that the stranger's act
was unforeseeable rests on the defendant, but the matter is
unclear (in *North Western Utilities* v. *London Guarantee &*
Accident Co. (1936), the Privy Council appeared to assume
that the defendant must prove both that the escape was due
to the act of a stranger and that this act was unforeseeable. In
Perry v. *Kendricks Transport* (1956) the Court of Appeal
regarded the burden of proof as resting on the plaintiff to
prove that it was foreseeable).

(3) *Contributory negligence*

This will no doubt constitute a defence in a suitable case,
though no actual authority exists.

(4) *Statutory authority*

It would be unusual if statute were expressly to authorise
the defendant to emit dangerous substances from his land.
On the other hand many statutory undertakings store such
substances on their land under statutory duties or powers. It
is a question of statutory interpretation whether the rule in
Rylands v. *Fletcher* applies to the activity (*Green* v. *Chelsea*
Waterworks Co. (1894)). Where the statute does not
mention the rule in *Rylands* v. *Fletcher*, the rule appears
to be that if the activity is carried out under a statutory *duty*
as opposed to a power, *Rylands* v. *Fletcher* is excluded
(*Dunne* v. *North Western Gas Board* (1964). This rule
applies even if, as in *Dunne's* case, the statute expressly preserves liability in nuisance. Where the activity is carried on
under a statutory *power*, *Rylands* v. *Fletcher* is available, at

least where the statute expressly preserves liability in nuisance (*Charing Cross* case, *supra*) and even though the activity does not exceed the terms of the power and there is no negligence. The effect of *Dunne* v. *North Western Gas Board* is to place outside the operation of the rule in *Rylands* v. *Fletcher* nationalised industries such as the various Area Gas and Electricity Boards, to whose activities the type of liability embodied in *Rylands* v. *Fletcher* would seem particularly appropriate. Thus, in *Pearson* v. *North Western Gas Board*, (1968), the plaintiff who suffered serious personal injuries and lost her husband and home as the result of an explosion which occurred underneath her house following an escape of gas from the defendants' gas main, was unable to recover in *Rylands* v. *Fletcher* because the defendants were under a statutory duty to supply the gas.

(b) *Consent of plaintiff*

Where there is an express consent by the plaintiff to the defendant's bringing the thing on his land, this will be a good defence to an action under *Rylands* v. *Fletcher* (*Att-Gen.* v. *Cory Brothers & Co.* (1921)). It is more normal for the plaintiff's consent to be implied from his conduct. The cases on implied consent fall into two categories. The first category is where the relationship of landlord and tenant exists between the defendant and the plaintiff. The tenant is deemed to consent to anything kept by the landlord on his premises at the time of the tenant's taking the lease. Thus a tenant of a shop in the defendant's theatre could not complain when his shop was flooded because of the freezing-up of a sprinkler system which the defendants had installed in their theatre to prevent fire (*Peters* v. *Prince of Wales Theatre Ltd.* (1943)).

The second category is where the plaintiff and defendant are occupants of different parts of the same building, there being no relationship of tenant and landlord between them, and something kept on the defendant's premises escapes into the premises of the plaintiff. Most of the cases concern the escape of water from premises on the upper storey to those on the lower. These cases have decided that the lower occupant cannot complain of such an escape (*Ross* v. *Fedden* (1872); *Anderson* v. *Oppenheimer* (1880)). The reason for this appears to be the same as in the case where the parties are landlord and tenant, namely, that the plaintiff must take the condition of the defendant's premises as he finds them at the time of taking occupation of his own premises, provided there is nothing unusually dangerous about their condition. This explanation involves the anomaly that consent is implied merely because the plaintiff has come to the nuisance. An alternative explanation, that the plaintiff consents to the presence on the defendant's premises of something from which he also obtains benefit, for example, a common water supply, is, however, insufficient to explain those cases where the plaintiff has failed to recover even though the element of benefit to himself is lacking (see, *e.g. Ross* v. *Fedden* (*supra*), where the presence of water in the building did not benefit the plaintiff).

Remoteness of damage

The rule as to remoteness of damage in *Rylands* v. *Fletcher* has never been authoritatively settled. Blackburn J. spoke of of liability for the "natural consequence" of the escape, which may suggest a similar rule to that laid down for negligence in *The Wagon Mound* (No. 1). On the other hand, it appeared to be assumed before the latter case that the Polemis rule of direct consequences would apply to *Rylands* v. *Fletcher* and the Privy Council in *The Wagon Mound* (No. 1) expressly excluded from the width of their remarks concerning remoteness the rule in *Rylands* v. *Fletcher*. It may be, therefore, that the direct consequences rule survives in relation to this tort.

Rylands v. Fletcher and other torts

In many cases *Rylands* v. *Fletcher* overlaps with other torts, especially nuisance and negligence. The differences between *Rylands* v. *Fletcher* and negligence are fairly obvious but it is quite common for both to be committed in a given case. Furthermore, where act of God or of a stranger is relied on as a defence, there is considerable administration because the availability of both defences turns on question of foreseeability.

The similarity between private nuisance and *Rylands* v. *Fletcher* has already been mentioned. Of course private nuisance can be committed in circumstances quite remote from *Rylands* v. *Fletcher*. Thus in many cases of nuisance there is no question of the defendant's bringing something on to his land. Where the case does concern the escape of something brought by the defendant on his land, the following are the more important differences between *Rylands* v. *Fletcher* and nuisance:

1. It is unlikely that *Rylands* v. *Fletcher* extends to the escape of intangibles such as noise. *Hoare & Co.* v. *McAlpine* (1923), in which liability was imposed for the escape of vibrations, has received criticism.

2. In *Rylands* v. *Fletcher* the defendant is liable if he has brought the thing on the land in the course of non-natural

use. In nuisance the requirement is that the defendant should have used the land unreasonably.

3. In *Rylands* v. *Fletcher* there is always liability for an escape caused by an independent contractor. In nuisance, liability is not invariably imposed for the acts of an independant contractor.

4. Other differences have already been mentioned. In *Rylands* v. *Fletcher* liability is strict and there is liability even for an unforeseeable escape. In nuisance it is probable that an unforeseeable escape is not actionable. *Rylands* v. *Fletcher* probably does not share the characteristics of private nuisance that the plaintiff must have an interest in land and that he cannot recover for personal injuries.

Status of Rylands v. Fletcher today

Rylands v. *Fletcher* is now recognised as a tort in itself, independent of, though resembling, nuisance. At one time it was thought that it might form the basis for the incorporation of a greater measure of strict liability into English law, either in the form of liability for hazardous activities, or in the form of enterprise liability. Neither of these developments has taken place. Instead by a series of restrictive decisions in particular the establishment of the defences of act of God, act of a stranger and statutory authority, the rule itself has become diminished in scope. Whether the rule in *Rylands* v. *Fletcher* should continue to survive in its present form will no doubt be a question which the Pearson Committee will consider.

17. LIABILITY FOR THE ESCAPE OF FIRE

In so far as there are any special principles applicable to liability for damage caused by fire, it is because of the former existence of a particular form of the action on the case by which a person was liable for the keeping of a fire on his land which spread to and caused damage on that of his neighbour. It is a disputed question whether liability was strict. In any event, the occupier was liable for the acts of members of his own household and of his servants, agents and guests (*Beaulieu* v. *Finglan* (1401)). In 1774 the Fires Prevention (Metropolis) Act afforded a protection to the occupier on whose land a fire "shall accidentally begin." The courts have given to this Act the interpretation that, unless there is intention or negligence in causing the fire to spread or the constituent requirements of a tort of strict liability are present, the occupier is not liable.

Negligence
Filliter v. *Phippard* (1847) decided that the Act of 1774 was no defence when the fire began through the defendant's negligence. Furthermore, the fact that the fire began accidentally and is allowed to spread through negligence does not make the statutory defence available (*Musgrove* v. *Pandelis* (1919)). In *Sochaki* v. *Sas* (1947) it was held that where a lodger left a fire in his room unattended and without a fire guard for a few hours, and the fire spread, *res ipsa loquitur* did not apply to prove his negligence. This case makes it clear that negligence must be proved even where the fire is intentionally lit, even though this appears to contradict the wording of the 1774 Act. The occupier is liable also for the negligence of his servant or independent contractor. The liability for the latter's negligence can no doubt be explained by the normal principles of the employer's liability for his contractor's actions (*infra*, p. 231) but in *Balfour* v. *Barty-King* (1957) was treated as a survival of the occupier's liability under the former action on the case.

Strict liability
There is liability where the conditions of liability under the rule in *Rylands* v. *Fletcher* are present and the Fires Prevention (Metropolis) Act will not provide a defence. In *Musgrove* v. *Pandelis* (1919) the defendant was held liable for

a fire which began in the carburettor of his car and spread to the plaintiff's premises, since the car was a *Rylands* v. *Fletcher* "object," and the keeping of a car in a garage was a non-natural use of land. The former finding seems artificial, the latter questionable. The approach in *Mason* v. *Levy Auto Parts* seems preferable. In that case the judge, in considering whether wooden stacking cases on the defendant's land were objects within the rule in *Rylands* v. *Fletcher*, thought that the correct test was whether they were likely to catch fire, and the fire spread to the plaintiff's land.

Other torts which may involve strict liability, for example, nuisance and breach of statutory duty, may be committed by means of fire. The existence of the form of strict liability embodied in the former action on the case has received recent confirmation in *H. & N. Emanuel* v. *G.L.C.* (1971). The defendants, the G.L.C., were held liable for a fire which spread from land they occupied to the premises of the plaintiff and caused damage there. The fire had been started by a contractor employed by the Ministry of Works which by the permission of the defendants had engaged him to clear the defendants' site of some houses. The fire had spread through the contractor's negligence. All three members of the Court of Appeal found the defendants liable under the *Beaulieu* v. *Finglam* principle, since the contractor was not a "stranger," and the defendants were therefore liable for his negligence, Lord Denning M.R. thought that the Ministry of Works contractor was not a stranger, because the occupier should have anticipated that he would light a fire and so had a duty to control him. This seems to involve reviving the old rule, under which liability may have been strict, and applying it in such a way that it is virtually equivalent to negligence.

18. LIABILITY FOR ANIMALS

INTRODUCTION

It is important to note that a person may be liable for the acts of his animals under the ordinary principles of torts not specifically associated with animals. Thus he may commit nuisance by keeping a noisy dog, or negligence by carelessly allowing his dog which he knows to be dangerous to mankind to escape and injure another person. The principles upon which a person will be held liable in negligence for the acts of his animals will be considered later in this chapter. First, however, it is necessary to consider those torts which are exclusively concerned with the acts of the defendant's animals, in particular, the common law torts of *scienter* liability and cattle-trespass. Both these torts embody a form of strict liability, but the reasons for the imposition of strict liability appear to differ. In the case of *scienter* liability, strict liability is imposed because the defendant has created a special risk by keeping a dangerous animal. In the case of cattle-trespass, strict liability is part of the give and take of an agricultural community in which each farmer expects to pay for the damage caused by his trespassing cattle irrespective of fault on his part. Both these torts had considerable obscurities attached to them and for this reason the law relating to liability for animals (including liability for negligence) was the subject of review by the Law Commission, the result of which was the Animals Act 1971, which came into force on October 1, 1971. Some understanding of the previous law is necessary in order that the legislative purpose behind this enactment be understood, and accordingly the pre-1971 rules relating to liability for animals will be described in outline.

STRICT LIABILITY AT COMMON LAW

The law previous to the Animals Act concerning strict liability for dangerous animals can be summed up in this way:

(i) A distinction was drawn between dangerous animals (*ferae naturae*) and harmless animals (*mansuetae naturae*). The former were animals belonging to a species regarded as in itself dangerous to mankind. The basis for classifying the species as *ferae naturae* was that its members had the propensity of attacking human beings. Examples of species actually held to be dangerous are the bear, elephant, zebra, leopard, and particular species of monkey. Animals which merely had the propensity to damage property (Colorado beetle, locust) were thus not *ferae naturae*. Nor it seems were animals dangerous to man through being likely to spread disease rather than through attacking him. The extent of the species' domestication, even outside the United Kingdom, was relevant evidence, along with the general characteristics of the species, as to whether it was *ferae naturae* (*McQuaker* v. *Goddard* (1940)—camel held to be *mansuetae naturae*). Once an animal was regarded as *ferae naturae*, however, it did not matter that in certain parts of the world it had been domesticated (*Behrens* v. *Bertram Mills Circus Ltd.* (1957)—Indian elephant held to be *ferae*). The keeper of an animal *ferae naturae* was strictly liable for damage done by it when acting in accordance with its dangerous characteristics.

All other animals, whether domesticated such as cattle and sheep, or wild such as rabbits were *mansuetae naturae*. In the case of an animal *mansuetae naturae*, the keeper was strictly liable for damage done by it if he knew that the particular animal had a propensity to attack human beings or other animals, and the animal acted in accordance with this propensite in causing damage. In the case of both types of animal, liability was enforced by the *scienter* action (*i.e.* the animal was kept by the defendant knowing of its dangerous nature) but only in the case of the animal *mansuetae naturae* was proof of *scienter* required.

(ii) In order to prove the *scienter*, the plaintiff had to prove that the particular animal had either attacked or shown a tendency to attack human beings or other animals, and that the defendant knew this. Proof that the animal had acted in accordance with a characteristic normally found in animals of that species was not enough (no liability for cat killing pigeons—*Buckle* v. *Holmes* (1926); nor for fillies committing playful attack on the plaintiff—*Fitzgerald* v. *Cooke Bourne (Farms)* (1964)). Proof of knowledge of the heightened aggressive tendencies of Alsatian dogs rather than dogs generally, or of bulls rather than cattle was equally insufficient. There was, however, some authority that knowledge of occasional characteristic aggressiveness by a particular species was enough (attack by bitch with pups—*Barnes* v. *Lucille Ltd.* (1907); by butting ram—*Jackson* v. *Smithson* (1846)).

(iii) The animal whether *ferae* or *mansuetae* had to be acting in accordance with the characteristic which led to its being regarded as dangerous in order to render its keeper liable; otherwise the damage was too remote, *Behrens* v.

Bertram Mills Circus (*supra*) showed that the risk created by an animal *ferae naturae* would not be defined narrowly (personal injuries inflicted by stampeding elephants recoverable even though they acted in fright). Further, provided the animal manifested its own dangerous tendency, any damage not excluded by the rules of remoteness was recoverable (for example damage to property inflicted by a dangerous bull attacking human being; or personal injury inflicted by a dog on the owner of another animal while attacking that animal in accordance with its known tendency (*cf. Whycherley* v. *Grave* (1967)). The rule might still operate restrictively. Damage to flocks caused by an animal *ferae naturae* does not seem to have been recoverable.

(iv) In order that the keeper should be liable, it was necessary to prove that the animal escaped from his control (*Rands* v. *McNeil* (1955)).

STRICT LIABILITY UNDER THE ANIMALS ACT 1971

Strict liability for dangerous animals is retained by the Animals Act. This may be welcomed, as well as the strengthening of strict liability by the abolition of the requirement of an escape by the animal and of the common law defences (if, in fact, such defences existed), of act of God and act of a third party. The Act has also left intact the common law position whereby some species of animals are conclusively presumed to be dangerous and some non-dangerous, so that in the case of the latter there is liability only where the particular animal has a known tendency to do harm. The basis chosen by the Act for classifying a species or a particular animal as dangerous seems questionable and likely to give rise to difficulties of interpretation.

Dangerous species

The dangerous species is defined by section 6 of the Act as follows: "A dangerous species is a species—

(a) which is not commonly domesticated in the British Islands; and
(b) whose fully grown animals normally have such characteristics that they are likely, unless restrained, to cause severe damage or that any damage they may cause is likely to be severe."

It may be noted that the dangerous species under this definition includes the animal such as the Colorado beetle which presents a danger only to property and also the animal likely to spread disease. Clause (a) of the definition shows that domestication of the species outside the British Isles is no longer relevant in determining whether it is dangerous. *McQuaker* v. *Goddard* is therefore no longer law of this point, although there would still be a question whether a camel came within section 6 (2) (*b*). The last words of section 6 (2) (*b*) cause difficulty. They require the court to take an animal not likely to cause damage, to imagine it causing damage, and to assess the probable consequences of such damage as severe or otherwise. No guidance is given by the Act as to the meaning of severe. The courts are therefore free to adopt a purely quantitative test, or perhaps to treat personal injuries as more severe than damage to property. In view of the tortuous nature of this definition it is legitimate to wonder why the Law Commission Report did not give examples of the type of animals envisaged by the words. Is a giraffe such an animal? There is no definition of species in the Act, although section 11 provides that the word includes sub-species or variety. The test is therefore presumably whether a sub-species or variety has characteristics which render it a dangerous sub-species or variety, in which case liability for its acts will be decided under section 2 (1). In *Cummings* v. *Grainger* (1977) the Court of Appeal held that an Alsatian guard dog fell within the provisions of section 2 (2). Such damage as it caused it was likely to cause within the particular circumstances of its acting as a guard dog, and these circumstances were known to its keeper (Lord Denning M.R. thought that only the severity of its bite was in the circumstances likely—but that also brought it within section 2 (2). The approach of the Court of Appeal meant that it did not have to answer the question whether the Alsatian was a variety of dog with dangerous characteristics bringing it within section 2 (1).

Liability for animals belonging to dangerous species

Section 2 (1) provides, "Where any damage is caused by an animal which belongs to a dangerous species, any person who is a keeper of the animal is liable for the damage, except as otherwise provided by this Act." It may be noted that, provided the animal has caused the damage, no further question of remoteness of damage can arise. If the animal is either likely to cause damage or if damage that it may cause is likely to be severe, it is irrelevant whether the damage it actually causes is the damage it is likely to cause or whether it is severe. While this simplifies the law it represents a considerable change.

Liability for animals not belonging to dangerous species

Section 2 (2) provides: "Where damage is caused by an animal which does not belong to a dangerous species, a keeper of the animal is liable for the damage, except as otherwise provided by this Act, if—

(*a*) the damage is of a kind which the animal, unless restrained, was likely to cause or which, if caused by the animal, was likely to be severe; and

(*b*) the likelihood of the damage or of its being severe was due to characteristics of the animal which are not normally found in animals of the same species or are not normally so found except at particular times or in particular circumstances; and

(*c*) those characteristics were known to that keeper or were at any time known to a person who at that time had charge of the animal as that keeper's servant or, where that keeper is the head of a household, were known to another keeper of the animal who is a member of that household and under the age of sixteen.''

The following points may be noted about this subsection:

1. It does not require the animal to inflict the damage in the course of an attack. It is thus wide enough to cover liability for infectious animals, for the animal which damages property without attacking it, and even for damage caused by a dog running into the highway and causing an accident.

2. Subsection (2) (*b*) appears to enact the common law position concerning domestic animals which cause damage through acting in a manner characteristic of the species. There is, therefore, still no strict liability for damage caused by a bull, unless that particular bull was known to have a propensity to cause that particular damage, or (*semble*) the bull was manifesting periodic sexual aggressiveness.

3. The difficulties of construing the phrase, "if caused by the animal, was likely to be severe," have already been considered in connection with the dangerous species (although the wording of section 6 is slightly different). The plaintiff's burden is increased within the context of this subsection because he must prove that the defendant knows this to be a characteristic of the particular animal. Where the animal acts in accordance with a characteristic of the species which is found only at a particular time or in particular circumstances, it is not clear whether the knowledge required of the defendant is of the characteristic of the species or of the particular animal involved.

4. The damage actually caused by the animal must be such that it is likely to cause it, or that if it did cause it, it would be likely to be severe. If the damage is of the latter type, it does not matter that it is not actually severe.

5. Subsection (*c*) is based upon the common law rules

which determine whether the knowledge of one person is treated as that of its keeper.

No necessity for escape

Neither subsection requires the animal to escape from the defendant's control in order that liability be established and the Law Commission Report makes it clear that this effect was intended. *Rands* v. *McNeil* (*supra*, p. 208) is therefore no longer law.

Liability for damage done by dogs

Section 3 of the Animals Act which replaces liability under the Dogs Acts of 1906 and 1928 provides that where a dog causes damage by killing or injuring livestock (for the definition of this, see below, p. 214), any person who is a keeper of the dog is liable for the damage except as otherwise provided by the Act. The defences in section 5 of the Act therefore apply to this form of liability. Section 3 maintains the principle of the Dogs Acts that there is liability even in the absence of *scienter* or negligence.

Section 9 provides a defence to an action for the killing of a dog which worries livestock.

Defences to actions brought under section 2 and section 3

Section 5 (1) and (2) establish the defences that the plaintiff was wholly at fault and that the plaintiff voluntarily accepted the risk. Section 6 (5) preserves the latter defence even where the risk is incidental to the plaintiff's employment. Section 10 of the Act makes it clear that the apportionment provisions of the Law Reform (Contributory Negligence) Act 1945 are applicable where the plaintiff has been contributorily negligent.

Section 5 (3) deals with the problem of whether it is a defence to an action based on section 2 that the injury was inflicted by the defendant's animal while the plaintiff was trespassing on the defendant's land. Section 5 (3) allows the defence if (a) the animal was not kept on the land for the protection of persons or property, or (b) the animal was kept there for the protection of persons or property and keeping it there for that purpose was reasonable. *Cummings* v. *Grainger* illustrates the operation of the defences under section 5 (2) and (3). In that case the plaintiff was savaged by an Alsatian guard dog in the defendant's scrap-metal yard. The plaintiff had followed her friend into the yard, the friend having gone in to collect his car. The friend was a licensee but the plaintiff was a trespasser. The yard had warning notices outside it, and the plaintiff testified that she knew, and was frightened of, the dog. The Court of Appeal held that the defence under section 5 (2) applied since the plaintiff had willingly accepted the risk of the dog's attack. The court's language suggests that any form of voluntary entry with knowledge of the risk is enough to establish the defence. It was also held that the keeping of the dog for the protection of property was reasonable, so that the defence under section 5 (3) applied. This rather surprising attitude to the question of reasonableness may change in the light of the Guard Dogs Act 1975, which makes it a criminal offence to keep a guard dog roaming free without a handler.

The omission of the defences of act of God and of a third party from section 5 means that these defences are not available to an action under section 2.

Keeper

Liability under section 2 of the Act is imposed upon the keeper of the animal. He is defined by section 6 of the Act as the person who owns the animal or has it in his possession; or is the head of a household of which a member under 16 owns the animal or has it in his possession. Section 6 also deals with the problem of wild animals in captivity which have escaped and returned to their wild state (particularly those indigenous to this country) by providing that the keeper of the animal at the time of its escape continues to be its keeper until another person becomes its keeper under the provisions mentioned above.

Cattle-trespass

Liability at common law

Cattle-trespass was committed at common law by one whose animals of the class of cattle entered land of the plaintiff, where the plaintiff did not permit the entry. Exceptionally it could be committed without unauthorised entry if cattle lawfully on land consumed or otherwise destroyed chattels belonging to the plaintiff on that land, for example, crops after severance from the land. "Cattle" were bulls, cows, sheep, goats, pigs, horses, asses and poultry (but not dogs and cats). The following were the chief features of liability at common law for cattle-trespass:

(i) Liability for cattle-trespass was strict.

(ii) It was actionable *per se* without proof of damage.

(iii) Liability was imposed upon the person in possession of the cattle at the time of the trespass. The owner out of possession seems not to have been liable.

(iv) The plaintiff in an action of cattle-trespass normally had to be the possessor of the land, but an exception to this

had been recognised in the case of the grantee of the crops of
the land, or of an exclusive right of pasture over the land. In
the case of damage done to a chattel on the land the plaintiff
had to be possessor of the chattel.

(v) Damages in cattle-trespass were not limited to damage
to the land itself. The courts also allowed as damages consequential upon the trespass personal injuries (as in *Wormald* v.
Cole (1954)) and damage suffered by the plaintiffs when
their train was derailed by the defendant's trespassing cattle
(*Cooper* v. *Ry. Executive (Southern Region)* (1953)).

(vi) There is little authority upon defences to cattle-trespass
and in view of the regulation of the general defences to the
strict liability in the Animals Act it is not proposed to
examine it. But two special defences must be mentioned. It
was a defence to an action of cattle-trespass that the animal
escaped from the highway into the plaintiff's land and that
the defendant was not negligent. This defence was available
whether the animal had itself escaped on to the highway or
had been taken there by the defendant. But a defendant
might be negligent in failing to remove his animals from the
plaintiff's land after they had entered it from the highway. It
is uncertain whether this liability was in negligence or
cattle-trespass. It is also uncertain whether the plaintiff's land
had to adjoin the highway in order that the defence be available. The better view appears to be that there was no such
limitation, since if the animal could gain access to the land
from the highway, that land ought to be regarded as sharing
the risks of such entry.

It was also a defence that the entry occurred because of
the plaintiff's failure to perform a duty owed to the defendant
to fence his land.

Liability under the Animals Act
The Act makes a few important changes in the law relating
to cattle-trespass but the general principles underlying the
tort are left undisturbed. Thus strict liability for cattle-trespass
is retained because of the necessity of providing a clear rule
whereby the losses caused by marauding cattle can be automatically adjusted. But consequential loss in the form of
personal injuries can no longer be recovered in cattle-trespass
since such loss cannot be regarded as part of the give and take
of the agricultural community. In order to establish liability
for personal injuries caused by invading cattle it will therefore
normally be essential to establish negligence unless the conditions of section 2 of the Act apply. The Act, however,
makes it possible for the occupier to recover for damage to
chattels on the land which are in his ownership or possession.
Section 4 (1) (*a*) does not allow the recovery in cattle-trespass

of damages where the person who suffers the damage does not own or occupy the land, and this exceptional case of cattle-trespass has therefore disappeared.

The following is a summary of the changes effected by the Act:

Livestock. Section 4 of the Act refers to livestock which is defined in section 11 to mean any animals of the bovine species, horses, asses, mules, hinnies, sheep, pigs, goats and deer not in the wild state. Livestock within the meaning of the Act appears to differ from the common law interpretation of cattle including deer and excluding poultry.

Damage. The tort is no longer actionable *per se*; damage must be proved arising from the entry. This may take the form of damage to the land itself or to chattels on the land owned or possessed by the occupier. Section 4 (1) (*b*) also allows the recovery of expenses reasonably incurred in keeping the livestock while it cannot be restored to the person to whom it belongs or while it is detained in pursuance of section 7 of the Act (*infra*, p. 214) or in ascertaining to whom it belongs, from the person to whom the livestock belongs.

Who is liable. The person liable is the person to whom the livestock belongs but section 4 (2) provides that for the purposes of section 4 livestock belongs to the person in whose possession it is. The owner out of possession of the livestock is therefore not liable.

Who may sue. The person who may claim is the person who has ownership of or who is in occupation of the land, but if the claim is for damage to chattels on the land such person must also show that he has ownership or possession of the chattels. Under the section therefore an owner out of possession of the land may now claim, but it seems that he will only be able to claim where his reversionary interest in the land is damaged (unless his claim is for damage to his chattels).

Defences. Section 5 recognises three defences to liability under section 4. Section 5 (1) excuses the defendant where the damage is due wholly to the fault of the plaintiff. Section 5 (5) confirms the special defence formerly available to actions of cattle-trespass that the animal strayed from a highway which it was lawfully using (the subsection does not make it a requirement of the defence that the plaintiff's land should adjoin the highway). Section 5 (6) confirms and extends the defence that the entry would not have happened but for the breach by the plaintiff of his duty to fence his land. At common law it appeared that the defence was available only where the duty to fence was owed by the plaintiff to the defendant. This limitation does not appear in the subsection. Further, the defence is available where there is a breach by any person having an interest in the land, for example, to the occupier of land when the breach of the duty to fence is committed by the owner out of possession. These appear to be the only defences possible to liability under section 4, but there may be also a reduction for the plaintiff's contributory negligence.

New remedy. Section 7 abolishes the old right of distress damage feasant with regard to animals (as to objects see *supra*, p. 56), and replaces it with a new right of the occupier of land to detain any livestock which strays on to that land.

LIABILITY FOR NEGLIGENCE

There may be liability for negligence both in the case of dangerous and non-dangerous animals under the existing law. Negligence is particularly important however in the case of animals which are of the class of harmless animals and which individually do not have dangerous characteristics known to their keeper. Several cases have established that there might be liability for failure to control such animals when they were taken by a person in control of them on the highway (*e.g. Deen* v. *Davis* (1935); *Aldham* v. *United Dairies Ltd.* (1940); *Gomberg* v. *Smith* (1963)). There might also be liability in negligence if such animals caused damage to other persons on the land of their keeper. There was however no duty of care, in the absence of "special circumstances" to prevent harmless animals from straying on to the highway (so held by the House of Lords in *Searle* v. *Wallbank* (1947).

Impressed by the evidence about accidents on the highway caused by straying animals, the Law Commission recommended the abolition of the rule in *Searle* v. *Wallbank.* The abolition of the rule is accomplished by section 8 (1). Now, therefore, an occupier of land owes a duty of care in relation to the straying of so-called harmless animals from his land on to the highway. But under section 8 (2), no breach of duty is committed by a person by reason only of the fact that he has placed animals on land if: (a) the land is common land, or is land situated in an area where fencing is not customary or is a town or village green; and (b) he had a right to place animals on that land (*cf. Davies* v. *Davies* (1975))—right to place animals on common land included a licence to place animals on such land given by the person with the right to place them there.

19. BREACH OF STATUTORY DUTY

The term, "breach of statutory duty," refers particularly to those cases where a civil action in tort is available for breach of a statute which appears to impose purely criminal penalties. Whether such action is available has been based by the courts upon an inference from the words of the statute of legislative intent, but as will be seen shortly such intent appears largely a legal fiction. As a tort, breach of statutory duty is something of a hybrid. In many cases, the behaviour which constitutes it amounts also to common law negligence, and for this reason it is sometimes called statutory negligence. This is particularly so in the case of industrial safety legislation passed for the protection of workmen in factories, which is generally construed as conferring a civil action on a workman injured by its breach. The statute here serves the useful purpose of particularising the standard of reasonable conduct expected of his employer, so that the workman does not need to show that the employer acted unreasonably. But breach of statutory duty, even in those cases where the statute merely defines the employer's obligation to take reasonable care, is usually more than mere statutory negligence. If the statutory duty is construed as absolute, a non-negligent failure to comply with it will be a breach. Further, where the statute imposes an obligation which would not be required of the employer to discharge his duty of care, liability is in every sense strict. Only where the effect of the statute is to impose an obligation upon the defendant merely to take reasonable care to do that which the ordinary law of negligence would in any case compel him to do can breach of statutory duty be entirely equated with negligence.

Requirements of the tort

The plaintiff in an action for breach of statutory duty must show: (i) that the statute was intended by Parliament to confer a civil remedy for its breach; (ii) that the statute imposed a duty upon the defendant; (iii) that the defendant was in breach of this duty; (iv) that the plaintiff suffered harm or damage which was not too remote a consequence of the breach of duty.

Was the statute intended to confer a right of action in tort?

The difficulties of extracting any consistent approach from

the decisions of the courts on this matter may perhaps be
illustrated by indicating that though actions in tort are allowed
for breach of factory legislation, the same is not true of
breach of road traffic regulations (*Phillips* v. *Britannia Hygienic
Laundry* (1923); *Clarke* v. *Brims* (1947); but *cf. Kelly* v.
W.R.N. Contracting (1968) in which an action for breach of a
parking regulation was allowed); or by comparing *Read* v.
Croydon Corporation (1938), in which an action was
allowed for breach of a statutory obligation to supply whole-
some drinking water, with *Square* v. *Model Farms Dairies Ltd.*
(1939) which held that the supply of infected bottled milk in
breach of statutory duty gave no civil action. One suggested
criterion is that the statutory action would be "unusual" (*cf.
Atkinson* v. *Newcastle and Gateshead Waterworks Co.* (1877)
—no action for breach of statutory obligation to maintain
water pressure so that fire brigade could not extinguish fire;
and *Cutler* v. *Wandsworth Stadium Ltd.* (1949)—no civil
action for breach of statutory obligation to admit bookmaker
to dog track). But in *Monk* v. *Warbey* (1935) a successful
action was brought against a motorist for breach of his statutory duty to insure his car. It is arguable that if common
law remedies exist, this is a reason for not adding to them—it
seems unlikely that the Theft Act 1968 or the Trade Descrip-
tions Act 1968 would be construed as conferring civil
remedies. Other suggested criteria for finding that a civil
remedy is intended are that the statute imposes no criminal
or other sanction (*Reffell* v. *Surrey C.C.* (1964); *Booth* v.
National Enterprise Board (1978); *Thornton* v. *Kirklees*
(1979)); that the statutory sanction is derisory or inadequate
(*cf. Groves* v. *Wimborne* (1898) on derisory penalties; *Meade*
v. *London Borough of Haringey* (1979) on the "inadequacy"
of the statutory remedy of complaint to a Minister); or that
the statute is for the protection of a recognised class of
persons. The first two suggestions can clearly have no general
validity. The third explains some cases but not others. For
example, although employees are a recognisable class of
persons for whose benefit a civil action has been found to be
conferred by safety legislation in factories and workplaces,
the courts generally refuse to extend a similar benefit to road
users who have suffered from breach of traffic regulations,
(*Phillips* v. *Britannia Hygienic Laundry* (1923)); or to
tenants subject to the protection of the Rent Acts for breach
of the latter (*McCall* v. *Abelesz* (1976)). The more general
the duty and the more elevated the level at which it is
imposed the less likely is the court to find a civil action to be
conferred (but *cf. Booth* v. *National Enterprise Board* (1978)
in which the court admitted the possibility of statutory
government directives to the National Enterprise Board giving

rise to civil actions). Although the decision is sometimes reached by a close examination of the relevant statute (*cf. McCall* v. *Abelesz*), very often the question looks to turn on matters of policy as much as of construction.

Statutory duty laid upon the defendant
The statute must imposed a duty rather than a power upon the defendant. The duty must be imposed upon the defendant (*Harrison* v. *N.C.B.* (1951)—duties imposed by Coal Mines Act 1911 in relation to shot-firing were imposed upon shot-firers rather than upon defendant employer).

Breach of duty
The defendant must be in breach of his statutory duty. Whether he is or not will raise, *inter alia*, a question of statutory interpretation. The court must decide whether the duty is a strict one, or whether it is one of reasonable care only. In *Galashiels Gas Co.* v. *Miller* (1949) it was held that the defendants' statutory duty to maintain a lift in good repair was strict, so that where the lift fell to the bottom of the lift-shaft, injuring the plaintiff, there was liability even though no negligence by the defendants could be established. In *John Summers* v. *Frost* (1955) it was held that the duty to securely fence "every dangerous part of any machinery" was a strict one, so that the employers were in breach of this duty in failing to fence a grindstone, even though the effect of fencing the machine was to make it unusable. On the other hand, the duty arising under section 48 (1) of the Mines and Quarries Act 1954, to take "such steps . . . as may be necessary for keeping the road or working-place secure" is a duty based upon foreseeability of danger and is therefore one of reasonable care. (*Robson* v. *National Coal Board* (1968)). The wording "so far as reasonably practicable" qualifying the employer's obligation also means that the obligation differs little if at all from the employer's common law duty (*Levesley* v. *Thomas Firth* (1953)). The court must also be satisfied that the statutory duty, as precisely interpreted, applies to the case before it. Thus the plaintiff in *Eaves* v. *Morris Motors* (1961) failed to show a breach of section 14 (1) of the Factories Act 1937, since that section only requires fencing of dangerous parts of machinery and not of materials that are inserted into machinery. Similarly, in *British Railways Board* v. *Liptrot* (1969) it was held that there is no duty to fence when what is dangerous is the machine as a whole rather than its particular parts—otherwise there would be a duty to fence vehicles.

Plaintiff must be a person protected by the statute

In general, employees of persons other than the employer subject to the statutory duty, and self-employed persons have been held to be outside the benefit of statutory duties and regulations for the purpose of suing in breach of statutory duty. Thus in *Hartley* v. *Mayoh & Co.* (1954) the plaintiff, a fireman, was electrocuted in the course of fighting a fire at the defendants' factory, because of the defendants' breach of statutory regulations. It was held that he could not recover from the defendants for breach of statutory duty because he was not a "person employed" in the factory within the meaning of the regulation (*cf. Herbert* v. *Harold Shaw* (1959); *Kearney* v. *Eric Waller* (1967)). Something may turn upon the interpretation of the statute in question. Thus it has been held that the phrase "any person" in section 29 of the Factories Act 1961, extends to all those who enter a factory to work for the purposes of the factory, and that, therefore, a window-cleaner who was employed as an independent contractor by the factory owner came within the ambit of the duty (*Wigley* v. *British Vinegars Ltd.* (1964)). Unless the wording of the statute appears clearly to envisage it, however, the courts will normally be reluctant to extend the benefit of statutory duties to outsiders. This may be explained either on the ground that courts believe in class benefit as the basis for allowing an action for breach of statutory duty, or as part of their general reluctance to impose duties on employers in respect of the safety of persons other than their own employees (*cf.* employers' common law liability, *supra*, p. 170).

On the other hand, if the plaintiff is within the protected class, it does not matter that he is acting outside the course of his employment (*Smith* v. *Supreme Wood Pulp Co.* (1968)), nor that he is trespassing upon his employer's machinery (*Uddin* v. *Associated Portland Cement Manu— facturers* (1965)) or premises *(Wedgewood* v. *Post Office* (1973)). Where such trespass shows an unreasonable failure to look after his own safety by the plaintiff, there will be a deduction for contributory negligence (to the extent of 80 per cent in *Uddin*, though in *Westwood* no deduction was made since no danger was foreseeable to the trespassing employee).

Damage

Normally the statute will be interpreted as conferring a right of action on the plaintiff only when he has sustained actual damage. But *Ashby* v. *White* (1703) shows that a statute may confer a right of action even without proof of actual damage (interference with the plaintiff's right to vote was

actionable *per se*). On the other hand, it appears likely that
the plaintiff must show some injury or grievance over and
above that suffered by the public generally. The action does
not serve as a private means of enforcing the criminal law (*cf.
Gouriet* v. *Union of Postal Workers* (1976)). The plaintiff
must show that the damage he suffered was that against
which the statutory duty was intended to guard and also that
it was not too remote a result of the breach of statutory duty.
These requirements must be examined in turn.

(1) *The harm suffered by the plaintiff must be that contemplated by the statute*

In *Gorris* v. *Scott* (1874) the defendant, who was trans-
porting the plaintiff's sheep on his ship, infringed a statutory
order under which animals on board ship were to be divided
into pens. The sheep were washed overboard and drowned
and it was found that this would not have occurred had they
been penned. The plaintiff's action for breach of statutory
duty failed because the purpose of the statute was to prevent
the spread of disease rather than to prevent the loss of animals
in the manner that occurred. It is necessary to distinguish the
rule in *Gorris* v. *Scott* from the rules relating to remoteness
of damage, since the loss the plaintiff suffered in that case
was clearly a foreseeable result of the defendant's breach of
duty. This was recognised by the House of Lords in *Close* v.
Steel Co. of Wales Ltd. (1962). An injury to the plaintiff
through fragments of a shattered drill being flung against him
would have been avoided but for the defendants' breach of
statutory duty in failing to fence the drill. The House of
Lords held that, even had the injury been foreseeable, the
plaintiff would not have recovered because the purpose of
the statute was to prevent the machine operator's body
coming into contact with the machine, rather than to prevent
the risk of fragments being flung out. These cases emphasise a
judicial tendency to confine breach of statutory duty within
narrow limits. A different approach arose in *Donaghey* v.
Boulton & Paul (1968) (plaintiff's fall through hole in roof
which would have been avoided by the provision of crawling
boards which defendants in breach of statutory duty failed to
supply was actionable though chief purpose of crawling
boards was to prevent falls through fragile material in the
roof).

(2) *That the damage was not too remote*

The onus of showing that the damage was not too remote
a result of the breach rests on the plaintiff (*Bonnington
Castings Ltd.* v. *Wardlaw* (1956)). The normal rule of
remoteness of damage applies to this tort so that the harm

the plaintiff suffers must be a foreseeable consequence of the breach of duty. In *Millard* v. *Serck Tubes* (1969) the plaintiff's arm was caught in a machine which the defendants had in breach of statutory duty failed to fence. Although the way in which the plaintiff's arm became caught was unforeseeable, the defendants were held liable to him in breach of statutory duty. The result of the case would undoubtedly have been the same had the action been one for common law negligence. Where the precise harm against which the duty was intended to provide a safeguard occurs, the defendant cannot successfully argue that it occurred in an unforeseeable way (*cf. Hughes* v. *Lord Advocate* (1963), *supra*, p. 111). The principle has been pushed a little further in cases in which the plaintiff's injuries have been held not too remote a result of the breach although the way in which he received them is unexplained (*Thurogood* v. *Van Den Berghs and Jurgens* (1951). *Allen* v. *Aeroplane and Motor Aluminium Castings* (1965), discussed *supra*, p. 141).

The plaintiff must also establish casual connection between his injury and the breach (*McWilliams* v. *Arrol & Co.* (1962)). There it was held that a failure to provide safety belts in breach of statutory duty was not actionable because there was evidence that the general practice of workmen on the site was not to wear the belts and the plaintiff could not show on the balance of probabilities that he would have been an exception.

Defences to the action

Volenti non fit injuria

For reasons of public policy this defence is not available to an employer in suits against him by his workmen, since he should not be able to escape from his statutory obligations by obtaining his workman's consent. The defence is, however, available where the employer is being sued on the ground of his vicarious liability for a breach of statutory duty imposed upon and committed by his workman, provided that the workman who commits the breach is not of superior rank to and in receipt of habitual obedience from the plaintiff (*I.C.I.* v. *Shatwell* (1965)—two workmen ignored statutory safety regulations imposed upon themselves and one was injured in consequence—held that *volenti* was a defence).

There may be policy reasons for making the defence unavailable in cases other than employer and workman but there is no authority on this point.

Contributory negligence

This defence is clearly available. Special rules relating to

the defence in relation to breach of statutory duty have
already been discussed (*supra*, p. 127).

Statutory duty delegated to or also laid upon the plaintiff

Where the performance of the employer's statutory duty
has been delegated to the plaintiff workman, and he has
failed to discharge it, with the result that he has suffered
injury, a difficult causal problem arises as to whether the
employer is liable. On the one hand, the employer is clearly
in breach of his duty, because the statutory duty is non-delegable. On the other, a person ought not to recover damages
for something that is entirely his fault. In *Ross* v. *Associated
Portland Cement Manufacturers Ltd.* (1964) the House of
Lords attempted to solve the question whether delegation of
the defendant's duty to the plaintiff was sufficient without
more to enable the court to say that the plaintiff was entirely
responsible for his own injuries. The employers in that case
were held liable for two-thirds of the plaintiff's injuries,
because they had delegated to him their statutory duty of
making safe his work fence without giving him proper
instructions, and he was not qualified to perform this task.
The employer's fault thus was different from and went
beyond that of the plaintiff in failing to make safe the work-
place.

Where, however, the employer's breach of statutory duty
is purely the result of the action of the plaintiff workman, no
action will lie against the employer because the workman was
the sole cause of his own injuries. This will be the case *a
fortiori* where the statutory duty is also laid on the workman
himself. Thus, in *Ginty* v. *Belmont Building Supples Ltd.*
(1959), the plaintiff failed to use a crawling-board while
working on a roof, in breach of statutory regulations binding
upon himself and his employers. He was injured as a result.
His actions for breach of statutory duty against his employers
failed because he was unable to show that they had committed
any breach of the statutory regulations other than that
committed by himself.

The House of Lords in *Boyle* v. *Kodak* (1969) has now
held that the employer's duty to instruct a workman about
the steps to be taken to avoid the commission of a breach of
statutory duty binding on that workman applies whenever
there is a risk that the workman will not be sufficiently
familiar with the regulations imposing such a duty, and even
if there was no foreseeable danger as a result of any breach. It
is clear, therefore, that the doctrine whereby the employer
may be found liable for a breach of statutory duty where his
fault is not co-extensive with that of the servant reaches
beyond the case where such fault would give rise to an action

for common law negligence (in the *Boyle* case, the result was an apportionment of damages between the employer and the injured plaintiff who was also at fault in not performing the statutory duty).

Extent and importance of breach of statutory duty

Statistically the tort is of very great importance today because of the large number of actions brought by workmen for breach by their employers of industrial safety legislation. Although in most of these cases the action for breach of statutory duty is duplicated by that for negligence, it has an independent importance since the statutory duty forms a particularisation of the standard of reasonable conduct expected of the employer and relieves the workman from having to prove a failure to comply with this standard. Physical safety is not, however, the only interest protected by the tort. Examples of the diverse interests that are protected are: the right to vote at a general election (*Ashby* v. *White* (1704)); the right of a shareholder to sue the company for breach of the statutory contract in the articles of the company (*Pender* v. *Lushington* (1877)); the right to compel the town clerk at the end of his term of office to hand over his accounts and books to his employers (*Lichfield Corporation* v. *Simpson* (1845)); the right of a homeless person to be provided with accommodation by a local authority (*Thornton* v. *Kirklees M.B.C.* (1979)).

20. VICARIOUS LIABILITY

This term used in connection with the law of tort refers to the situation where one person is liable for the commission of a tort by another. The outstanding case in English law is the liability of a master for the torts of his servant committed in the course of the latter's employment. Liability for the acts of an independent contractor is based upon the breach of a personal, non-delegable duty of the employer rather than on vicarious liability.

The relationship of principal and agent is, generally speaking, irrelevant for determining questions of vicarious liability for tort. The agent is employed to bring his principal into contractual relation with third parties. He may be either a servant or independent contractor (according to principles discussed below), and upon this will turn the question of the principal's liability for the torts he commits. In two cases, however, the status of agent is relevant to determining the existence of vicarious liability in tort. If an agent, acting within the scope of his apparent or usual authority, makes a fraudulent misrepresentation to a third party, causing him to act to his loss, the principal is liable in the tort of deceit. Cases on the liability of car owners for the acts of persons who drive the car at the request of the owner and for his purposes have also been rationalised in terms of agency (*infra*, p. 234).

VICARIOUS LIABILITY IN THE CASE OF MASTER AND SERVANT

Rationale

It is now recognised that the reason for imposing liability upon the master for the torts of his servant committed in the course of his employment is one of policy. Vicarious liability achieves the dual purpose of providing a financially responsible person as defendant and of providing the master with an inducement to institute maximum standards of safety within the enterprise. At the same time the limitation that the tort must have been committed during the course of the servant's employment shows that this is a form of enterprise liability, rather than that the master is an insurer of the servant's wrongdoing.

Who is a servant?

Several tests have been propounded by courts for deciding this question. But it seems that these tests are for the guidance of the court rather than principles of law, and that each case must be resolved on its own special facts. No one test has paramountcy over another and where they produce a different result, the court must make up its mind on the evidence and on its overall impression. One test that was at one time regarded almost as conclusive was whether the employer could determine the way in which the work was to be done, the test of control. With the increase in technical knowledge and skill, this test has become a great deal less useful, since in practice the employer will let the servant alone in his performance of tasks demanding such knowledge. If it is argued that the employer must be able to control the overall manner in which the work is done, this element would seem to be present also in the case of work done by independent contractors. Other factors which will enter the court's consideration are the method of payment (for example, wages or a lump sum) and who supplies tools, premises, equipment. An alternative test put forward by Lord Denning in 1952 has won some acceptance today. He contrasted the servant who is normally employed as an integral part of his employer's business (giving as examples the ship's master, the chauffeur, and the newspaper reporter) with the independent contractor whose services are accessory to the business (examples being the ship's pilot, the taxidriver, and the freelance contributor). The two tests of control and integration may produce different results. Thus in *Morren* v. *Swinton and Pendlebury U.D.C.* (1965) an engineer employed by a local authority was held to be its servant though subject to no control by it in relation to the carrying out of his work, on the ground that the terms of his contract made him sufficiently integrated into the business of the authority. On the other hand, in *Market Investigations* v. *Minister of Social Security* (1969), a woman interviewer, employed by the plaintiffs, who was subject to exact control as to the method of conducting interviews, was held to be the plaintiffs' servant, though it seems doubtful whether she was sufficiently integrated into the employer's business to satisfy the integration test. In *Ready-Mixed Concrete Co.* v. *Minister of Pensions and National Insurance* (1968) it was stated that there must be sufficient control by the employer, and there must be no provisions in the contract inconsistent with service in order to establish a contract of service. However, it is not clear why control should be essential nor why the existence of certain terms pointing away from service should always outweigh a greater number of terms pointing towards it. The correct test of service seems to be whether a preponderance of the terms of the contract point towards it. Some may do this by establishing control, others integration, and others, such as the power of appointment and dismissal, may point to service though they establish neither control nor integration. It must be pointed out that it is not for the parties themselves to determine the nature of the contract they have entered into, so that express provision in the contract that a person is not a servant will not prevail against other factors which indicate service (*Ferguson* v. *Dawson* (1976)). A particular problem in relation to the police force has been removed by the Police Act 1964. A policeman is not in the position of servant to anyone. Section 48 of the Act makes the chief officer of police for any police area liable for torts committed by constables under his direction and control on similar principles to those determining the master's liability for the torts of his servant. Any damages and costs awarded are to be paid out of the police fund.

Cases on borrowed servants typify the problems of complicated factual analysis which have to be faced by courts. The servant may be so completely "taken over" that, at least as far as the doctrine of vicarious liability is concerned, he becomes the servant of the borrower; otherwise he will merely be his independent contractor (contractually speaking, however, he will remain throughout the servant of his original master). In *Mersey Docks and Harbour Board* v. *Coggins and Griffiths Ltd.* (1947), a crane driver employed by the Board had been hired together with his crane to another company and while with that company had by his negligence injured the plaintiff. The crane driver was held to be still a servant of the Board because of the following factors: he continued to be paid by the Board which alone had power to dismiss him; the borrower could give him directions as to the work to be done but could not instruct him in the operation of the crane. These factors outweighed the fact that the contract of hire provided that the crane driver should become the servant of the hirers, since this, as far as vicarious liability was concerned was for judicial rather than contractual determination. Other factors which may affect the decision are whether the servant lent is technically skilled (since the service of an unskilled servant is more easily transferred), and whether the servant is lent for a specific task or for the general purposes of the transferee.

Employer's personal duty

Little remains, nowadays, of the former theory of vicarious liability under which the master was liable because he had committed through his servant a breach of duty personal to himself, although it is true that some of the older cases seem to support it (*e.g. Broom* v. *Morgan* (1953); *Conway* v. *Wimpey* (1951); *Smith* v. *Moss* (1940)). It cannot meet the insuperable difficulty that if it were correct it would not matter whether the failure to discharge the duty was through the default of a servant or independent contractor, whereas there are numerous cases in which liability exists for the acts of a servant but not an independent contractor. The correct basis for vicarious liability is therefore that the master is liable for torts committed *by the servant* in the course of his employment. This is not to say that in no case can the employer be held liable for the breach by another person of a duty personal to the employer. In fact, this is the basis for the employer's liability for the acts of an independent contractor. Where such a personal duty exists, it may help to avoid difficult questions as to whether there is vicarious liability for the acts of a servant. In cases of medical negligence in the course of hospital treatment, for example, doubts may exist whether the particular person negligent is a servant of the hospital. Thus although radiographers (*Gold* v. *Essex County Council* (1942)), house-surgeons (*Collins* v. *Hertfordshire County Council* (1947)), whole-time assistant medical officers (*Cassidy* v. *Ministry of Health* (1951)) and anaesthetists (*Roe* v. *Minister of Health* (1954)) have been held to be servants of the hospital, a doubt remains about persons such as consultant surgeons. It may be, however, that a hospital is liable for the negligence of its independent contractors on the basis that it owes its patients a personal, non-delegable duty of care (as in other cases of liability for independent contractors' torts). If this is so, it makes no difference whether the particular person negligent is a servant or an independent contractor (apart from the difficulty of "collateral negligence, *infra* p. 233).

Another example of the concept of a personal duty binding the employer avoiding a problem as to whether vicarious liability exists is the case of *Morris* v. *Martin* (1966). The defendants had accepted the plaintiff's mink coat for cleaning. They handed the coat to their servant to be cleaned and the servant stole it. Difficulties exist as to whether theft by a servant can be regarded as being done in the course of his employment (in fact this question was answered in the affirmative, *infra*, p. 230). The defendants were, nevertheless, held liable because they were in breach of their personal duty as bailees of the coat to look after it.

A final point needs clarification. The "servant's tort" theory of vicarious liability does not require that the plaintiff must identify the tortfeasor, provided it is clear that the tort must have been committed by one of the defendant's servants acting in the course of his employment (*cf. Grant* v. *Australian*

Knitting Mills (1936)). If it is shown that the tortfeasor must have been one of a number of servants or independent contractors employed by the defendant, liability will exist only if there is a personal duty on the defendant.

Course of employment
The limitation has been established that the tort must be committed during the course of the servant's employment, and this requirement must now be examined. It may be noted that many of the decisions on whether a servant has acted in the course of his employment turn on questions of degree rather than logic. The present century has seen an extension of the limits within which the servant is recognised as acting in the course of his employment.

Substantive limits and duration of employment
The servant must be doing the work he has been employed to do. In *Rand* v. *Craig* (1919) the defendant employed servants to carry rubbish and deposit it in a named place. Instead they deposited it on the plaintiff's land. The defendant was held not liable to the plaintiff since the servants were acting outside the course of their employment. Here the area of employment was defined by the employer's express instructions. Similarly if the servant goes on a "frolic of his own" during his working hours he will be acting outside the course of his employment. By this term is meant some action of the servant which is so totally unrelated to the work the servant is employed to do that it cannot be understood to be a part of it. Whether the servant is on such a frolic often turns on questions of degree.

If the servant is performing work that he is employed to do in an improper way, he will be acting within the course of his employment. In *Century Insurance Co. Ltd.* v. *Northern Ireland Road Transport Board* (1942) the House of Lords held that a lorry driver who caused a fire by striking a match to light a cigarette while transferring petrol from his lorry to an underground tank in the plaintiff's garage was acting in the course of his employment because he was doing in an unauthorised way that which he was employed to do. The distinction between doing an act which is no part of the servant's employment and doing authorised work in an improper manner is also relevant where the act in question been specifically prohibited by the master. If the prohibition is regarded as delimiting the scope of the servant's employment, the prohibited act will be outside the course of employment. If what is prohibited is an improper method of carrying out the servant's authorised tasks, it will be within the course of employment (so in *Limpus* v. *London General*

Omnibus Co. (1862) the defendants' bus driver who raced his bus with another belonging to a rival company despite the fact that the defendants had expressly warned their drivers not to race, was held to be acting within the course of his employment). The question of the effect of prohibitions on the servant's conduct causes difficulty in the case of the servant who gives unauthorised lifts to third parties in his employer's vehicle. If such a person is injured by the negligence of the employee, courts have based the non-liability of the employer on the fact that the servant was not acting in the course of his employment (*Twine* v. *Bean's Express* (1946); *Conway* v. *Wimpey* (1951) in which it was also explained by reason of the plaintiff's status as a trespasser on the vehicle). In *Rose* v. *Plenty* (1975) a milk roundsman had, contrary to the instructions of his employer, made use of the services of the plaintiff, a thirteen-year-old-boy, for the purpose of assisting him in delivering milk. The plaintiff was injured by the negligent driving of the float by the roundsman. The Court of Appeal by a majority held the employer of the milk roundsman vicariously liable for his negligence to the plaintiff. All three members of the Court of Appeal treated the question as turning on whether the roundsman was acting in the course of his employment the plaintiff's status as a trespasser on the float did not affect the duties owed to him by the servant and the vicarious liability of the employer depended upon whether the servant and not the employer had committed a tort. The majority were able to distinguish the earlier cases on the ground that in them the plaintiffs were receiving gratuitous lifts whereas here the plaintiff was being used for the purpose of the employer's business. Although the case seems rightly decided, the distinction it draws is not very satisfactory. In the earlier cases, it is not clear why the employer's prohibition is regarded as delimiting the sphere of the servant's employment, since apart from the prohibited act, the servant was carrying out his duties in a normal fashion (see also *Iqbal* v. *London Transport Executive* (1974)—a bus conductor who was prohibited from driving the bus was acting outside the course of his employment when he drove it; *Stone* v. *Taffe* (1975)—a public house manager in giving an unauthorised after-hours party in the public house was not acting outside the course of his employment).

In some cases difficulty has arisen because the servant has performed some act which is not part of the servant's normal employment, but which by implication may be within the scope of his employment. Thus a servant may have an implied authority to defend his master's property, using physical force if necessary. If such a servant uses an unreasonable amount of force against one whom he reasonably suspects to be stealing from his master (so being deprived of the defence of defence of property), his master will be liable for the servant's act which is merely a wrongful way of performing something within the scope of the servant's employment (*Poland & Sons* v. *Parr* (1972)). On the other hand a servant, though he may have an implied authority to detain one whom he suspects to be obtaining his master's goods without paying for them, has no authority to do this when such payment has been made. So in *Warren* v. *Henley's Ltd.* (1948) the servant, a garage attendant, accused the plaintiff of attempting to leave without paying for petrol supplied to him. Later, after the plaintiff had paid, the servant assaulted him. The garage was held not liable because the servant had not acted in the course of his employment (for a recent illustration, see *Keppel Bus Co.* v. *Sa'ad Bin Ahmad* (1974)).

In order to be acting within the course of his employment, the servant must commit the tort during his actual hours of employment. For example, a servant who returned to his work without his master's permission after the premises had been closed would not be acting within the course of his employment. But a reasonable extension to normal working hours will be recognised by the courts as not outside the course of employment, for example, the servant who stays for a short time in order to finsih a job, or one who leaves taps running in a washroom which he visits after completing his working day, so damaging the plaintiff's property (see *Ruddiman & Co.* v. *Smith* (1889)).

Criminal conduct by servant

The problem here is whether the servant who commits a crime or acts dishonestly entirely for his own benefit is acting within the course of his employment. The mere fact that the servant has committed a crime is clearly not enough to take his act outside the course of his employment—thus, the commission by a servant of a breach of statutory duty while performing his authorised work would be inside the scope of his employment. Even where the servant has acted for his own benefit the master may be held liable. Whether the servant's act will be regarded as within the course of his employment will depend upon whether it can be regarded as a wrongful performance of the work which the servant is employed to do. Thus in *Morris* v. *Martin* (1966), the master was held liable for the theft of the mink coat by the servant to whom it had been entrusted for cleaning (for this explanation of the decision based upon conventional principles of vicarious liability, see the judgment of Diplock L.J.). The Court of Appeal was in agreement that if the theft had been a servant who had no duties in relation to the coat, the master would not have been liable. In *Lloyd* v. *Grace, Smith & Co.*

(1912) the master, a firm of solicitors, was held liable for the fraud of its conveyancing clerk who had induced the plaintiff to convey two cottages, which she wished to sell, to him, representing that this was necessary for their sale. This was clearly a wrongful performance of the work the clerk was employed to do. Furthermore, the plaintiff was justified in relying on the representation of the clerk since by employing him as a conveyancing clerk the defendants had invested him with apparent authority to make representations of that sort.

Acts simultaneously inside and outside course of employment

Although there are only *obiter dicta* in support, it seems correct to say that the servant may be acting inside the course of his employment *vis-a-vis* one person, and outside it *vis-a-vis* another. In *Twine* v. *Bean's Express Ltd.* (1946) the defendants' servant, the driver of a vehicle belonging to the defendants, had given a lift to the plaintiff contrary to the defendants' instructions, and by his negligent driving of the vehicle had caused him injury. The employers were held not liable to the plaintiff because the servant's act was wholly outside the course of the servant's employment, rather than an improper means of carrying it out. But Lord Greene M.R. expressed the view that as far as persons other than the plaintiff were concerned the driving of the van was inside the course of employment, so that had they been injured by the negligent driving they would have had an action against the employer. This view appears sound in principle.

LIABILITY FOR THE ACTS OF AN INDEPENDENT CONTRACTOR

The liability of one who has employed a contractor to do work may be personal under the ordinary rules of tort, rather than vicarious. So, he may have instructed or authorised the contractor to commit a tort, or by his negligent instructions may have contributed to the contractor's commission of a tort, or he may have committed a tort of strict liability through the contractor (as in *Rylands* v. *Fletcher* (1868)). In certain cases there may be liability for the negligence of a contractor although the employer is not personally at fault and no tort of strict liability has been committed. Such liability has been based by English courts on a breach by the employer of a non-delegable duty of care binding on himself. Liability is therefore still personal rather than a vicarious liability for the contractor's negligence. This formulation is misleading in so far as it suggests that liability is other than strict. The employer of the independent contractor is not liable for his *fault* in delegating to the contractor. Indeed it many cases it would be negligent not to employ a contractor. Furthermore the liability of the employer of an independent contractor is in one respect stricter than the vicarious liability of an employer for the torts of his servant. The employer of the contractor has no overall control of the way in which the work is done—the employer of a servant has such control.

There is no reason of policy comparable to the case of the employer of servants why liability should exist for the negligence of an independent contractor in every case. Contractors are usually financially responsible persons; their employers are often not. Policy reasons have dictated that liability should exist in two categories of case: (i) the person who has commissioned work involving exceptional risk to the public is liable for the negligence of a contractor in carrying out that work: (ii) certain persons (who will in the normal course of events be financially responsible), and who have a duty of care for the protection of other persons by reason of their relationship to them, are not allowed to delegate the performance of that duty to a contractor. The two categories will be examined in turn.

(1)   *Exceptional risks*

The leading case on this category is *Honeywill and Stein* v. *Larkin Brothers Ltd.* (1934). The defendants had employed a contractor to take flashlight photographs inside a cinema. They were held liable for his negligence in starting a fire because the work commissioned was "extra-hazardous." This category also includes liability for work commissioned on the highway, which involves unusual hazards both because of the large number of people whom it may affect and because of the dangers of motorised traffic. Thus in *Holliday* v. *National Telephone Co* (1899) the contractor, a plumber, was employed by the defendants to solder tubes through which the defendants' telephone wires were to be passed. The telephones wires were situated on the highway. The contractor carried out his work negligently and the plaintiff, a passing pedestrian was injured by molten solder. The defendants were held liable to the plaintiff. In an action for failure to maintain the highway brought against the highway authority, it is no defence for the highway authority to show that it had arranged for a competent contractor to carry out or supervise the maintenance of the highway (section 1 (3) of the Highways (Miscellaneous Provisions) Act 1961. *Salsbury* v. *Woodland* (1970) held that the category of work done on the highway should not be extended to work done near the highway; also that the felling of a tree near the highway did not involve unusual hazards to other persons. *Matania* v. *National Provincial Bank* (1936) also seems to be a case falling within this category. Where the contractor had created by his negligence a nuisance, it was held that the employer was liable only if the work created a special risk of the creation of a nuisance.

(2) *Non-delegability of duty of care for protection of a class of persons*

The employer's personal duty of care to provide for the physical safety of his workmen by providing proper plant, premises, staff and system of work is the most obvious, in fact the only clear, example of the duty of care falling within category (2). Policy dictates that the employer, normally a financially responsible person, should not be able to escape from the duty of care by transfering it to another person even one who may also be financially responsible (he may of course, have remedies in contract or by way of contribution proceedings against a negligent contractor). The duty of care which hospitals owe to their patients for their treatment may, as suggested above, be another example of this category but the law is not yet clear.

It should be mentioned that neither the list of categories in which liability may exist for the negligence of a contractor, nor the list of cases in those categories is closed.

Collateral negligence by contractor

If the contractor is negligent in some matter which is an integral part of the task which has been entrusted to him, the employer is liable (assuming that on the above principles liability for the contractor's negligence exists). If, however, the negligence consists in some collateral act, not a necessary part of the contractor's function, the employer is not liable for such negligence. But what negligence of the contractor is collateral? In principle it seems that in cases within category (2) above, the concept should not apply at all. If the reason behind this category is that the workman should not be denied a remedy against the employer, as well as against the contractor, this applies whether or not negligence is collateral. *Padbury* v. *Holliday and Greenwood Ltd.* (1912), the case which established the doctrine, was a case within category (1). The contractor had been employed to fit window casements into premises situated on the highway. The contractor's servant negligently left a hammer lying on the window sill, and the hammer was knocked down when a gust of wind blew the window open. The plaintiff, a pedestrian on the highway, received personal injuries as a result. The defendants who had employed the contractor, were held not liable for his neglignece, because the negligence was collateral. The servant's negligence here was clearly collateral to the contractor's method of performing the work, but this seems irrelevant since the employer is not held liable for the contractor's negligence because he personally should have supervised the work. On the other hand the negligence was certainly not collateral to the risk created by the work commissioned, and this seems the true test. The correctness of this decision is therefore open to doubt.

LIABILITY OF CAR OWNERS

It has been established for some time that a car-owner who has delegated the driving of a car to another person while remaining a passenger in the car is liable for the negligence of the driver, on the ground that he has retained control over the vehicle. This is personal rather than vicarious liability. In *Ormrod* v. *Crosville Motor Services Ltd.* (1953) an extension to this rule was recognised, when the owner of a car which was being driven from London to Monte Carlo at the owner's request and for his benefit but in which he was not himself travelling was held liable for the driver's negligence. The ratio of the case is that where the driving is done at the request of the owner and for his purposes, the driver is the owner's agent, and the owner is vicariously liable for his negligence.

A recent case, *Launchbury* v. *Morgans* (1971) concerned the liability of the owner of a car whose husband borrowed it daily for work. She knew that the husband occasionally stopped out late for a drink, and acquiesced in this, provided he got someone else to drive him home if he was unfit to drive. After one such evening, the husband was killed and the plaintiffs, passengers in the car, were injured through the negligence of the husband's friend who was driving the car for the husband. In the Court of Appeal, the wife was held vicariously liable for the negligence of the friend on the ground that the car was being driven for her purposes, either on the ground that it was in the wife's interest that the husband should be driven home safely, or that in the case of a "matrimonial" car almost any journey undertaken by either spouse in it has a joint matrimonial purpose. The House of Lords refused to accept either argument. The fact that the wife had an interest in the driving did not mean that it was done for her purposes. Furthermore, the innovation of the "matrimonial" or "family" car was one for the legislature rather than the courts to make. The decision had unfortunate practical consequences for the plaintiffs since it meant that they could not recover from the wife's insurers. Now that insurance against liability to passengers in a motor vehicle is compulsory, the wife herself could be sued in similar circumstances for breach of statutory duty for permitting the car to be driven without insurance cover. More importantly, the plaintiffs would have an action against the Motor Insurers Bureau which by agreement among insurance companies pays out in cases where insurance against third party liability is compulsory but insurance cover does not exist (but only in cases of personal injury. It may therefore still be important to establish that the driver was driving the car as agent of the owner where the third party suffers damage to his property). The House of Lords did not disapprove of *Ormrod* v. *Crosville Motor Services* and presumably the doctrine laid down by that case survives intact. Some of the other cases in which owners have been held liable for the negligence of those whom they have permitted to drive their cars must, however, be of dubious authority in the light of the judgments in the House of Lords (*cf.* especially, *Parker* v. *Miller* (1926); *Carberry* v. *Davies* (1968)).

21. DEFAMATION

INTRODUCTION

The tort of defamation protects a person's interest in his reputation. Thus, if the defendant has made an untrue statement, or what amounts to a statement, which is defamatory of the plaintiff, the plaintiff has a right of action against him unless the defendant can establish one of the special defences available to an action for defamation. It is important to note that the tort protects the plaintiff's reputation as it appears to other people. This means that publication of the statement by the defendant to persons other than the plaintiff himself is an essential part of the tort—the purpose of the tort is not to protect the injured feelings of the plaintiff (on the other hand it appears to be accepted that there is defamation if the statement is made to a person who disbelieves it—see, for example, Lord Reid in *Morgan* v. *Odhams Press* (1971), the justification for this being, according to Lord Reid, the annoyance caused to the plaintiff). The tort goes beyond protecting the mere personal reputation of the plaintiff and extends to the protection of the reputation of his commercial and business undertakings.

The rules of the tort represent an attempt to strike a balance between two important and often competing interests, the public interest in freedom of speech (which is often a private interest also), and the private interest in maintaining one's reputation. The difficulty of achieving this balance is perhaps indicated by the fact that, though liability for a defamatory statement is strict and substantial damages may be recovered from one who makes such a statement, a large variety of defences exist for the protection of one who makes such a statement. It is also the case that many of the rules of the tort, though reasonably well settled as matters of law, are notoriously uncertain in their practical application. This again supports the idea of the law treading a knife-edge between two conflicting positions.

The recovery of substantial damages for a defamatory statement, especially from one who is ignorant of the defamatory nature of the statement, has led to criticism in recent years. Certain statutory defences (*infra*, pp. 247-252) mitigate the hardship of this in the case of innocent defamation by allowing the defamer to escape liability by making, for example, an offer of amends to the plaintiff. The inequity of allowing the recovery of substantial damages by one who has suffered a mere injury to reputation remains. It is true that the remedy of damages is necessary as a deterrent to the calculated use of defamatory statements as a means of selling newspapers and periodicals. But the amount of damages recovered for defamation seems often disproportionate to the actual effect in financial terms the statement may have.

SLANDER AND LIBEL

Defamation comprises two torts, slander and libel. The distinction was formerly of purely procedural effect, slander being actionable in the common law courts while libel was purely within the jurisdiction of the Star Chamber. After the common law courts succeeded to the jurisdiction of the Star Chamber over libel, the distinction was maintained and unfortunately acquired substantive force. Broadly speaking, it can now be said that slander is committed by one who publishes the defamatory statement orally, libel by one who publishes it in writing. The effect of the distinction is that in the case of slander proof of special damage is, with four exceptions, an essential part of the plaintiff's cause of action; libel is on the other hand actionable *per se*. The distinction receives some justification from the greater triviality and lesser potentiality for doing harm of spoken rather than written words. But it still seems unfortunate for several reasons. In the case of slander which is not actionable *per se*, the plaintiff often has no means at all of vindicating his reputation. The distinction can also be criticised both for the difficulties that arise in drawing it and for its arbitrary nature. The line between slander and libel may be drawn on the technical ground that slander has its impact on the aural sense, libel on the visual. Thus libel would include defamatory pictures, statutes, and conduct such as hanging the plaintiff in effigy. This distinction becomes increasingly arbitrary with the development of methods of communication which, though operating through the ear, are clearly as potent in the spreading of defamatory material as the written word, the most obvious examples being films, radio and television, and gramophone records. If, on the other hand, a purely technical test is replaced by one which attempts to draw the line between slander and libel on the ground that libel is a more serious form of defamation than slander, there is again difficulty in deciding what such a test should be and how it is reconcilable with the English cases. One possibility is that slander refers to a transient statement, libel to one with some degree of permanence. Another is that for the statement to amount to libel it should have considerable potential for doing harm to reputation. Both these tests have obvious difficulties in their applications.

The only English case which suggests that the test is anything other than a mechanical one depending upon the mode of publication of the statement is *Forrester* v. *Tyrrell* (1893) in which it was held that reading out a defamatory written statement is libel. It is weak authority for a test of permanency, but does not distinguish according to whether the listener to the statement realises that a written statement is being read. It is contradicted by *Osborn* v. *Boulter and Son* (1930) in which two members of the Court of Appeal thought that the dictation of a letter to a typist and the reading out of the letter aloud after dictation amount to slander alone (although the person dictating is liable in libel if the letter is subsequently published by his authority). In *Youssoupoff* v. *Metro-Goldwyn-Mayer Pictures Ltd.* (1934) it was held that a film which suggested as a matter of historical fact that the plaintiff had at one time been raped was libellous, but as the defamatory meaning was conveyed by a combination of pictorial representations and sound, the case is no support for the view that a defamatory anecdote told in a film is libel. Defamatory statements made in broadcasts whether through radio or television are, under the Defamation Act 1952, to be treated as published in permanent form by which it appears to be meant that they are libel. So, under the Theatres Act 1968 are statements in theatrical performances. However, the uncertainty about other media such as films, gramophone records, and recorded tapes, as well as statements made through trained parrots and skywriting, remains. The Report of the Committee on Defamation (Cmnd. 5909) recommended abolition of the distinction between libel and slander. The Committee was satisfied that this would not lead to an undue increase in frivolous actions brought in respect of spoken words.

Slander actionable per se

In four cases the plaintiff does not have to prove special damage as part of his cause of action in slander:

(1) *Imputation of crime*

It is slander actionable *per se* to impute to the plaintiff the commission of a crime for which he may suffer or have suffered imprisonment.

(2) *Imputation of disease*

The disease imputed must be infectious or contagious and

the imputation must be that the plaintiff is presently suffering from it.

(3) *Imputation in respect of office, profession, calling, trade or business*

At common law an imputation that a schoolteacher had committed adultery with a school cleaner was not actionable *per se* under this rubric—it reflected discredit on the schoolteacher as a man rather than on the man as a schoolteacher. But section 2 of the Defamation Act 1952 makes it slander actionable *per se* where the words are calculated to disparage the plaintiff in his office, profession, calling, trade or business, though not spoken of him in the way of such office, profession, calling, trade or business.

(4) *Imputation of unchastity to a woman under Slander of Women Act 1891*

Such imputation includes one of lesbianism (*Kerr* v. *Kennedy* (1942)).

Special damage in slander not actionable per se

Material loss such as loss of employment, loss of contracts through refusal by persons to contract with the plaintiff and loss of hospitality from friends proved to have provided food and drink on former occasions is special damage for the purpose of the tort. Nervous shock and illness arising from mental distress do not appear to be recoverable in slander, although the rule in libel is different, and no satisfactory explanation appears to exist for this difference.

Where the damage is suffered because of a third party's action, this may make it too remote (*Lynch* v. *Knight* (1861) damage too remote where husband made wife leave home when he heard she had almost been seduced before marriage). But the third party's action must be unforeseeable; for this reason the rule that damage caused by repetition of the slander is too remote is questionable (*Ward* v. *Weeks* (1830)). There is certainly liability when the repetition is performed in the course of a legal or moral duty, or where the defendant intends the repetition.

PRINCIPLES OF DEFAMATION

It now remains to consider those principles which are applicable to both libel and slander. In order to establish the defendant's liability in defamation, the plaintiff must show that the defendant has published a statement about him which is defamatory.

Defamatory nature of the statement

The requirement that the statement should bring the plaintiff into hatred, contempt or ridicule, formerly the accepted definition of a defamatory statement, is now recognised to be inadequate in the light of decisions that to impute to the plaintiff that she has been raped (*Youssoupoff's* case, *supra*, p. 238) or is insane is defamatory. The test that the statement should lower the plaintiff in the esteem of right-thinking men also fails to explain these cases. These tests fail to appreciate that the reaction of society as a whole to the statement may be irrational and emotional and may make people inclined to shun the plaintiff when what is imputed to him is a misfortune rather than a misdeed. Thus to say of the plaintiff that he is illegitimate, impotent or has cancer is almost certainly defamatory.

Another problem arises where the statement is calculated to bring the plaintiff into disfavour with a certain section of the community which is not an ordinary cross-section of the community and whose reaction to the statement is questionably right-thinking. Although there is little English authority on the point it has been held that to call a person a German in time of war with Germany is defamatory; it also seems likely that it is defamatory to call a person a Communist. These problems become more intractable when the statement imputes something to the plaintiff upon which there are deep divisions within the country. Is it defamatory to say that a worker is a non-unionist, or has worked during a strike, or that a student is a demonstrator? The answer to each question is, it is submitted, yes, on the ground that the statement is calculated to bring the plaintiff into disfavour with a sufficiently sizeable section of the community. This must receive some qualification, however, in the light of the decision of the Court of Appeal in *Byrne* v. *Deane* (1937). In that case it was held that it was not defamatory to say of a member of a club that he had supplied the police with information about an illegal gaming machine kept at the club, because a person who supplies such information ought not to be less well-thought of by his fellows. There seems no reason of policy behind this decision, since a court's decision that the statement was defamatory would not mean that the court condoned the offence. The court's preference for the ideal rather than the actual attitudes of the club members may therefore be questioned. The result of the case seems to be that where the court classifies the attitude of the section of the public concerned as anti-social or perverse it will not hold the statement defamatory.

Circumstances of time, place and occasion will often be relevant in determining whether a statement has a defamatory content. Thus it is only defamatory to say of a person that he is a German if a state of war prevails between Germany and this country. The relevance of occasion explains why mere vulgar abuse spoken in the course of quarrelling is normally not defamatory. To call another a bastard in the course of a skirmish would not be defamatory, since the listeners would understand that the statement was not intended to contain any substratum of fact. But if the statement was intended to convey that a factual basis existed for the statement, or if its listener would reasonably interpret it in this way, then the statement would be defamatory even if uttered as abuse. Thus to call a man a pansy or a turncoat might be actionable.

Statements imputing incompetence to the plaintiff in his trade or profession are actionable in the same way as attacks upon his character. Thus to suggest that the goods manufactured by the plaintiff are of inferior quality or that a film critic is an incompetent member of his profession is undoubtedly defamatory. Equally it is possible for a trading association such as a company to sue in defamation (*South Hetton Coal Co.* v. *Norther Eastern News Association* (1894)). It has also been held that a trade union (*Willis* v. *Brooks* (1947)), and a local authority (*Bognor Regis U.D.C.* v. *Campion* (1972)) can be defamed, although under the present trade union legislation the trade union may not have sufficient legal personality to sue (*E.E.P.T.U.* v. *The Times* (1980)). It may be noted that dead persons cannot be defamed.

In order that a statement be defamatory it must be untrue, but not every untrue statement is defamatory. To say that the plaintiff has ceased to be in business is not defamatory since this can have no damaging effect upon the plaintiff's reputation (*Ratcliffe* v. *Evans* (1892)). If such a statement is made maliciously and if it causes the plaintiff actual damage, the plaintiff has another cause of action against the defendant (*infra*, p. 285).

Interpretation of defamatory statements: Innuendo

The test to be applied is whether the words of the defendant in their ordinary and natural sense defame the plaintiff. The whole of the defendant's statement must be looked at, not merely that which the plaintiff relies on as being defamatory. This is important because what follows an *ex facie* defamatory statement may qualify or explain it (as in, "Lord X, you are a thief. You have stolen my heart"). Where the plaintiff is relying on the words having a defamatory meaning which is not explicity stated, but which can be collected from the words in their ordinary and natural sense, the plaintiff does not have the burden of proving such extended meaning, and it is for the judge to decide whether the words are capable of bearing that meaning. The plaintiff does not have to allege such extended meaning in his peadings, though in some cases it may be prudent for him to do so. In this situation the plaintiff is said to be relying on a "false" innuendo, false in the sense that the burden of proving such innuendo does not rest upon him. In *Lewis* v. *Daily Telegraph* (1964) the defendant newspaper stated that the Fraud Squad of the City of London Police were investigating the affairs of the plaintiff's company. The House of Lords held that, though the natural interpretation of these words was that the plaintiff was reasonably suspected of fraud, and were therfore prima facie defamatory, they could not bear the interpretation that the plaintiff had actually been guilty of fraud, so that the defendant could justify the statement by proving the facts stated. If the defendant has stated therefore that A reasonably suspects B of fraud, this is only defamatory if it is not true; if on the other hand he says that A has told him that B has conmitted fraud, this is apparently defamatory in the sense that B has actually been fraudulent (*M'Pherson* v. *Daniels* (1829)). The distinction though not difficult to draw is difficult to justify.

Where the defamatory meaning cannot be collected from the actual words used, and the plaintiff is relying upon knowledge by those who have received the statement of facts which render it defamatory, the plaintiff is said to rely on a "true" innuendo. In *Tolley* v. *J.S. Fry and Sons Ltd.* (1931) the plaintiff, a well-known amateur golfer, was depicted in cartoon likeness in the defendants' advertisement, the suggestion in the advertisement being that he had a fondness for the defendants' chocolate. The advertisement was held to be defamatory because it suggested that the plaintiff had infringed his amateur status by accepting payment for appearing in the advertisement. This meaning could not have been derived from the advertisement alone; the plaintiff therefore had to prove that there were persons who knew of him as an amateur golfer and who would read the meaning he alleged into the advertisement. Where the plaintiff is relying on facts not stated in the defendant's statement in order to prove its defamatory nature, he must give details of these facts in his pleadings. He must therefore also prove the existence of such facts on the balance of probabilities.

The interpretation of the statement is along with other matters of law for the judge rather than the jury. He must decide, *inter alia*, whether the statement is capable of being defamatory in the sense that it is capable of bearing the meaning that the plaintiff puts upon it. If it is, the jury, which decides questions of fact, then decides whether it is actually defamatory. The interpretative function of the judge allows him to exercise considerable control over the outcome of an action, and can be abused (see, for example, the surprising decision in *Capital and Counties Bank* v. *Henty* (1882) in which it was held that the defendants' statement to their customers that they would not receive in payment cheques drawn on the plaintiff bank was incapable of being defamatory, although it caused a run on the bank).

Reference to the plaintiff

There must be such sufficient reference to the plaintiff in the defendant's statement that it may reasonably be concluded that it is defamatory of the plaintiff. This does not mean that the plaintiff must actually be named in the statement. All that is required is that the defendant has supplied sufficient particulars to enable the plaintiff to be identified as the subject of the statement. Where the defendant's statement is made of a large class of people which includes the plaintiff ("All lawyers are crooked," or "All West Indians are idle") an action in defamation will generally not succeed although the statement may constitute a criminal offence, for example, seditious libel, or an incitement to a breach of the peace. But if the class referred to is so small that the defendant's statement may be regarded as being defamatory of each member of it, then the defendant may be successfully sued by each member. Thus where seventeen defendants had been indicted for murder, the defendant's statement that all took part in the murder was actionable by each of them (*Foxcroft* v. *Lacy* (1613)). Furthermore, a statement made about a class which would ordinarily be too large to allow members of the class to sue may be actionable by individual members of that class if there is evidence that the statement particularly refers to them. So in *Le Fanu* v. *Malcolmson* (1848) a statement in an article by the defendant imputing cruelties to Irish factory owners was found by the court on a reading of the article as a whole to refer to factory owners in Waterford including the plaintiff. Reference to the plaintiff by the defendant's statement need not be intentional. There is sufficient reference if the defendant has used a fictitious name to identify a person in a work intended to be fictional, provided that it was believed by certain persons to refer to the plaintiff (*cf. Hulton* v. *Jones* (1910) in which one Artemus Jones, a churchwarden of Peckham was said in a newspaper article to be conducting an amorous liaison with a woman not his wife the real Artemus Jones, a barrister who was not a churchwarden and who did not live at Peckham recovered £1,750 damages because several people testified to the fact that they thought the statement referred to him). Equally a true statement about one person may be defamatory of another person with the same name (*Newstead* v. *London Express Newspaper* (1931)—a newspaper statement that Harold Newstead, a thirty-year-old Camberwell man had been convicted of bigamy was true of a Camberwell barman of that name but untrue of the plaintiff, a Camberwell barber aged about thirty. The statement was held to be defamatory of the plaintiff. Finally it is clear that the statement need not expressly refer to the plaintiff, provided persons reading it or hearing it would take it as so referring. In *Cassidy* v. *Daily Mirror Newspapers* (1929), a newspaper photograph of Cassidy with a woman, together with a statement that the two had become engaged was held to be defamatory of Cassidy's wife who would have been assumed by those reading the statement who knew her to have been living in sin. The result of this case has been confirmed by *Morgan* v. *Oldhams Press* (1971). In that case an article in the defendants' newspaper stated that a girl, who had been an accomplice of a dog-doping gang, had been kidnapped by members of the gang. The girl in question had, to the knowledge of people who read the article, stayed with the plaintiff during the period mentioned in the article and in the area indicated by the article. The articles was held to be defamatory of the plaintiff. This is an astonishing decision. It would not seem to matter whether the statement is true, provided that in the minds of certain people it implicates the plaintiff, and this implication is false. So a newspaper which publishes a correct statement that a certain person has been murdered may be held liable to anyone whose friends believe him to have committed the murder.

Whether the statement is capable of being understood as referring to the plaintiff is a question of law for the judge. Whether it in fact refers to him is a matter for the jury to decide.

Publication

Publication of the statement to persons other than the plaintiff himself is an essential requirement of defamation. This requirement is clearly satisfied where the defendant has intentionally made the statement to another person, but it is enough if the defendant should have foreseen its publication. Several cases have turned on whether the sender of a letter should foresee that it will be opened and read by someone other than its intended recipient. There is no publication when a father opens his son's letter, nor when a butler opens a letter to his employer even though it is unsealed. But it is to be expected that a postcard will be read, that clerks employed by the plaintiff will open letters addressed to him at his place of business and which appear to be business letters, and that a husband will open a letter which though sealed and addressed to his wife looks like a circular (on the last point see *Theaker* v. *Richardson* (1962)). There will also be publication if a Post Office official opens the letter in the course of his duties, for example, to check that it was the class of mail which ought to be placed in an unsealed envelope. Where the defendant has no reason to suspect that his statement is being published, as in the case where the statement is overheard by one whose presence is reasonably unsuspected by the defendant, there is no publication (*White* v. *Stone Lighting and Radio Ltd.* (1939)).

It is also relevant in deciding whether there has been publication to consider the person to whom the statement has been made. Where a statement has been typed or printed at another's request, there is no publication when the statement is handed back to its author (*Eglantine Inn Ltd.* v. *Smith and Smith* (1948), a Northern Ireland decision—the typist or printer may be liable for its subsequent distribution under principles to be discussed below). Publication by the defendant to his wife is also not enough though publication to the wife of the plaintiff is. In general the person to whom publication is made must be able to understand the statement —there is no publication by speaking the words to a deaf person who cannot lip-read, nor to an infant who is below the age of understanding. Where the defendant's words have some special sense which can only be appreciated by one who knows of facts not stated by the defendant, it must be shown that publication has been made to such persons, though it is not necessary that any of them should be called to give evidence that he did so understand the defendant's words (*Hough* v. *London Express Newspapers Ltd.* (1940)). Publication by dictating the statement to a typist is sufficient (*Pullman* v. *Hill and Co.* (1891)).

One who repeats a defamatory statement made by another person is liable if the repetition constitutes a publication even if he does not know that the statement is defamatory. The original maker of the statement is liable for such republication if he has authorised it, or, it seems, if it is reasonably foreseeable. On these principles, the author, publisher, and printer of defamatory material and even such mechanical distributors as newsagents, bookshops and libraries are liable in defamation for the dissemination of the material among the public (for the defences available in the case of innocent defamation, see pp. 246-247). All, it seems, are principals in respect of the publication (although as between themselves one may be the agent of the other) and they will be treated as joint tortfeasors. The printers in *Eglantine Inn* v. *Smith* (*supra*) were held liable on these principles because they clearly envisaged the distribution of the defamatory material among the public, and could therefore be taken to have authorised it. More difficulty exists where the defendant has not authorised its subsequent publication, for example, where he has made a speech at which reporters are present, or has told defamatory matter to a reporter without authorising him to publish it. English law is unclear about the liability of the maker of the statement, but the question probable depends upon the foreseeability of the later publication.

Failure to remove defamatory matter may constitute publication (held *obiter* in *Byrne* v. *Deane* (*supra*) where the court considered that failure to remove the libel from the club notice-board amounted to publication). But the limits of this rule are ill-defined. There must be control by the defendant over the place where the statement appears and an expectation that he will keep it under periodic review. *Byrne* v. *Deane* was followed in the American case of *Hellar* v. *Bianco* (1952) in which failure to remove a libel from the wall of a toilet was held to be actionable defamation.

Nature of the liability for defamatory statement

Liability for publication of the statement requires, as noticed already, fault, in the form of intention or negligence on the defendant's part. Furthermore it seems clear that the defendant must intentionally make a statement (for example if the defendant's computer produced a defamatory statement through some mechanical defect, the defendant would not be liable). The defendant need not, however, know of the defamatory nature of the statement. He is liable, for example, if he does not know of facts which make the statement defamatory of the plaintiff, or if he does not realise that the statement refers to the plaintiff. Defamation is therefore in this sense a tort of strict liability (the "reference" cases, *supra*, p. 243, make it clear that liability is strict, although in all of them it is arguable that the defendant was at least negligent; in *Hulton* v. *Jones*, in failing to make it clear that the statement was intended to be fiction, in *Cassidy* and *Morgan* in failing to make proper enquiries, and in *Newstead* in failing sufficiently to identify the correct Harold Newstead).

DEFENCES TO DEFAMATION

Innocent defamation

The common law position whereby an innocent defamer could be held liable to pay substantial damages was clearly unjust. The rigour of the law has been mitigated in two respects.

(1) *Mechanical distributors*

Mechanical distributors of a libel, for example, newsagents, carriers, booksellers and circulating libraries are liable for publication of the libel despite ignorance of its existence. *Vizetelly* v. *Mudie's Select Library Ltd.* (1900) gives the mechanical distributor a defence if he can show that he neither knew nor ought to have known of the existence of the libel in the work he was distributing.

(2) *Unintentional defamation*

Printers and publishers. The printer and publisher (other than a mere mechanical distrbutor) (the term "publisher" no doubt covers broadcasts on radio or television) of a defamatory statement cannot make use of the defence based on *Vizetelly's* case but may establish a defence based upon section 4 of the Defamation Act 1952. Under the terms of this section the publisher may make an offer of amends to the aggrieved party. This means an offer: (a) to publish or join in the publication of a suitable correction and apology; and (b) to take such steps as are reasonably practicable on his part for notifying persons to whom copies have been distributed that the words are alleged to be defamatory of the party aggrieved. If the offer of amends is accepted by the party aggrieved and duly performed, no proceedings for libel or slander may be taken against the party making the offer. If the offer of amends is not accepted by the party aggrieved, it is a defence to an action for libel or slander to prove that the words were published innocently in relation to the plaintiff. Innocent publication is defined in such a way as to include the various types of unintentional reference to the plaintiff in the cases considered above. It is also required, however, that the defendant must have exercised all reasonable care in relation to the publication and there must be some doubt whether each defendant in those cases could have established this. The defendant must also show that if he was not the author of the words, that the words were written by the author without malice. The difficulty of proving both the defendant's own lack of fault and the author's lack of malice has caused this section to be of little use to defendants. The Committee on Defamation Report (Cmnd. 5909) recommended that the latter requirement should be dispensed with.

Justification

Defamation cannot be committed by telling the truth however deleterious an effect the truth may have on another's reputation. For the law protects the plaintiff against imputations about his actual character, rather than one he is generally thought to possess. The defendant, however, has the onus of establishing the truth of what he has said—he must justify the statement. The defendant justifying need only show that his statement was substantially accurate. A statement that the plaintiff had been sentenced to a fine or three weeks' imprisonment was justified by showing that he had actually been given the alternative of two weeks in prison (*Alexander v. North-Eastern Ry. Co.* (1865)). Further, section 5 of the Defamation Act 1952 provides that the defence will not fail if the truth of several charges is not established provided that, having regard to the truth of the remaining charges, the charge not proved does not materially injure the plaintiff's reputation. If, for example, the defendant states the plaintiff's conduct amounts to obtaining property and pecuniary advantage by deception under the Theft Act 1968, whereas in fact his conduct amounts to only one of these offences, the defendant could, it seems, justify by proving this. In such a case, however, there is nothing to prevent the plaintiff relying in his statement of claim on the one defamatory statement which the defendant cannot justify. A low award of damages might be expected here, although the defendant cannot adduce in mitigation of damages the fact that the plaintiff committed the other offence (*infra,* p. 258). The Report of the Committee on Defamation recommended that section 5 of the Defamation Act 1952 should be amended to allow the defendant to refer to the whole of his statement in his defence of justification, so preventing the plaintiff from relying on a defamatory passage while omitting other material which the defendant can justify.

The defence of justification is vitally bound up with the interpretation of the statement (*cf.* for example, the distinction drawn in the cases discussed above (p. 242) between a statement that X suspects Y of fraud and a statement that X says Y is guilty of fraud. The former can be justified by proof of X's suspicion; the latter only be proving that Y has committed fraud)).

An extraordinary twist to the defence of justification has been provided by the Rehabilitation of Offenders Act 1974. The Act has introduced the notion of a "spent" conviction. Where a person has received a sentence for a crime, which generally speaking must not exceed 30 months' imprisonment, and where a certain period of time varying from five to 10 years has elapsed since the conviction (the rehabilitation period) the conviction becomes spent and the convicted person is entitled to be treated in law as though he had not been committed, charged with, prosecuted for, convicted of or sentenced for that offence. A person who publishes any of these facts may nevertheless rely upon the defence of justification (or any of the other defences to defamation). In the case of justification the Act expressly provides that this defence cannot succeed if the publication is proved to have been made with malice. The Act thus establishes the first infraction of the principle that truth is an absolute defence to the publication of defamatory material. It is worthy of note that section 13 of the Civil Evidence Act 1968 prevents the convicted person re-opening the issue of his guilt in proceedings for defamation by providing that the conviction is conclusive evidence of this fact.

Fair comment

It is a defence to an action of defamation that the defendant's words were fair comment upon a matter of public interest. More latitude is allowed to the defendant in establishing this defence than the previous one. In so far as his words consist of comment he is not required to show the objective correctness of his views. Indeed it is the difficulty of determining what is the correct view on so many matters that has led to the recognition of this defence. But the courts have placed on the extent of the defence a number of restrictions which must now be considered.

Matter of public interest

The matter commented on must be one of public interest. Thus, it may concern the conduct of public officials, the government of the country both central and local, works of art and other matters submitted for public consideration, and other matters of public concern (such as the running of relig ious institutions) of which an exhaustive list cannot be given. The private life and conduct of anyone is not a matter of public interest, unless it throws light upon such matters as his fitness to hold public office.

Comment on true facts

The basis of the defence of fair comment is that the defendant is stating his honest opinion about certain facts. It is essential, therefore that his statement must contain, or refer to, facts upon which a comment can be based. If no such factual basis is stated, the allegation itself is treated as one of fact and must be justified-fair comment is not available as a defence. If, for example, the defendant has stated that X is a coward without more, fair comment is no defence, and he must prove the truth of the allegation. If, however, he alleges X to be a coward because he failed to volunteer for military service during the war, this is comment, and is protected provided he honestly believed it. Fair comment is, therefore, an important bastion of freedom of speech, allowing persons commenting on public affairs to indulge in criticism of a virulent or outspoken nature. The factual content of the statement need not be expressly stated and may be derived by implication from its context. Also, provided the defendant has referred to facts upon which he is commenting, these facts themselves do not need to support the allegation. These points emerge from the case of *Kemsley* v. *Foot* (1952). The defendant, a journalist, had written an article in a newspaper condemning the newspaper, the "Evening Standard" for its unethical standards in publishing a certain story. The article was headed "Lower than Kemsley." The House of Lords held that, taken in conjunction with the article itself, the headline could be regarded as an intended slur on the journalistic standards of the Kemsley press, and that a sufficient factual content existed in it (*i.e.* that Lord Kemsley was the proprietor of certain newspapers) to allow the defendant to plead the defence of fair comment.

What facts must the defendant prove in order to establish the defence of fair comment? Three types of fact must be distinguished in order to answer this question. The first are facts necessary to establish the minimum factual content of the statement in order to make available the defence of fair comment. This minimum factual content must be accurately stated though, as *Kemsley* v. *Foot* indicates, the requirement is easily satisfied. Second are facts stated by the defendant in his statement which go to establish the fairness of the comment. The former rule was that the defendant had to prove every factual allegation in his statement—comment had be on facts truly stated. Under section 6 of the Defamation Act 1952, however, this is no longer necessary. The section provides that a defence of fair comment shall not fail by reason only that the truth of every allegation of fact is not proved if the expression of opinion is fair comment having regard to such of the facts alleged or referred to in the words complained of as are proved. This section refers only to the defence of fair comment and not to justification. The defendant must prove the truth of every defamatory allegation of fact in his statement, even though he could establish fair comment in relation to the facts he can prove (see *Truth (N.Z.) Ltd.* v. *Holloway* (1960)). Third are facts which the defendant has not stated in his comment but which he relies on to establish the fairness of his comment. Clearly the defendant will not fail by reason of a failure to prove one or more of such facts-the only relevance of such failure is that it tends to show the comment could not have been made fairly. The defendant in *Kemsley* v. *Foot*, for example, would have needed to prove quite a lot more by way of factual basis for his comment than that it referred to Lord Kemsley and his newspapers.

Because the defendant may have to prove the truth of factual allegations, whereas in the case of comment need only show that it is fair, it is clearly important to distinguish between what is fact in the defendant's statement and what is comment. This may, however, be a troublesome question. If the defendant has criticised a certain play because of the inadequacy of its plot, this is comment and it is irrelevant that the majority of leading drama critics would disagree with the defendant's views. If, however, the play is based on true events, a criticism which failed to make this clear and at the same time castigated the weakness of the plot would be factually inaccurate and the plea of fair comment would fail for this reason. The mere fact that the truth of the defendant's comment may be tested either empirically or by hearing evidence on the matter does not necessarily deprive it of the status of comment, provided it is a fair comment in the light of what is known to the defendant. This is because what the defendant is expressing is an opinion as to the truth of the fact, rather than advancing it as fact itself. The defendant runs the risk, however, that the court will treat his statement as a factual allegation and require him to justify it. This is well illustrated by *London Artists* v. *Littler* (1969) in which the defendant, relying on the fact that the owners of a theatre wished to get a certain play produced by the defendant out of their theatre by a certain time, and the fact that the actors in the play all gave notice of termination of their contracts through the same agent at the same time and in the same form, alleged the existence of a plot between the artists and the theatre owners. The Court of Appeal treated this as a factual allegation and required the defendant to justify it.

A particular instance showing the difficulty of drawing the line between fact and comment is that in which the defendant imputes motives of dishonesty or self-seeking to the plaintiff. Such an allegation is treated as one of comment, but in evaluating the fairness of such a comment the law adopts a stricter test than that applying generally in cases of fair comment. The defendant must here show a reasonable basis of fact for the making of such imputations. Such basis was not present in *Campbell* v. *Spottiswoode* (1863) in which the defendant alleged that the plaintiff's motive in attempting to organise a religious campaign to spread the doctrines of Christianity among heathens was to increase the sales of the plaintiff's own newspaper (*cf.* however, the remarks of Lord Denning M.R. in *Slim* v. *Daily Telegraph* (1968) to the effect that even in cases where dishonesty is alleged, the only test of the fairness of the comment is whether the defendant honestly believed it).

Where the defendant is relying on the proof of certain

facts for the purpose of establishing the defence of fair comment, the plaintiff is entitled to be given particulars of those facts under the rules of pleading. But he is not entitled to be informed in advance by the defendant what aspect of the alleged defamatory publication is fact and what is comment (*Lord* v. *Sunday Telegraph* (1971)). This is a matter for the court to decide. Under the so-called "rolled-up plea," a defence to defamation which purported to combine justification and fair comment into one defence, R.S.C., Ord. 82, r. 3 (2) requires the defendant to specify in advance what part of his publication is fact and what is comment. But the Order has meant that the use of the plea is now obsolete. Of course, if the defendant pleads only fair comment, and the courts finds that there are defamatory allegations of fact in his statement, his defence will fail unless the court gives him leave to justify.

Fairness of the comment

Given the truth of the facts on which the defendant has commented, the court must then decide on the fairness of the comment. Courts are loth to pronounce comment upon true facts unfair, since the defence of fair comment is an important bastion of freedom of speech. Lord Denning remarked in *Slim* v. *Daily Telegraph* that the defence of fair comment is available to an honest man expressing his honest opinion on a matter of public interest, no matter how wrong, exaggerated or prejudiced that opinion. The defence will only fail therefore if either the comment is so blatantly unfair that no honest man could have written it, or if it is proved that the defendant had no genuine belief in the truth of what he said. There are two exceptions to this principle. Where the defendant's comment imputes dishonesty or dishonourable motives to the defendant (as in *Campbell* v. *Spottiswoode, supra*), the comment must be one which could reasonably be made on the facts known to the defendant. Secondly, in the case where the defendant's comment is actuated by malice towards the plaintiff, this will render his comment unfair even if he honestly believed in the comment and even though the comment itself would have been fair if made by one who genuinely believed it to be true (*Thomas* v. *Bradbury, Agnew & Co.* (1966)). This rule appears to have the effect of precluding one who is proved to be malicious towards the plaintiff from commenting unfavourably on the plaintiff or his work. The Report of the Committee on Defamation made the satisfactory suggestion that the only test of the fairness of the comment should be whether the defendant believed it. This suggestion would apply to both the special cases considered in this section.

Burden of proof
The onus is on the defendant to establish that the facts on which he commented were true, that the comment was such as an honest man might make, and that the matter commented on was one of public interest. The plaintiff must prove malice on the part of the defendant. The judge decides whether the matter commented on is one of public interest. The other questions that arise in relation to the defence must be decided by the jury.

Privilege
It may be a defence to an action of defamation that the statement was made on a privileged occasion. Such privilege may arise in the public interest (for example, the public interest in the freedom of reporting certain matters to be considered shortly) or in the private interests of the persons between whom the statement is communicated. If the occasion is one of absolute privilege, this is a complete defence to proceedings for defamation, however irresponsible or malicious the statement may be. If the occasion is one of qualified privilege, the privilege may be defeated by proof that the defendant was malicious.

Absolute privilege
The following are subject to absolute privilege:

(i) statements made in the course of parliamentary proceedings; this privilege extends to all reports, papers, votes and proceedings published by, or under the authority of, either House of Parliament. It is not possible to refer to a speech made in Parliament in order to establish malice in relation to a speech made outside Parliament (*Church of Scientology of California* v. *Johnson-Smith* (1973)).

(ii) communications between high-ranking officers of state;

(iii) statements made during the course of judicial proceedings, whether by the judge, counsel or witnesses:

(iv) a fair and accurate report in any newspaper or in a wireless broadcast of proceedings publicly heard before any court exercising judicial authority within the United Kingdom, if published contemporaneously with the proceedings;

(v) communications between solicitor and client; the privilege may be limited to communications made with reference to forthcoming litigation, other communications enjoying only qualified privilege.

Qualified privilege
On occasions of qualified privilege there is for various rea-

sons not the same paramount need to protect the freedom to make the statement as in the cases considered above. Accordingly proof of malice by the maker of the statement will destroy the privilege.

Occasions of qualified privilege. Qualified privilege may arise when a statement is made for the protection of the public interest, or for the protection of the private interest of one or more persons. Examples of the former category are a statement made to the police by a member of the public giving information about the commission of a crime, and a complaint about misconduct or neglect of duty by a public officer made by a member of the public to the proper authority.

Qualified privilege in the public interest also attaches to a number of reports of the proceedings of public bodies. For example, at common law qualified privilege exists in respect of fair and accurate reports of parliamentary proceedings and of judicial proceedings. The latter privilege is wider than the statutory absolute privilege in respect of such reports in that it is available whatever form the report takes and no matter at what time it is made, and also in that it extends to the reporting of the proceedings of administrative tribunals. Various reports receive qualified privilege under section 7 of the Defamation Act 1952, for example, of public meetings, of the proceedings of a local authority, or of the proceedings at the general meeting of a public company (the privilege is forfeited if the publisher has unreasonably refused to publish a reasonable statement by the plaintiff by way of explanation or contradiction of the published statement) or, *e.g.* of public legislative proceedings in any of Her Majesty's Dominions, of proceedings of international organisation such as the United Nations or its constituent bodies, or of the proceedings in public of the International Court of Justice (in these cases the privilege is not lost by refusal to publish a statement on behalf of the plaintiff by way of explanation or contradiction). These are examples of cases where the public not only has an interest in the making of the statement but also in receiving the statement. This is not true of all statements made in the public interest. Thus information about a crime alleged to be committed by the plaintiff should normally be supplied to the police rather than to the public at large.

Where the interest is that of the speaker alone, the recipient must have a legal, moral or social duty to protect the interest. Where it is that of the recipient alone, the speaker must have a legal, moral or social duty to communicate the statement. It seems clear, also, that qualified privilege applies when each party has an interest to be protected by the making of the statement, whether the interests are distinct or common to

both parties. Equally, where one party has a duty to make
and the other to receive, the statement, qualified privilege
applies (*Riddick* v. *Thames Board Mills* (1977). The cases
very often do not fit easily into any one category. The chief
requirement is that the statement should be made for the
genuine protection of an interest or the performance of a
duty.

A case which illustrates the operation of these principles is
Watt v. *Longsdon* (1930). In that case the defendant, a
company director, received some defamatory allegations
about the plaintiff, an overseas employee of the company, in
a letter. The allegations were of drunkenness, dishonesty, and
sexual immorality. The defendant showed the letter to the
chairman of the board of directors of the company, and to
the plaintiff's wife. The former communication was held to
be subject to qualified privilege because of the common
interest of the defendant and the chairman in the plaintiff's
conduct. The communication to the wife was, however, held
to be not subject to qualified privilege because although the
wife had an interest in her husband's conduct, the defendant
had no duty of any sort, moral, social or legal to make
communications about such conduct to her. The case does
not rule out the possibility of a third party having a duty to
communicate to one spouse details about the behaviour of
the other; on the facts however the defendant was behaving
as an officious intermeddler in the plaintiff's marital affairs.

Excess of privilege and malice

It is necessary to distinguish these two matters because the
House of Lords decision in *Adam* v. *Ward* (1917) has made it
clear that they are different. The defendant may exceed the
privilege by publishing the statement to persons other than
those to whom publication is necessary for the protection of
an interest. For example, it will not normally be necessary
for the protection of a private interest to publish a statement
in the press and if this is done the privilege will be forfeited.
Similarly, the privilege may be forfeited if extraneous matter
not germane to the privilege is included in the defendant's
statement (as in *Tuson* v. *Evans* (1840) in which the defendant's statement that the plaintiff owed him rent included the
further statement that the plaintiff was dishonest). The prohibition upon publication of an otherwise privileged statement to third persons without an interest in receiving the
communication does not mean that any publication of this
sort automatically causes the forfeiture of the privilege. Publication to clerks and typists of the defendant is within the
privilege provided it is reasonable and within the ordinary
course of business. So also is a company protected if it sends

a copy of its auditor's report to the printers with a view to its circulation among shareholders. In these cases there was doubt whether the privilege protecting the publication to typists was original or ancillary to the publication of the statement to a third party on a privileged occasion (the cases in which the privilege had been recognised concerned subsequent publication of the statement to a third party, for example, *Osborn* v. *Boulter* (1930)). If there was no subsequent privileged publication because, for example, the defendant decided not to send the letter or because he sent it to the plaintiff himself, a doubt remained whether publication of the statement to the typist amounted to defamation. In *Bryanston Finance Co.* v. *De Vries* (1975), the Court of Appeal, in dealing with the second of the two factual situations, decided that publication to the typist was privileged because the privilege was an original one. The conclusion has convenience if not logic to support it.

Qualified privilege may also be lost where the defendant has published a statement which does not exceed the privilege but can be proved to have been actuated by malice towards the plaintiff in making the statement. Malice for the purposes of qualified privilege means that the defendant has no honest belief in what he has said. However prejudiced, irrational or wrong-headed he may be, his belief in the truth of the statement prevents a finding of malice (recently affirmed by the House of Lords in *Horrocks* v. *Lowe* (1974), *cf.* the similar principles governing fair comment). There is an exception to this where the defendant has made use of the privilege for some improper purpose other than the legitimate protection of an interest. Here the defendant's honest belief in the truth of the statement will not protect him (*e.g. Winstanley* v. *Bampton* (1943)—the defendant who in publishing the statement was motivated by feelings of spite or anger towards the plaintiff was malicious though he honestly believed its truth (*cf.* also *Angel* v. *Bushell & Co.* (1968)).

Malice and joint publication

The question of the effect upon the liability of joint publishers of the malice of one of them arises in connection with the defences of fair comment and of qualified privilege, and it may be assumed that the same considerations apply to both defences. Where each joint publisher has a separate and independent privilege, he will not be affected by the malice of one joint publisher. Thus in *Egger* v. *Viscount Chelmsford* (1965) members of the Kennel Club came to a decision that the plaintiff should not be allowed to officiate as judge at a dog show and communicated this in a letter to a third party. The letter was covered by qualified privilege but it was found that several members of the committee had been malicious in reaching their decision. The Court of Appeal held that their malice did not affect the privilege of the other members of the committee since each had a separate, independent privilege. Where the privilege of each joint publisher is not a separate privilege, but is a privilege derivative from one of their number the position is less clear. Are the printer and publisher of a work, who enjoy the same privilege as its author, affected by the malice of the author if the privilege is qualified? In *Egger* v. *Viscount Chelmsford* it was held that the secretary of the Kennel Club who wrote the letter on the instructions of the Committee and who was found to be not personally malicious was not liable, (by Lord Denning M.R. and Harman L.J. because an innocent agent should not be "infected" by his principal's malice, by Davies L.J. because the secretary had a separate and independent privilege). It may be assumed that the reasoning of the majority applies to protect all other innocent agents of the author. Where an employee maliciously publishes a defamatory statement on a privileged occasion, the employer is vicariously liable (so decided by the majority of the Court of Appeal in *Riddick* v. *Thames Board Mills* (1977)).

Consent
    It is a defence that the plaintiff consented to the publication of the defamatory material (see *Cookson* v. *Harewood* (1932)).

Apology
    In order to establish the defence of apology under section 2 of the Libel Act 1843, the defendant must show that the libel was inserted in a newspaper or other periodical "without actual malice" and "without gross negligence" and that the defendant inserted a full apology for the libel either before the commencement of the action or at the earliest opportunity afterwards. The apology must be accompanied by a payment into court of money by way of amends. Apology is a complete defence to the plaintiff's action, but if it fails the defendant will be penalised in costs even though his payment into court exceeded the amount of damages awarded by the jury (though the apology may still go in mitigation of damages). This has meant that apology is an unpopular defence, since the effect of a payment into court under Order 22 of the Rules of the Supreme Court is to make the plaintiff responsible for costs incurred after the payment if the damages awarded by the jury do not exceed the payment, and this procedure is therefore preferable. It is nevertheless

still advisable to publish an apology which may go in mitigation of damages.

REMEDIES

Damages

The primary remedy for defamation is the action for damages. Libel is actionable *per se*, as are certain forms of slander. In the case of defamation actionable *per se*, damages are at large. Therefore aggravated damages (*i.e.* increased damages arising from the circumstances of the tort's commission, *infra*, p. 311) and parasitic damages (*i.e.* for injury to interests other than reputation, for example, injured feelings, *infra*, p. 311) may be awarded. Furthermore in the case of defamation actionable *per se*, the plaintiff does not need to prove his loss—general damages may be awarded in respect of damage which is presumed to have occurred from the fact of the tort's commission (though sometimes the court will refuse to presume such damage. Contemptuous damages of a farthing were awarded to the plaintiff in the *Newstead* case, (*supra*, p. 244)). Exemplary damages can no longer be awarded in actions for defamation unless the defendant has calculated that his profit from publication of the defamatory matter will exceed the amount of damages awarded to the plaintiff, (see, for example, *Cassell* v. *Broome* (1972) confirming on this point the speech of Lord Devlin in *Rookes* v. *Barnard*)). The Report of the Committee on Defamation recommended the complete abolition of exemplary damages in defamation. The defendant is entitled to plead in mitigation of damages that the plaintiff's reputation is bad, but the court is here concerned with the plaintiff's reputation as it is and not as it ought to be. The defendant cannot therefore adduce specific events by way of detraction from the character the plaintiff is generally thought to possess (*Plato Films* v. *Speidel* (1961)). The Report of the Committe on Defamation recommended abolition of this rule.

The courts are reluctant to issue interlocutory injunctions in cases of defamation, and will not do so when the defendant intends to plead justification or fair comment. Furthermore, the issue of a writ will not be allowed by the court to stifle further comment upon any matter—such further comment is only a contempt of court if there is a real risk, as opposed to a mere possibility, of interference with the administration of justice (*Att-Gen* v. *Times Newspapers* (1973)).

22. THE ECONOMIC TORTS

There is no general principle of liability in tort for intentionally causing another economic loss. The defendant may not be liable for causing such loss even though he has been malicious (*Allen* v. *Flood* (1898)) or has competed in an "unfair" manner (*Mogul S.S. Co.* v. *McGregor Gow & Co.* (1889)). English courts have attempted to solve the problem of imposing liability for causing economic loss by creating a series of exceptions to a general principle of no liability. These exceptions appear to turn on the existence of one or more of three factors:

(i) An improper motive in the defendant. Though malice is generally irrelevant, it may not be so where the defendants have acted in combination.

(ii) The existence of a right in the plaintiff. The courts are more ready to give their protection when the defendant has interfered with a right of the plaintiff or something analogous to a right. The tort of interference with contract protects the plaintiff's enjoyment of his contractual rights. Intangible rights of property such as copyright, patents, and registered trade marks are protected by actions in tort. The tort of passing-off recognises a right in the name and appearance of the plaintiff's goods or services, clearly an analogous right to that of the other forms of intangible property.

(iii) The means used by the defendant. The defendant may incur liability because the means he has used are unlawful (interference with contract, conspiracy, intimidation and unlawful means) or because he has told a lie (deceit and injurious falsehood).

It has been suggested that there is a principle of liability underlying all the economic torts to the effect that it is tortious intentionally to damage another by means of an act which the actor was not at liberty to commit (Weir (1964) C.L.J. 225). It will be seen in the course of this chapter that the principle is difficult to harmonise with cases in which the defendant was held not liable for causing loss through the use of unlawful means (p. 268). In *ex parte Island Records*, Lord Denning M.R. held that whenever the defendant was causing damage to the plaintiff by interfering with his trade or calling by means of an unlawful act, the plaintiff was entitled to an injunction to stop him. The other member of the majority in the Court of Appeal did not lay down so broad a proposition. In any case it is likely that Lord Denning was referring to equitable relief rather than to liability in tort.

In many cases of liability for causing economic loss the result is achieved by influencing a third person to act to the plaintiff's loss. This result is inherent in the notion of an economic interest which generally presupposes an advantageous relationship with another person. However, it is possible for the economic torts to be committed otherwise than through the medium of a third party, and in the case of deceit this is invariably true. Another point of importance is that although the intention of causing the plaintiff loss is not a sufficient condition, it is generally a necessary one of liability. Negligence in relation to an economic interest is not enough unless the conditions of *Hedley Byrne* liability are fulfilled.

The economic torts have been subject to considerable legislative intervention in recent years in an attempt to regulate industrial conflict. The Industrial Relations Act 1971 took away the immunity from actions in tort which trade unions had enjoyed since 1906, and created new causes of action against them for causing economic loss. With the repeal of the Industrial Relations Act by the Trade Unions and Labour Relations Act 1974, the immunity of trade unions has been restored although some measure of tortious liability has been retained (for discussion of this point, see *infra*, p. 331).

INTERFERENCE WITH CONTRACT

In *Lumley* v. *Gye* (1853) the principle was established that an action lay, at the instance of the other party to the contract, against one who induced a party to a contract to break it.

The facts in *Lumley* v. *Gye* were that the defendant persuaded a singer, who was under contract to sing at the plaintiff's theatre, to sing at the defendant's theatre instead. The defendant knew of the singer's contract with the plaintiff. The court held that these facts disclosed a cause of action in tort.

Previous to this case, although it was recognised that a master could sue one who enticed his servant away from his services, there appeared to be no general principle of protection of contractual rights. The case is, therefore, an important milestone in the recognition and protection by the courts of purely economic interests. As long as *Lumley* v. *Gye* marked the boundaries of the tort, the law was reasonably clear. Developments which have taken place since *Lumley* v. *Gye* have clouded the picture. In the first place it is now established that action lies for indirect interference causing a breach of contract, rather than direct persuasion. The probability is that in the case of indirect interference, the defendant must have used unlawful means. Secondly, it is no longer clear that the defendant must have induced a breach of contract.

Elements of the tort

Actionable interference with contract
Until recently, lip-service, at least, has been paid to the view that the defendant's act must induce a breach of contract. If, for example, A persuades B to terminate lawfully his contract with C, C could not sue A under *Lumley* v. *Gye*. The view that the defendant's act must induce a breach was difficult to reconcile with cases in which the defendant's act had made it impossible for the other party to the contract to perform (see, for example, the facts of *G.W.K. Rubber Co.* v. *Dunlop* (1926); *J.T. Stratford* v. *Lindley* (1965) (*infra*, p. 263). On facts such as these, it is arguable that no breach had been committed by the defendant. The possibility of frustration of the contract in these circumstances may also be present. That an actionable breach is not necessary is shown by *Torquay Hotel Co.* v. *Cousins* (1969). In that case the defendants were officials of the Transport and General Workers Union (T.G.W.U.). The union had a dispute over recognition with the Torbay Hotel in Torquay. The plaintiffs, who owned the Imperial Hotel in Torquay, became involved in the dispute through the act of the managing director of the Imperial Hotel, who made a statement which was reported in the press to the effect that the local Hotels Association would "stamp out" the T.G.W.U. in Torquay. As a result of this the defendants decided to stop supplies of oil reaching the Imperial Hotel. The Imperial had a contract for the supply of fuel oil, as ordered, with Esso. Esso drivers were members of the T.G.W.U. and would clearly not cross the latter's picket lines. One of the defendants telephoned Esso and informed them that because of the dispute supplies of oil to the plaintiffs would be stopped. No oil was, in fact, ordered or delivered, although Esso informed the managing director of the Imerial Hotel that they could not supply him with oil. Esso was protected from liability for breach of contract in these circumstances by reason of a *force majeure* clause in the contract. Nevertheless the Court of Appeal held that a prima facie case of inducing a breach of contract under the *Lumley* v. *Gye* principle had been established. Russell and Winn L.JJ. thought that it was sufficient that Esso were in breach of contract although protected from liability by the *force majeure* clause. Lord Denning M.R. proceeded on a

broader plane. He thought that where there was direct interference with a contract, which all three members of the
Court of Appeal thought to exist in this case, there was no
need for a breach at all. Lord Denning's view may be seen as
a logical development from the earlier cases. It would mean,
however, that conduct which is perfectly lawful, in itself and
in its result, might be found to be tortious. It seems doubtful
whether the need to protect economic interests justifies this
extension.

Act constituting an interference

In deciding what acts amount to an interference with contract, a distinction is sometimes drawn between direct interference and indirect interference. Examples of the former are
persuasion of the other contracting party, and physical
restraint aimed against him; of the latter, industrial action
taken against him. It is suggested, however, that the more
fundamental distinction is between persuasion of one of the
parties to the contract to break it, and the doing of an act
which, whether directly or indirectly, has the effect of preventing performance of the contract. The latter category
would include both physical and industrial action against a
contracting party. In the case of prevention of performance,
it seems probable that the defendant is liable only if he has
used unlawful means. Indeed it is possible to view the use of
unlawful means to prevent the performance of a contract as
part of the wider tort of causing loss by unlawful means
(*infra*, p. 268). This would mean that the difficulties mentioned above of deciding whether the tort of interference
with contract is limited to interference inducing a breach
would disappear where the defendant has used unlawful
means. This view would also make it possible to safeguard to
some extent the original *Lumley* v. *Gye* principle by requiring, *pace* Lord Denning in *Torquay Hotel* v. *Cousins*, that, in
cases of persuasion, the persuasion must induce a breach of
contract.

(1) *Persuasion*

The defendant's persuasion must induce (*i.e.* cause) a
breach of contract. It is not necessary that the defendant
should stand to profit from the breach, nor is the line that is
drawn between persuasion and mere advice to break the contract a sound one, since it simply restates the issue as to
causation. If the defendant, whether through persuasion or
advice, has induced a breach of contract, he is liable. The
defendant's persuasion may take the form of a dealing with a
party to the contract which the defendant knows to be a
breach of that contract (as in *B.M.T.A.* v. *Salvadori* (1949)).

In principle there ought to be liability only if the dealing has induced the breach. If the party to the contract had already decided to break his contract before the dealing, the latter has not caused the breach. This derives a measure of support from *Batts Combe Quarry* v. *Ford* (1943)—acceptance of a gift known to be given in breach of contract was not actionable under *Lumley* v. *Gye.*

Finally, in relation to persuasion, further mention must be made of *Torquay Hotel Co.* v. *Cousins.* In that case all three members of the Court of Appeal thought that there was direct interference with the contract because of the telephone call made by the defendants to Esso. Since, however, the purpose of the phone call was merely to inform Esso that its drivers would not be allowed to deliver oil to the plaintiff, it seems wrong to equate this with persuasion. Such interference should have been regarded as coming within the second category of prevention of performance of the contract.

(2) *Prevention of performance of the contract*

In the first place, the defendant may have physically prevented the performance of the contract. In *Lumley* v. *Gye*, for example, had the defendant unlawfully detained the singer, thereby falsely imprisoning her, the result in law would have been the same. In *G.W.K. Co.* v. *Dunlop Rubber Co.* (1926) a car manufacturer contracted with the plaintiff that tyres manufactured by the plaintiff should be displayed on his cars appearing at an exhibition. The defendant replaced the plaintiffs' tyres on cars on show at the exhibittion with tyres of his own manufacture. He was held liable to the plaintiff under *Lumley* v. *Gye* principle. Also coming within this category is the use of industrial action against a contracting party which has the effect of making it impossible for him to perform his contract. In *J.T. Stratford Co,* v. *Lindley* (1965) the defendants, who were officials of the Watermen's Union, wanted negotiating rights for the union in respect of three union members employed by a company called Bowker & King. The other 45 employees of Bowker & King were members of the Transport and General Workers Union. J.T. Stratford, the chairman of Bowker & King, had refused negotiating rights in respect of these employees to both unions, but he later concluded an agreement covering all his employees with the T.G.W.U. The defendants thereupon instructed members of their union not to handle barges belonging to J.T. Stratford & Co. (of which J. T. Stratford was chairman and which was controlled by him) and which had been hired out to customers, nor to handle barges which were to be or had been repaired by that company. The result of this embargo was that the company's barge-hiring and barge-repairing businesses were crippled. The House of Lords found that a prima facie case of interference with contract had been made out in respect of the barge-hiring business, since the defendants must have realised that the barges were hired out under contracts which required their return to the company on completion of the contract. In respect of the barge-repairing business sufficient knowledge of the contracts for repair could not be proved to justify a finding that there was a prima facie case of liability under the same principle. In any case, an interlocutory injunction was issued against the defendant to cease their embargo.

Until the *Stratford* decision it had generally been thought that where the interference took the form of prevention of performance of the contract rather than direct persuasion, the defendant must have used unlawful means. The means used might be a tort (for example, the tort of trespass in *G.K.W. Co.* v. *Dunlop Rubber Co.*), or a breach of contract (assumed to be the case in *D.C. Thomson & Co.* v. *Deakin* (1952), although in that case since no breach of contract had been committed it was not possible to establish unlawful means). The judgments of the House of Lords in the *Stratford* case, however, are curiously equivocal on the question whether unlawful means are necessary in the second category of interference. Lord Pearce actually said that it was unnecessary to decide whether the refusal of union members to work the plaintiffs' barges was a breach of their contracts of employment so as to constitute unlawful means. Lord Reid and Viscount Radcliffe thought that a breach of the contract of employment had been committed, but appeared to think this was relevant only to liability for causing loss by unlawful means rather than to liability under the *Lumley* v. *Gye* principle. Viscount Radcliffe and Lord Donovan seemed to treat the case as essentially one of causing loss by unlawful means rather than of interference with contract. Only Lord Upjohn treated the case unambiguously as one of interference with contract and he clearly thought that there was a requirement of unlawful means in this tort. Admittedly the action was for an interlocutory injunction and the House of Lords had only to be satisfied that the plaintiffs had a prima facie case. Even so, the lack of clarity in the judgments is unsatisfactory. If there is no requirement of unlawful means in interference with contract coming within the second category, this surely should have been stated more explicitly.

Knowledge of the contract by the defendant

The requirement of knowledge of the contract by the defendant is illustrative of the requirement of the economic torts generally that the defendant must intend to cause loss. The rule is generally stated in terms of actual knowledge (*British Industrial Plastics* v. *Ferguson* (1940), though there has been some relaxation of this requirement. Thus where, as in *J.T. Stratford & Co.* v. *Lindley* the existence of a contractual relationship between the company and the hirers of its barges must have been obvious to the defendants together with the fact that their action would bring about a breakdown of those contracts, sufficient knowledge existed. In *Emerald Construction Co.* v. *Lowthian* (1966) it was held that where the defendant knows of the existence of a contractual relationship, he commits the tort if he intends to bring that contract to an end even if he assumes that it can be lawfully terminated. No case yet has countenanced the possibility of "constructive knowledge" of the contract being enough.

Damage

It appears to be the law that the plaintiff must prove that he has suffered damage arising from the interference.

Only the party not in breach can sue under the *Lumley* v. *Gye* principle. Since it is clear that in the "prevention of performance" cases, the other party may also suffer economic loss, and since the tort may extend beyond interference producing a breach of contract, it is not obvious why in appropriate cases the party against whom action has been taken to produce the interference shoud not sue.

CONSPIRACY

The tort of conspiracy is committed when two or more persons conspire together to injure the plaintiff, or when they together use unlawful means with the result that the plaintiff is injured. It is a wider tort than inducement of a breach of contract in that its field of protection is not limited to rights arising under contract. Conspiracy became a potentially important tort when it was decided that it lay even where the conspiracy was to perform a lawful act, provided the defendant intended to injure or damage the plaintiff. In the sphere of economic interests in particular, conspiracy appeared to be a means of getting round the rule of English law that an act done intentionally to infringe the economic prosperity of another person was not *per se* tortious. Despite the dubious logic which accepted that what is done by one person is not actionable but will be actionable if done by two, this did seem to promise some redress in cases where people suffered damage caused intentionally by their trade competitors. However, it eventually became established that a combination to cause economic damage to another person is not actionable unless the predominant purposes of the defendants is to cause that damage. If, for example, they are acting in the furtherance of their own interests, no action for conspiracy will lie against them. Thus, in *Crofter Hand Woven Harris Tweed Co. Ltd.* v. *Veitch* (1942) the defendant union officials instructed dockers to refuse to handle yarn sent from the mainland of Scotland for delivery to the plaintiffs' factory in the Outer Hebrides. The plaintiffs depended entirely upon these supplies in order to weave cloth. The defendants had no trade dispute with the plaintiffs but wished to reduce the competition provided by the plaintiffs' business for other mills on the island which employed union labour, so that the employers could increase wages. The House of Lords held that this was not conspiracy since the defendants' predominant purpose was the protection of members of their union. The case may be compared with *Quinn* v. *Leathem* (1901). The plaintiff had been employing non-union labour, but was willing for his men to join the union and was willing to pay their fines and entrance money. The defendant union officials refused this offer and ordered that the men be discharged and compelled to walk the streets for 12 months. The plaintiff refused to do this, and the defendants then brought pressure to bear on a customer of the plaintiff as a result of which he stopped dealing with the plaintiff. The plaintiff recovered for this loss in conspiracy. In view of the plaintiff's offer, the defendants had acted vindictively and not in protection of their legitimate interests. The interests furthered by the combination need not be economic nor need the action be in the private interests of those combining in order to come within the protection of the *Crofter* case (*Scala Ballroom (Wolverhampton) Ltd.* v. *Radcliffe* (1958)— legitimate combination aimed against the plaintiff who operated a colour bar). But the courts have a power to say whether the interest is one that can legitimately be protected. Thus, in the *Crofter* case, Viscount Maugham thought that a conspiracy aimed against the religious views, or the politics or the race or colour of the plaintiff would be actionable. Viscount Simon thought the same would follow where those combining did so because of a bribe offered to them by a third party.

It appears that the burden of showing that the predominant intention of the defendants was to injure him, lies on the plaintiff (a majority of the law lords in the *Crofter* case were in favour of this view). Where damage disproportionate to the purpose of the defendants has been inflicted upon the plaintiff, this does not in itself make the defendants liable, but is evidence that their primary intention was to injure the plaintiff.

Conspiracy by agreement to use unlawful means

This type of conspiracy may have the advantage that it does not appear to be limited by the requirement of the *Crofter* case that the defendants' predominant purpose must be to injure the plaintiff, although it seems necessary that the defendants must have as part of their purpose the infliction of injury or damage on the plaintiff. Since, however, the individual use of unlawful means to inflict damage on another person is normally actionable, conspiracy adds little here, unless the effect of a conspiracy is to render actionable the use of unlawful means which if used by individuals would not be actionable.

INTIMIDATION

The tort of intimidation consists in a threat to commit an unlawful act (or that an unlawful act will be commited), intending as a result of the threat to produce damage to the plaintiff, and actually producing such damage. The existence of this tort, long in doubt, was finally confirmed by the House of Lords in *Rookes* v. *Barnard* (1964). The defendants were three officials of the A.E.S.D. Union, two of whom were employed by B.O.A.C. A branch of the union had, at a meeting at which the defendants were present, passed a resolution under which it was agreed that all union labour would be withdrawn unless the plaintiff, who was not a member of a union, was dismissed by B.O.A.C. The union had an agreement with B.O.A.C. providing for 100 per cent union membership. There was also in the agreement a "no strike" clause which the defendants later conceded to be incorporated in the contracts of employees subject to the agreement. The defendants notified B.O.A.C. of the union resolution and B.O.A.C. thereupon lawfully terminated the plaintiff's contract of employment. The plaintiff was held to be entitled to damages for his loss from the defendants. The ground for the decision was that the individual acts of the defendants amounted to the tort of intimidation, since each had threatened B.O.A.C. with an unlawful act, namely, a withdrawal of labour in breach of the "no strike" clause (or in the case of the official not employed by B.O.A.C. the commission of an unlawful act by other persons). The combination to utter such threats was therefore an actionable conspiracy not protected by section 1 of the Trade Disputes Act 1906 (the then equivalent of section 13 (4) of the Trade Union and Labour Relations Act 1974).

It will be noticed that three parties were involved in *Rookes* v. *Barnard*, the defendants, the plaintiff and B.O.A.C. Where only two parties are involved, *i.e.* where the plaintiff receives a threat which causes him to act to his own loss, there is less reason for the existence of the tort of intimidation since the plaintiff will normally have other remedies against the defendant. Thus if he is threatened with a breach of a contract to which he and the defendant are parties, his contractual remedies will normally protect his interest in having that contract performed. If threatened with physical violence he can sue in tort by using a *quia timet* injunction. There are cases, however, in which the existence of a tortious remedy may be necessary in a two party situation. It has been held, for example, that an agreement in restraint of trade is unlawful means for the purpose of an action for causing loss by unlawful means (*Brekkes* v. *Cattel* (1971)). Yet if the plaintiff were to receive a threat from the defendant that he and another person intended to enter into such an agreement unless the plaintiff complied with the threat, the plaintiff has no remedy unless the defendant carries out the threat (in which case the agreement can be declared void under the Restrictive Trade Practices Act 1956, and damages awarded to the plaintiff). Equally, it appears that a conditional threat of future physical violence if the plaintiff does not comply with the condition does not constitute assault (see above). If the plaintiff is denied the remedy of intimidation here, having acted on the threat to his loss, he may have no other remedy.

CAUSING LOSS BY UNLAWFUL MEANS

The question of whether liability in tort exists for the infliction of economic loss by unlawful means is a difficult one. It is probably true to say that in the case of the intentional infringement of a penal statute causing economic loss, the question is identical with the question of whether an action for breach of statutory duty will lie (although in *Williams* v. *Hursey* (1959), an Australian case, the High Court of Australia thought that a combination to violate a penal statute was actionable though no action for breach of statutory duty lay). In other cases everything depends upon whether the court concludes that the predominant purpose of the illegality is its sole purpose. In *Chapman* v. *Honig* (1963) the Court of Appeal held that a landlord who had issued a notice to quit in circumstances in which it was a criminal contempt of court (because it was designed to punish the tenant for having given evidence in court against the landlord) was not civilly liable to the tenant, since the sole purpose of the illegality was to ensure the due administration of justice. Again in *Hargreaves* v. *Bretherton* (1950) it was held for a similar reason that no civil action lay against one who had given perjured evidence. On the other hand, the mere fact that the illegality has to do with the administration of justice will not necessarily defeat the plaintiff. In *Acrow (Automation)* v. *Rex Chainbelt Inc.* (1971) it was held that where the defendant, in order to defeat an injunction which the plaintiff had obtained against a third party withheld supplies from the plaintiff (a civil contempt), this was the tort of causing loss by unlawful means. The distinction between this and the two earlier cases may be that the purpose of the illegality was here fairly obviously to safeguard individual rights as well as to ensure the due administration of justice.

Many of the cases in which actions have been allowed have concerned action taken against third parties with the intention of causing the plaintiff loss. In *Tarleton* v. *McGawley* (1794) the defendant fired a cannon at a canoe of natives who were trading with the plaintiff's ship as the result of which one was killed and the others returned to land. The plaintiff recovered damages for the loss of his trade from the defendant. In *J.T. Stratford & Co.* v. *Lindley* Lord Reid and Viscount Radcliffe thought that the economic loss the plaintiff suffered through loss of future contracts with barge hirers (not recoverable under interference with contract) was recoverable under this tort, since the defendants had used unlawful means in inducing breaches of the employees' contracts of employment with the barge hirers. In *Rookes* v. *Barnard* Lord Reid, speaking *obiter*, thought that a breach of contract committed with the intention of causing a third party loss is actionable by that third party if loss occurs. Privity of contract was not a fatal objection because the third party was complaining not of the non-performance of the contract, but of the intentional infliction of damage on him through its breach. *Pace* Winfield (p. 492), the cases do not bear out the suggestion that the tort of causing loss by unlawful means is limited to three party situations (*cf*, the *Acrow (Automation)* case). Nor is there any foundation for his suggestion that in three party situations the illegality of the means must be found to be so primarily by reference to the third party. Recent cases, for example, have held that an agreement which appears to be one which would be declared void under the Restrictive Practices Act 1956 is unlawful means for the purpose of this tort (*Daily Mirror Newspapers* v. *Gardner* (1968); *Brekkes* v. *Cattel* (1971)), though clearly such illegality is not aimed at anyone in particular (an agreement which is void as being in restraint of trade at common law is not unlawful means so as to give a civil action to persons

injured by it—*Mogul Steamship Co.* v. *McGregor* (1927). The
reality seems far more complex than Winfield suggests. The
tort of unlawful means seems to give to courts the same sort
of discretion to create new causes of action as the tort of
breach of statutory duty.

Defences

(a) *Trade Disputes*
   Clearly the torts discussed in this chapter have a considerable potential part to play in the area of trade disputes.
Governments of varying political complexions however, have
seen fit to limit the possibility of tortious liability arising
here. The trade union itself was given immunity from actions
in tort by the Trade Disputes Act 1906. This immunity was
removed in 1971 but was restored, with some exceptions in
1974. It is discussed at p. 331. There remains the possibility
of actions in tort against the trade union official or member.
The law on this topic is contained in sections 13 and 15 of
the Trade Union and Labour Relations Act 1974, as amended
by section 3 (2) of the Trade Union and Labour Relations
Amendment Act 1976, and as further amended by sections 15,
16 and 17 of the Employment Act 1980. Section 13 embodies
the principle that where the action taken is "in contemplation or furtherance of a trade dispute" this is a defence to
certain actions in tort that would otherwise be available.
Section 13 (1) as amended provides: an act done by a person
in contemplation or furtherance of a trade dispute shall not
be actionable in tort on the ground only-(*a*) that it induces
another person to break a contract or interferes, or induces
another person to interfere, with its performance. or (*b*) that
it consists in his threatening that a contract (whether one to
which he is a party or not) will be broken or its performance
interfered with, or that he will induce another person to
break a contract or to interfere with its performance. Section
13 (1) (*a*) deals with liability for inducing a breach of or interference with a contract; section 13 (1) (*b*) with intimidation,
where the act threatened relates to a contract. It may be
noted that the provisions apply to all contracts, not merely
to contracts of employment, an extension introduced by the
1976 Act. Section 13 (3) provides: for the avoidance of
doubt it is hereby declared that-(*a*) an act which by reason of
subsection (1) . . . above is itself not actionable; (*b*) a breach
of contract in contemplation or furtherance of a trade
dispute; shall not be regarded as the doing of an unlawful act
or as the use of unlawful means for the purpose of establishing liability in tort. This section removes doubts that might
exist as to whether an act not actionable under section 13 (1)

might still be unlawful so as to give rise to tortious liability.
Section 13 (4) completes the picture by providing that an
agreement or combination to do or procure the doing of any
act in contemplation or furtherance of a trade dispute shall
not be actionable in tort if the act is one which, if done
without any agreement or combination, would not be actionable in tort. This confers immunity from liability in conspiracy
not only upon acts to which section 13 (1) confers immunity
but also upon conspiracies to commit crimes, provided the
crime is not also a tort. The immunities confered by section
13 do not of course cover the whole field of tort. No protection is given, for example, to the commission of assault or
battery in the furthance of a trade dispute.

"in contemplation or furtherance of a trade dispute".
The interpretation of this phrase is clearly of paramount importance in deciding whether the immunities conferred by section 13 apply. The definition of trade dispute is in section 29
(1) of the 1974 Act. This provides that a "trade dispute" means
a dispute between employers and workers (which terms
include employers' associations and trade unions, s. 29 (4))
or between workers and workers, which is connected with
one or more of the following:

(a) terms and conditions of employment, or the physical
conditions in which any workers are required to work;
(b) engagement or non-engagement, or termination or
suspension of employment, or the duties of employment of
one or more workers;
(c) allocation of work or the duties of employment as
between workers and groups of workers;
(d) matters of discipline;
(e) facilities for officials of trade unions;
(f) machinery for negotiation or consultation, and other
procedures, relating to any of the foregoing matters, including the recognition by employers or employers' associations
of the right of a trade union to represent workers in any such
negotiation or consultation or in the carrying out of such
procedures.

Existence of the trade dispute
The definition of "trade dispute" is a broad one. Nevertheless it is clear that the question of the existence of the trade
dispute is determined objectively. The trade dispute must
actually exist (*per* Lord Diplock in the *Express Newspapers*
case). An example of a case where a trade dispute was found
not to exist is *BBC* v. *Hearn* (1977). The defendant union

officials were restrained by injunction from instructing their members to commit breaches of their contracts of employment with the BBC by preventing the television broadcast by satellite of the F.A. Cup Final to overseas countries including South Africa of whose apartheid policy the union disapproved. There was no trade dispute within the terms of section 29 (1) between the union and its members, and the BBC. Nevertheless the Court of Appeal recognised that the defendants could have converted the dispute into a trade dispute within section 29 (1) (a) by demanding that it should be a term of their members' contracts of employment that they should not be required to broadcast to South Africa. The requirement of section 29 is that the dispute need only be "connected with" terms and conditions of employment. It seems, therefore, that most disputes are capable of being converted into trade disputes. In *N.W.L. Ltd.* v. *Woods* (1979) the defendants were officials of the International Transport Federation, a federation of trade unions representing transport workers. ITF had a policy aimed against shipowners who flew flags of convenience on their ships rather than the flag of domicile, and were thereby enabled to avoid negotiating rates of pay with unions in their own countries and so to engage cheap, Asiatic labour. The defendants issued instructions to their members at the port of Redcar to "black" the plaintiffs' vessel, which was flying a flag of convenience, unless the plaintiff signed an agreement that they would enter into articles with the crew on the standard ITF terms. The crew itself were quite satisifed with their terms of employment. The plaintiffs claim for an interlocutory injunction (*infra*, p. 276) against the defendants to stop the blacking failed. Lord Diplock thought it was quite unarguable that the dispute was not connected with terms and conditions of employment. Even if the demands being made of the employer were unreasonably or might drive him out of business, this did not change the character of the dispute. Nor did it matter whether the predominant purpose of the defendants was not to improve the conditions under which Asiatic seamen were employed, but to "drive Asiatic seamen from the seas" provided there was a dispute connected with terms and conditions of employment. Lord Scarman thought that the connection with terms and conditions must not be a sham. Thus there would be no such connection where the defendant was pursuing a private grudge, or acting out of sheer vindictiveness (thus approving the cases of *Huntley* v. *Thornton* (1957); *J.T. Stratford Co.* v. *Lindley* (1965)).

"in contemplation of furtherance".
The latter two decisions could equally well have been

explained on the basis that the defendant was not acting in contemplation or furtherance of a trade dispute. A decision to pursue a private grudge under the guise of a trade dispute clearly does not contemplate or further the dispute. What, in general, is the test the words lay down? Do they mean that the act must actually be capable of furthering the interests of a party to the dispute, or is an honest belief that it is so capable enough? The latter, subjective formulation has been approved by the House of Lords in *Express Newspapers Ltd.* v. *McShane* (1980) and *Duport Steels Ltd.* v. *Sirs* (1980). Questions of the "remoteness" of the action taken from the dispute and its parties were relevant to showing only that the belief was not honestly held. Lords Salmon and Keith in the Express case suggested that the belief must be a reasonable one, but only in the sense that if no reasonable person could have entertained it, this would not do.

Secondary action
The House of Lords decisions in *Express Newspapers* v. *McShane* and *Dupont Steels Ltd.* v. *Sirs* recognise that immunity may exist in relation to action taken against non-parties to the trade dispute, provided it is believed that this action will conduce to an eventual favourable resolution of the dispute. Such action is referred to as secondary action. In *Express Newspapers Ltd* v. *McShane*, for example, a dispute existed between the National Union of Journalists and the Newspaper Society, a body representing proprietors of provincial newspapers. The NUJ called a strike among its members in the Press Association, a news agency which supplied news copy to both provincial and national newspapers. The strike response was only partial. The defendant NUJ officials therefore instructed its members working for the national press (including the plaintiff newspaper) to "black" copy emanating from the Press Association. This action was held to be within the protection of the "contemplation or furtherance" formula, since the defendants had a bona fide belief that the solidarity of the strike at the Press Association would be increased thereby, thus increasing pressure on the Newspaper Society.

In order to restrict the immunity attaching to secondary action, section 16 of the Employment Act 1980 was passed. The section is complex, but its broad effect may be stated as follows. The immunities conferred by section 13 (1) (a) and (b) and the consequential immunities in section 13 (3) and (4), that exist in relation to action taken to "interfere" with contracts of employment with employers not party to a trade dispute are abolished where the effect of the action is to produce "interference" with contracts which are not contracts of employment. Certain secondary action, however, remains within the protection of section 13. Section 16 (3) excepts secondary action designed to prevent the supply of goods or services between an employer who is a party to the trade dispute, and the employer under the contract of employment to which the secondary action relates. The secondary action has to be likely to achieve that purpose. Section 16 (4) excepts secondary action designed to prevent the supply of goods or services to another person through an associated employer of the party to the dispute, the goods or services being in substitution for those which but for the dispute would have fallen to be supplied by the employer party to the dispute, the contract of employment to which the secondary action relates being with either the associated employer or the recipient, and the secondary action being likely to achieve its purpose. Section 16 (5) deals with secondary picketing and is considered in the next section.

Picketing
   Picketing is not itself a tort. It may however form the basis of recognised torts such as public nuisance through obstruction of the highway (see *Hubbard* v. *Pitt* (1976), or trespass on the highway. Economic torts such as conspiracy or interference with contract may also be committed by pickets. Section 15 considerably curtails the immunity which a person picketing in contemplation or furtherance of a trade dispute previously enjoyed. Picketing is declared to be lawful if it is done in contemplation or furtherance of a trade dispute by a worker at or near his own place of work (or in the case of a worker dismissed because of a trade dispute, his former place of work) or by a trade union official at or near the place of work of a member of that union whom he is accompanying, and whom he represents, and in both cases for the purpose only of peacefully obtaining or communicating information, or peacefully persuading any person to work or abstain from working. The so-called flying picket is now clearly an unlawful picket. Where however picketing has the effect of producing secondary action as defined in section 16 (*i.e.* in relation to contracts of employment with employers not party to the dispute and producing an interference with commercial contracts), section 16 (5) preserves the immunity from liability in tort existing under section 13 provided the picketing complies with the requirements of section 15. Thus a person picketing at his place of work in furtherance of a trade dispute is not liable in tort if he peacefully persuades the employees of an employer not party to the dispute to break their contacts of employment by, for example, not delivering goods to his employer's premises.

Acts to compel trade union membership

The effect of section 17 is to remove any immunity conferred by section 13 where a person has taken action of the sort referred to in section 13 aimed at a contract of employment, or at any other contract through the medium of a contract of employment, for the purpose of compelling workers to become members of a particular trade union, where none of those workers works for the employer under the contract of employment to which the action relates. For example, a trade union official who in an attempt to produce a "closed shop" agreement with employer X persuaded the workers of employer Y to break their contracts of employment by boycotting X would not enjoy immunity under section 13.

(b) *Justification*

The extent of this defence is ill-defined. It may enable a court to indicate disapproval of a contract which is nevertheless legally enforceable. For example, in *Drimelow* v. *Casson* (1924) the defendants, who were representatives of certain theatrical unions, induced theatre proprietors to break their contracts with the plaintiff, a theatre manager. This was held to be justified on the ground that the plaintiff paid his chorus girls such low wages that they were compelled to turn to prostitution. Only in rare cases of this sort will the defence succeed since it is not normally for the court to speculate whether a legally enforceable contract deserves to be enforced, nor generally, upon the justifiability of action which is otherwise illegal.

INTERLOCUTORY INJUNCTIONS

An important weapon in the trade dispute is the interlocutory injunction. By means of this a party to a trade dispute may obtain an immediate injunction against industrial action taken against him pending trial of the action. Because of the nature of trade disputes, the interlocutory proceedings almost invariably constitute the real trial of the action. A trade union would hardly wish to wait a number of years for the final determination of the dispute to find whether a particular strike was legal. The plaintiff in order to obtain an injunction in interlocutory proceedings needed to show that the balance of convenience lay in his favour (which normally he was able to show by proving that he would suffer irreparable damage before the action came to trial) and that he had a prima facie case of proving an actionable wrong. The House of Lords decision in *American Cyanamid Co.* v. *Ethicon* (1975), however, changed the latter requirement to one that the plaintiff need only establish that there was a serious question to be tried. In response to this decision, the legislature added section 17 (2) to the Trade Union and Labour Relations Act 1974. This requires the court, in exercising its discretion whether to grant an interlocutory injunction, to have regard to the likelihood of the defendant establishing a defence under sections 13 and 15 of the Act. The intention seems to have been to re-establish the previous rule that the plaintiff must establish a prima facie case of the defendants liability to succeed. In the *N.W.L.* case, the *Express* case and the *Dupont Steels* case, all members of the House of Lords were agreed that this is now the law, although opinions differed as to whether section 17 (2) had changed the law established by American Cyanamid, or was merely declaratory of the position in relation to trade disputes which that case did not affect. Certain reservations were made. Lord Diplock in *N.W.L. Ltd.* v. *Woods* thought that the defendant would have to establish a high degree of likelihood of a "trade dispute" defence succeeding where the consequences of his action were likely to be disastrous to the employer, to third parties, to the public or to the nation. Lord Fraser in the Dupont case thought that the court might grant an injunction even where no prima facie case existed where the health or safety of the public were threatened; Lord Scarman in the *Express Newspapers* case where the freedom of the press was seriously threatened.

23. THE ECONOMIC TORTS: PASSING-OFF

The tort known as passing-off protects primarily the person whose trade competitor passes off his goods or services as that person's. It is often said that in this tort the courts are recognising a proprietary right in the description or appearance of the goods or services, a right of intangible property akin to such things as copyright, patents, and design (which now receive the protection of statute). In a way all rights protected by the law of torts are proprietary in the sense that the protection they enjoy is universal—they are *iura in rem*. But it seems true to regard passing-off as a proprietary type of tort, in a particular sense, since in it the plaintiff is complaining not of damage inflicted upon himself or his property by the defendant, but of the defendant's unauthorised use of something which belongs to the plaintiff. In this, passing-off strongly resembles conversion, the other tort with a predominantly proprietary purpose. Passing-off is the "purest" of the economic torts. Its purpose is almost exclusively the protection of economic interests. Furthermore, passing-off has become of increasing importance since the courts by allowing numerous extensions of it have used it as a means of controlling unfair trade competition. This has meant, however, that the boundaries of the tort and its extensions are somewhat ill-defined. In order to commit passing-off, the defendant must have done something to suggest that the goods or services which he is selling to the public are those of the plaintiff. The following are some of the methods of passing-off that have been recognised by the courts.

Use of the plaintiff's trade mark
Although it is now possible to register trade marks under the Trade Marks Act 1938 and to bring a statutory action for their infringement, the action for passing-off is still available where the defendant has used the plaintiff's trade mark on his goods, and may be necessary, for example, where the plaintiff has not complied with the statutory requirements for registration.

Use of plaintiff's trade name
In *Powell* v. *Birmingham Vinegar Brewery Co.* (1896), the plaintiff sued to protect the name "Yorkshire Relish" which

the plaintiff used for the sauce he manufactured. The action was successful.

The trade name may be derived from the area in which the goods are manufactured. Thus, successful actions have been brought to protect the trade names "Stone Ales," "Chartreuse" liquers, and "Champagne." The last case (*J. Bollinger* v. *Costa Brava Wine Co. Ltd. (No.* 2) (1961) concerned an action by a manufacturer of champagne against the defendants who described their wine, produced in Spain, as "Spanish champagne." It was held that the word "champagne" was still generally regarded as referring exclusively to wine produced in the Champagne district of France. that the prefix "Spanish" did not prevent the possibility of purchasers being misled into thinking they were purchasing such wine; that the plaintiff could obtain an injunction to prevent the defendant's use of the name, although he was only one of the wine producers in the Champagne district.

The Spanish Champagne case has been approved and extended by the House of Lords in *Warnink* v. *Townend* (1979). The plaintiffs were one of a number of producers of advocaat, a drink consisting of a mixture of eggs and spirits. The defendants manufactured a drink in England which they marketed as "Old English Advocaat," and which was made from dried eggs and Cyprus sherry. Because of the sherry base it sold at a cheaper price than the plaintiffs product. The House of Lords granted the plaintiffs an injunction against the defendants use of the name advocaat for their product. That name had acquired an exclusive meaning that spirits and not wine were used in its manufacture. Thus the Spanish champagne ratio protecting products exclusively associated with a particular region has been extended to products exclusively associated with a particular process.

When the plaintiff is alleging that he alone has the right to use words which simply describe the goods or their characteristics, he has a difficult burden of proof to discharge in that he must show that these words have acquired the status of a trade name. This was achieved by the successful plaintiff in *Reddaway* v. *Banham (George) & Co. Ltd.* (1896) where an injunction was obtained to protect the name "Camel Hair Belting." It is possible, though not decided, that where the trade name ceases to be exclusively identified with the plaintiff and comes to be regarded as a description of the product itself, he can no longer sue to protect it. It may be, however, that the explanation is that his acquiescence in its use by others over a period of time allows the defendant to establish a defence of consent.

Use of defendant's name

It is sometimes said that there is nothing to prevent a person trading by or describing his goods by his own name. But it is clear that this is not so where the use of the name is fraudulent (*Croft* v. *Day* (1843)), nor where, though innocent, it creates avoidable confusion with that of that plaintiff (*Baume & Co. Ltd.* v. *A.H. Moore Ltd.* (1958)). Where confusion is unavoidable it seems that the defendant is entitled to use his own name, unless the plaintiff can prove that in the minds of the public the production of goods under a certain name is exclusively associated with himself (*Parker-Knoll* v. *Knoll International* (1962)). Where the plaintiff and defendant are not in competition with each other, the plaintiff may still succeed against the defendant for using a name identical with or similar to his own, provided the use of the name is calculated to cause him damage. The action is for a tort analogous to passing-off (*Harrods Ltd.* v. *R. Harrod* (1923) is one of a number of examples).

Imitating appearance of plaintiff's goods

There are common-sense limitations to this method of committing the tort. Thus, where the similarity between the goods is in their functional rather than their decorative aspects, the courts are normally unwilling to interfere.

Action for torts analogous to passing-off

The courts have also allowed actions in some cases where no action for passing-off would lie, if the case is analogous to passing-off. For example, though no action for passing-off will lie where plaintiff and defendant are not in economic competition (see *McCulloch* v. *May Ltd.* (1947)—plaintiff, a children's broadcaster who used the name "Uncle Mac" unsuccessful in action of passing-off against defendants who manufactured a cereal, "Uncle Mac's Puffed Wheat"), it seems to be accepted that an action for a tort analogous to passing-off will lie if the defendant's act is calculated to cause damage to the plaintiff's reputaion or livelihood (held so in *Sim* v. *H.J. Heinz Co. Ltd.* (1959) and *Borthwick* v. *Evening Post* (1888)—in that case an injunction by the proprietor of the *Morning Post* against the defendants to prevent them calling their evening newspaper the *Evening Post*, was refused only because the defendant's act was not calculated to cause the plaintiff damage).

An action analogous to passing-off was also available in *Sales Affiliates Ltd.* v. *Le Jean Ltd.* (1947). The plaintiffs marketed materials which were used in a permanent wave process known as "Jamal." There was evidence that this process was exclusively associated in the trade with the plaintiff's materials. The defendant hairdressers used other materials when asked by their customers for the "Jamal" treatment. This was held to be a tort analogous to passing-off the latter not being available because the defendant had not sold goods or services to the public which they had represented as those of the plaintiffs.

Other requirements of passing-off and the analogous torts

Act calculated to deceive

It is a question of fact whether the defendant's act is calculated to deceive. Evidence may be received from persons actually deceived but such evidence is not necessary.

Defendant need not know of the infringement

It is settled that passing-off can be committed by one who is acting in complete good faith and without negligence. This emphasises the proprietary nature of the action and here also it resembles conversion.

Damage

It is unnecessary to prove damage in an action of passing-off. Further, the court may, as in the case of libel, presume that damage will flow from the defendant's act and thus award substantial damages though no actual damage is proved. It is, however, doubtful whether damages can be claimed from the defendant for the period before he knows of the infringement. In the action for the analogous tort the plaintiff must show that the defendant's act is calculated to cause damage to his business or reputation.

Other forms of unjust trade competition

Some forms of trade competition are outside the scope of an action of passing-off or the analogous action. An example of this is *Cambridge University Press* v. *University Tutorial Press* (1928). The defendants claimed that a book published by them was the book prescribed for study by an examination board for its examination. In fact the book published by the plaintiffs had been prescribed. The plaintiffs' action against the defendants failed. Clearly, people could not have been misled into believing that they were buying the plaintiff's book; but if the use if the plaintiff's name is actionable if calculated to cause him damage (*supra*, p. 279), why should not also be the use of a quality with which the plaintiff is exclusively associated (another example would be a claim by garage A that it was the last before a motorway, whereas this was true of garage B)? There seems to be no real difference of principle between the *Cambridge University* case and *Sales*

Affiliates v. *Le Jean*, in which the plaintiff was successful. For similar reasons, it seems that the law will not protect the plaintiff whose "scoop" newspaper story is published without acknowledgement by the defendant, or the dog-racing stadium broadcast commentaries of whose races are relayed from a vantage point outside the stadium (*Victoria Park Racing and Recreation Grounds Co. Ltd.* v. *Taylor* (1937)).

Where an action for passing-off, or the analogous tort, is not available, there is still a possibility of obtaining an injunction, if the court considers that the defendant is infringing a right of property of the plaintiff. The availability of the injunction depends therefore upon the extent to which courts are willing to recognise new rights of intangible property. So far, however, the courts have confined its availability to cases where the defendant is abusing information entrusted to him in confidence by the plaintiff (*cf. infra*, p. 300). Whether the protection will be extended to cases where the defendant is not breaking a confidence is a problem for the future.

24. THE ECONOMIC TORTS: DECEIT AND INJURIOUS FALSEHOOD

DECEIT

The tort of deceit is committed by one who makes a fraudulent misrepresentation to another who acts upon it to his detriment. The tort is not limited to the recovery of financial loss (in *Burrows* v. *Rhodes* (1899) the plaintiff recovered for physical injury suffered through his participation in the Jameson raid which he joined on the strength of a false representation by the defendant). Deceit has become of reduced importance since a duty of care in respect of statements was recognised by the House of Lords in *Hedley Byrne* v. *Heller and Parnters Ltd.* (1963). But differences in the measure of damages in deceit (*infra*, p. 284) may mean that it is still worthwhile to attempt to prove fraud rather than negligence. It is still necessary to prove fraud in the making of the statement where either the requirements of *Hedley Byrne* or of the Misrepresentation Act 1967 (*supra*, p. 80) cannot be met.

Requirements of deceit
The requirements of deceit are as follows:

(i) the defendant must make a false representation;
(ii) he must either know that it is false or make it recklessly, not caring whether it is true or false;
(iii) he must intend that the plaintiff act or fail to act on the representation;
(iv) the plaintiff must suffer damage as a result of his reliance on the representation.

False representation
The term "representation" has acquired a restricted meaning given to it by courts of equity in deciding whether to grant the equitable remedy of rescission. Representations about the future intentions of the representor, opinions and representations of law are excluded. The term is similarly limited in the tort of deceit. But a statement of future intention is actionable if at the time of making it the defendant did not have that intention, since there is sufficient factual content in the representation, *viz.* that at the time of making it he did have that intention (*Edgington* v. *Fitzmaurice*

(1885)). Similarly a statement of opinion is at least a representation that the defendant actually holds that opinion. In *West London Commercial Bank Ltd.* v. *Kitson* (1884) a representation about the effect of a private Act of Parliament was held to be actionable in deceit, but it cannot be predicated whether this would be true of a representation about the general law. There is also liability for stating half-truths, ambiguities, and for action taken to conceal the truth (*Schneider* v. *Heath* (1813)—defendant took steps to conceal from a prospective buyer that his ship had rotten timbers). There is authority in support of the view that one who knows that events subsequent to the making of a statement make it no longer true is liable, as is one who subsequently discovers the falsity of the statement, if the statement is left uncorrected (this does not extend, however, to one who changes his mind after an accurate statement of future intention).

Knowledge of the falsity
There is some difficulty where the representation is made by a person other than the defendant. Where a servant acting in the course of his employment commits deceit, the master is vicariously liable. The same applies to a principal, where his agent has committed the tort, provided the agent has authority to make representations in the relevant matter. There is also liability if a fraudulent principal makes the representation through an innocent agent. But it is not possible to make the principal liable where his agent has innocently made a misrepresentation of whose untruth the principal would have known (*Armstrong* v. *Strain* (1952)). There would, of course, be liability if the principal knew that the agent was making the misrepresentation.

Intention that plaintiff should act on the representation
It is not necessary that the representation should be made to the plaintiff himself. Thus, in *Langridge* v. *Leny* (1837), the plaintiff's father bought a gun from the defendant who knew that the father intended his sons to use it. The defendant fraudulently represented that the gun was sound. He was held liable to the plaintiff who was injured when the gun burst on firing. Clearly the defendant *intended* the sons to act upon the statement though he did not *desire* it, since whether they did or not became immaterial to him after the completion of the father's purchase. On the other hand, in *Peek* v. *Gurney* (1873) it was held that statements in a prospectus issued by the defendant were intended by him to be acted upon only by those who acquired shares by subscription from the company (to whom the prospectus would have been issued) and not by subsequent purchasers of the shares on the

market. The fact that it is foreseeable that the plaintiff should act on the representation is, therefore, not enough. This rule, though satisfactory for negligent statements, seems open to criticism where fraudulent statements are concerned.

Plaintiff's reliance on the representation

It must be shown that the representation was at least one of the reasons for the plaintiff acting as he did. Thus, in *Smith* v. *Chadwick* (1884), the plaintiff had bought shares in a company on the faith of a prospectus which contained the untrue statement that a certain person was a director of the company. Since the plaintiff had never heard of this person, he could not show that he relied on the statement in the prospectus and his action therefore failed.

Plaintiff must suffer damage

The normal claim in deceit is for economic loss, but personal injury and damage to property are also recoverable.

Remedies

An action for damages is the virtually invariable remedy for deceit. In *Doyle* v. *Olby (Ironmongers) Ltd.* (1969) the plaintiff bought a business from the defendants about which the latter had made various fraudulent misrepresentations including one to the effect that all the trade was over the counter whereas, in fact, the employment of a traveller was necessary, The plaintiff recovered the following items as damages: (i) the difference between the price he paid for the business and its actual value; (ii) expenditure incurred in the course of running the business, *viz.* rent, rates, and the interest on a bank overdraft. In contract the plaintiff would have recovered only the difference between the value of the business as represented and its actual value, since in contract the plaintiff is put into the position he would have been in had the representation been made good; in tort he is put into the same position as if it had never been made. The damages awarded for the first item included the reduction in value through the plaintiff's being unable to afford to employ a traveller. This suggests that in deceit damages will be awarded even though they are caused by the plaintiff's impecuniosity, a more favourable measure than in tort generally (cf. *Liesbosch (Dredger)* v. *S.S. Edison (Owners)* (1933)). Lord Denning went to far as to say that the defendant was liable for all loss flowing directly from the fraud, whether foreseeable or not. *Mafo* v. *Adams* (1970) decided that exemplary damages may also be recovered in deceit though only if the case comes within one of the three categories laid down by Lord Devlin in *Rookes* v. *Barnard* (*infra*, p. 312). A sum may also be awarded in respect of the plaintiff's mental or physical suffering arising from the fraud (*Shelley* v. *Paddock* (1980)).

Lord Tenterden's Act

Under the Statute of Frauds 1677 a guarantee was unenforceable unless it was in writing and signed by the guarantor or his agent. After the action for deceit was created in 1789, it became possible to circumvent the statute by suing in deceit rather than on the guarantee itself. This resulted in the passing of Lord Tenterden's Act in 1828 which provided that a false representation as to credit could not be sued upon unless made in writing and signed by the representor or his agent. The Act is limited to fraudulent representations—it does not apply where the representation is made negligently (*W.B. Anderson* v. *Rhodes (Liverpool)* (1967)). The curious result is produced that the defendant might be able to defeat an action brought in respect of an oral representation as to credit by establishing his own fraud, though whether the courts would allow him to succeed is not clear.

INJURIOUS FALSEHOOD

Injurious or malicious falsehood consists in the making of a false statement by the defendant about the plaintiff or his property which is calculated to cause him damage and as a result of which the plaintiff suffers damage. The tort is a generalisation from specific cases. It was called slander of title to make a verbal attack on another person's title to land as a result of which the land lost value or a purchaser could not be found for it. Slander of goods consisted in a similar attack on the plaintiff's chattels. The close relationship of these torts to defamation itself is indicated by their name. In *Ratcliffe* v. *Evans* (1892), however, the Court of Appeal found that these torts formed part of a wider principle by virtue of which any intentionally false statement made by the defendant about the plaintiff or his property was actionable, even though it was not defamatory, if it resulted in damage to the plaintiff. In that case the defendant published a statement in his newspaper that the plaintiff's firm had ceased to exist, knowing that this was untrue. The plaintiff recovered damages from the defendant in injurious falsehood for the loss of custom he suffered as a result of the statement.

Elements of the tort

The following are the chief elements of the tort:

(1) *There must be a false statement about the plaintiff or his property*

Where the statement does not refer to the plaintiff or his

property, this does not appear to be tortious even though the plaintiff suffers damage as a result. If, for example, on the facts of *Ratcliffe* v. *Evans*, another firm which enjoyed advantageous business relations with the plaintiff's firm had also suffered economic loss as a result of the loss of custom suffered by the plaintiff's firm, this would not have been recoverable from the defendant. This requirement of injurious falsehood appears to be the reason why statements such as that made in *Cambridge University Press* v. *University Tutorial Press* (*supra*, p. 280) are not actionable as that tort.

(2)   *The statement must be calculated to cause the plaintiff damage*

Because of the courts' policy whereby they will not allow advertising campaigns by rival business men to be conducted in court, the defendant is not liable if his statement is a mere puff, extolling his own product, even at the expense of the plaintiff's. Thus, in *White* v. *Mellin* (1895), the defendant sold infant food produced by the plaintiff in his shop. He affixed to the bottles in which the food was sold, labels stating that a certain food (produced by the defendant) was better in several respects for infants than any other. This was held not to be injurious falsehood. Where, however, the defendant has made a disparaging statement about the plaintiff which goes beyond a mere puff, the requirement that it is calculated to cause damage to the plaintiff is fairly easily satisfied. In *Lyne* v. *Nichols* (1906) a statement by a newspaper proprietor that the circulation of his newspaper greatly exceeded that of the plaintiff's rival newspaper was held to be actionable. Again, in *De Beers Abrasive Products* v. *International General Electric Co. of New York* (1975), where the defendant had circulated in the international trade market a pamphlet which purported to give the findings of laboratory experiments concerning the effectiveness of an abrasive maufactured by the defendants and another manufactured by the plaintiffs, the experiments concluding that the defendant's abrasive was superior, this was held to be more than a mere puff and was capable of amounting to slander of goods.

(3)   *The statement must be made to a third party or parties*

The gist of this tort is that third parties, influenced by the statement, act to the loss of the plaintiff. The plaintiff must therefore show that the statement has come to the knowledge of third parties. Whether, if this happens by the negligence of the defendant, or accidentally, the tort is commited, is uncertain. In the former case, at least, it seems there should be liability.

(4) *The statement must be made maliciously*

This requirement causes most difficulty in connection with this tort. Although malice seems originally to have been necessary only where it was necessary to rebut a "privilege" claimed by the defendant (for example, in cases of slander of title, the defendant himself might have claimed an interest in the land), it now seems to be accepted as applying to all the forms which the tort may take. But the meaning of malice here is dubious. If the defendant makes a statement knowing it to be false, and the statement is calculated to cause damage to the plaintiff, it might be thought that malice is easy to establish. Can the defendant rebut this evidence of malice by showing that he acted for the plaintiff's good? For example, if the defendant makes a false statement about the plaintiff's business to a third party causing that person not to award a profitable contract to the plaintiff, ought the defendant to be able to excuse himself on the ground that he considered it not in the plaintiff's best interest for him to undertake this contract? None of the cases seem to have gone this far, and in *White* v. *Mellin* (*supra*) the House of Lords thought (*obiter*) that either an intention to injure the plaintiff, or a knowledge of the statement's falsity would be enough. It is settled that malice may be established although the defendant was acting to further his own trade interests. Thus, in *Joyce* v. *Motor Surveys Ltd.* (1948), the defendants wished to evict the plaintiff from the tenancy of one of their garages, because they wished to sell their business with vacant possession throughout. They told the Post Office that he had changed his address, and told the tyre manufacturers' association that the plaintiff had ceased trading there (the plaintiff was a tyre dealer). This was held to constitute injurious falsehood. The burden of proving malice lies on the plaintiff.

(5) *Damage*

The plaintiff must show that he suffered damage as a result of the statement. This will normally be pecuniary, though there seems no reason to exclude a claim for physical damage where this has occurred. Where he is claiming that he suffered loss of custom as a result of the defendant's statement, it is not always necessary to call the evidence of particular customers who have ceased trading with him as a result of the statement. In *Ratcliffe* v. *Evans* (*supra*), for example, the plaintiff was allowed to succeed on proof of general business loss, rather than the loss of particular customers. Whether the plaintiff is allowed to do this will depend largely upon the type of falsehood and the circumstances of its utterance. Section 3 (1) of the Defamation Act 1952 further alleviates the position of the plaintiff by allowing him to succeed without proof of special damage at all, (a) if the words complained of are published in writing or other permanent form, and are calculated to cause pecuniary damage to the plaintiff; or (b) if the words are calculated to cause pecuniary damage to the plaintiff in respect of any office, profession, calling, trade or business carried on by him at the time of the publication.

Since most actions for injurious falsehood occur when the plaintiff has suffered such damage, and the majority of these concern damage to the plaintiff's trading interests, the necessity to prove damage will now only rarely arise. Where the requirements of the Act are fulfilled, the subsection places injurious falsehood in the same position as regards proof of damage as libel and slander actionable *per se. Fielding* v. *Variety Incorporated* (1967) shows both the close association between defamation and injurious falsehood and the fact that it may be advantageous to prove the defamatory nature of the statement. The defendants' magazine had published a statement that a play, "Charlie Girl," produced by the plaintiff had been a "disastrous flop." In fact the play had been a great success. The plaintiff recovered £1,500 for libel and £100 for injurious falsehood, the difference being due to the fact that damages for injury to feelings may be awarded in defamation but in injurious falsehood the plaintiff is limited to his actual loss.

Injurious falsehood and negligent statements

It was pointed out in an earlier chapter (p. 000) that injurious falsehood is in danger of being swallowed up by liability in negligence. But *Ross* v. *Caunters* (1980) shows that where A has by a negligent statement made to B caused B to act to C's loss, C can only succeed against A if a sufficient degree of proximity exists between them. If not, C must still establish that A committed injurious falsehood.

25. INTERFERENCE WITH FAMILY RELATIONSHIPS

INTRODUCTION

The law on the subject of torts which interfere with family relationships at one time bristled with anomalies. Most of the worst of these have been removed by the Law Reform Miscellaneous Provisions Act 1970, which has abolished the torts of enticement, seduction (including rape) and harbouring of a child, enticement of a spouse and harbouring of a wife. Section 4 of the Act removes a husband's right to damages from a co-respondent for his adultery with his wife. The only important torts of interference with family relationships which survive are a parent's action for loss of his child's services and the husband's action for loss of his wife's consortium. Even these torts are in many respects irrational, and it is probable that there will soon be further reform in this area of the law (more sweeping changes were envisaged by the Working Paper of the Law Commission on this subject —the changes effected by the Act of 1970 are merely part of these). The Law Commission in its Report on Personal Injury Litigation-Assessment of Damages (No. 56) has recommended the abolition of the parent's action for loss of his child's services, and the husband's action for the loss of his wife's consortium.

It is noteworthy that the surviving torts supply a very incomplete protection for family relationships. A child has no action for injury to its parents, even though as a result of the injury the child has suffered loss of financial support or has incurred medical expenses on the parent's behalf. The first loss will no doubt be defrayed when the parent himself recovers tort damages, although by that time it may be too late; for example, the child may have lost a business opportunity. These remarks apply also to the case of the wife, where her husband suffers injury. She cannot obtain damages for loss of her husband's consortium (*infra*, p. 291). Where, however, the tort has caused the death of the parent or husband, before either has been able to bring his own action, dependants can obtain the full measure of their loss of financial support by taking action under the Fatal Accidents Acts 1846—1959.

PARENT'S ACTION FOR LOSS OF CHILD'S SERVICES

Nature of the defendant's act

The parent must prove that the defendant committed a tort against the child, leading to the loss of service, other than a tort committed in the course of rape. For example, the defendant may have injured the child by committing battery, or negligence.

Proof of loss of services

The parent in his action, which derives from the same source as the master's action for the loss of his servant's service, *i.e.* the *actio per quod servitium amisit*, must establish that he was in receipt of services from the child and that he has been deprived of these as the result of the defendant's act. In theory, therefore, the action is intended to recompense the parent for his economic loss. In practice the courts are willing to place an economic value on the most trivial of domestic services, for example, the making of a cup of tea (*Carr* v. *Clarke* (1818)) or the milking of cows (*Bennett* v. *Allcott* (1787)); indeed the presence of a child under the age of majority in the parent's household is normally enough to imply the fact of service (*Jones* v. *Brown* (1794)). Furthermore, the fact that such services will not be replaced at the parent's expense (for example, by engaging a housekeeper) is irrelevant. But the child must be of a sufficient age to be capable of rendering service—so the parent had no action when his two-year-old child suffered an illness through the defendant's tort (*Hall* v. *Hollander* (1825)). The fact that the child has attained its majority is irrelevant provided service by it is proved. The only difference appears to be that with such a child, service will not be presumed merely from the fact that the child lived in the same household as its parent (*Bennett* v. *Allcott* (*supra*)—that case is an illustration of the ease with which service may be otherwise established).

Plaintiff in the action

The parent's enjoyment of the child's services is part of his right to the custody of the child, a right which normally persists until the child reaches his majority. Custody was at one time held to be the right of the father alone. Now, however, at least where the spouses are living together, each is jointly entitled to custody, and the mother also may bring the action for loss of services (as she may also do when she alone has custody, for example, when her husband is dead). The action may also be brought by any other person who has custody of the child, and who is in receipt of its services, for example, an adoptive parent or a foster parent.

Measure of damages

The damages that can be awarded in this tort are limited to the actual pecuniary loss suffered by the parent. Aggravated damages in respect of injury to the parent's feelings or emotional distress caused by the child's condition cannot be recovered (*Flemington* v. *Smithers* (1826)). But the parent is not restricted to claiming an amount representing the value of the lost services. He is also entitled to claim any out-of-pocket expenses reasonably incurred because of the tort, *e.g.* medical expenses (*Bates* v. *Stone Parish Council* (1954)).

Defences

Contributory negligence by the child does not appear to be a defence, since the parent's action is distinct from that of the child (so held for the analogous action by husband for loss of wife's consortium—*Mallet* v. *Dunn* (1949)). Does this mean that consent by the child will not bar the parent's action? Consent by the parent clearly does so (for example, consent to operation on child).

Conclusion

The tort by its very nature is anomalous. Its requirement that the parent must establish loss of service makes the basis of the claim extremely artificial. In the first place, it means that in many cases the parent receives a financial sum purporting to represent the economic value of the services, but in fact operating more like a payment by way of solatium for the parent's grief. In the second place, the requirement of service bars the reasonable claim of the parent who has incurred expenses on behalf of a child from whom he is not in receipt of service.

HUSBAND'S ACTION FOR LOSS OF CONSORTIUM

A husband may claim damages in respect of a tortious injury to the wife the result of which is that he is deprived of her consortium (which may be described as companionship and support) and her services. Although the action depends upon proof of a tort committed against the wife, the husband's action is quite distinct from that of the wife. So his action is not affected by the wife's contributory negligence (*Mallet* v. *Dunn* (1949)—*quaere*, the effect of other defences available against the wife).

There is a great deal of uncertainty about the types of damage which can be claimed in an action for loss of consortium. Three types of damage must be distinguished: (1) damage arising from loss of the wife's companionship; (2) damage arising from the loss of the services of the wife; (3)

medical and other out-of-pocket expenses reasonably incurred by the husband. There is no doubt of the husband's right to claim under the third head in his action for loss of consortium. Furthermore, it does not matter that there has never been any actual loss of consortium, for example, if the wife receives medical treatment at home. For this reason, the courts have sometimes based the husband's right upon his legal obligation to maintain his wife, so necessitating expenditure by him in the event of her injury.

Under the second head of damage, it seems, it has always been recognised that the husband may claim for the expense of hiring services during a period of total loss of consortium, for example, while the wife was in hospital. There has been uncertainty about the availability of such a claim when cohabitation has been resumed. In *Best* v. *Samuel Fox & Co.* (1952) the House of Lords were equally divided on the question whether the husband could maintain an action when his consortium has merely been impaired, rather than totally lost. Recent cases, however, have favoured the husband's claim where he has been deprived of services during a period when consortium is merely impaired. So in *Cutts* v. *Chumley* (1967) where the wife was rendered totally incapable by her injuries of rendering services, the husband received £5,000 damages representing the future expense of employing a housekeeper to look after the three young children of the marriage. Even where the husband has not had to incur expense in order to replace the wife's services, the court may allow a claim by him. For example, in *Lawrence* v. *Biddle* (1966), a husband who would be required to do more work in the house because of the wife's injury was awarded £40 damages. The definition of such damage in the Australian case of *Toohey* v. *Hollier* (1955) as being of a "material and practical kind because of greatly reduced capacity of his wife to perform the domestic duties, to manage the household affairs and give him her support and assistance" expresses the matter best.

The first head creates the most difficulty. There is no doubt that the husband may claim damages for loss of consortium during the period when he has been totally deprived of his wife's society, even though during this period he has incurred no expense. The only basis for such damage is therefore loss of companionship. It seems very doubtful whether any further damages can be awarded in respect of such intangible matters as diminution of conjugal happiness after resumption of cohabitation (although in *Best* v. *Samuel Fox* (*supra*), Lord Reid, consistently with his view that the action protected impairment as well as total loss of consortium, thought that the husband would have a claim where the wife became sexually frigid as a result of the injury).

Another problem arises where the husband claims for loss of earnings arising from the fact that he has given up his employment in order to visit his wife in hospital. This loss is allowable as damages only if the visits will have the effect of shortening the wife's stay in hospital and therefore the period of loss of consortium, or of maintaining consortium between husband and wife, and thereby reducing the damages that wold have to be paid for loss of it (*Kirkham* v. *Boughey* (1957); *McNeill* v. *Johnstone* (1958)).

Since the basis of the claim for loss of earnings is that they substitute damages that would otherwise be awarded for loss of consortium, it seems unlikely that loss of earnings could be recovered beyond the amount of those damages (see, for example, the judgment of Lord Devlin in *McNeill* v. *Johnstone*). Where the husband does not make loss of consortium the basis of his claim, he cannot recover loss of earnings, though giving up his employment in order to be near or with his wife, even though he acted reasonably (*Kirkham* v. *Boughey*, *supra*—the husband gave up lucrative employment in Africa in order to be near to and visit his wife in hospital. Since he and his wife lived separately while he was in Africa, he could not make the maintenance of consortium the basis of his claim for loss of earnings).

MASTER AND SERVANT

The torts involving a master's claim for the loss of services of his servant are survivals from the days when servants were regarded as part of the master's family circle. It remains a tort to deprive the master of the services of his servant by enticing him or harbouring him although both actions are now obsolete. The *actio per quod servitium amisit* is of rather greater importance since it allows a master to recover from a person who has deprived him of the services of his servant by tortiously injuring the servant. The tort may be one resting on proof of intention or negligence, so that in the case of the latter the action is an exception to the rule that negligence will not lie for purely pecuniary loss. The importance of this tort was, however, considerably reduced by the decision in *I.R.C.* v. *Hambrook* (1956) that it was limited to cases where the service was menial or domestic.

CONCLUSION

It has long been recognised that the English law concerning tortious interference with family relationships is irrational.

Certain persons are given a right to sue for loss of services or society. Others with an equally valid claim are not. The Pearson Commission recommended the abolition of all the torts considered in this chapter. Instead they recommended that the injured person himself should be able to recover damages for the loss of his capacity to render services gratuitously to certain relatives (defined in the same way as the recommended class for bringing the Fatal Accidents Act 1976 claim (*infra*, p. 303). Damages should be assessed on the basis of what is reasonable.

26. MALICIOUS PROSECUTION AND ABUSE OF PROCESS

MALICIOUS PROSECUTION

Malicious prosecution is committed by one who maliciously and without reasonable and probable cause institutes criminal or civil proceedings against the plaintiff, the result of the proceedings being in the plaintiff's favour, and the plaintiff thereby suffering damage. The formidable series of hurdles the plaintiff must surmount in order to succeed in this tort accounts both for the rarity of actions for it and for the low proportion of those which succeed. It is questionable whether the public interest in the bringing of criminal prosecutions requires such extensive protection at the expense of the private interest in not being brought unnecessarily to court. The action for malicious institution of civil proceedings is highly unusual and there is some doubt whether it exists at all. A civil action may, however, fail because it is an abuse of the process of the court (*cf. Goldsmith* v. *Sperrings Ltd.* (1977). *Riddick* v. *Thames Board Mills Ltd.* (1977)).

Prosecution

The defendant must be the person "actively instrumental" in causing proceedings to be brought against the plaintiff. In the large number of prosecutions brought by the police, the prosecutor is the police officer who conducts the prosecution, even though he may have acted on the advice of his superior officers in deciding to prosecute. A private person who gives information to the police or to a magistrate as the result of which a prosecution is brought is not the prosecutor, since the decision to prosecute is not his. If, however, he agrees with the police to prefer charges and later signs the charge-sheet, he is the prosecutor, although the decision to instruct counsel to prosecute was taken by the police (*Malz* v. *Rosen* (1966)). Although it used to be thought that the mere laying of an information or bill of indictment before a magistrate was not a sufficient commencement of the proceedings to constitute a prosecution, unless the magistrate issued in consequence a summons against the plaintiff or a warrant for his arrest, it now appears to be the law that, if the magistrate has begun to inquire into the merits of the case, this may amount to a prosecution provided the plaintiff suffers damage thereby (*Mohamed Amin* v. *Jogendra Kuma Bannerjee* (1947)).

Termination of the proceedings in the plaintiff's favour

This requirement of the tort is satisfied even though the plaintiff has won on a technicality such as a defect in the indictment or excess of jurisdiction in the court.

Absence of reasonable and probable cause

The plaintiff has the difficult onus of proving the negative, that there was no reasonable and probable cause for the institutuon of proceedings against him. Such absence may be established in one of two ways; (i) the plaintiff may show that the prosecutor had no honest belief in the probable guilt of the plaintiff. (ii) he may show that despite the prosecutor's honest belief in the plaintiff's probable guilt, the facts which the defendant honestly believed would not lead a man of ordinary prudence and caution to that conclusion.

Both means of discharging the plaintiff's onus require the court to inquire into the prosecutor's state of mind. If dishonesty on the defendant's part is established, it is irrelevant that the facts as found by the jury would have led a man of prudence and caution to believe in the plaintiff's probable guilt. The second method involves an inquiry into the facts honestly believed by the defendant and then an objective determination whether these facts ought to have caused him to believe in the plaintiff's guilt. The jury as the tribunal of fact will answer the question whether the defendant was dishonest and if they find he was this will determine the question whether there was reasonable cause. If they find the defendant to be honest, the jury must determine what facts the defendant honestly believed, and it is for the court to decide whether these were capable of furnishing reasonable and probable cause.

The fact that the defendant took advice before instituting proceedings seems logically relevant only to whether he was dishonest, not also to whether or not the facts he believed constituted reasonable cause. But several recent cases have indicated that this fact may be sufficient to determine both issues in the plaintiff's favour (*Malz* v. *Rosen* (1966)—private person prosecuting on advice of police; *Glinski* v. *McIver* (1962)—(*obiter*)—police officer acting on advice of his superiors, for example, the legal department of Scotland Yard). To take advantage of this rule, the defendant must communicate all the facts which he knows to the other person.

Malice

The plaintiff must prove that the defendant was actuated by malice in bringing the prosecution. This is achieved by showing that the defendant's motive in bringing the prosecution was not the vindication of justice. If it can be shown that the defendant had no honest belief in the plaintiff's guilt malice is easily enough established. Even where he has such belief, however, it is possible to establish malice if it can be proved that the defendant brought the prosecution for some ulterior purpose of his own rather than the desire to see justice done. It is apparently enough if the defendant prosecutes in order to make an example of the plaintiff to deter others (*Stevens* v. *Midland Counties Ry.* (1854)). Generalised ill-will towards the plaintiff will also point to malice, on the defendant's part, but feelings of anger and resentment arising from the facts on which the defendant based his decision to prosecute are not.

The judge decides whether there is evidence of malice to go to the jury. The jury decides whether there was malice in fact.

The two issues of malice and absence of reasonable and probable cause must be kept separate by the judge in advising the jury. Thus, though malice exists, there may still be reasonable cause for bringing the prosecution and no inference can be drawn of the absence of reasonable cause from the presence of malice. Where, however, reasonable cause is absent, this does not *ipso facto* establish malice but may justify an inference of malice (*Johnstone* v. *Sutton* (1786)).

Damage

The tort of malicious prosecution requires proof of actual damage. Because damages are not at large, the plaintiff cannot recover for his distress or humiliation arising from the prosecution even though he has succeeded in showing malice on the part of the defendant. Actual damage may be proved under one or more of three heads established by *Savile* v. *Roberts* (1698).

These are:

(i) damage to reputation. The charge against the plaintiff must be necessarily defamatory of him, not merely capable of being understood in a defamatory sense, malicious prosecution being narrower here than defamation. To accuse the plaintiff of pulling the communication cord in a train is not defamatory (*Berry* v. *British Transport Commission* (1962)).

(ii) damage in respect of the personal security of the plaintiff. Mere exposure of the plaintiff to the risk of imprisonment because of the charge seems enough (*Wiffen* v. *Bailey and Romford U.C.* (1915)—*contra*, Diplock J. *obiter* in *Berry's* case).

(iii) pecuniary loss. The plaintiff may recover the difference between actual costs awarded him and the amount of his defence costs (*Berry's* case), but unsatisfactorily this does not appear to be the rule where civil proceedings were instituted against the plaintiff.

ABUSE OF PROCESS

It is a tort maliciously and in the absence of reasonable cause to make use of a legal process against the plaintiff (other than the mere swearing of false evidence—see *Hargreaves* v. *Bretherton* (1958)) as the result of which the plaintiff suffers damage. In *Roy* v. *Prior* (1970), for example, the defendant obtained a bench warrant for the plaintiff's arrest by giving evidence which the plaintiff alleged to be false that the plaintiff was evading service of a witness summons. As a result the plaintiff was arrested. The House of Lords held that the plaintiff had a good cause of action against the defendant if he could show that the defendant acted maliciously and without reaosnable cause.

Abuse of process sometimes needs to be distinguished from false imprisonment. If the defendant wrongfully arrests the plaintiff, this is false imprisonment however genuine the defendant's belief in the plaintiff's guilt. If, however, he procures the arrest of the plaintiff by another person, by making use of a legal process, this is too indirect to be false imprisonment. It is only a tort if the defendant has abused the process by acting maliciously and without reasonable cause. Thus it is not false imprisonment, though it may be abuse of process, to give false information to the police as a result of which they arrest the plaintiff (*Grinham* v. *Willey* (1859)). Where, on the other hand, the police are acting as mere agents of the defendant in effecting the arrest, as when they refuse to effect an arrest unless the plaintiff signs the charge-sheet, this is sufficiently direct to be false imprisonment (*Hopkins* v. *Crowe* (1836)).

27. INNOMINATE AND DOUBTFUL TORTS

INNOMINATE TORTS

In this chapter will be discussed a number of cases which cannot be classified under previously mentioned categories. Innominate torts are those which escape classification either because the interest protected is an unusual one, or because they are analogous to torts which protect a well-recognised interest. There is a large variety of torts of the former class of which only a few examples can be given. It is a tort actionable *per se* for a member of a common calling to refuse to provide services to the public. So an innkeeper is liable in tort for refusing to provide accommodation which he has available to the plaintiff (*Constantine* v. *Imperial Hotels Ltd.* (1944)). It is a tort actionable *per se* to interfere with another person's right to vote (held so far as the Returning Officer of a constituency was concerned in *Ashby* v. *White* (1703), although this person now has a statutory defence to such an action). It is tortious to interfere with a right of franchise enjoyed by another, an example of such a franchise being the exclusive right to carry for hire goods or passengers by means of boats across a river or arm of the sea.

Innominate torts which are analogous to nominate torts have been discussed in various sections of this book. So, for example, those with a reversionary interest in land or in chattels can sue in tort for damage done to such interests though they cannot comply with the strict requirements of trespass or conversion (*supra*, pp. 43, 52). Other examples discussed above are torts analogous to false imprisonment (*supra*, p. 16) or passing-off (*supra*, p. 277).

DOUBTFUL TORTS

In some cases there is doubt whether an existing civil remedy is based on tort. Two leading examples are discussed here.

Interference with occupation

Although the phrase "right to work" is an emotive one and although no such generalised legal right exists, it is undoubtedly true that courts will sometimes intervene to protect the plaintiff in the exercise of his occupation or profession.

What is not clear is whether the type of intervention that the court makes justifies the view that the defendant has committed a tort. Many cases have concerned the explusion of the plaintiff from membership of an association which controls the entry into or right to practice a given occupation. The courts will intervene here if the expulsion is *ultra vires* or otherwise in breach of the association's rules, by way of an injunction or a declaration that the plaintiff has been improperly expelled (*Lee* v. *Showmen's Guild* (1952); *Abbott* v. *Sullivan* (1952)). The remedy in such cases is often explained as resting on contract—the rules of the association have contractual force as between the members of the association. In *Abbott* v. *Sullivan* the Court of Appeal considered whether the expelled member had any claim in damages for breach of contract or in tort but decided against both. Since the right to claim damages is an essential characteristic of a tort, the case does not support the view that the right is based on tort. On the other hand it is clear that the situations in which the courts will protect a person's occupation are not limited to cases where there is a breach of contract. In *Nagle* v. *Feilden* (1966) the Court of Appeal refused to strike out a cause of action in which the plaintiff claimed that the Stewards of the Jockey Club had refused her a trainer's licence solely on the ground that she was a woman. In *David* v. *Abdul Cader* (1963) the Privy Council refused to hold that an allegation that the defendant had maliciously refused the plaintiff a licence to run a cinema disclosed no cause of action. Nor did they rule out the possibility of damages being recovered. These cases could not have rested on contract, and it may be therefore that a new tort, though not yet in existence is in the process of creation.

Breach of confidence

Courts have for many years been willing to restrain by injunction the disclosure of confidential information, whether of a personal (see *Gee* v. *Pritchard* (1818); *Argyll (Duchess)* v. *Argyll (Duke)* (1967)) or of a commercial character (*Cranleigh Precision Engineering* v. *Bryant* (1965)). It is possible to obtain damages in lieu of an injunction in such cases under Lord Cairns' Act 1858, but the award of damages, like that of the injunction itself, lies within the discretion of the court (*infra*, p. 323). Furthermore, as the remedy is equitable, damages could not be awarded against a bona fide purchaser of the information for value and without notice. It is clearly therefore advantageous to show that the user of confidential information commits a tort, since in that case damages are obtainable as of right, and perhaps, from anyone who obtains the information in whatever circumstances. *Seager* v. *Copydex* (*No.* 1) (1967) suggests that a tort is committed by one who makes use of confidential information. In that case, damages were awarded against the defendants who had made use of the plaintiff's design for a carpet grip, which the plaintiff had entrusted in confidence to the defendants. The damages awarded were tortious in character, on the analogy of conversion, rather than equitable in lieu of an injunction (see *Seager* v. *Copydex* (*No.* 2) (1969)). A new tort may therefore have been created. Whether it has, and what are its features, must be left for resolution by the courts (Megarry V.C. in *Malone* v. *Commissioner of Police* (1979) would give no decided view on the first question). Whatever the basis of the remedy it is not available in respect to the disclosure of iniquity. Lord Denning M.R. in *Fraser* v. *Evans* (1968) thought that a general defence of "just cause or excuse" for breaking the confidence existed. The Court of Appeal in *Woodward* v. *Hutchins* (1977) refused the remedy to pop-stars against their former press agent since those who seek to be presented before the public only in a favourable light must accept that the picture may need to be redressed by adverse publicity. This is a considerable restriction on the remedy since it seems most likely to be availed of by public figures. The remedy is not available in respect of telephone-tapping, since one who entrusts a confidence over the telephone accepts the risk that it may be overheard (*Malone's* case); in any case the police who conducted the tap would have the defence of just cause for breaking the confidence if it gave information about crime.

PRIVACY

Privacy already receives a considerable degree of incidental protection under existing legal remedies, for example, nuisance (*cf. Lyons* v. *Wilkins* (1899)), trespass to land (*cf. Hickman* v. *Maisey* (1900)), defamation (*cf. Tolley* v. *Fry* (1931) (1931)), infringement of copyright (*cf. Williams* v. *Settle* (1960)), and the action for breach of confidence. There is, however, no tort of infringement of privacy itself, despite several abortive attempts to pass legislation creasting one. (*Malone* v. *Commissioner of Police* (*supra*) is the latest decision to confirm this point). In this Britain is very different from the United States in which protection of privacy is comprehensive. The Younger Committee Report on Privacy (Cmnd. 5012), however, recommended no basic change in the law, although recommending that there should be a new tort of unlawful surveillance by technical device. Part of the problem with protection of privacy is that it interferes with freedom of speech, the view prevailing in this country that this should rule out a remedy for infringement of privacy altogether rather than that the publisher should be required to justify his publication on the ground that it was in the public interest or made without malice. Another problem with the protection of privacy is that there appears to be no consensus among those who support it as to the best method of achieving it and in particular whether this should be done through criminal sanctions or civil remedies. The Rehabilitation of Offenders Act 1974 is a good example of the complications that may be involved. It contains criminal penalties for the disclosure of spent convictions, a civil remedy for defamation against a person who reveals another person's spent conviction, and a number of exemptions from liability in relation to the non-disclosure or denial of a previous spent conviction.

28. DEATH IN RELATION TO TORT

The former rule was that the death of either party extinguished the defendant's tortious liability. To this there were a few minor exceptions. Apart from this, it was also a rule of the common law that a third party could not bring an action in respect of the death of another person as the result of a tort (*Baker* v. *Bolton* (1808)). Both these rules could be productive of injustice and both have now largely been abrogated by statute. The major injustice was to deny third parties such as dependants an action in respect of the death. This was remedied by a series of Acts called the Fatal Accidents Acts. The effect of these, since they allow dependants a tortious action in respect of the death of another, has been to create a new tort. The substantive effect of these Acts must be contrasted with the merely procedural significance of the Law Reform (Miscellaneous Provisions) Act 1934, which allows tortious actions to survive as part of the estate of the victim or against the estate of the tortfeasor. Despite the differing effects of these statutes, they are best treated in conjunction since claims under both are commonly made when actions are brought in respect of death as the result of a tort.

FATAL ACCIDENTS ACTS, DEATH CREATING LIABILITY

By a series of Acts now consolidated in the Fatal Accidents Act 1976, it is possible for a dependant to bring an action when the death of the person upon whom the dependency exists has been caused by the tort of another, provided the person killed would have been able to bring an action and recover damages for such tort. The relation of dependency can only be established by certain relatives who are defined by the Act as follows: wife, husband, children, grand-children, father, mother, step-parents, grandparents, brothers, sisters, uncles, aunts, and their issue, adopted and illegitimate dependants and step-children. Furthermore, such persons must establish a relation of dependency on the person killed. The nature of this will be explored later. It is still true that apart from these exceptions created by statute, it is impossible for a tortious action to be brought in respect of another's death. An employer cannot sue where his servant is negligently killed, though he has an action where the servant is merely injured. The Acts have created an important exception to the general principle that negligence causing purely pecuniary loss is not actionable.

Nature of the relatives' action

The Act of 1846 requires the death to be caused by the "wrongful act, neglect or default" of the defendant. These words are clearly wide enough to cover all torts, and in substance the relatives' action is an action for tortiously causing the death of another person. As such, it has been said to be "new in its species, new in its quality, new in its principle, in every way new" (words spoken by the court in an 1884 case). It is, however, a requirement of the Act that the wrongful act of the defendant could have been made the subject of a successful action for damages by the person injured had he survived to bring such action. (Section 1 (1)). This has been interpreted by the courts to mean that anything which has the effect of extinguishing the liability of the defendant to the deceased in his lifetime (for example, settlement of the action by the deceased, expiration of a limitation period on his action) has the same effect on the relatives' action. It is also provided by section 5 that contributory negligence by the deceased operates to reduce the amount the relatives can recover. Though a new cause of action, therefore, the relative's action is treated as very similar to that of the deceased himself. But the relatives' claim is not affected by any contract under which the deceased limits the amount payable by the defendant (*Nunan* v. *Southern Railway* (1924)). Similarly in *Pigney* v. *Pointers Transport* (*supra*, p. 116) the relatives' claim succeeded even though the deceased had died by his own hand. The death was not too remote because it was a foreseeable result of the injury the defendant had inflicted on the deceased. Nor was *ex turpi causa* a defence to the relatives' claim although the deceased had committed a felony. Where the nature of the dependency itself is *turpis causa* the action will fail (see *Burns* v. *Edman* (1970)—action by criminal's widow failed.)

Nature of the dependency

The courts have in the absence of specific legislative provisions devised rules of their own about the interest of the relatives which is protected by the action. This interest will be described here as their dependency, although it is not so described in the Act itself. The dependency must be of a financial nature; the relative must suffer pecuniary loss as a result of the death. Thus the action is not available to give damages to the relatives for their mental suffering as a result of the death. The financial advantage must be a reasonable probability; if it is too speculative the courts will reject it. So where the deceased was a child of four years to whom the father intended to give a good education, the action was not allowed. Where on the other hand the deceased had gratuitously assisted his father in his business in the past, and where the deceased had made gifts of money to his father during a period of unemployment, the action was allowed because it was reasonable to expect such charity would recur (*Barnett* v. *Cohen* (1921); *Franklin* v. *S.E. Ry.* (1858); *Hetherington* v. *N.E. Ry.* (1882)).

One case (*Sykes* v. *N.E. Ry.* (1875)) holds that the dependency must arise from a family rather than business relationship. So where a son was employed by his father under a contract of service, the father did not have an action for loss of these services when the son was killed. The father had not established any dependency on the son since he was paying him the going rate for his services. Where the dependant is being paid more than the value of his services by the deceased, he is entitled to recover the excess from the defendant (*Malyon* v. *Plummer* (1964)).

Although a pecuniary advantage is insisted on, this may be of a quite indirect nature. Thus the services of a wife or a daughter in performing ordinary domestic tasks have a financial value, even though in their absence the employment of outside help would not be considered. An unusual benefit was recognised in *Davies* v. *Whiteways Cider Co.* (1974). The deceased's dependants had in his lifetime received gifts which because of his death within seven years of the gift attracted estate duty. The amount of this was held to be recoverable in the dependants' action.

Assessment of damages

It is impossible to lay down firm rules on this matter: so much depends on the individual case and the nature of the dependency involved. Where the deceased's resources include earnings, the amount of future earnings lost is worked out on similar lines to those governing the assessment of such loss generally (*infra*, pp. 312-314). Contingencies affecting both the deceased and the relatives must be assessed by the court, but statute now prevents the assessment of the likelihood of a widow's remarriage or actual remarriage to be used as a ground for reducing damages (Law Reform (Miscellaneous) Provisions) Act 1971, s. 4 (1)). However, furthermore in the case of the child's claim under the Fatal Accident Acts, the likelihood of remarriage of the widow may be a relevant factor and is one which the court is not precluded from taking into account.

Benefits arising from the death may go in reduction of

damages but the Act themselves has prohibited deduction in the case of money paid under an insurance policy taken out against the deceased's life, pensions, gratutities or bene- fits (which section 4 (2) defines as social security benefits payable as a result of the death). As in non-fatal cases the courts refuse to make deductions for voluntary services rendered by third parties which go to replace the loss of dependency. So in *Hay* v. *Hughes* (1975), the court refused to make a deduction from the damages received by children who had lost both parents in a road accident and had then been looked after free of charge by their grandmother.

In the case of inherited property, also, the courts are slow to make deductions. In the first place, if the property would in any case have been inherited by the same person, only the amount attributable to the acceleration of the benefit is deducted. Secondly, where a widow inherited a house from her husband which she would continue to use as a dwelling, no deduction was made because the continuing residential requirement of the widow meant that no real financial benefit accrued to her (*Heatley* v. *Steel Co. of Wales* (1953)).

SURVIVAL OF CAUSES OF ACTION AFTER DEATH

It has been already stated that the common law rule was that the death of either the tortfeasor or his victim normally rules out the possibility of an action in tort. The common law was totally changed by the Law Reform (Miscellaneous Provisions) Act 1934 which provides that on the death of any person all causes of action subsisting against or vested in him shall survive against, or as the case may be, for the benefit of, his estate. Section 1 (4) defines the concept of a subsisting cause of action to include the case where the defendant dies before damage necessary to establish the cause of action has occurred, but such damage has occurred thereafter.

Defamation is now the only tort to which the Act does not apply. The Committee on Defamation recommended that actions in defamation should survive against the estates of defendants, that in certain circumstances the estates of defamed persons should be allowed to bring the action, and that near relatives of deceased persons should have an independent right to sue for a declaration and injunction (but not damages) for defamatory statements about the deceased made with five years of his death.

Action on behalf of the estate of victim

The action differs from that brought under the Fatal Acci- dents Acts in that it is the deceased's own action which is brought. It is therefore brought on behalf of his estate by his personal representative, the amount recovered passing as part of his estate to those entitled under the rules of succession.

What damages may be claimed

Damages are awarded to the estate under the same heads of damages as in the normal tortious action, for example, in actions for personal injury, pain and suffering, loss of amenity, loss of expectation of life, and loss of earnings. In the case of those heads of damages which have both a past and a future element, the court will take into account the death of the victim, and make no award in respect of the future element. Thus damages for pain and suffering, for loss of amenity, and for loss of earnings will be limited to the period from the injury until death. The award in respect of these heads will thus normally be small, although if the victim survives a lengthy period before his death quite a substantial sum may be awarded (for example, the award of £2,000 for loss of amenity to the victim in *Andrews* v. *Freeborough* (1962) who survived for a year in an unconscious state before dying).

Damages for loss of expectation of life do not have the same built-in limitation, not having a future element, and there were signs that estates of tort victims would be awarded substantial damages under this head. This tendency received a check, however, in the House of Lords decision in *Benham* v. *Gambling* (1941) which laid down judicial policy for the award of damages under this head. The principles established by the case apply not only to actions by the victim's estate, but to actions by the victim himself. Most important there is an arbitrary ceiling upon awards of damages under this head. This was assessed in *Benham* v. *Gambling* as £200, but, inflation being taken into account, is now £1,250 (*Gammell* v. *Wilson* (1980)). The courts have thus administered their own corrective to the legislature's perhaps erroneous decision in allowing tortious actions to survive for the estate's benefit. Within the limit, damages will vary not so much with the length of life that is lost as with the loss of future happiness that the death entailed. The character and habits of the deceased, his personal circumstances and state of health are clearly relevant matters from which this can be inferred. But the victim's own estimate of his future prospects of happiness is irrelevant—the test is to this extent objective. Actual life expectancy is relevant where the victim is very old, since the brevity of the remaining life-span will go in reduction of damages. Also where the victim is a young child the amount of uncertainty involved in assessing his future prospects will again cause a reduction. Such matters as the wealth and social status of the deceased are irrelevant, the courts recognising that wealth is not synonymous with happiness.

Damages for loss of expectation of life are objective in the sense that they do not include suffering caused by the victim's knowledge of the reduction of his life expectancy—such suffering may however be compensated in damages awarded for pain and suffering.

Funeral expenses

These may be recovered as damages from the tortfeasor if they have been met out of the deceased's estate.

OVERLAPPING CLAIMS UNDER FATAL ACCIDENTS AND LAW REFORM ACTS

The persons who can claim as relatives of the deceased under the 1846 Act or as being entitled to his estate under the 1934 Act are not necessarily the same, and where this is the case, both claims will have to be met in full by the defendant. It is normal, however, for the deceased's dependants to be the same persons as those entitled to his estate; in such a case both claims will normally be heard at the same time before the same court. Double compensation will be avoided because the court is entitled, in assessing damages for loss of dependency under the Fatal Accidents Act to take into account sums of money received as the result of the death which go to mitigate the loss of dependency. So damages received by the estate may operate to mitigate damages received under the Fatal Accidents Act. It operates in this rather than the reverse direction because damages awarded to the estate under the 1934 Act are based on the wrong to the deceased and these could hardly be reduced by sums of money recovered by living persons under the Fatal Accidents Act. In theory this opens up the possibility of a dependant obtaining double compensation by bringing the Fatal Accidents claim first. At the moment it is not clear why he should not succeed.

What damages received under the 1934 Act are deductible from those received under the Fatal Accidents Act? It seems clear that in relation to the so-called non-pecuniary aspects of the estate's claim, damages for these are deductible in full. So damages for loss of expectation of life, for pain and suffering, and for loss of amenity must be deducted (see, for example *Murray* v. *Shuter* (1975)). In relation to the pecuniary aspects of the claim, a distinction must be drawn between loss of earnings before the death and loss of future earnings. The former are not deductible, since the dependant could have expected the money they represent to be used for his benefit during the deceased's lifetime (*Murray* v. *Shuter*—surprisingly no deduction was made for the deceased's living expenses). In relation to future earnings, the House of Lords has decided in *Pickett* v. *British Rail Engineering Ltd.* (1978) that a living plaintiff is entitled to recover damages for loss of earnings during the "lost years" (*i.e.* those extra years of life the deceased would have enjoyed but for the defendant's tort). It is also now clear that this claim passes to the estate (*Gammell* v. *Wilson* (1980)); (*Kandalla* v. *B.E.A.C.* (1980)). The damages awarded must be reduced by the deceased's own future living expenses. The nature of the assessment is very similar to the method of assessing damages for loss of dependency under the Fatal Accidents Act, and it is assumed that where the same person is entitled under both Acts, the awards will cancel each other out. Where different persons are entitled, the decision in Picket has created the possibility of a person obtaining substantial compensation under the 1934 Act although he was not a dependant of the deceased and also of the defendant having to pay effectively the same damages twice.

Pearson Commission Report

The Pearson Commission had a number of recommendations to make about claims arising out of death. The most important are: an extension in the class of relatives entitled to bring the Fatal Accidents claim, allowing, in particular, a claim by persons accepted by the deceased as "children of the family," and by divorced spouses: the abolition of damages for loss of expectation of life, and the introduction of an action for loss of society resulting from death and capable of being brought by a husband or wife in respect of each other's death, by a parent for the death of an unmarried minor child, and by an unmarried minor child for the death of a parent; that courts should be entitled to take into account the actual remarriage of a widow before the trial in assessing damages under the Fatal Accidents Act; that damages for pecuniary loss in the lost years should not survive for the benefit of the deceased's estate. though damages for pain and suffering and loss of amenity should continue to do so. that benefits derived from the deceased's estate should be disregarded in assessing damages for loss of dependency under the Fatal Accidents Act.

29. REMEDIES

DAMAGES

The most common and important remedy in the law of tort is the award of damages. The principles upon which damages are awarded have, where relevant, been discussed in connection with the individual torts. In this chapter the general principles relating to damages will be set out, together with an examination of the rules governing the assessment of damages for personal injury. The fundamental principle governing the assessment of damages in nearly all cases is that the plaintiff should be compensated for the injury he has received. This point should always be remembered in considering the effectiveness of the law.

Classification of damages

(1) *Contemptuous and nominal damages*

Both these types of damages are similar in that they signify the award of a token sum to the plaintiff equivalent in law to no damages at all. But they differ in purpose. Nominal damages are awarded in order that the plaintiff's right should be vindicated although he has not suffered anything for which substantial damages could be awarded (for example, the right to vote in *Ashby* v. *White* (1703)). Contemptuous damages are awarded where the court, though vindicating the plaintiff's right is also signifying disapproval of his having brought the action. The award is therefore of the smallest coin of the realm. Contemptuous damages are particularly appropriate in the case of torts where the damages are at large, and the court wishes to "penalise" the gold—digging plaintiff who claims a large amount of general damages (as in the award of ¼d. to Harold Newstead, *supra*, p. 244). There is the important difference between contemptuous and nominal damages that where the former are awarded the plaintiff is unlikely to be awarded costs. Neither can be awarded where the tort is not actionable *per se*, since their award is tantamount to a finding that the plaintiff has suffered no damage.

(2) *Special and general damages*

Two senses of this distinction must be noted. "Special damage" is used to denote that damage which the plaintiff must establish as part of his cause of action when suing for a tort not actionable *per se*. When the plaintiff is suing for a tort which is actionable *per se*, the court may award damages for damage which is presumed to occur from the mere fact of the tort's commission though none is proved. Such damages are referred to as "general damages." The term, special damage, may be further divided into that damage of which it is possible for the plaintiff to give a precise, pecuniary estimate in advance, and that of which it is not. The former damage receives an award of damages which is called, confusingly, special damages; the latter is compensated by an award of general damages. The importance of this distinction is for the purposes of pleading. Special damages must be strictly pleaded and proved. General damages do not require such strict pleading and proof. It may be observed that damages for loss of earnings up to the date of trial are special damages. Damages for loss of future earnings are general damages. It is common, however, to refer to both as the "pecuniary" aspects of the plaintiff's claim, distinguishing them from damages for pain and suffering, loss of amenity and loss of expectation of life where again the damages are general damages).

(3) *Damages at large; aggravated damages*

In the case of torts actionable *per se*, damages are said to be at large. The court is able to award substantial damages even though no actual damage is proved by the plaintiff. Damages may be presumed to have occurred from the mere fact of the tort's commission (*cf.* particularly, defamation and nuisance). Another consequence of the damages being at large is that the court is free to award aggravated damages where the injury to the plaintiff is aggravated by such matters as the defendant's conduct or the distress or humiliation suffered by the plaintiff (see, for example, *Loudon* v. *Ryder* (*No. 2*) (1953)).

(4) *Parasitic damages*

These are damages given for the infringement of some interest which is not protected at all or not primarily protected by the tort in question. So, in an action for conversion, damages have been awarded for loss of reputation (*Thurston* v. *Charles* (1905)). In a woman's action for negligence causing her personal injuries, damages were awarded in respect of the loss of her husband's consortium, even though no action could have been brought in respect of this alone (*Lampert* v. *Eastern National Omnibus Co.* (1954)).

This case shows that the "parasitic interest" may be one not protected by other torts.

(5) *Exemplary or punitive damages*

In all the cases discussed so far, the amount of damages the court may award reflects as far as this is possible the injury or damage inflicted upon the plaintiff. In the case of exemplary or punitive damages this is not the case; extra damages are awarded in order to punish or make an example of the defendant. The House of Lords in *Rookes* v. *Barnard* (1964) confined the award of such damages to three situations:

(i) where the tortious action consists in oppressive, arbitrary or unconstitutional conduct by a government official;

(ii) where the defendant has calculated to make a greater amount out of his commission of the tort than he will have to pay in damages to the plaintiff (*Drane* v. *Evangelou* (1978)).

(iii) where statute authorises the award of such damages. In *Cassell & Co.* v. *Broom* (1972) the House of Lords confirmed the existence of these limitations upon the power to award exemplary damages. It must be noted that aggravated damages may serve a purpose similar to exemplary damages, with the limitation that they can only be awarded where the tort is actionable *per se*, and with the difference that in theory they are conpensatory, being awarded to assuage the plaintiff's injured feelings.

Damages for personal injuries

Two types of "loss" are inflicted upon one who suffers personal injuries. He may suffer actual financial loss such as loss of wages or reduction in his earning capacity. And he may suffer reduction in his enjoyment of his life, through pain and suffering and inability to participate in his usual activities, whether of a temporary or permanent nature. It is clear that the latter loss is incompensable in monetary terms. To allow a plaintiff £1,000 for the loss of a leg is assuagement rather than replacement. Nevertheless, English law compensates the injured person for both types of loss. Many of the difficulties in the law of damages are caused by the attempt to evaluate the non-pecuniary claim.

In considering the award of damages for personal injuries, damages in respect of the non-pecuniary aspects of the plaintiff's claim will be considered first.

(1) *Non-pecuniary damages*

There are a number of recognised heads of non-pecuniary damages. These are damages for loss of expectation of life, for pain and suffering, and for loss of amenity. The first of these is considered elsewhere (*supra*, p. 307).

Pain and suffering. This is pre-eminently the head of

damages which reflects the subjective effect the injury has upon the plaintiff. He is entitled to be compensated both for pain and suffering he has experienced up to the date of the trial and for such as he will experience in the future. The sum awarded may be in respect not only of the physical pain involved but also the mental anguish the plaintiff experiences, for example, in knowing that his expectation of life has been reduced or that his capacity to enjoy life has been reduced. No award for pain and suffering can be made where the plaintiff is rendered permanently unconscious by the injury and does not regain consciousness (*Wise* v. *Kaye* (1962)).

Loss of amenity. There was doubt for some time whether in the case of injury such as loss of a leg, damages were given to compensate the plaintiff's subjective appreciation of the effect of the injury, or for the injury itself. If the former, damages for loss of an amenity would be merely part of damages awarded for pain and suffering. In *Wise* v. *Kaye*, however, the Court of Appeal awarded £15,000 damages for loss of amenity although the plaintiff could have had no appreciation of the effect of her injuries upon her, and this decision was upheld by the House of Lords in *West and Son Ltd.* v. *Shephard* (1964). It is now clear, therefore, that loss of amenity is a distinct head of damages from pain and suffering. Cases such as *Wise* v. *Kaye* and *West* v. *Shephard* render the compensatory function of the award of damages almost a fiction.

(2) *Pecuniary damages*

The plaintiff will recover as special damages his loss of earnings up to the time of the trial, and medical expenses actually incurred by him (including the cost of private medical treatment). He seems also able to recover medical or other out-of-pocket expenses incurred on his behalf by a third party, provided their incurrence was reasonably necessary, and the plaintiff would feel under a moral obligation to reimburse the third party. The plaintiff is also able to recover as general damages loss of future earnings through reduction in his earning capacity. The method of assessment is to take a number of years' purchase (corresponding to the number of years of working life that would have been left to the plaintiff but for his injury), to multiply this by the annual sum of earnings lost by the plaintiff, and to adjust the sum arrived at to reflect contingencies such as the shortening of the plaintiff's working life through other events, and the benefit the plaintiff receives from receiving an immediate lump sum. The method of adjustment is to shorten the "multiplier," *i.e.* the number of years of working life left to the plaintiff. Even in the case of young working adults, the maximum multiplier is about 18 years. Courts refuse to admit in evidence actuarial tables showing the life expectancy of persons in the plaintiff's position (*Taylor* v. *O.Connor* (1971); *Mitchell* v. *Mulholland* (1972)). Furthermore, a number of cases, the latest being *Cookson* v. *Knowles* (1978), have established that the possibility of future inflation is not to be taken into account in making the award. It is of course impossible for courts to know in advance whether inflationary conditions will continue to exist in, say, 15 or 20 years' time. But the present fact of inflation has led to the possibility of serious undercompensation of plaintiffs. The fact that the sum received may be invested and that at the prevailing high interest rates it might be possible to counteract inflation is only partially an answer. To be valid it would require the investment of all interest—but the plaintiff must meet his living expenses and will have to spend interest for that purpose. Furthermore tax is deducted from the capital sum on the basis of the present annual rate for the plaintiff's earnings—but if inflation continues it is likely that a lesser rate of tax or no tax at all would be leviable on that figure. Given the present system of compensation by way of a lump sum and the impossibility of predicting the distant economic future, the courts may well have no choice in the matter. The Pearson Commission proposal to introduce damages by way of periodic payments (considered below, p. 320) would simplify the problem.

In *Pickett* v. *British Rail Engineering* (1979), the House of Lords held that a living plaintiff could obtain damages for loss of earnings during the "lost years" (*i.e.* those years of life expectancy lost to the plaintiff through the tort of the defendant). The problem that this causes by reason of the survival of the action after death has already been considered (*supra*, p. 306). In relation to the plaintiff himself, however, the decision seems just, since the plaintiff receives a sensible loss by being deprived of his future earning power during his lifetime. Another recent development is that damages for loss of earning capacity is firmly recognised as a head of damages by the courts (see *Moeliker* v. *Reyrolle & Co.* (1976)). A plaintiff who has retained his job despite his injury may nevertheless be less employable by reason of the injury—he is entitled to compensation for this.

In relation to medical expenses, the plaintiff is not compelled to take free treatment under the National Health Service, even though it is readily available (Law Reform (Personal Injuries) Act 1948, section 2 (4) *cf.* the huge amount awarded under this head to the plaintiff in *Lim* v. *Camden Health Authority* for the cost of private medical treatment in the future). Where the plaintiff will need future nursing, but is likely to receive this gratuitously from third parties such as his parents, the court will put a value on these services and award damages to the plaintiff for them (*Taylor* v. *Bristol Omnibus Co.* (1975). Damages will also be awarded to the plaintiff in relation to services rendered gratuitously by third parties before the trial (even if the plaintiff has no moral obligation to compensate the third party—*Donnelly* v. *Joyce* (1973)). Where, however, the plaintiff has received or will receive free nursing from a state institution, no damages will be awarded in respect of this (*Cunningham* v. *Harrison* (1973)).

(3) *Deductions*

The difficulty of the problem whether an incidental benefit received by the plaintiff as a result of his injuries should be deducted from the damage he receives is explained because of competing considerations of policy; fears of over-compensation and an excessive rise in liability insurance premiums if the benefit is not deducted, and of under-compensation if it is, particularly if the view if taken that the amount of damages awarded is generally inadequate. The law on this matter seems something of a compromise. If the purpose of the benefit is to compensate for those aspects of the plaintiff's loss which are capable of yielding to a precise pecuniary estimate, then it is deductible, since the function of damages is compensatory. Where, on the other hand, the benefit is not clearly directed towards any particular part of the plaintiff's loss, so that it may cover those aspects of his claim which are not capable of being precisely estimated (for example, pain and suffering) it is not deductible because it is impossible to decide whether to allow him to keep the benefit would represent over-compensation. Examples of the former class of case are the deductibility of wages or sick pay paid by an employer to his employee while the latter is off work (*Receiver of Metropolitan Police District* v. *Croydon Corporation* (1957); and of unemployment benefit (*Foxley* v. *Olton* (1965)), although in the same case it was said that national assistance was not deductible on the unsatisfactory ground that its payment was discretionary. The deductibility of income tax from awards of damages for personal injuries (*British Transport Commission* v. *Gourley* (1956)) is explicable on similar grounds. By special legislative provision (s. 2 of the Law Reform (Personal Injuries) Act 1948), half the amount of social security benefits such as industrial injury benefit, disablement benefit and sickness benefit is deductible from damages for a period of five years. The prime example of the second class of case is money payable under an accident insurance policy. This is not deductible from damages (*Brad-*

burn v. *G.W. Ry.* (1874)), nor are charitable gifts by third
parties for the same reason. These cases also turn to some
extent on policy. The courts are unwilling to deprive a person
of the benefit of his own thrift. To make charitable payments
deductible creates the risk of such charity drying up.

The distinction drawn above, however, has become much
blurred if not altogether erased in recent cases. Most important is the House of Lords decision in *Parry* v. *Cleaver* (1970).
In that case it was held that a disability pension payable by
an employer to his employee was not deductible from
damages. The pension was contributory and thus in the
nature of insurance. This, in the opinion of the majority, outweighed the fact that it was earnings-related and clearly
intended to replace lost earnings. In *Cunningham* v. *Harrison*
(1973) the Court of Appeal held that an *ex gratia* payment of
half pay for the remainder of the employee's life by his
employer was not deductible, since it was in the nature of a
charitable payment. In *Daish* v. *Wauton* (1972) the same
court held that the financial benefit of being housed free in a
National Health Service institution was not deductible, either
because it partook of charity or because it was contributory
(even though the particular plaintiff had made no contribu-
tions). Despite the generosity of these decision towards
accident victims, the rule that unemployment benefit is
deductible has survived *Parry* v. *Cleaver*, even though it is
contributory (*Nabi* v. *British Leyland* (1980)). Supple-
mentary benefit, which is, unlike national assistance, not discretionary and which is not contributory, is also deductible
(*Mehmet* v. *Perry* (1977)). The Pearson Commission took
the view that all social security benefits should be deducted
from damages.

In the *Receiver for Metropolitan Police District* case, it was
held that an employer who had continued to pay his
employee's wages during his absence from work had no
action in quasi-contract against the third party who by his
tort had caused the absence from work. The court thought
that it made no difference whether or not there was a contractual obligation to make the payment. Since wages are
deductible from the award of damages (though see *Cunningham* v. *Harrison* (*supra*), it follows that the employer
has no hope of being recompensed by the employee, so that
the *actio per quod servitium amisit*, where available, is his
only remedy. Where, on the other hand, a third party has
rendered gratuitous services to the plaintiff because of the
injury, it now appears to be settled that the plaintiff can
recover in his own action the value of such services, even
if the third party has no moral claim against the plaintiff to be recompensed (*Donnelly* v. *Joyce* (1973)—the plain-

tiff's mother gave up her job in order to care for him. The plaintiff was allowed to recover the value of the services rendered. *Roach* v. *Yates* (1938) is to similar effect).

(4) *Itemisation of damages and overlap*
  In *Fletcher* v. *Autocar and Transporters* (1968) the Court of Appeal expressed its disapproval of a method of awarding damages under which individual amounts were assessed for the different heads of damages and the total sum was then awarded as damages. This they thought would tend to produce over-compensation, particularly if no account was taken of possible overlap between these heads of damages. Thus where the plaintiff indulged in an expensive pastime such as golf, the loss of amenity involved in not being able to play golf was to some extent compensated in the financial saving to the plaintiff. This approach was also manifested in *Smith* v. *Central Asbestos Co.* (1972) in which the Court of Appeal thought that a high award in respect of future earnings would to some extent compensate for the loss of amenity involved in asbestosis. There is some inconsistency in the Court of Appeal's approach to this problem since it is difficult to see how the question of overlap can be examined without the court making at least a notional itemisation of damages. In any case the court must now itemise its awards for the purpose of awarding interest. Different rates of interest apply to each head—*Jefford* v. *Gee* (1970)). The justice of the Court of Appeal's approach to overlap is also not readily apparent. If the plaintiff has lost one expensive amenity, this seems no reason to deprive him of the opportunity of replacing it with another expensive pastime which the injury does not prevent him from indulging.

(5) *Interest*
  Since many actions in tort take years to resolve, the question of interest on damages is important. The court is now bound to award interest on damages where the plaintiff recovers more than £200 unless it is satisfied that there are special reasons why it should not be given (section 22 of the Administration of Justice Act 1969). The principle adopted by the courts (see *Jefford* v. *Gee* (1970); *Cookson* v. *Knowles*; *Pickett* v. *British Rail Engineering*) is that interest is only awarded on money which the plaintiff has been kept out of by the defendant's wrongful act. Thus there can be no interest awarded on damages for loss of future earnings. In relation to loss of earnings up to the date of trial, the plaintiff is entitled to interest at half the short-term interest rates during that period on the whole sum, the justification for this being that interest on the first instalment of wages should

bear the full interest and thereafter on a declining scale to the
last instalment which should bear no interest at all. Interest
on damages for non-pecuniary loss bears interest at the full
short-term interest rate from the date of service of the writ.

Duty to mitigate damage

The plaintiff must not do anything to increase the amount
of damage he has suffered. Nor must he omit to take reasonable action to reduce such damage (*HMS Flying Fish* (1865)
—damages reduced because plaintiff refused to accept aid
after a collision at sea.) Mention must be made here of the
decision in *Liesbosch Dredger* v. *Edison* (1933), a decision on
damage to property but one which illustrates a general
principle of the law of damages as a whole (the principles
upon which damage to property is compensated are too
complex for treatment in this book—the reader should consult
the specialist works). In the *Liesbosch* the defendants' ship
had by negligent navigation sunk the plaintiffs' dredger. The
plaintiffs, who were working under a contract with the port
authority, could not afford to buy a replacement dredger,
which would have been available, and in order to carry out
their contract had to hire a replacement. Rates of hire were
high and the substitute dredger was more costly to work than
the Liesbosch. The plaintiffs claimed this extra economic loss
as damages from the defendants, but the House of Lords
refused to allow them anything beyond the normal measure
of damages, *i.e.* the cost of buying a replacement dredger,
and costs and loss of profit incurred until it could have been
regarded as ready for work. The reasoning was that the plaintiffs' extra losses were caused by their own lack of means,
which must be regarded as a new cause not flowing from the
defendants' negligence. Lawyers have always been sceptical
of the "new cause" theory. The impecuniosity of the plaintiff was a pre-existent condition rather than a subsequent
development and the normal rule is that the tortfeasor takes
the victim as he finds him. The rule looks therefore more like
one of policy, no doubt deriving from the same source as the
rule about negligence causing purely pecuniary loss—a desire
to shield the defendant from having to meet all the financial
consequences of his act. It is no doubt a rational argument
that persons in the position of shipowners carrying out
commercial contracts should foresee the disastrous financial
consequences of the loss of the ship and the inability to buy
a replacement, and should take steps to provide against the
event. Against this it is arguable that where the plaintiff's
lack of means is based upon the refusal by the defendant to
pay him damages until a court has determined his liability,
the extra loss should fall upon the defendant.

The question arose again before the Court of Appeal in *Dodd Properties* v. *Canterbury City Council* (1980). Contractors (the second and third defendants) of the first defendant council had caused damage to the plaintiffs' building in 1968. Liability on the part of both contractors was admitted in 1978. The council also was found to be liable at the trial. In 1970, the time at which it was first feasible to carry out repairs, the cost of repairs was some £11,000. By 1978 it had risen to some £30,000. Cantley J. found that the defendant had the means to carry out the repairs in 1970, but had made a "reasonable, commercial" decision to postpone the carrying out of repairs until he was certain of being paid for them by the defendants, all of whom denied liability. The effecting of repairs would have increased the "financial stringency" of the plaintiffs who had been trading on a bank overdraft for some years. He held himself bound by the Liesbosch to award the plaintiffs only the 1970 cost of repairs. On this he was unanimously reversed by the Court of Appeal. The decision in the Liesbosch was distinguishable, applying only to impecuniosity, not to financial stringency. If that was so, the only question was whether the plaintiffs had acted reasonably in not taking steps to mitigate their damage in 1970 by having the repairs done then. On this point the Court of Appeal accepted the finding of Cantley J. The decision seems a just one, but the distinction it lays down is unsatisfactory. The impecunious person in the plaintiff's position would have been in an even worse position, since he would have faced the inevitability of loss through his inability to take action. A question arises, therefore, whether the Liesbosch decision is an absolute rule to be applied in all cases of impecuniosity.

Once-and-for all assessment of damages

Damages are awarded in a lump sum and are not subject to review. The award of damages in respect of any one cause of action is therefore final. This causes hardship in the type of case of which *Fetter* v. *Beale* (1701) is an example, where the plaintiff's injuries are greater than appears at the trial. In that case the court refused to alter its original award on subsequent application to it by the plaintiff. The principle established by this case does not apply when the plaintiff is suing in respect of a different cause of action (as in *Brunsden* v. *Humphrey* (1884) in which it was held that the defendant's negligence in causing the plaintiff personal injury and damage to his property gave rise to distinct causes of action so that action in respect of the latter did not prevent a subsequent action for the former). For the same reason, it does not apply where the defendant has committed a continuing tort since fresh causes of action arise in respect of such tort from day to day as long as it is being committed.

Pearson Commission Report

The Pearson Commission made some wide-ranging proposals concerning the award of damages for personal injury. Only a minimum of comment is possible here.

(1) *Heads of damage*

The Commission recommended abolition of damages for loss of expectation of life. Instead a claim for loss of society through the death of another person should be introduced (for the cases in which this could be brought, *supra*, p. 314). Damages for pain and suffering and for loss of amenity should continue to be awarded, but damages for non-pecuniary loss should not be awarded in cases of permanent unconsciousness of the plaintiff. No damages for non-pecuniary loss should be awarded for such loss suffered during the first three months after the injury. This proposal, which would eliminate a large number of small claims, is the less attractive in the light of the fact that the Report favours the retention of fault-based tort compensation as a whole. It is presumed, in view of the Commission's terms of reference, that the recommendation is not intended to apply to injuries inflicted intentionally. In relation to damages for pecuniary loss, the Commission made two recommendations that have been anticipated by court decisions: that damages for loss of earning capacity, and for loss of earnings during the "lost years" should be recoverable. The repeal of section 2 (4) of the Law Reform (Personal Injuries) Act 1948 was recommended; instead it should be enacted that the expense of private medical treatment should be recoverable as damages only if it was reasonable on medical grounds that it should be sought.

(2) *Periodic payments*

The Commission made important recommendations concerning periodic payments. In the case of future pecuniary loss caused by death or serious and lasting injury, the court must award damages in the form of periodic payments, unless the plaintiff satisfies it that a lump sum would be more appropriate. The court would have a discretion to award periodic payments where injury is not serious and lasting. This would not interfere with out-of-court settlements which could continue to be made on a lump sum basis. The plaintiff could apply to the court at any time for commutation of a periodic into a lump sum award. Periodic awards of damages would be subject to review in the light of changes in the plaintiff's medical condition, and would be revalued annually in line with the movement of annual earnings. The right to the periodic award should "descend" to dependants for the time the deceased would have lived but for his injury. If enacted these provisions should remove the injustices caused by the erosion of the value of damages by inflation; also by the rule in *Fetter* v. *Beale*.

(3) *Assessment of damages*

The Commission recommended that all social security benefits, whether past or future, should be fully deducted f.rom damages, whether for pecuniary or, where relevant, non-pecuniary loss. Such a rule would further eliminate numerous small claims in tort. Otherwise the Commission favoured the retention of the somewhat illogical rules established by the courts as to the deductibility of collateral benefits. In relation to the assessment of damages for loss of future earnings, a majority of the Commission recommended a modification of the assessment of the "multiplier" to take into account inflation and the fact that different earnings attract different tax rates. The application of the "modified multiplier" would produce the result that highly taxed plaintiffs with large earnings losses over a lengthy period of time would be compensated on the basis of a multiplier exceeding the length of working life left to them (with a consequent vast increase in awards).

THE INJUNCTION

A court may, in addition to awarding damages to the plaintiff, or without awarding damages, issue an injunction. This is a peremptory order to the defendant (disobedience of which is punishable by imprisonment) to abstain from (prohibitory injunction) or to take (mandatory injunction) certain action. The injunction is a discretionary remedy and will be issued only where it is "just and convenient" to do so (the words are taken from section 45 of the Supreme Court of Judicature Act 1925).

Types of injunction

A prohibitory injunction will take the form of an order to the defendant to stop committing a tort such as, commonly, trespass or nuisance. The mandatory injunction orders the defendant to perform a certain act, for example, the pulling down of a building which infringes the plaintiff's right to light. An injunction of the former type may cause less hardship to a defendant in that it may afford him a large amount of choice as to how he complies with it. So an order to discontinue a nuisance caused by fumes may be obeyed in a number of ways, which is not true of an order to pull down a building. For this reason a stronger case has normally to be made for the grant of a mandatory than a prohibitory injunction. Interlocutory injunctions must be distinguished from *quia timet* injunctions. The former type of injunction is claimed by the plaintiff in interlocutory proceedings taking place before the actual trial of the action, the justification for its issue being that otherwise the plaintiff may suffer irreparable damage before the trial of the action takes place. The interlocutory injunction has been heavily relied on in recent years by those who have been threatened with heavy economic losses as a result of strikes (*supra*, p. 275). The interlocutory injunction is distinguishable from the *quia timet* injunction on the ground that the plaintiff is alleging that the defendant is actually committing (or has committed) a tort against him. The *quia timet* injunction is available where no tort has been committed by the defendant but the plaintiff apprehends the possible future commission of a tort by the defendant. An injunction which is a final one issued after the trial of the plaintiff's action is called perpetual.

Torts restrainable by injunction

There appears to be no tort against which an injunction will not be awarded, although some torts, notably trespass to land and nuisance, are particularly apt for the issue of the remedy, and others, such as assault and malicious prosecution will nearly always be redressed by damages. Where it is doubtful whether the wrong committed by the defendant is a tort, this does not mean that an injunction will not be granted. Examples have already been given (*supra*, pp. 299-301) of the issue of injunctions in cases where the tortious character of the defendant's conduct is debatable. Furthermore, under Lord Cairns' Act 1858 the courts may award damages in such cases (see *infra*). Eventually the courts may award damages as of right in cases of this sort, thereby treating them as torts. If this is the case, the injunction may be seen as a way of extending the boundaries of the law of tort.

Exercise of court's discretion

The court may take a number of factors into account in deciding whether to grant an injunction, for example, whether damages are an adequate remedy (if the tort is continuing or there is a likelihood of repetition, damages are probably inadequate); the defendant's difficulty in complying with the injunction in view of the expense involved or its impracticability; the conduct of the plaintiff, in particular acquiescence on his part. Although the courts will consider the defendant's convenience in exercising their discretion, they will also consider the justice of the case. If the defendant has incurred expenditure after notice of the plaintiff's right and in wilful violation of such right, an injunction may be granted though its effect is to cause this expenditure to be wasted (*Daniel* v. *Ferguson* (1891)).

Lord Cairns' Act 1858

The court has jurisdiction under Lord Cairns' Act 1858 to award damages either in addition to or in substitution for an injunction. Although originally intended for the purely procedural purpose of giving the Court of Chancery a general power to award damages, the Act has a substantive effect also in allowing the award of damages in cases where no tort or breach of contract has been committed, provided an injunction is at least theoretically available. The award of such damages, like the injunction itself, is within the discretion of the court. Where the award is made in substitution for an injunction, it covers future damage as well as damage that has already occurred; this is not so with normal damages. Damages can even be awarded under this Act where a *quia timet* injunction is sought (*Leeds Industrial Co-operative Society Ltd.* v. *Slack* (1924)).

OTHER REMEDIES

The plaintiff may choose in some cases to sue for an account of the profits the defendant has made through committing the tort. This is particularly the case where the tort is passing-off or another of the torts involving trade competition. It has been mentioned in an earlier chapter (*supra*, p. 39), that in detinue the plaintiff may claim restitution of his property in addition to or as an alternative to a claim for damages. The remedy of self-help has already been dealt with in Chapter 5.

30. EXTINCTION OF TORTIOUS LIABILITY

Tortious liability may be extinguished in any of the following ways.

DEATH

The death of the tortfeasor extinguishes his liability in the case of defamation only.

JUDGMENT

Judgment obtained against a tortfeasor has the effect of converting his liability on the cause of action into liability on the judgment, so that further actions cannot be brought against him in respect of that cause of action. So, for example, a judgment obtained in conversion bars a subsequent action in quasi-contract for the proceeds of sale of the chattel. Where the same facts give rise to distinct causes of action (*supra*, p. 319) judgment obtained on one cause of action will not bar a later action based on the other.

Satisfaction of judgment

Judgment obtained against one of several joint or concurrent tortfeasors does not release the others (*supra*, p. 119). But satisfaction of the judgment by one of them releases the rest. Where tortfeaors are neither joint nor concurrent, satisfaction by one will not normally release the others except in special circumstances. If however A and B have successively converted C's chattel, satisfaction of the judgment by A will release B since C thereafter no longer has the right to possesssion of the chattel.

WAIVER OF TORT

The problem here is whether the election by the plaintiff to pursue one of two alternative remedies means that he cannot go back on this decision and pursue the alternative remedy. At one time it was thought that by choosing one remedy the plaintiff must be taken to have waived the other. But the House of Lords in *United Australia Ltd.* v. *Barclay's Bank Ltd.* (1941) found that the cases relied on for this turned on the extinction of tortious liability through judgment rather than waiver. The pursuit of one remedy only constituted waiver where the remedies were inconsistent with rather than alternative to each other. So a landlord who chooses to sue for a forfeiture of the lease rather than for rent which is due cannot sue for rent due from the date of the forfeiture proceedings even though judgment in the latter is not obtained (*Jones* v. *Carter* (1846)). On the other hand in the *United Australia* case the plaintiff company's institution and subsequent discontinuance before obtaining judgment of proceedings in quasi-contract against another company for improperly obtaining the proceeds of a cheque payable to the plaintiffs was held to be no bar to an action in conversion against the defendant bank which cashed the cheque.

VOLUNTARY TERMINATION

1. Accord and satisfaction

Liability in tort may be extinguished by an accord and satisfaction. This means an agreement between the parties (accord) backed up by consideration (satisfaction), the intention being that liability under the agreement should replace the liaiblity in tort. The normal "settlement" of a tortious action operates in this way, the plaintiff agreeing to accept a certain sum and in return agreeing not to institute proceedings against the defendant. The consideration for the accord may be executory or executed; the difference is between the plaintiff's agreement to release the defendant in consideration of his promise to pay £100, and in consideration of his actual payment of that sum.

2. Release

This term signifies an agreement binding the victim of the tort whereby the tortfeasor is released from liability though he provides no consideration. The usual form of a release in English law is by deed, although this does not appear to be essential.

LIMITATION

The principle of limitation is that by lapse of time a right of action becomes no longer enforceable. The relevant limitation periods for tortious actions are contained in two statutes, the Limitation Act 1939 and the Limitation Act 1975. The fomer laid down a six-year limitation period for all torts, with the exception of an action for the recovery of land which must be brought within twelve years of the accrual of the cause of action. The latter Act has preserved a change first introduced by the Law Reform (Limitation of Actions,

etc.) Act 1954, under which the period in respect of actions
for damages for negligence, nuisance or breach of duty, when
the damages claimed by the plaintiff include damages for
personal injuries, is three years. When the plaintiff claims
both for damage to property and personal injuries in the
same action, the three-year period applies to both.

"Personal injuries" for the purposes of the Act include any
disease and impairment of a person's physical or mental condition. It is doubtful whether the latter words include injury
to feelings where the tort protects these parasitically (as in
defamation). The Act's specification of negligence and nuisance seems futile in the light of the likely interpretation by
the courts that breach of duty includes all torts (for example,
negligent trespass in *Letang* v. *Cooper* (1965); battery in
Long v. *Hepworth* (1968)).

Effect of limitation

The effect of the expiry of a relevant period is generally
procedural rather than substantive. The right of action is
rendered unenforceable rather than extinguished altogether.
So, for example, a limitation defence must be pleased. So
also, the court may allow the plaintiff to amend his writ by
adding a defendant against whom the limitation period has
expired when satisfied that the plaintiff has made a genuine
mistake (*Rodriguez* v. *Parker* (1967)). In the case of conversion, detinue and the action for recovery of land the plaintiff's title to the property is extinguished by expiry of the
limitation period. Without this rule the property in question
would be unmarketable.

Accrual of cause of action

Under both statutes the limitation period begins to run
from the date on which the cause of action accrued. There
are two requirements for determining such date. In the first
place there must be a person capable of suing and being sued.
Secondly, the cause of action must be complete.

(1) *Person capable of suing and being sued*

A special dispensation exists under section 22 of the
Limitation Act 1939 when the potential plaintiff is a minor
or of unsound mind at the time the cause of action accrued.
The limitation period does not commence until the disability
ceases, or he dies. In the case of an action for personal injuries,
the plaintiff had under the 1954 Act to prove also that he
was not at the time the right of action accrued to him in the
custody of a parent. Section 2 of the Limitation Act 1975
has removed this requirement so that the claim of persons
under disability in respect of personal injuries is now governed

by the same principles as claims for other damage. The dispensation granted to persons under disability by section 22 of the 1939 Act does not extend to allowing the cessation of a limitation period which had commenced before the plaintiff became subject to disability.

(2) *Completion of cause of action*

In the case of torts actionable *per se*, time runs from the moment the defendant acted; in the case of torts which require proof of damage, from the moment damage occurs. In the case of continuing torts where a fresh cause of action arises *de die in diem*, each new cause of action has its own limitation period (*Coventry* v. *Apsley* (1691)). Nuisance and trespass to land are torts which often may give rise to such continuing causes of action. Where a tort is actionable only upon proof of damage, a difficulty may arise as to when such damage has occurred. In *Cartledge* v. *E. Jopling and Sons Ltd.* (1963) the House of Lords held that time ran when pneumoconiosis affected the plaintiff's lungs even though he could not have discovered this at the time even by an X-ray examination. In *Sparham-Souter* v. *Town and Country Development (Essex)* (1976), however, the Court of Appeal held that, where the plaintiff had purchased a house built on defective foundations, time did not run until the plaintiff could with reasonable diligence have discovered the defective state of his property. The *Sparham-Souter* case was referred to without disapproval by the House of Lords in *Anns* v. *London Borough of Merton* (1977) but the issue of limitation was not before the House in that case and there appears to be no real distinction between the *Cartledge* and the *Sparham-Souter* cases.

Cartledge v. *Jopling* led to the passing of the Limitation Act 1963, which was superseded by the Limitation Act 1975. Section 2A (4) of this Act provides that *in actions for personal injuries* the limitation period is three years from the date of accrual of the cause of action or from the date of the plaintiff's knowledge of it. Section 2A (6) provides that the knowledge required is knowledge: (a) that the injury in question is significant; (b) that the injury is attributable in whole or in part to the act or omission which is alleged to constitute negligence, nuisance or breach of duty; (c) of the identity of the defendant, including (defendant) if it is alleged that the act or omission was that of some person other than the defendant, of the identity of that person. Knowledge that any acts or omissions did or did not, as a matter of law, involve negligence, nuisance or breach of duty is irrelevant. Even where the plaintiff's case falls outside the statutory limits there is a discretion in personal injury cases to set them aside under section 2D of the 1975 Act. Six criteria for the exercise of this discretion are laid down by section 2D (3) of the Act. The discretion conferred is a broad one and is not limited to exceptional cases. For example, it was exercised in the plaintiff's favour where the delay in bringing the action was due to the fault of his legal advisers (*Firman* v. *Ellis* (1978)); where the delay has caused no prejudice to the defendants (*Buck* v. *English Electric Co.* (1978); where the plaintiff was reluctant to bring litigation against his employer for fear of jeopardising his job (*McCafferty* v. *Metropolitan Police Receiver* (1977)).

The Act of 1939 makes special provision for the case of fraud. Where the plaintiff's action is based upon the fraud of the defendant, or where the right of action has been concealed by the defendant's fraud, time does not begin to run until the plaintiff has or, with reasonable diligence, could have discovered the fraud. The tort of deceit appears to be the only cause of action in tort based on fraud. But in *Beaman* v. *A.R.T.S. Ltd.* (1949) the court's interpretation of fraud in connection with the concealment of a right of action shows that a consciousness of wrongdoing rather than legal fraud is sufficient. Steps taken to conceal the right of action are also unnecessary (fraudulent concealment where bailee in time of war disposed of chattel without attempting to communicate with bailor).

In the case of successive causes of action in conversion or detinue or conversion and detinue in respect of the same chattel (whether committed by the same or different persons), the Act of 1939 provides that time runs from the first of these. This, coupled with the fact that section 3 (2) provides that the effect of the expiry of the limitation period on conversion or detinue is to extinguish completely the former owner's title, ensures that he cannot sleep on his rights for too long.

Death and period of limitation

In the case of the survival of a cause of action in tort for or against the estate of a deceased person, the normal periods of limitation apply (see Proceedings against Estates Act 1970). The Fatal Accidents Act claim is subject to special provisions under section 2B and 2C of the Limitation Act 1975. The dependants' claim is barred if the injured person's claim would itself be barred under the time-limits set up by section 2A of the Act (*supra*), and no account may be taken of such time limits being overriden under section 2D (section 2B) (2)). The action if not so barred must be brought within three years of the date of death or from the date of the knowledge of the dependant for whose benefit the action is brought, whichever is the later (section 2B (3)). "Knowledge" is defined in the same way as in section 2A. Where more than one dependant brings the action, the knowledge of each is assessed individually (section 2C). The power under section 2D to override the time limit applies to the dependants' action also.

31. PARTIES

CORPORATIONS

It is clear law that a corporation, as a legal person distinct from its members, may commit torts and may have torts committed against it. The commission of torts by a corporation clearly requires some action on the part of the human agents of the corporation. Thus the corporation is vicariously liable for the torts of its servants committed in the course of their employment. The corporation may incur personal liability where the human agent is so much in control of the corporation that his actions may be regarded as those of the corporation itself. In *Lennard's Carrying Co.* v. *Asiatic Petroleum Co. Ltd.* (1915) it was found that the managing director of a company was the "directing mind and will of the corporation" so that fault on his part constituted "actual fault" on the company's part for the purposes of a statute. Where the personal liability of the corporation is concerned it does not seem to matter that the act is *ultra vires* the corporation (*Campbell* v. *Paddington Borough Council* (1911)). Where, on the other hand, a servant is acting *ultra vires* the corporation his action may be outside the scope of his employment. Thus in *Poulton* v. *L. & S.W. Ry.* (1867) the defendants were held not liable for the act of a station master who had detained the plaintiff for non-payment of a fare. The railway company itself had no power to detain in these circumstances. It is unsafe to conclude from this case that corporations are never liable for the torts of their servants where the corporation is carrying out an *ultra vires* activity. In *Poulton's* case the station master clearly had no authority express or implied from his superiors to act in the way he did.

UNINCORPORATED ASSOCIATIONS

(1) *Generally*

Unincorporated associations in general have no legal personality distinct from that of their members. In theory, therefore, all members should be joined as co-plaintiffs or co-defendants in an action in tort. Where, however, all the members of the association have an identical interest in defending an action, it is possible to bring a representative action against certain members who are sued as representing the members as a whole. So in *Campbell* v. *Thomson* (1953) a representative action against two members of a club was held to be correctly brought, where the members were allegedly all individually in breach of their duties towards the plaintiff as his employers and as occupiers of the club premises. Where such an action succeeds, judgment can be enforced against the separate property of any member—there is no limitation to "club" property. The same considerations will determine whether members of an unincorporated association can bring a representative action in tort.

(2) *Trade unions*

Trade unions are a special type of unincorporated association. They have since 1871 been endowed by statute with the capacity to sue and be sued in the name of the union, thus avoiding the difficulty of representative actions. Furthermore the liability of trade unions appears to be enforceable only against union property (*Bonsor* v. *Musicians' Union* (1956) though the theoretical explanation for this is still a matter of some doubt. A statutory immunity from liability in tort was conferred upon trade unions by section 4 (2) of the Trade Disputes Act 1906. This immunity briefly disappeared under the provisions of the Industrial Relations Act 1971, but has now been restored by section 14 of the Trade Union and Labour Relations Act 1974. The immunity also prevents the bringing of representative actions against trade union officials representing themselves and all the other members of the union. Such officials can, however, still be sued in their personal capacity.

The Act of 1974 has created several important exceptions to the immunity of trade unions from liability in tort. Actions in tort can be brought in respect of:

(a) any negligence, nuisance or breach of duty (whether imposed on them by any rule of law or under any enactment) resulting in personal injury to any person; or

(b) without prejudice to (a), breach of any duty so imposed in connection with the ownership, occupation, possession, control or use of property (whether real or personal).

Such liability must not arise, however, from an act done in contemplation or furtherance of a trade dispute.

THE CROWN

Until 1947, the Crown enjoyed virtually complete exemption from liability in tort. The Crown Proceedings Act of 1947 took away this immunity, however, with the result that the

Crown's liability is now determined on the same principles as that of a private person. Whether the Crown is liable for breach of statutory duty depends upon whether the statute binds the Crown; unless the statute expressly provides that the Crown is bound or unless it is bound as a matter of necessary implication, the Crown will not be bound. Where a common law duty is replaced by a statutory duty it is therefore a matter of importance whether the statute binds the Crown (*cf.* the Occupiers' Liability Act 1957, which expressly binds the Crown).

There are still certain exemptions from liability. The Sovereign herself cannot be sued in tort in her private capacity. Section 2 (5) of the Act of 1947 prevents the Crown from being sued for acts done or omitted to be done by persons in the exercise of their judicial office, or by any person in the execution of the judicial process (*cf. infra,* for the personal immunities of participants in the judicial process). Section 10 of the Crown Proceedings Act prevents a member of the armed forces from suing another member of the armed forces in tort for death or personal injury inflicted on him in circumstances where the injury would be attributable to service for the purposes of his pension.

THE POST OFFICE

The Post Office which now has separate legal personality of its own distinct from that of the Crown has an immunity, formerly enjoyed by the Crown, from liability in tort where loss or damage has been suffered by any person by reason of anything done or omitted to be done in relation to anything in the post.

PARTICIPANTS IN JUDICIAL PROCESS

A judge in a superior court of record acting within his jurisdiction is not liable in tort for acts done or words spoken in his judicial capacity even though he has acted maliciously or corruptly. In the case of judges of inferior courts, for example, county and magistrates' courts, the judge has immunity except where he has acted maliciously or corruptly or in excess of his jurisdiction. A similar immunity to that of the judge of an inferior court applies to officials who perform administrative functions. Other participants in the legal process, for example, parties, witnesses, counsel and jurors, enjoy absolute privilege from liability in defamation and other torts in respect of statements made by them in the course of the proceedings. The statement must have some relevance to the matter before the court.

HUSBAND AND WIFE

The special position of spouses, both as regards liability in tort *inter se* and towards third parties, has now been almost totally abrogated by statute. The Law Reform (Married Women and Tortfeasors) Act 1935 put the wife into exactly the same position as any other person when she had committed a tort against a third party and abolished the husband's vicarious liability for his wife's torts. The Law Reform (Husband and Wife) Act 1962 removed the surviving anomaly, that of prohibiting actions in tort between the spouses. The court has power to stay the proceedings if no substantial benefit will accrue to either party or if the case can more conveniently be dealt with under section 17 of the Married Women's Property Act 1882.

PERSONS WHO ARE INSANE

Insanity is not a recognised defence to an action in tort. Where a tort requires proof of a specific intention, it might be expected that inability to form that intention through insanity would preclude liability and this receives support from *Morriss* v. *Marsden* (1952) (schizophrenic held liable in battery because he intended to commit the attack although he did not know that what he was doing was wrong). It has been suggested that insane persons are less capable of committing torts requiring intention and a specific state of mind such as malice (Clerk & Lindsell, para. 185). Torts of strict liability can no doubt be committed by such persons, but whether they can commit negligence is an open question.

MINORS

There is no minimum age of tortious responsibility. Minors, like insane persons, are judged by ordinary principles of tort. There is no authority to indicate at what age an ability to form a tortious intention is acquired. Does a minor of tender years who tears up a pound note commit conversion? Contributory negligence cases (*supra*, p. 100) indicate that a minor of quite advanced years will not be judged by the same standards as an adult. Different considerations may affect his liability for negligence—in *Gorely* v. *Codd* (1967) a sixteen-year-old boy was held liable for his negligence in the use of an air-rifle.

A minor cannot be sued in tort where the action in tort is a means of enforcing a contract which does not bind him. So, for example, in *Jennings* v. *Rundall* (1799) where the defendant hired the plaintiff's horse to be ridden for a short and rode it for a much longer journey with the result that it was injured, he was held not liable in trespass. But in *Burnard* v. *Haggis* (1863) where the minor hired a mare which was not to be used for jumping, and allowed a friend to ride and jump it, he was held liable in trespass. His action was not merely a wrongful performance of the contract—it went totally outside its terms.

PARENTS

There is no general principle whereby a parent is vicariously liable for the torts of his children. His liability exists, if at all, under the ordinary rules of tort. So, for example, he may be liable in negligence for giving a dangerous gun to his child (*Newton* v. *Edgerley* (1959)—cf. *Donaldson* v. *McNiven* (1952)).

BANKRUPTS

The effect of section 30 (1) of the Bankruptcy Act 1914, which provides that demands in the nature of unliquidated damages arising otherwise than by reasons of a contract, promise or trust are not provable in the bankruptcy, is that most tortious claims cannot be so proved. The bankrupt himself remains liable in tort and may be sued for the full amount of the claim. The bankrupt retains the right to sue in tort where the claim is for the infringement of a purely personal interest. Where the claim is for the protection of the bankrupt's property, it vests in the trustee in bankruptcy. Examples of the former are claims in defamation, battery and false imprisonment; of the latter, conversion and passing-off.

ASSIGNEES

Rights of action in tort can generally speaking not be assigned. The rule reflects the personal character of causes of action in tort, although of course this is not true of all of them. There are certain exceptions to the rule, most importantly, the right of the insurer by way of subrogation to pursue rights of action previously belonging to the insured, after he (the insurer) has discharged his liability on the policy. It is also possible to assign a right of action on a judgment debt which arises from an action in tort. So also is it possible to assign the proceeds of what may be recovered in a tortious action (*Glegg* v. *Bromley* (1912)).

Unborn Persons

It is still not certain whether English law recognises for any purposes legal personality in the unborn human child between the moment of conception and of birth. The Congenital Disabilities (Civil Liability) Act 1976 avoids answering this question while at the same time providing a practical solution to a problem it presents. Under section 1 (1) where a child is born disabled but alive, a person may be held liable to the child if he is "answerable to the child in respect of the occurrence" which produced the child's disablement. "Occurrence" is defined by section 1 (2) as one which-(a) affected either parent of the child in his or her ability to have a normal, healthy child; or (b) affected the mother during her pregnancy, or affected her or the child in the course of its birth, so that the child is born with disabilities. Under section 1 (3) a person is answerable to the child if he was liable in tort to the parent, or if he was in breach of a legal duty to the parent without producing any actionable injury to that parent. Liability of the mother, though not of the father, to the child is expressly excluded, except where the mother is driving a motor vehicle when she knows or ought to know herself to be pregnant. The Pearson Commission was in favour of extending a similar immunity to the father as the mother enjoys.

The Act recognises certain defences. Under section 1 (4), in the case of an occurrence preceding the time of conception the defendant is not answerable to the child if either or both parents knew the risk of their child being born disabled; if the father is the defendant, this subsection does not apply if he knew of the risk and the mother did not. The defendant is able to rely under section 1 (6) on a contract term excluding his liability in a contract with the parent affected. Because of the Unfair Contract Terms Act 1977 this is of reduced importance. Negligence of the parent affected has the effect of reducing the child's damages under section 1 (7). The Pearson Commission favoured abolition of this rule.

INDEX